American Intelligence and the
German Resistance to Hitler

Widerstand: Dissent and Resistance in the Third Reich

Andrew Chandler, *Series Editor*

American Intelligence and the German Resistance to Hitler

A Documentary History

edited by

Jürgen Heideking
& Christof Mauch

with the assistance of Marc Frey

WestviewPress
A Division of HarperCollinsPublishers

Widerstand: Dissent and Resistance in the Third Reich

Copyright © 1996 by Westview Press, Inc., A Division of HarperCollins Publishers, Inc.

Published in 1996 in the United States of America by Westview Press, Inc., 5500 Central Avenue, Boulder, Colorado 80301-2877, and in the United Kingdom by Westview Press, 12 Hid's Copse Road, Cumnor Hill, Oxford OX2 9JJ

Library of Congress Cataloging-in-Publication Data
American intelligence and the German resistance to Hitler : a
documentary history / edited by Jürgen Heideking and Christof Mauch
with the assistance of Marc Frey.
    p.   cm. — (Widerstand, dissent and resistance in the Third Reich)
  Includes bibliographical references and index.
  ISBN 0-8133-2687-7 (hc)
    1. World War, 1939–1945—Secret service—United States—History—
Sources.   2. United States. Office of Strategic Services—History—
Sources.   3. World War, 1939–1945—Military intelligence—United
States—History—Sources.   4. Anti-Nazi movement—History—Sources.
I. Heideking, Jürgen, 1947–   . II. Mauch, Christof, 1960–   . III. Frey,
Marc, 1961–   .   IV. Series
D810.S7A58   1996
940.54'8673—dc20
                                                            95-22614
                                                            CIP

The paper used in this publication meets the requirements of the American National Standard for Permanence of Paper for Printed Library Materials Z39.48-1984.

10   9   8   7   6   5   4   3   2   1

Contents

1942

1943

1944

1945

Acknowledgments

The present edition grew out of a research project, supported by the Volkswagen Foundation, on foreign contacts of the German resistance during World War II. The editors could not have undertaken the project of searching, collecting, logging-in and selecting the documents in this volume without the most generous backing of this foundation. They are also proud to have earned financial support from the American Council of Learned Societies in New York and the Roosevelt Instititute in Hyde Park, New York.

It would be difficult to do justice to the quantity of careful work involved in preparing the documents for publication. An acknowledgment can only barely begin to recognize the long hours of dedicated work put in by several members of Tübingen and Köln University who contributed importantly to this volume by transcribing documents, proofreading, performing clerical tasks and doing routine research. These colleagues and assistants include: Sigrid Schneider in Köln and Katharina Hauser, Annemarie Jakschitsch, Johannes Kleinschmidt and Michael Lingk in Tübingen. Among those who read and commented on the manuscript in whole or in part is Petra Marquardt-Bigman in Washington, D.C. We will always be obliged for her commentaries and critical feedback. Furthermore, we should like to extend our thanks to the archivists in the National Archives in Washington, D.C., in particular to Lawrence MacDonald and John Taylor, who have been a source of assistance, inspiration and friendship.

Jürgen Heideking
Christof Mauch

Abbreviations

AFHQ	Allied Forces Headquarters
AG	Army Group
Antifa	Antifaschistische Bewegung (Anti-fascist Movement)
AWCC	Archives of the World Council of Churches, Geneva
BBC	British Broadcasting Corporation
BDO	Bund Deutscher Offiziere (German Officer's League)
BRAL	Bureau de Recherches d'Action à Londres (London Bureau of Information and Operation)
CALPO	Comité Allemagne Libre pour L'Ouest (Free Germany Committee in the West)
CCC	Combined Chiefs of Staff
CDF	Central Decimal File
CGT	Conféderation Générale du Travail (General Workers' Confederation)
CIA	Central Intelligence Agency
CIC	Counterintelligence Corps
CLNAI	Comitato di Liberazione Nazionale per l'Alta Italia (National Liberation Committee of Upper Italy)
CO	Commanding Officer
COI	Coordinator of Information
Comintern	Communist International
CP	Communist Party
DAF	Deutsche Arbeitsfront (German Labor Front)
DFB	Deutscher Freiheitsbund (German Freedom Movement)
DGER	Direction Générale des Etudes et Recherches (General Headquarters for Study and Research)
DMI	Director(ate) of Military Intelligence, Great Britain
DNB	Deutsches Nachrichtenbüro (German News Service)
DNVP	Deutschnationale Volkspartei (German National People's Party)
DND	Das Neue Deutschland (The New Germany)
EAM	Greek National Liberation Front
ETO	European Theater of Operations
FAB	Freiheitsaktion Bayerns (Freedom Movement for Bavaria)
FCC	Federal Communications Commission
FNB	Foreign Nationalities Branch
FRUS	Foreign Relations of the United States
Gestapo	Geheime Staatspolizei (Secret Police)
GHQ	General Headquarters
IS	Intelligence Service

ISK	Internationale[r] Sozialistische[r] Kampfbund
ITF	International Transport Workers Federation
ITFU	International Federation of Transport Workers
MB	Mutual Broadcasting
METO	Mediterranean Theater of Operations
MG	Military Government
MI	Military Intelligence
MID	Military Intelligence Division
MO	Morale Operations
MP	Military Police
NA	National Archives, Washington, D.C.
NATO	North Atlantic Theater of Operations
NSDAP	Nationalsozialistische Deutsche Arbeiterpartei (German National Socialist Workers' Party)
OKW	Oberkommando der Wehrmacht (Supreme Command of the Armed Forces)
ONI	Office of Naval Intelligence
OSS	Office of Strategic Services
OWI	Office of War Information
POEN	Provisorisches Österreichisches Nationalkommitee (Provisional Austrian National Committee)
POW	Prisoner of War
PSF	President's Secretary's Files
PW	Prisoner of War
PW	Psychological Warfare
PWB	Psychological Warfare Board
R&A	Research and Analysis Branch
RM	Reichsmark (German Mark)
SA	Sturmabteilung (Storm Troopers)
SAP	Sozialistische Arbeiterpartei (Socialist Workers Party)
SCAF	Supreme Commander of the Allied Forces
SD	Sicherheitsdienst (Security Service of the SS)
SED	Socialist Unity Party
sgd	signed
SHAEF	Supreme Headquarters of the Allied Expeditionary Forces
SI	Secret Intelligence
SO	Special Operations
SOE	Special Operations Executive (British)
SPD	Sozialdemokratische Partei Deutschlands (Social Democratic Party of Germany)
SS	Schutzstaffel (Guard Detachment of the Nazi Party)
TCA	Training Corps Assignment
TOD	Time of Departure
TOR	Time of Receipt
US	Unconditional Surrender
USMC	United States Military Command
USN	United States Navy
USNR	United States Navy Reserve
USSR	Union of Soviet Socialist Republics
X–2	Counter-Espionage Branch of the OSS

Editorial Methods and Principles

The editors started their work on the project with the assumption that this volume is not only a compendium of historical documents but also a form of literature. In selecting material for this book, we have tried to assemble a collection that conveys a sense of the unfolding of events over time. Furthermore it is the objective of this edition to recover the various levels and perspectives that the OSS records provide on the topic of the German resistance. Well over a hundred thousand documents were screened by the editors during the process of selection.

The documents are organized in chronological order and, for ease of reference, are numbered in sequence. On a few occasions, we have changed this order and taken together several documents that speak of a single episode. In this situation, documents within each "cluster" bear alphabetical designations next to the number of the cluster. Each document is preceded by a headnote that identifies its date, origin and subject matter. In instances where the release date differs from the date of the document itself, that fact is indicated in a date line or in a footnote. The archival location of each document is provided in a footnote.

The text of each document in this volume is reproduced as it appears in the original, with only minor editorial intervention. For example, underlined passages have been silently converted to italics and obvious slips of the pen and errors in typesetting have been corrected. Further silent standardization includes the positioning of the date line at the top right. Spelling errors remain if they seem essential to the particular style of a document. Conjectural readings and illegible and missing words are enclosed in square brackets, as are explanatory additions by the editors, such as abbreviations or translations. Questionable errors are marked with a [sic]. If the original document was footnoted, these footnotes are printed in italics in order to distinguish them from the editors' notes. Likewise, handwritten passages or signatures are printed in italics.

Several text passages had to be omitted in order to avoid repetition and digression. Editorial omissions of no more than one page are indicated by a bracketed ellipses ([...]), longer editorial omissions by an ellipses with no bracket (...). The editors have summarized the substance of longer omissions in footnotes so that the character and content of each document could be retained.

To supplement the documents, the editors have prepared an index containing biographical and subject information and an introductory essay. The primary purpose of the essay is to facilitate the reading of the documents and to provide an overall perspective of the historical events. Extensive footnotes supply the reader with background information and references to other documents in the collection. The footnotes do not indicate sources of information unless the material has a unique aspect that appears to require attribution. In general, the annotation research involved extensive study of the archival collections and of the primary and secondary sources listed in the Notes on Sources and Bibliography at the end of the volume.

J. H.
C. M.

Introduction

The German Resistance Viewed
from an American Perspective

On 31 October 1944, Germans turned on their radios and unexpectedly heard the voice of a man believed to have been dead for more than three months—either killed by his own hands, as their government claimed, or murdered by the Nazis, as it was rumored in the country. However, the speaker, who identified himself as Colonel General Ludwig Beck, the former Chief of Staff of the German Army, claimed to have survived the purge following the failed attempt on Hitler's life. He also claimed to remain in command of a strong anti-Nazi resistance movement. Appealing to their sense of duty and patriotism, the General told his listeners that the war was criminal folly and urged them to prepare for the final revolt against Nazi rule.

Nothing is known about the reaction of ordinary Germans to this broadcast, but news of General Beck's "resurrection" found its way into the presses of several Western and neutral countries. But anyone who listened to the radio during the following weeks to get more information or precise orders were disappointed. They had fallen victim to a psychological warfare tactic designed by the U.S. Office of Strategic Services (OSS) to undermine German morale by creating the impression of widespread resistance inside the "Third Reich." In reality, Beck had been dead since 20 July 1944, and organized opposition to Hitler no longer existed in Germany. When the Nazis successfully jammed a second OSS broadcast, the psychological warfare experts turned to other, more promising activities.

Half a century after the end of World War II the issue of German resistance to Nazism still instigates public controversies in Germany and in the United States. Some German conservatives deny Communist resistance fighters the right to be honored together with conservatives such as Stauffenberg and Beck; U.S. critics suspect that Germans are trying to "balance" the Holocaust with 20 July 1944 commemorations. The questions are still passionately debated whether Germans can claim to have resisted the Nazi regime in a similar way as, for example, the French, the Italians, the Serbs or the Norwegians, and whether the attempt on Hitler's life should become part of the "founding myth" of the Federal Republic of Germany. Unfortunately, in the heat of political controversy not many people pay close attention to the historical record. Without reliance on sources, however, it is impossible to reconstruct the facts and, equally important, the ideologies and mentalities of wartime.

By presenting the German opposition as seen through U.S. eyes, this book offers a new and hitherto missing perspective that might help clarify the public debate about the German resistance. We have profited by the recent transfer of the OSS records from the CIA (Central Intelligence Agency) to the National Archives. An archivist praised this move as an "acquisition of unprecedented significance." The United States is the first country to open its World War II intelligence records to domestic and foreign researchers making the OSS the only modern secret intelligence agency whose activities and ideologies can be studied in detail.

Observing oppositional forces in Germany was only one of many tasks undertaken by the OSS, which had been set up in June 1942 "to collect and analyze strategic information and to plan and operate special services." Under the energetic leadership of General William J. Donovan, who had been appointed by President Roosevelt as Coordinator of Information (COI) after Pearl Harbor, the OSS soon began to operate on a world-wide basis, employing about 13,000 people at its height in late 1944. Nevertheless, the OSS files reveal that the headquarters in Washington, D.C., were preoccupied with German resistance matters and gave high priority to information concerning the morale of the German home front. The OSS records, therefore, add significantly to our knowledge about the German resistance, even though not all the reports from the outposts in London, Bern, Stockholm, Madrid and Istanbul are considered reliable. In addition, the OSS files provide a glimpse of the views of what was perhaps the best informed governmental agency, whose internal debates reflected various shades of opinion in the Roosevelt administration as a whole.

The documents made available in this volume are a small but fairly representative selection from the OSS records concerning German resistance activities. They give answers to the following questions:

1. What did the U.S. government know through the efforts of the OSS about German opposition and resistance against the Nazi regime?
2. How did the OSS perceive this so-called German underground in terms of military-political value and ideological orientation?
3. How did the OSS react to the efforts of German resistance circles to establish contacts (commonly referred to as "peace feelers" in London and Washington) with the Western governments?
4. In what ways and to what extent did the OSS support or try to manipulate German resistance forces?

This introduction intends to place the documents in their historical context rather than interpret them. The reader is free to draw his or her own conclusions and to connect the events and opinions of the past with the debates of today. In addition, the editors of this volume hope to stimulate further research on the secret history of World War II and foster a more open attitude toward the declassification of intelligence records.

Early Considerations of Psychological Warfare Against Nazi Germany, April 1942 to May 1943

In the spring of 1942, the office of the COI and the State Department began to grapple with the problem of devising a coherent and viable psychological warfare strategy directed against Germany [documents 2 and 3].[1] At that time the U.S. administration believed in Winston Churchill's concept of bringing about the downfall of the Nazi regime by "setting Europe ablaze." Churchill's idea involved both massive bombing and the support of anti-Nazi forces in the occupied countries. To this end, the British had created a new instrument of subversive warfare, the Special Operations Executive (SOE). In the United States, as a starting point, war planners listened to Paul Hagen, alias Karl Frank, a socialist immigrant from Austria, who offered to establish contacts with resistance groups in Germany and made proposals for a collaboration with the German "underground" [1]. This strategy was aimed at separating the Nazi rulers from the German people. From very early on, COI and OSS pinned their hopes on the working classes as "natural enemies" of National Socialism and Fascism [4]. It was expected that the large numbers of foreign workers and prisoners of war forced to toil in German factories would strengthen the opposition potential of the German labor force [6].

The OSS believed that the labor movement would become the most important ally in the common struggle against the Axis powers. This belief was confirmed by a group of left-wing German immigrants whom Donovan had drafted from the New School of Social Research in New York for the Research and Analysis Branch (R&A) of his new organization. Led by Franz Neumann, Herbert Marcuse and Max Horkheimer, they explained the rise of National Socialism in terms of a historic contradiction between the progressive working classes and the authoritarian German ruling elites, who had enlisted the Nazis to consolidate their threatened position. This interpretation, which combined the Marxist doctrine of class struggle with the egalitarian idealism of the New Deal, not only fixed the ideological point of view of many R&A members but had a considerable impact on the outlook of the OSS and the administration in general. One of the first practical consequences was the establishment of an OSS Labor Section, headed by Arthur J. Goldberg, with branch offices in London and Bern as points of contact with the German "underground" [11].

The question of the timing and content of a major propaganda offensive against Germany was still in the balance when Allen W. Dulles took over the OSS station in Bern in November 1942. From this neutral look-out he soon got in touch with emissaries of the resistance [7, 8]. Distinguishing between "good" and "bad" Germans was no easy task, however, since even a high-ranking SS official tried to sound out his views on a possible peace initiative [39]. In February 1943, in the aftermath of the German defeat in Stalingrad, Dulles reported on the effort

---

1. Throughout this book documents will be referred to by bracketed numbers.

of German groups to eliminate Hitler. Having been told by the prominent Swiss psychologist C. G. Jung that Hitler would rather commit suicide than surrender his power to internal or external enemies [9], Dulles now considered the removal of the Führer to be the necessary beginning of the end for Nazi Germany. However, he did not yet see any organized opposition in Germany, and he thought the best way of getting rid of Hitler would be to "create the impression that we desire that he remain" [10]. In the meantime the psychological warfare options of the OSS had become severely limited by a shift in British propaganda [5] and by Churchill and Roosevelt's agreement on the "unconditional surrender" formula at the Casablanca conference in January 1943.

Nevertheless a comprehensive political warfare program was drawn up by R&A in May 1943, based on the assumption that "fear is the predominant element making for the fighting and productive strength of the German people." On one hand, the memorandum by historian William L. Langer, the head of R&A, contained the usual verdict of "the German counter-revolution composed of Army leadership, big business, East Elbian Junkers, and high civil servants." On the other hand, Langer thought the time had come to tell the German people "that they must now actively oppose the regime, that they must refuse to become partners in crime." In his opinion, the Nazi regime tried to counteract the growing opposition "by compelling ever larger strata in German society to participate actively in the commission of atrocities against foreign peoples and in the spoliation of foreign countries." Although the German government had never informed its own people about the terrible war crimes, "this knowledge is undoubtedly being disseminated by foreign propaganda and by the actual experience of the German soldier." In order to split the masses from the hard-core Nazis, therefore, the Allies should guarantee the German people the right of self-determination, laid down in the Atlantic Charter, and officially repudiate a partition of Germany [12]. Both recommendations ran counter to the official U.S. policy that had already begun to embrace the idea of a "German dismemberment." With the Allied landings in Italy and the sudden collapse of the Fascist regime in July 1943, the debate over the best way to terminate the war entered a new phase.

In Expectation of a Sudden German Collapse, August 1943 to April 1944

The Moscow Free Germany Committee

German defeats in the summer campaign against the Soviet Union and the armistice concluded between the new Italian government under Marshall Badoglio and the Allies in early August 1943 gave rise to speculations about an imminent collapse of the Third Reich. These speculations were fueled by the Soviet sponsorship of a "Free Germany Committee" in Moscow, composed of German political refugees, mostly Communists, and captured German officers and soldiers. The OSS paid close attention to the activities of the Committee, trying to discover the underlying Soviet intentions [14, 15]. Obviously, the Committee was a propaganda weapon designed to speed the disintegration of the German army, but it could also be seen as a warning that the Soviet Union was in a position to make a separate deal with Germany should the Western Allies disregard Moscow's political interests. In a report dated 26 November 1943, R&A noted that the Committee "addressed its appeals much less to the masses than to those sectors of the ruling class likely to be interested and capable of overthrowing Hitler" and that its strategy presumed "that an Army *putsch* against Hitler is the shortest path to social revolution" [29].

The real or imagined successes of the Free Germany Committee brought the deficiencies of the Anglo-American political warfare efforts into even sharper relief. As early as August 1943, Irving H. Sherman from the OSS Counterintelligence Branch had opened the debate about whether the Western Allies should respond to the Soviet initiative by setting up their own "Committee of German Exiles" [13]. Similar ideas were advanced by the OSS Morale Operations (MO) experts in London (where a branch office of the Free Germany Committee had been set up) and by OSS Istanbul, which had established a good working relationship with a group of German emigrants including a future mayor of West Berlin, Ernst Reuter [17, 18, 26]. But because of their political implications, which aroused the suspicion of the State Department, these projects stood no serious chance of being realized. Among those urging a more activist course and advocating a political appeal to the German people was Allen Dulles who opined "our political warfare has lagged behind our military warfare. … If we take concerted measures in both the psychological and military fields of warfare, we can crack Germany and end the war this year." [16].

The same conclusion was drawn independently by British Intelligence experts in early September 1943. Comparing the situation in 1943 with that of 1918, they were of the opinion that a German "collapse" was imminent [19a]. Their American counterparts, confronted with this prognosis, were less optimistic, pointing to the different political backgrounds of the two situations and to the totalitarian nature of the Nazi regime [19b, 19c]. This exchange of opinions, which attests to the powerful impact of historical examples and memories on people's minds, contributed to the sense of growing weakness and destabilization of Germany. From this time on, the OSS constantly updated the probabilities and possible patterns of a German collapse, while the military authorities began to formulate contingency plans for a sudden termination of hostilities.

During the fall of 1943 the OSS took great pains to get a clearer picture of the general mood in Germany and the strength of German opposition to the Nazis. The main source of information was once again Allen Dulles who, in a fairly restrained and guarded manner, reported on various loosely connected resistance circles. He also transmitted a memorandum from Willem Visser't Hooft, General Secretary of the World Council of Churches in Geneva, describing oppositional activities of the German Protestant Church [20, 27, 28, 30]. The view of the German Socialist opposition was presented in a very detailed report by Willy Brandt who, from his exile in Sweden, kept in contact with labor activists and intellectuals in Germany and occupied Europe. From time to time he secretly visited Germany, which allowed him to gather first-hand information for Western intelligence agencies [21, 40]. In its first comprehensive report on the German opposition in late September 1943, R&A maintained that "the underground has experienced some revival and expansion since the outbreak of war." Admitting that the "individual undergrounds were still atomized into small groups within the city, the town and the factory," the analysts emphasized the psychological and moral dimensions of the resistance. They cautioned "that within a totalitarian state the strength of an underground movement does not depend upon numbers. Totalitarianism and a wide-spread underground are a contradiction in terms. ... Even as it is the record is a tribute to human endurance and courage, and the revelation of a great hope" [22]. The growing resistance activities, therefore, seemed to promise an outbreak of the desired "social revolution" in Germany at least during or immediately after the military collapse. To encourage and foster this development, R&A submitted a detailed plan for making better use of the revolutionary potential of the foreign workers in Germany [23], and the OSS Labor Branch engaged in a number of projects to infiltrate Germany and cooperate with German labor elements [33].

The Morde-Papen Conversations

Whereas R&A concentrated almost exclusively on the possible contribution of the German working classes to the Allied war effort, two very different and bolder approaches were attempted by other OSS agencies with the aim to speed up the collapse of the Nazi regime. In early October 1943, U.S. journalist Theodore A. Morde went on an OSS-sponsored mission to Turkey, where he twice met with Ambassador Franz von Papen, whom he considered as a possible "German Badoglio." Morde tried to convince the conservative former Reich chancellor that he must bring about Hitler's removal from power as an essential precondition for peace and the survival of his country. Von Papen signaled his readiness to cooperate in principle but asked for territorial and political guarantees to be given by the President of the United States [24a]. Donovan passed the Morde report to Roosevelt, commenting optimistically that "it contains an idea that your skill and imagination could develop." The President, however, following the advice of Robert E. Sherwood from the Office of War Information and Adolf A. Berle from the State Department, denied a passport to Morde who had suggested that he would continue his contact with von Papen [24b, 24c, 24d]. This decision constituted a humiliating defeat for Donovan in his struggle to enhance his agency's prestige in the administration, and it made him more cautious in dealing with politically sensitive questions. OSS Istanbul stayed in contact with a German banker who was close to von Papen, but they knew "that the character and scope of our Department's functions rule out entirely any political initiatives or engagements" [39].

The Herman Plan

The outcome of the Morde-Papen affair did not augur well for another, more serious effort to establish German-U.S. contacts in neutral Turkey. The initiative came from the German opposition in Army, government, Church and bourgeois circles, which for several months had been coalescing around Carl Goerdeler, former mayor of Leipzig, General Ludwig Beck and Admiral Wilhelm Canaris, head of the Abwehr (Army Intelligence). Probably on the suggestion of Canaris, Count Helmuth James von Moltke, a legal adviser to the Abwehr, used two official missions to Turkey to get in touch with U.S. Minister in Cairo, Alexander Kirk, whom he knew from Kirk's time as Ambassador in Berlin. In October 1943, OSS agent Alfred Schwarz notified Washington that von Moltke had offered to negotiate a "working agreement concerning full co-operation" between the German High Command and the U.S. Joint Chiefs of Staff [25]. Since for political reasons Kirk refused to come to Istanbul, in December von Moltke shared his ideas with German emigrants and members of the OSS in Istanbul. This exchange of views resulted in a written "Exposé on the Readiness of a Powerful German Group to Assist Allied Military Operations Against Germany," code-named "Herman Plan" by the OSS [31]. Admitting the moral and political necessity of an "unequivocal military defeat and occupation of Germany" as well as "the justification of the Allied demand for unconditional surrender," the plan proposed the virtual opening of the Western front to the Allies and the retreat of German troops in the east to the vicinity of the German-Russian border that had been established in 1940. OSS Istanbul recommended the Herman Plan as the best chance "of ending the War in the West at one stroke, and sav[ing] perhaps many hundred thousand lives" [32].

This positive view was echoed by Professor Karl Brandt, a German emigrant teaching at Stanford University, whom in late February 1944, after a long period of hesitation, Donovan asked for a critical evaluation of the plan [37a]. When the Herman Plan and the Brandt Memorandum were reviewed by leading members of the OSS, however, a cautious and negative attitude prevailed. Critics doubted whether the German group was able to deliver on its promises, and they feared that a coup d'état would give rise to another nationalistic stab-in-the-back legend after the war. In particular, however, they objected to the implicit anti-Soviet tendency of the Herman Plan, which, if revealed, could seriously damage the Great Alliance. William Langer and Donovan himself wanted to forestall this danger by passing to the Soviets the information concerning these contacts in Turkey [37b]. Finally, on 3 April 1944, the OSS Planning Group decided to inform neither the Russians nor even the Joint Chiefs of Staff, but to allow OSS Istanbul to continue the Herman connections and to "play upon this group as a possible instrument of double agents or in any way coldly calculated to promote the success of the invasion, without any regard for the German individuals involved" [37c].

This attitude on the part of the OSS was not fully in accord with developments on the diplomatic level: At the October meeting of the Foreign Ministers in

Moscow as well as the Teheran Conference of the "Big Three" in late November, the Allies had promised to exchange any information concerning German peace feelers. On the one hand, this agreement was thought to dispel Stalin's fears of a separate agreement between the Western powers and Germany. On the other hand, it gave the British and U.S. governments some reassurance concerning the future role of the Moscow Free Germany Committee. By insisting that the Herman Plan was purely an intelligence matter, the OSS Planning Group found a convenient way to get around these cumbersome diplomatic restrictions.

The OSS and the Conspiracy Against Hitler, January to September 1944

While Donovan and his colleagues were scrutinizing the merits of the Herman Plan in Washington, its principal author, Helmuth James von Moltke, had already been arrested by the Gestapo. His arrest, in combination with a serious crisis of the OSS in Istanbul caused by the collapse of the "Dogwood circle," which had been infiltrated by double agents prevented the resumption of talks in Turkey. From that time on, the Beck-Goerdeler group relied almost exclusively on OSS Bern as its channel to the Western Allies. In late January 1944, Allen Dulles for the first time used the code name "Breakers" to refer to a "German oppositional group … composed of various intellectuals from certain military and government circles" [34]. Adam von Trott zu Solz from the German Foreign Office and Abwehr agents Hans Bernd Gisevius and Eduard Waetjen served as emissaries and principal informants, enabling Dulles to keep OSS Washington informed about the progress of the movement to overthrow Hitler and the Nazi government [35, 36, 39]. It took Washington some time to realize that all these signals originated from just one source in Germany.

At the same time, the OSS did not lose sight of the labor underground and the possibility of anti-Nazi sympathies among the common German soldiers. On one hand Allen Dulles was prepared to cooperate with the Swiss branch office of the Communist Free Germany movement in producing propaganda material and smuggling it into the Reich [38]. On the other hand he warned OSS Washington about a trend to the radical left, which in his opinion was intensified by a "complete ignorance as to the ultimate objectives and the practical ideas for the future of Europe maintained by the [Western] Allied powers." Under these circumstances, the moderate labor leaders were afraid "that even if the Allies achieve military victory, the peace will be quickly lost and a new dictatorship may take the place of the present one in central Europe" [41]. Setting up an Anglo-American propaganda committee was still out of the question, but the OSS Planning Group at least permitted "the use of prisoners of war to transmit surrender appeals to their previous comrades." Having no political content, such activities "would probably not require consent of high political circles in the U.S. or England" [42].

U.S. suspicion of the Soviet-sponsored Free Germany Committee was temporarily allayed when Donovan, after consulting Soviet military and diplomatic circles in Washington, reported to the President that because of lack of success "the Committee has been shelved for the time being and is only held in reserve." Allegedly, the Soviet government was committed to "the elimination of all representatives of the German ruling class, including the big Prussian landowners, industrialists, etc." Yet, "Stalin does not entertain any idea of Germany turning Communistic. He is, however, believed to favor the development of a Popular Front which would offer Russia greater liberty of movement" [47].

On 16 May 1944, OSS Washington passed a condensed version of Dulles's latest "Breaker" messages to the State Department and to the White House [43], followed by additional information on the German opposition received via Madrid [44]. This practice of forwarding "raw intelligence" to the highest political and military authorities was continued right up to the assassination attempt on Hitler on 20 July 1944 [45, 47, 48, 49]. Dulles remained skeptical of "Breaker's's" chances for success, mainly because he found it difficult to believe that the Gestapo and the SS were unaware of the conspiracy. He confined himself to listening to his German interlocutors and reporting their offers and proposals back to Washington, stressing the Western orientation of the "Breakers" as a counterpoise to the growing influence of the Soviet Union in central Europe. The Joint Chiefs of Staff, the State Department and the White House took notice of these messages but without displaying any special interest or giving specific instructions in response. Their attention was absorbed by the dramatic events unfolding in Normandy after the Allied landings on 6 June 1944 that seemed to foreshadow the rapid military collapse of Germany. Now that the invasion had succeeded and the interallied European Advisory Commission in London was already preparing the zonal division of Germany, the British and U.S. governments were less inclined than ever to respond to political or military overtures from the German opposition.

In the hours following the attempt on Hitler's life, Dulles had to rely on Swiss newspapers and radio broadcasts since his German informants either went into hiding or lost their contacts to the resistance group [50]. In the main his reporting was accurate, with the exception that he described the bomb explosion, which had taken place in Hitler's East Prussian headquarters, as having taken place in the Berchtesgaden area of the Bavarian Alps. His hastily drawn up proposals suggest how the Allies might have reacted had the "Breakers" gained a foothold in Berlin or other German cities. Dulles soon recognized, however, that "the movement appears to be breaking," and he correctly predicted that "the blood purge will be ruthless" [51]. This and the following telegrams or radiotelephone messages from Dulles were transmitted to the President by Donovan, who was full of praise for Dulles's achievements [53, 54, 57]. At the same time the OSS began to exchange information on German opposition matters with British intelligence, who obviously lacked insight into the conspiracy [56].

In comparison with Dulles's empathy for the German opposition forces, the prevailing mood in Washington was much less sympathetic to the "Breakers" movement. Donovan's Special Assistant Wallace R. Deuel lamented that "the Fourth Reich now has its alibi for the present war." He assumed that "the Generals will now try to make a deal with Russia, since they and Hitler together have failed catastrophically to conquer the Soviets" [55]. Psychologist Walter C. Langer was convinced that the Nazis themselves had staged the assassination attempt in order to eliminate their rivals and to "strengthen the myth that Hitler is under the protection of Divine Providence," a view that was shared by German Socialist and Communist emigrants in Sweden [58, 63]. In their comprehensive report of 27 July 1944, the R&A experts presented all the available empirical data but judged them from a narrow ideological perspective. Basically they saw the coup d'état, as they termed it, in light of an internal power struggle of the German elite that indicated the beginning disintegration of the Nazi regime and the weakening of German morale. In a sweeping statement they characterized the plotters as "bankrupt generals, nationalist intellectuals, and (possibly) nationalistic Social Democrats and civil servants" who had tried to sell themselves to the West for what they believed to be "the ultimately necessary war against the USSR." These were not the social and political forces on which R&A pinned their hope for Germany's democratic future: "The extermination of the group thus does not impede the political regeneration of Germany" [60]. Donovan himself came to the conclusion that it would be "of more benefit to humanity" if the Germans "battle it out inside Germany without help from us." He objected to making the "Breakers" correspondence available to the Russians because the OSS had refrained from giving the group any assistance or assurances [61]. The instrumental approach preferred by the OSS Planning Group was taken up by the MO Branch when it directed the European outposts to confuse the SS by denouncing German officers and Nazis as being involved in the conspiracy [59, 62, 85].

In the months following the 20 July events, the OSS tried to piece together the additional evidence on the "Breakers" movement and its brutal suppression by the Nazis as it became available. Dulles suspected that the Eastern-oriented wing of the group was still active, a view that gained some plausibility by news of ongoing German-Russian contacts in Sweden [64, 69]. During an interview in the Vatican, the Pope's German secretary, Father Georg Leiber, told his OSS visitors about several earlier assassination attempts against Hitler that had failed like the last one. He also revealed that Konrad Adenauer, former mayor of Cologne and a leader of the Catholic Center party (who was to become the first chancellor of the Federal Republic of Germany) had refused to join the resistance movement, "since he believed that the Nazi regime should bear the onus of losing the war before the opposition should attempt its overthrow." [65]. This interview was part of a systematic effort by OSS to learn more about the attitude of the Catholic and Protestant churches, their organizations and their clergy, whom they considered as important elements for the post-war reconstruction of Germany [52, 70a, 70b, 70c, 71]. In September 1944, OSS Madrid landed an intelligence coup by procuring an eyewitness account of the dramatic events that had taken place on 20 July in the German Ministry of War, the headquarters of the conspirators against Hitler [67]. The ruthlessness demonstrated by the Nazis in tracking down and executing the remaining participants and sympathizers of the "Breakers" movement gave credence to a report received by Dulles that Hitler had ordered the liquidation of all foreign workers [66]. In January 1945 when Dulles became aware that Helmuth James von Moltke's execution was imminent, the OSS induced the State Department to start a diplomatic rescue operation. Unfortunately, this last-minute effort failed to save the life of a man judged by OSS as thoroughly democratic, liberal and European-minded [83a, 83b].

OSS Propaganda and Subversive Warfare Against Germany, October 1944 to May 1945

Undeterred by the destruction of the conservative-liberal opposition to Hitler, the OSS intensified its campaign to foster a popular resistance movement by means of propaganda and special operations. Part of this strategy was the "resurrection" of General Beck and the production and dissemination of newspapers such as *Das Neue Deutschland* purporting to represent a growing "Peace Party" inside Germany [68, 72]. OSS Stockholm offered to distribute leaflets in Germany indicating "existence of powerful underground movements within country" [74]. The black radio program *Capricorn* featured a German speaker, "Hagedorn," who gave orders from a nonexistent "underground" movement to his listeners. As it later turned out, *Das Neue Deutschland* and Hagedorn convinced a number of Germans that an organized resistance existed in their country [97a, 97b, 98].

To make OSS propaganda more effective, Paul Mellon from the MO Branch suggested the enlistment of C. G. Jung "in view of his intimate knowledge of the individual German mind." Mellon's own ideas about Germany as a "pagan nation" that had always been "subject to the powerful sway of its own barbarian soul" came close to the concept of "collective guilt," which also underlay the Morgenthau Plan [75]. Such a wholesale condemnation of the German people was not shared by the R&A experts, who endeavored to establish criteria for distinguishing Nazis from non-Nazis and anti-Nazis [73]. The growing tension between a punitive approach to the German problem, which was gaining support as news spread about the genocide committed against the European Jews, and the partly class-oriented, partly pragmatic OSS approach is also reflected in the continuing debate over the "unconditional surrender" formula. When in the fall of 1944, contrary to all expectations, German military resistance stiffened on the Western front, the OSS and the U.S. Joint Chiefs of Staff favored a propaganda line that would counter Goebbels's predictions of complete national annihilation should the war be lost. It proved to be next to impossible, however, to overcome the reservations raised by the supreme political authorities in London and Washington [76, 81a, 81b].

On a practical level, OSS at least succeeded in employing German prisoners of war for propaganda activities behind enemy lines in northern Italy [78, 79]. In France, the OSS cooperated with the left-wing German resistance group CALPO (Comité Allemagne Libre pour L'Ouest) in matters concerning Secret Intelligence

(SI) as well as Special Operations (SO) [82, 96]. The idea of arming the foreign workers in Germany for a revolutionary mass uprising was still under discussion in late January 1945, but owing to the rapid advance of the Allied armies after that date it had no chance of being implemented. The most ambitious project concerned the "long-range penetration" of Germany by OSS intelligence missions, which began in the fall of 1944 with the recruitment of German agents in England. By the end of the war, the OSS could boast of having sent more than 100 such missions into the Reich that had succeeded not just in surviving (which seemed to be difficult enough) but in relaying messages back to Allied military headquarters [99]. That all of these activities were part of Donovan's still more ambitious scheme of building up a permanent U.S. central intelligence agency is evident from his memorandum of 1 December 1944 to President Roosevelt, as well as from his instructions to Dulles [77, 80]. This plan, however, was cut short by President Truman's order to dissolve the OSS at the end of September 1945. Supporters of a permanent intelligence organization had to struggle for another two years until the CIA was founded in 1947.

OSS and the Beginning of the Cold War in Europe, January to October 1945

In the final months of the war, mutual mistrust began to strain the relations between the Western Allies and the Soviet Union. In this respect, Allen Dulles played an important role by raising the alarm about the Russian intentions in Central Europe and by engineering a separate surrender of German troops in northern Italy. In January 1945, Hans-Bernd Gisevius, who finally with OSS assistance had been able to escape from his hideout in Berlin, confirmed Dulles's fears of a German drift into the Soviet orbit [86, 87, 89]. Dulles now saw the danger of the Soviets installing the Free Germany Committee as the German government in a similar way as they had used the Communist Lublin Committee to outmaneuver the London-based Polish government-in-exile. In order to be prepared for this eventuality he offered to gather "quietly and without formality ... certain individual Germans" who could advise the Western Allies on German political matters. At the same time Dulles, fearing that the Russian armies might overrun the whole of Germany, revived the idea of getting in touch with German officers who were willing to facilitate the surrender of German troops in the West [90]. Activities of this kind were in principle authorized by the OSS, although Donovan insisted that Dulles was not allowed to give guarantees of personal security and that "none of the group should be encouraged to believe that we are fostering any German committee for political purposes." [92].

Actually, Dulles had already established "secret channels" to the Supreme German commanders in France and Italy. His reports of 25 January and 26 February 1945 prove that he was aiming at nothing less than opening the entire Western front [88, 91]. Because of difficulties on the German side and vigorous protests from Stalin against what he saw as separate peace negotiations, Dulles's "Operation Sunrise" suffered many delays until it resulted in the surrender of the German forces in Italy only a few days before the final capitulation [93, 94]. During the last weeks of the war, the line between German opposition groups and Nazi opportunists seeking to save themselves by aiding the United States became even more blurred. Dulles's readiness to deal with Bavarian Nazis must be understood in the context of his worries about a last-ditch SS defense in the Alpenfestung and his desire to forestall further territorial gains by the Soviets in the East [95a, 95b].

The last three documents published in this volume illustrate the fact that the OSS remained vitally interested in questions concerning the German resistance even after the war had ended. From their Wiesbaden headquarters, an "OSS research team" started in early June 1945 on an investigative trip through West Germany, accompanied by the leader of a Socialist resistance group. They brought back tales of frustration about attempts at organizing resistance circles foiled by the Gestapo or disrupted by Allied bombing raids and about lack of direction, leadership and unity. It became clear that a working class "underground" had never materialized although many people had suffered for their political beliefs or oppositional behavior [100].

The conservative resistance, which had almost succeeded in killing Hitler and overthrowing the Nazi regime, did not fare better under close U.S. scrutiny. A consolidated interrogation report drawn up by the Counterintelligence Division of the U.S. Army in September 1945 emphasized the lack of "a true democratic spirit" on the part of the conspirators. The authors were convinced that "the total defeat of Germany seems a far better guarantee for world security than might have been created by a peaceful entry of Allied armies into Germany in July or August 1944." [101].

The Field Intelligence Study on the "Political Implications of the 20th of July," undertaken between June and October 1945 by R&A expert Franklin Ford, together with Gisevius's book *To the Bitter End*, marks the beginning of a history of the resistance. Starting with the observation that claims of participation in the conspiracy had become a political asset in occupied Germany, Ford approached his topic on the basis of solid documentary evidence and with scholarly detachment. His conclusion remains valid to the present day: "Dramatic as it was and costly though it proved to potentially valuable leadership for post-war Germany, the conspiracy cannot be taken as endowing all who were connected with it with a special degree of political reliability and moral worth." [102]

1942

Document 1 · 10 April 1942

Memorandum by Paul Hagen[1]: How to Collaborate with the Anti-Nazi Underground in Germany[2]

How to Prepare Collaboration with the Anti-Nazi Underground Movement

Introductory Remarks

There is an anti-Nazi potential in Germany, which up till now has not been utilized. It has hardly been recognized in its importance for political warfare. The following proposals show a practical way how to prepare effective steps to open up this hitherto neglected front. It may be remembered that American armies have worked with underground movements previously, in Asia as well as in South America.

I. How large is the anti-Nazi potential in Germany? Some idea about its present importance may be conceived by the fact that the economic damage resulting from the spontaneous differentiation in Germany, mostly expressed in passive resistance, slowdown of work and decrease of productivity in Germany's production centers, may easily out-balance the amount of lease-lend help given by the United States to its European allies. From September 1941 to March 1942 the average monthly deliveries amounted to about three hundred million dollars.[3] Under the assumption that the value of German war production at the present time amount to about three billion dollars monthly, a deficit of only 10 per cent of this production resulting out of the mentioned passive resistance, would be the equivalent of the monthly lease-lend deliveries. There is reason to believe that the

---

1. NA, RG 226, Entry 106, Box 12, Folder 88. Pseudonym for Karl B. Frank. Frank, an Austrian Socialist writer and founder of the anti-Nazi underground movement Neu Beginnen, had entered the United States in December 1939. Ever since then he was trying to establish contacts with U.S. intelligence circles.

2. This memorandum was presented to Allen W. Dulles who, at that time, was working in the New York City bureau of the Coordinator of Information (COI), the predecessor of the OSS. In a letter to William J. Donovan, Dulles explicitly favored Hagen's proposals. On 12 May 1942, Allen W. Dulles forwarded the Hagen Report to Arthur J. Goldberg in Washington who in June 1942 had founded the OSS Labor Section and become head of its outpost in London.

3. On 11 March 1941 $6 billion of lend-lease aid had been approved by Congress.

decrease of productivity resulting from anti-Nazi and anti-war feeling in Germany is higher than this 10 per cent.[4] The way to influence the existing spontaneous differentiation is two-fold. First, the political way of stating the most effective war aims and the propaganda. This is not to be discussed in this memorandum. Secondly, the organized collaboration with existing nuclei of underground groups and circles, their encouragement and organizational strengthening.

II. The first necessary step would be the careful study of these groups, their personnel and their contacts. That could be done through a special agency in cooperation with such people experienced in underground work, carefully selected as trustworthy to the cause of an Allied victory and the defeat of Nazism. This agency would have to work out a plan how to make contacts; first in the few border places in Europe where inside contacts still can be reached, in consequence, with the inside groups themselves. Existing contacts to representatives abroad of such inside groups have been practically cut off during the war but with systematic effort they could be reorganized. The agency should consist of a working mixed party of Intelligence officers of the army and some carefully selected people who have been active in the mentioned underground movement. A small staff of a few dozen experienced people should be prepared, supported with technical facilities (papers, etc.) to look up as soon as possible old contacts in Sweden, Switzerland, etc., where contacts to inside groups might possibly be reorganized.

III. At the same time another staff, selected by the same agency could set up a research office in America, to analyse and study carefully German newspapers and above all, all of the available local newspapers, reviews, books, etc. Very valuable information could be found in these publications, in the editorial as well as in the advertisement sections, where a surprising amount of information is available and could be digested by real experts with regional and local knowledge who would rightly be able to interpret such publications. It would be possible to use several dozens [sic] qualified people for this job, among trustworthy refugees. This section could have an official research institute affiliated with it, which would be able to coordinate knowledge and expert experience of many things; emigrations from Germany, Jewish refugee knowledge, technical and economic facts, etc. It might even be possible to get additional military information through such a careful digest of this material. It would certainly produce important political information. That would be one of the sources available at a time when mere Intelligence work is less successful, considering the totalitarian blockade of information behind the Nazi lines.

IV. Another section of the agency could train trustworthy refugees for investigation, help in questioning war prisoners and similar people. Here again the surplus information available would come from a more intimate knowledge of local dialects, local [...] social conditions, etc.

---

4. *Some documents about this point may be found in the forthcoming book* Will Germany Crack *by Paul Hagen. Harper & Brothers. May 1942.*

V. Special care should be given to the "expeditionary" staff and preparing the reorganization of contacts in Switzerland, Sweden, unoccupied France and occupied France, maybe also Ankara. Several of the German underground groups did have trustworthy people in all of these places. In Sweden as well as in Switzerland contacts may be reorganized from reliable elements of the labor organizations like the Swiss Social Democratic party or the Swedish Social Democratic party. There have always been individuals, particularly in the youth groups of these parties who were working together with the border organizations of the German underground movement before the German expansion. There may be at the present time very few reliable anti-Nazi Germans approachable in Switzerland; most of them have been imprisoned but there still are Swiss people who are sympathetic with the movement.[5] The same is true for unoccupied and occupied France. (It isn't the purpose of this memorandum to give concrete details.) Another branch to develop would be a careful investigation of contact possibilities with anti-Nazi personalities and groups in South America. It is well known that the Nazis use South America for their contacts. The situation would have to be studied carefully by very qualified and reliable emissaries and visitors sent from the agency, making a thorough research in order to find for the beginning a few reliable collaborators.

VI. In the later period it could be conceived that collaborators of this agency could be dropped the parachute way in order to make direct contact with people inside if the border contacts wouldn't be successful enough.

VII. It may be also conceived that a kind of recruiting activity could later be developed if the number of war prisoners has grown. In the many thousands there would certainly be a few dozen people who could be enthusiastic to join a coordinated anti-Nazi underground movement. A larger group could be neutralized and the Nazi influence could be checked, which is important for the preparation of the coming democratic change in Germany.

VIII. Finally, a close contact should be established with the American propaganda center, the Coordinator's office,[6] for instance, in order to synchronize special propaganda to Germany with the organizational and research achievements of the agency.

IX. The greatest success possible could be achieved if people elected for the work with the agency would have the feeling that they are not used as agents but as special nuclei of anti-Nazi Germans, treated as part of the organized vanguard of a coming democratic Germany—in another word—treated as allies and not as agents.

If there should be any interest in the general principles of this plan, it would be easily possible to make a more concrete plan.

---

5. This is a reference to the practise of internment that Swiss authorities applied to emigrés without valid residence permits.

6. I.e., the Coordinator of Information (COI), the first U.S. central intelligence agency headed by William J. Donovan.

Document 2 · 23 April 1942

Memorandum by Adolf A. Berle, Assistant Secretary of State[1]: Political Propaganda Campaign Directed Toward Germany

SECRET

I. Political Propaganda Campaign Directed Toward Germany

I believe that the time is due (if not overdue) for an all-out political campaign to upset the Nazi Government in Germany. The conditions appear favorable, and there is a very fair chance of a successful outcome. On the other hand, the risk is negligible.

II. Underlying Conditions

It will be recalled that the German political overturn in 1918 began *not after but before* the defeat of the German armies in the field. A movement to create "arsols" [arsons?] and the slight evidences of internal revolt appeared in the Spring of 1918, that is to say, before the main drive began. This drive was by no means defeated in July of 1918; yet in that month the first division revolted. From that time there was progressive deterioration until the revolution in October.

Somewhat the same conditions prevail now, and for the same reasons.

Although the German armies are successful in the military sense, the underlying situation appears to have deteriorated to a point where defeat or disintegration seems almost certain unless peace is made, giving Germany access to supplies from the Western Hemisphere prior to the end of this year.

---

1. NA, RG 226, Entry 106, Box 9, Folder 70. From 1938 to 1944 Adolf A. Berle was Assistant Secretary of State. His duties included coordinating U.S. and foreign intelligence activities and negotiating with Allied governments in exile as well as postwar planning.

...²

The deaths on the Russian front have been so widespread and are so widely known in Germany that there is already evidence leading to the belief that contingents sent to the east consider that they are probably condemned to death. Already the morale factor in that sense is beginning to deteriorate.

In summary, it is therefore an army into which have been introduced roughly a million more or less untrained men of unsuitable age, whose very presence is notice both to the German civilian population and to the German army that the country is beginning to get into straits.

A third factor is the obviously growing concern of Germany at the British bombing. This, relatively ineffective in the year 1941, has begun to be extremely serious in the west of Germany. In part it has contributed to the growing economic derangement (it will be recalled that the German Staff plan assumed that the Anglo-American air forces would destroy much of German industries). In larger part, it has at length proved to Germany that her civilian population is not immune from direct military attack.

III. Political Factors

The political factors implicit in this situation are more obscure, but such evidence as we have indicates that they are beginning to be active.

It is fairly well established that one group of German generals has been actively canvassing the possibility of a change of government, so as to place Germany in a better position to make peace.³ This is not to indicate that I think any kind of peace could be made with the German militarists—which I think would be disastrous—but merely to point out that in that respect, conditions are somewhat similar to those which prevailed in the Spring of 1918.

It is also already clear that Germany is cautiously seeking some avenue by which she can open peace negotiations, and is gradually adapting her propaganda to that end. Again, this is only interesting as showing the lack of confidence which the German Government has in its own position.

It is interesting to note that reading of the Japanese-German intercepts⁴ makes it plain that Germany has given up any real hope that Japan will be of any great

---

2. The omitted passage gives some details about German General Staff documents relating to the invasion of the Soviet Union in 1941. They had been obtained through intelligence channels.

3. In June 1942 the British Embassy officially informed the State Department that during the past few months there had come to the attention of the British authorities a number of indirect approaches from persons claiming to represent anti-Nazi groups in Germany. The Secretary of State replied orally to the British that there had been no such peace feelers of a tangible nature reaching the United States.

4. Beginning 1941 U.S. military intelligence agencies were able to intercept and decode the Japanese diplomatic messages to and from Berlin.

assistance to her in this regard. Indeed, her feeling towards peace is itself in the nature of a betrayal of the Japanese interest.

Catholic sources continually report the search for the nucleus of a non-Nazi Government. Originally it seems they were thinking of a military clique; later advices speak of their attempt to set up a civilian group based on the old civil servants who have survived.

Finally, we have indisputable evidence of the growing corruption and disorganization of the German administrative and second-string machinery. General Sikorski[5] reported his ability to purchase, in German-occupied Poland, arms sufficient to equip 4 divisions. Isolated indications of a somewhat similar situation in France suggest that there also the German political machinery is coming to be in bad shape.

It may be noted that the recent elevation of the S.S. (Himmler's Guards) as a separate arm[6] suggests that the Nazi Government is itself worried about the situation.

Finally, it may be noted that the timeliness of a political attack was recognized by Stalin in his January speech, and less clearly echoed shortly thereafter by Anthony Eden.[7]

IV. Political Factors in the Occupied Countries

In German-occupied Europe the political situation is increasingly adverse.

The attempt of the Quisling Government to secure domination over the religious and educational institutions of Norway seems to have provoked a crisis.

The entry of Laval into the French Cabinet, coupled with the excecution of many hostages by the German authorities in occupied France seems to have intensified the feeling there.

General Sikorski reports a growing organization in Poland. The Yugoslav resistance has never been thoroughly broken.

...

Technical Details

Certain technical matters ought to be tied up.

I have been told that most of the German army are now fitted with headphones and short-wave radio receivers, since the German orders are transmitted in this way. I am likewise told that it is possible to handle short-wave broadcasting so

---

5. At the time Vladyslaw E. Sikorski was Prime Minister of the Polish government-in-exile and Commander in Chief of the Polish forces fighting with the Allies.

6. The so-called Waffen-SS.

7. This is a reference to a parliamentary debate on 4 March 1942, during which Secretary of State for Foreign Affairs, Anthony Eden, was made to comment on Stalin's recent distinction between Germans and Nazis. Eden declared that it should be made impossible for Germany to rearm again; at the same time, however, he emphasized the importance of Germany's economic recovery.

that it reaches these receivers. It is thus possible to talk directly to considerable segments of the German army.

The precise arguments addressed to particular segments of the German army can be developed at length. One of them should be that the Japanese, if they are victorious, do not contemplate giving the slightest help to Germany

A. A. Berle, Jr.

Document 3 · 8 May 1942

Letter from Allen W. Dulles (COI New York) to COI William J. Donovan: Suggestions for Psychological Warfare[1]

SECRET

I have read Berle's most interesting memorandum dated April 23, 1942.[2] The timeliness of the program outlined depends largely upon the accuracy of the analysis of the present situation in Germany. As set forth in this memorandum this picture is somewhat more optimistic from our point of view than I would have judged it to be, but Berle, of course, has access to material not available to me.

Certainly the time will come when a propaganda drive based on a comprehensive statement to be made by the President should be undertaken. I should be inclined to feel it might be too soon to undertake this now. If Germany had initial successes in the Russian campaign our propaganda drive might be quickly forgotten and it then would be hard to repeat it later. If, however, the summer campaign does not result in a knock-out blow for Russia, it would seem to me that it might then be desirable to start our propaganda campaign some six months hence as winter draws near—when Germany will be approaching her fourth winter of war, when even though surfeited with victories she will find herself still no nearer to peace.

---

1. NA, RG 226, Entry 106, Box 9, Folder 70.
2. Document [2].

As to the nature of the propaganda campaign I have a couple of suggestions in connection with Berle's memorandum. (1) I doubt whether we can warm over and repeat the Wilsonian technique. It was magnificent at the time and very effective, but if there is any one thing which the Germans have now been taught to mistrust it is the Wilson doctrines.[3] Hitler has dinned into their consciousness a story, largely false, of the alleged deceit practiced upon Germany before the last Armistice. Every man, woman and child in Germany has heard this. The President's message must and I believe can have a new approach and a fresh appeal. (2) With respect to the desirability of a campaign for the immediate up-set of the Nazi Government, as suggested in the opening paragraph of Berle's memorandum, the following point may be worth considering: a quiet suppression of Hitler and the Nazi Party by the military and the taking over of control by the latter might not be in our interest; what would be more desirable would be to fan the flames of hatred between the two groups by subtle propaganda and otherwise; keeping Hitler in power until there were some military reverses and then having an open struggle for power, possibly an open revolution, between the Nazi authorities and the military authorities. I am not sure but that Hitler, once the myth of infallibility has been shattered—and it already has been strained by the Russian campaign—would not be something in the nature of an asset to us. When Hitler falls it should not come through a quiet coup d'etat but as the result of open conflict between the Nazi and military elements. It seems to me that our propaganda over the next few months should be directed along the lines of building up the rift between the Nazi Party and the Military, rather than an attempt at this time to propagandize for the elimination of Hitler.

---

3. In World War I, Woodrow Wilson had tried to define precise war aims, otherwise known as the famous Fourteen Points. When the Germans accepted the U.S. terms, Wilson agreed to an armistice. In retrospect this action was judged by many, including President Roosevelt, to have been ill-advised.

Document 4 · 22 July 1942

Memorandum by Heber Blankenhorn (OSS Washington)[1]: The Labor Factor in Psychological Warfare Plans for Western Europe

SECRET

The Labor Factor

Introductory Summary

The most important factor in the psychological warfare situation in Western Europe Theatre is analyzed in the outline herewith. It is the labor factor.

The industrial labor population is the largest and likeliest target for anything this country can say to affect enemy morale.

The same holds for occupied countries. The industrial labor populations recently deprived of their own free organizations are the element most open to American influences and the most likely to do something about it.

Quantitatively and qualitatively, labor on the continent constitutes *the* American objective. Other elements of the populations, if affected by what America says, can do little in turn to affect the war unless they obtain labor backing.

In occupied France, Czecchia [sic], the Lowlands [Low Countries], etc., it is the factory workers, railwaymen, miners, etc., whose activities against the enemy have been important. In many areas they keep their unions intact or maintain underground their union habits and connections. It is their principal form of cohesion. Their unions moreover had accustomed them to international labor relationships, to which they still look, especially to affiliated types such as the American and British union federations.

---

1. NA, RG 226, Entry 139, Box 135, Folder 1813. Heber Blankenhorn, who had been the head of the Psychological Subdivision of G-2 (Counterintelligence) during World War I and a prolific author on psychological warfare strategy, was appointed by William J. Donovan to lead the North African propaganda campaign against the Germans.

In Germany it was industrial labor which first felt the weight of Nazi domination. It has been the first element of the German population to show some disillusion with the Nazi war.

The soldier drawn from industrial labor families was the part of the enemy armed forces whose morale was most affected by psychological war in 1918. What revolt there was in Germany in 1918 centered in labor organizations. In broad outline, the situation is the same today. American psychological warfare can direct much ingenuity at various classes, and the war will be little affected. *What the psychological war over Europe is about is labor*. Whoever reaches labor reaches the vitals of war morale, enemy and allied.

The exceptions to this generalization are numerous, and some appear in the analysis herewith. But it is deemed that the generalization calls for emphasis because American psychological warfare, such as it is so far, is remarkable for its disregard of the labor factor. Where strategy indicates the largest opportunity, the meagre performance so far has scattered to everything except labor.

Continental labor, due to special restrictions, is not easy to reach. Workmen lack shortwave sets. The principal medium, leaflets distributed by planes from a task force based in Britain, has not even been planned for.

Considerations of basic plans, of what to say, by what spokesmen, to what labor elements, are outlined in the analysis following.

H. B. [Heber Blankenhorn]

[...]

The Labor Factor

I. Importance of Labor Factor

The labor situation has attained such importance in this war that it requires separate treatment as [a] *distinguishable factor* in the plans drafted by P.W.B. [Psychological Warfare Board].

This is especially true for the Western Europe Theatre, where the size and influence of labor organizations have been greater than in any other war zone. ...[2]

II. Demarcations of Labor Situation

The labor situation in Western Europe Theatre falls into four main divisions:

A. Labor in *enemy* countries.
   In Germany and Italy the destruction of autonomous labor organizations was followed by the imposition of new, government-dictated formations.

---

2. The omitted passage contains long lists of international labor organizations as well as references to enemy acts regarding labor organizations.

Current information on the morale, performance or non-performance of these "corporations", etc., is essential to P.W.B. plans.

B. Labor in enemy-held, or *enemy-dominated* countries.

Despite the enemy dissolution of *national* free labor bodies in occupied countries, the survival of *local* labor bodies is reported in many areas. *Underground*, rather than formal, relationships are reported among many memberships of dissolved free labor federations. Current information on the morale of former union members, and other underground organizations is of capital importance to P.W.B. plans.

C. Labor in *neutral* countries.

Especially in Sweden and Switzerland, because of their proximity to enemy lands, and because their labor organizations' affiliations are anti-Axis, current information of labor morale and labor underground relationships is of potential practical value to P.W.B. plans.

D. Labor in Britain

As the expected base of psychological warfare directed to the continent, and as the base of refugee labor international federations, current information of the British labor situation is essential to P.W.B. plans. Its importance is increased by the fact that foreign relationships of American labor unions have been closest with the British.

Expert analysis of British labor information is essential because of the existence of a labor *political* organization participating in the British government.

Note: The above demarcations are concerned primarily with labor *economic* organizations. It is recognized that most of the European economic organizations have labor *political* relationships; some unions may be political bodies. But the present analysis endeavors to exclude *labor political* organizations.

Policies relating to political bodies, such as the British Labor Party, the labor or socialist parties represented in various governments-in-exile, or the Communist party of U.S.S.R. are solely the concern of the President and other policy-making agencies of the government. P.W.B. plans have no concern with such policy, except as stated by the government.

[...]

III. Psychological Objectives

The objectives of psychological warfare in this theatre correspond to the demarcations above:

(a) In *enemy* lands.

1. To *divide labor*, especially in munition plants, from the government.
2. To re-enforce distrust of the army command among *soldiers* from industrial labor families.
3. To increase hatred of war among the *women* of labor families.

Other objectives, more generally applicable to enemy populations apply

also to labor. The above three objectives comprise the main points precisely aimed at labor.

(b) In *enemy-held*, and enemy-dominated lands.

1. To *slow down* labor, employed in munition plants producing for the enemy.
2. To *encourage sympathy* for allied war aims and toleration for allied war
   acts, such as bombings of munition plants.
3. To *spread active support* of allied war efforts, through *sabotage*, instigat-
   ing demands for protection from air raids, etc.
   In enemy-dominated areas, such as unoccupied France,—to *re-enforce
   resistance* to Fascist "labor charters" and to forced labor in Germany.

(c) In *neutral* lands.

1. To *encourage sympathy* with allied war aims.
2. To *impede production* destined for enemy war effort.
3. To further *active cooperation* with allied labor, for information of enemy
   morale, *transmittal of propaganda* to labor in enemy lands, etc.
   Swedish and Swiss labor represent promising opportunities for the above
   objectives.

(d) In *Britain*

To furnish British labor, largely through cooperation of American labor,
with information and other means, for supporting objectives (a), (b) and
(c).

British labor is in no sense an objective of propaganda, but its *informed
cooperation* is deemed essential in order to reach labor in enemy, occupied and neutral lands.

[...]

IV. Means of Attaining Objectives

The methods available, of course, condition all psychological warfare. P.W.B.
plans have to take account first of all of the means for carrying them out. This is
especially true of the labor situation on the continent. Labor is *difficult to reach*
for three reasons.

(a) *Labor* on the continent is *subject to suspicion and surveillance.*

In Germany and Italy the elaborate organizations "for the benefit" of labor are
in fact government *espionage organizations* for the control of labor. In enemy-held
lands the occupying forces distrust labor more than any other class. Labor leaders
who refuse to be Quislings[3] live as marked men, frequently picked as hostages.

Enemy fears, of both occupied and unoccupied France, *center on labor* as the
origin of possible revolts in aid of an allied invasion.

P.W.B. plans have to take account of the fact that any labor responses to allied
efforts,—e.g. sabotage,—are subject to the most extreme penalties. Current information of the most precise nature on this point is essential to P.W.B. plans.

---

3. I.e., collaborators, named after the Norwegian Nazi Vidkun Quisling.

(b) Labor on the continent exhibits *inherited distrust* of certain *Allied govern-ments.*

E.g. British labor reports that its cooperations with labor on the continent have been limited by these distrusts.

(c) Labor's *means of communication are inferior* or restricted.

In Germany and Italy short-wave receiving sets are practically non-existent among laboring families. Residence and travel of laborers are restricted. In occupied lands the same lacks and restrictions prevail. As a partial offset, "grapevine" or underground communications are reportedly more effective among laborers.

The three principal *means* of reaching labor are (a) by radio; (b) by printed matter; (c) by underground agents.

...[4]

V. What to Say
...[5]

General directives concern first the spokesmen who will be most effective among laborers on the continent. Labor is impressed:

(1) By President Roosevelt. His name carries weight not only as an anti-Axis protagonist but as the sponsor of a program of legislation protecting labor in the *U.S.*

(2) By American labor leaders. No governmental statement that American labor supports the national war aims can compare with statements of that fact from labor spokesmen. Where the names of leaders are not well known to continental labor, the names of their organizations are known.

(3) By workers in American munition plants of German, French, Belgian, Norwegian, etc. descent. Labor is always impressed by simple statements from workmen about their jobs, their pay, their rights, and their war aims.

General directives—always to be applied to news events as much as possible—should cover a number of labor specific points. They should continually emphasize American wages and working conditions, in comparative terms dealing with the lower levels in the country whose labor is addressed. Directives should emphasize the following general American labor conditions:—The right of free self-organization protected by law even in war time.

Freely negotiated collective bargaining contracts even in war time.

Voluntary abrogation of the right to strike pending the duration of the war.

No laws protecting labor abrogated during the war; list these laws.

---

4. The omitted passage deals with technical details of how to reach the labor underground.
5. The omitted passage deals with the labor situation in France and Czechoslovakia.

Freedom to protest to the government and to benefit by war labor commissions, on which free labor has equal representation.

Freedom to advocate its own war programs; each should be cited.

Freedom to better its conditions during war time; particularly cite wage raises, government housing projects, etc.

Freedom to associate with international labor organizations; cite all international labor war conferences.

Freedom to contribute to the war effort; cite labor—management committees.

Labor's confidence in American war effort; cite facts of production as from labor spokesmen; cite successes (when they occur) of U.S. planes, tanks, etc.

The net aim should be to convey an impression of American industrial might, including the welfare of labor and labor support of *free* labor conditions.

Conversely labor conditions in enemy and enemy held countries should be listed and specified as conditions which American labor will never accept.

Other directives should deal with enemy coercions and reprisals on labor; cite all American labor expressions of sympathy with labor in Czechoslovakia, Norway, etc.; cite labor expressions of horror of enemy executions and other reprisals on labor.

Document 5 · 15 August 1942

Telegram from Myron Taylor (OSS Stockholm) to OSS Washington[1]: German Criticism of British Policy

#2161. Victor, for Bruce from Hopper. A reliable German informant has given me the following information which is in reality a military analysis of the present situation submitted for the sake of the common cause. This informant knows the personalities and politics of both the Soviet and Nazi regimes, he was a former leader of the German National Party[2] and an important Swedish editor considers him highly qualified because of previous interpretation of events taking place inside Germany and because of accurate information given in the past.
[...]

My informant believes that shift from anti-Nazi to anti-German propaganda by British is all wrong. That opposition within Germany needs a leader outside preferably in U.S.A. such as Masaryk in the last war,[3] that encouragement of elements within to remove Hitler is important. Forty percent of total population can be expected to support the opposition and is made up of trade union groups, Catholics and Prussian police. Encouragement of anti-Nazis within Germany by the U.S.A. is important.
[...]

---

1. NA, RG 59, CDF 103.91802/733. This telegram was sent via the American Legation in Stockholm and the Department of State.

2. Most of this type of information reached OSS Stockholm through Edgar Klaus and Bruno Peter Kleist. Neither of them, however, had been "a former leader of the German National Party." Thus, the informant referred to here cannot be identified.

3. During World War I, Thomas G. Masaryk worked from London and the United States for the liberation of Czechoslovakia both by establishing an intelligence system and by organizing an underground propaganda movement inside Czechoslovakia. From 1918 to 1935 he was President of the Czechoslovak Republic.

Document 6 · 16 December 1942

Memorandum by OSS Adviser Kurt Bloch[1]:
The Opposition Potential of the
Foreign Workers in Germany

[SECRET]

The German Opposition

...

Pre-Nazi Germany always fluctuated between two concepts of the "state," the so-called Rechtsstaat (government by law) and the so-called Polizeistaat (government by the police). These two concepts were primarily distinguished by the relationship postulated between the "state" and the individual.

[...]

The Nazi State, however, is sharply distinct from either of the traditional German concepts of government. [...] Under the rule of the Nazis, a curious social retrogression has taken place in Germany where a new tribal consciousness has been fostered instead of traditional nationalism. Gradually, over a period of ten years, the German people have been reduced to a tribe, with typical tribal marriage rules, with a totem symbol and with many irrational magical tribal rituals. Its chieftain, Adolf Hitler, typically combines the features of war leader, medicine man and saint. This retrogressive development has meant that social life in Germany has reverted to forms obsolete within the confines of Western civilization for centuries.

...

Within this general setting, Adolf Hitler functions in many capacities. Popularly he is supposed to lead a virginal life and to abstain from drink, meat and

---

1. NA, RG 226, Entry 100, MF INT 13-GE–599. Kurt Bloch, an economist who had emigrated from Berlin via London and Shanghai to the United States, was a member of the Institute of Pacific Relations from 1938–1942. At the request of the Foreign Nationalities Branch of the OSS he wrote a twenty-page study of the status of the anti-Hitler opposition within Germany, an extract of which is printed here.

tobacco; all these forms of abstemiousness are the traditional properties of saint-hood. They were indispensable for the fantastic and sacrilegious position of holiness into which he has been removed by all the tricks of propaganda. His halo now sanctions all Nazi lawlessness and immorality.

It is the declared policy of the United Nations to destroy Nazism. If, however, you remove the Nazi saint and his closest friends from the tribal scene, you are not likely automatically to cause a return to traditional observance of human and moral law; it would be much more likely that the destruction of the Nazis would be followed by a furious war of everybody against everybody else. With foreign or civil war removed as outlet for the criminal instincts now sublimated by the German tribe into national virtues, you are likely to face a lawless society without authority.

[...]

Secondly, it is important to visualize that Nazi Germany today differs in one other important aspect from all modern Western society we know of: through the extensive use of foreign labor in Germany. While in general the application of the principle of national self-determination in Central and Eastern Europe has not proven an easy success, the present condition of Germany forestalls its application to Germany; undoubtedly the largest body of friends on whom the United Nations can count in Germany, are the alien workers forced to labor for their German masters. In October 1941, the Royal Institute of International Affairs estimated the total foreign labor employed in Germany at 3 1/2 million men and women. This figure seemed too low at the time. The present total can scarcely be less than seven million. Clearly these foreigners are the primary source of opposition inside Germany. Owing to the treatment received at the hands of the Germans in their own country as well as in Germany, they are primarily an anti-German opposition. They are common people of the nations who are our Allies. On the list of any oppositional forces in Germany, they are Number One, nor could we afford to forget them in political warfare nor in any part of the postwar settlement of European and German problems. (It is a rather unpleasant property of all literature on postwar Germany that this important element of friends in Germany on whom the United Nations can count is overlooked in favor of a motley crowd of various German opposition groups of uncertain size and character.)

These foreign residents of Germany, however, are not only Number One on the list of the opposition forces in Germany, they also constitute an important element in determining the strength and direction of the German opposition itself. With one foreign worker for every ten German people, i.e., one foreign worker for each German soldier, and no less than one foreign for each four German workers, no German in Germany, in his political and social reasoning, can possibly forget that there are millions of non-German enemies in Germany whose primary political and social emotions are bound up with their hatred of the Germans as such, and who are willing to rise from their present state of subjection by force, against their masters whenever opportunity offers. While there are occasional reports on "fraternization" between foreign and German workers, it seems to be substantially true that such cases are rare exceptions.

The foreign workers have been established not only as a foreign group but also as a distinct socially inferior group, banned from inter-marriage and all the amenities of social life; kept in confinement, with low pay, long working hours, and largely given work which German workers are not asked to perform. In other words, the foreign workers constitute the lowest stratum of the German working class; owing to their presence, the German worker can no more feel—if he ever did—like the down-trodden hero of the revolutionary future. Today the German worker is a man who has to lose much more than his chains, namely: the German standard, with its distinct and undeniable superiority as compared with that of the alien worker.

The conditions under which a German political opposition inside Germany could operate differ, therefore, radically from the conditions under which an opposition generally operates in dictatorial countries. Italy and Spain, e.g., are free of such distortions of their national past and far from having rejected the heritage of Western civilization. Their social structure is free of important hostile alien elements spread all over the country. In Japan, the presence of a much smaller body of Koreans—about one million—has entailed positive measures aimed toward Japanese-Korean assimilation. Nowhere else has a nation been transformed into a tribe with slaves rounded up by the armed forces of the tribe and held in forms of communal dependency.
[...]

1943

Document 7 · 13 January 1943

Telegram from Allen W. Dulles (OSS Bern)[1]
to OSS Washington: German Efforts
to Establish Contact with Americans

SECRET

TOR: 1/16/43 2:43 pm

#278. Burns for Victor. Axis nationals and those of Axis controlled countries are trying to communicate with us as a result of the Russian offensive[2] which is deeply affecting public opinion. In Zurich I saw a friend [Hans Bernd Gisevius][3] of 474 [Willem Visser't Hooft][4] and 476 [Gero von Schulze-Gaevernitz][5] on Sunday, a German who is a friend of Neimuller [Niemöller][6] and who is thought to be working closely with Schacht.[7] He said that it is very important that encouragement be offered to the effect that negotiation with the United Nations for a durable peace could be instituted if the Nazi leaders were eliminated by the group resisting them. If this were not done, he said, chaos and revolution would ensue since Hitler would take up Bolshevism rather than give in to the western powers. He added that his friends did not want to risk their lives unless there is some hope

---

1. NA, RG 226, Entry 134, Box 307. Shortly before German forces occupied Southern France in November 1942, Allen Dulles had crossed the Swiss border and established himself as head of the OSS-outpost in Bern under the cover of "Special Representative for the President of the U.S."

2. On 8 January 1943, the Soviet Supreme Command summoned the German Sixth Army, which had been encircled in Stalingrad, to surrender.

3. Identified by Allen W. Dulles in cable #13/14 of 15 January 1943.

4. The Dutch theologian Willem Visser't Hooft acted as Secretary General of the newly formed World Council of Churches in Geneva.

5. Gero von Schulze-Gaevernitz, a U.S. citizen with German background, was one of Allen Dulles's closest collaborators.

6. Martin Niemöller, a leader of the confessional church movement in Germany, had been sent to a concentration camp by the Nazis in 1937.

7. Since 1937 Hjalmar Schacht was in contact with conservative circles of the German opposition against Hitler.

of success for the movement. It is my personal opinion that there has as yet been no serious organization of the movement.

Document 8 · 14 January 1943

Telegram from Allen W. Dulles (OSS Bern) to OSS Washington: Adam von Trott's Criticism of the Western Allies[1]

SECRET

TOR 1/16/43 6:13 pm

#314. The following telegram, which gives the views of a German who is a member of the opposition group, regarding whose identity a separate report is being made,[2] is a summary of a report written by 474 [Visser't Hooft].

It appears that the fact that their approaches are meeting with no encouragement or understanding is a source of deep disappointment to the opposition.[3] The answer is always given that Germany must suffer a defeat of her armed forces regardless of what new regime may be created. The view is taken that the opposition is taking tremendous risks to continue its activity, and that it will cease, by reason of the failure of the western powers to understand the oppressed peoples living in occupied countries and the Germans themselves, unless conversations are continued. There is consequently a tendency on the part of the opposition to believe that the Anglo-Saxon countries are merely theorizing and are filled with pharisaic condemnation and bourgeois prejudice.[4] The orientation towards the

---

1. NA, RG 226, Entry 146, Box 235.

2. In cable #13/14 of 15 January 1943, OSS Bern identified the oppositional German as Trottzusolz [Adam von Trott zu Solz]. Trott, a member of the German Foreign Office, was described by Allen Dulles as a "friend of [Sir Stafford] Cripps and understood to be well known to [Edward C.] Carter, Council Pacific Relations and perhaps also to my brother [John Foster Dulles]." Right until the attempt against Hitler, Dulles remained in touch with Adam von Trott through a cut-out.

3. Adam von Trott zu Solz had been trying to approach Visser't Hooft on several occasions since April 1942.

4. In his report to Allen Dulles, Visser't Hooft had explained that "to sit in judgment over the Germans will mean to turn a repentant sinner into a hardened sinner."

east is brought about by a belief that fraternization is not possible between the present Governments, but it is possible between the German and Russian peoples. Both peoples have experienced great suffering and have broken with the bourgeois way of living; both are slowly returning to the Christian traditions in a spiritual but not necessarily ecclesiastical way, and both are looking for a radical solution of their social problems. Russian soldiers are not hated by the Germans, on the contrary, they are respected.

According to the opposition, there is no belief in a decisive development in a military sense but only in a social one. Even after the German Army is thrown back by the Russians, when the latter's campaign comes to a halt, a revolutionary situation may spring up on both sides. Another important element in this respect is the fraternization between workers imported from abroad and German workers.[5]. The generals are ceasing to be a political factor, and the bourgeois and intellectual opposition is becoming less important there as a result of the fact that Hitler finds himself forced to play up to the laboring classes and to give them increasingly important positions. The conclusion of the memorandum is as follows: "Following Hitler's fall, a completely new Europe will be based on the brotherliness and experience of the oppressed common people".

I am transmitting the foregoing report solely because it may be of interest in connection with the program of psychological warfare and not because I am of the opinion that there is any serious organization of the opposition group[s] in Germany or that, short of a complete military victory for the United Nations,[6] they should expect or be lead to expect any encouragment from us or any dealing with us.

---

5. See document [23].

6. In the course of the Casablanca Conference (January 1943), Roosevelt and Churchill had agreed on a policy of *Unconditional Surrender* for Germany.

Document 9 · 3 February 1943

Telegram from Allen W. Dulles (OSS Bern) to David K. E. Bruce (OSS London)[1]: C. G. Jung's Analysis of Hitler's Mind

SECRET

TOR: 2/3/43 3:27 pm State Department

#41, 42, 43. To 105 [David Bruce] from Burns. I have been in touch with the prominent psychologist, Professor C. G. Jung.[2] His opinions on the reactions of German leaders, especially Hitler in view of his psychopathic characteristics should not be disregarded. It is Jung's belief that Hitler will take recourse in any desperate measures up to the end, but he does not exclude the possibility of suicide in a desperate moment. Basing his statement on dependable information, Jung says that Hitler is living at East Prussia headquarters in underground quarters,[3] and when even the highest officers wish to approach him, they must be disarmed and X-rayed before they are allowed to see him. When his staff eats with him, the Fuehrer does all the talking, the staff being forbidden to speak. The mental strain resulting from this association has broken several officers, according to Jung. Jung also thinks that the leaders of the army are too disorganized and weakened to act against the Fuehrer. [...]

---

1. NA, RG 226, Entry 134, Box 307. David Bruce was head of the OSS outpost in London.

2. Mary Bancroft, an intimate friend of Allen W. Dulles and student of C. G. Jung, had introduced the two to each other.

3. Between 23 November 1942 and 17 February 1943, Hitler was indeed staying at his isolated East Prussian headquarters, the so-called Wolfsschanze near Rastenburg.

Document 10 · 4 February 1943

Telegram from Allen W. Dulles (OSS Bern) to OSS Washington: Psychological Warfare Suggestions Against Germany[1]

SECRET

TOR: 2/8/43 7:50 pm

#827. From Burns for Victor. [...]

In answer to direct or indirect suggestions from German sources that there was an endeavor by groups to eliminate Hitler, the most effective reply that I have found is that so far as I was aware, Hitler was proving to be a great asset to us, and that there was not anything we could think of which would be more contributive to our military success than his keeping supreme command of the German armed forces. A line of this nature, enhanced by emphasis upon military errors made on prestige grounds following after Stalingrad[2] and possible disaster in the Caucasus, seems to be very effective. I am still of the opinion that if Hitler were to disappear, the end of Germany would begin, and for that reason his disappearance is favored by me. However, the most effective way of speeding this is to create in Germany the impression that we desire that he remain.

Concerning the present German effort at levee en masse, I would suggest that the Rathenau letter, dated October 9, 1918, to German Minister of War, Sceuch [Scheüch],[3] regarding this subject might be used effectively.

---

1. NA, RG 226, Entry 134, Box 307

2. On 31 January 1943, the Sixth Army under General Paulus had surrendered to the Soviets.

3. On his first day in office (October 9), the Prussian War Minister Heinrich Scheüch was approached by German industrialist Walther Rathenau. Rathenau suggested not to accept the American conditions of peace. His proposal for a last-minute effort at *levée on masse* was, however, rejected both by Scheüch and General Ludendorff of the Supreme Command of the Army.

Document 11 · 23 February 1943

Memorandum from Arthur J. Goldberg to OSS Director William J. Donovan: The Labor Division of the Office of Strategic Services[1]

Labor Division of the Office of Stategic Services

Very early in the work of the Office of Strategic Services it was recognized that the labor movements in Axis and occupied countries were important allies in the common struggle against the Axis powers. These labor movements had declared war on Hitler and Mussolini long before Pearl Harbor. In every Axis and occupied country they constituted the bulwark of the movements of resistance. Although their organizations were dissolved, they nevertheless waged an unremitting struggle underground. Not only did these labor movements wage internal warfare in the form of sabotage and resistance but also they constituted a valuable link with the outside world and a potential source of valuable and strategic information. Carrying on as they did and do under the most difficult of circumstances, they required help in many forms in order to continue and intensify their activities.

In recognition of this, the Office of Strategic Services established a Labor Division, staffed with men who had an understanding of the labor forces which had carried on the underground war against the Axis. This Labor Division has:

1. Established contact with underground labor organizations in virtually all of the occupied countries and in the Axis countries too,
2. Extended substantial help to these underground movements in the form of financial subsidies, facilities for communication, equipment and materials indispensable for carrying on underground activities, etc.

To win the confidence and support of these labor elements has been a difficult and arduous task. They all share a traditional antipathy toward cooperating with

---

1. Archives of the Army War College, Fort Carlisle, Pa., William J. Donovan Papers, Box 67, File 267. Prepared at the request of General William J. Donovan after a discussion with Goldberg on 22 February 1943.

governmental agencies. This is contrary to the established policy of the continental labor movement. In order to establish intimate collaboration, it was necessary to break down this traditional attitude. No existing intelligence service of the Government was or is in a position to do this. They lack the personnel and sympathetic point of view which are essential in order to obtain the cooperation of labor elements. The relationships which have been established between the underground labor movements and the Labor Division of the Office of Strategic Services proves the necessity for an agency which can carry on political and psychological warfare free from the limitations inherent in the functioning of the orthodox military departments. The fact is that neither the Military Intelligence Division nor the Office of Naval Intelligence has developed any relationships of any consequence with important underground labor groups nor were such relationships established by the Psychological Warfare Branch of MID [Military Intelligence Division] during the period of its existence. This was due to two reasons: (1) the lack of appreciation by MID and ONI [Office of Naval Intelligence] of the value of these contacts, and (2) the lack of confidence of the underground labor groups in the military and naval intelligence services.

We are entering upon a period of the war in which it becomes more important than ever to capitalize upon the forces of internal resistance behind enemy lines. We have underway, in collaboration with the underground labor groups, elaborate plans and projects to coordinate military invasion of enemy-held lands with widespread internal resistance. The success of these plans will mean much in the shortening of the war and in the lessening of our casualties. They will also mean much in the restoration in enemy and occupied countries of democratic institutions which the underground labor movements are uniformly pledged to reestablish.

Document 12 · 17 May 1943

Memorandum from William L. Langer (OSS Research and Analysis Branch) to OSS Director William J. Donovan: New Possibilities for Psychological Warfare in Europe[1]

SECRET

The Nazi Defeat in Tunisia, the Impending Invasion of Europe, and U.S. PW [Psychological Warfare]

The unprecedented rapidity with which the Nazis surrendered in Tunisia,[2]. the impending invasion of Europe, and Mr. Churchill's visit in the United States[3] make it necessary to re-examine the strategy to be adopted by the United States in PW operations in Europe.

PW operations against Europe will have to be distinguished according to targets. The targets are:

1. Germany's ally: Italy
2. Germany's satellites: Bulgaria, Romania, Hungary, Slovakia, Croatia, and Vichy France
3. occupied Europe
4. Germany proper

---

1. NA, RG 226, Entry 92, Box 301, Folder 39. This memorandum was prepared by a Psychological Warfare (PW) Subdivision in the Research and Analysis Branch of OSS, and forwarded by William L. Langer, Harvard historian and chief of R&A, to William Donovan. Further copies were forwarded to PW board members James Grafton Rogers, Edmund Taylor, John Magruder and Walter C. Langer.

2. On 13 May the German Africa corps had surrendered in Tunisia. Some 252,000 Axis soldiers were taken prisoner

3. From 12 May until 25 May 1943, Roosevelt and Churchill were meeting in Washington for the Trident Conference. The Americans were determined to get a firm commitment by the British to a cross-channel invasion; also a target date for D-Day was set.

This memorandum is concerned only with Germany while special memoranda will be submitted for Poland and Czechoslovakia.

We desire from:

1. the people in occupied Europe active co-operation with the invading army;
2. the people in the satellite states (Hungary, Slovakia, and Croatia) active sabotage of the efforts of their governments to assist Germany's war effort;
3. the German people at least the resolve not to participate further in crimes committed against the peoples in occupied Europe and a slowdown campaign in the factories.

These are, as far as Germany goes, minimum requirements.

[...]

Whether we get the cooperation from the German people will depend to a considerable extent on the gratifications that we may be able to offer to them. In order to determine this, we must find out the elements that enter into the moral picture of Germany.

1. The German soldier fights supremely well. That appears to be the universal judgement. But he has surrendered without qualms and, in part, even with pleasure, when military defeat was certain. He has done so in Tunisia, though he apparently did not do so in Russia. How can we explain this fact: The surrender in Tunisia and the resistance before Stalingrad may, indeed, provide us with an answer.

The German soldier fights well not because he is a passionate Nationalist desirous of dying a hero's death, not because he is an ardent Nazi who wants to establish a New Order, but because his approach to fighting is largely technological. Fighting is a business and has to be carried out efficiently. Such an attitude gives tremendous strength as long as the machine functions in which he is incorporated, but makes for weakness once the machine breaks down.

He, nevertheless, fought well in Russia because he was afraid of the Russians.

It has always been my contention that fear is the predominant element making for the fighting and productive strength of the German people. Innumerable instances could be given, but it will be sufficient to draw attention to a State Department cable from Bern, May 1 1943 (OSS No.18140),[4] which maintains that the main reason why the Germans are fighting so well is that their propaganda has been able to play upon their fear.

2. This fear takes many forms and has many causes. I would summarize it in the following way:

a. Middle classes and considerable sections of the workers are afraid of Russia. While the German regime has never informed its own people of the atrocities and

---

4. Not printed.

spoliation committed in eastern territories, this knowledge is undoubtedly being disseminated by foreign propaganda and by the actual experience of the German soldier.

The Germans begin to realize that Russia will demand reparations and that the reparations cannot be paid either in money or in machinery alone. They are afraid that Russia will insist on the transfer of millions of German workers to Russia in order to assist in the reconstruction of the destroyed territory. This fear is strongest among the middle classes and considerable parts of the workers, while it is far less strong in the [former] conservative groups and especially among the Junkers[5] and the officers Corps who always had a high appreciation of the so-called realism of Russian policy and were willing to make bargains with Russia. It is my belief that the foreign policy tradition of Bismarck is still alive among these groups.

We should exploit this fear of Russia to the utmost, not by pointing out the difference between Russia and Anglo-America but by stressing the humane treatment given to German war prisoners, and to the peoples in countries liberated from the Axis.

[...]

Germany has already reached a point where certain controls are beginning to break down. We know that fraternization between German and foreign workers has already gone beyond words and expressed itself in actual help given to foreign workers [...]. We have reason to believe that productivity of the German worker is declining, and we may assume that this is partly due to slowdown tactics, or to sabotage [...].

The Nazi regime counteracts this growing opposition by compelling ever larger strata in German society to participate actively in the commission of atrocities against foreign peoples and in the spoliation of foreign countries.

It is my conviction that the time has now come to tell the German people that they must now actively oppose the regime, that they must refuse to become partners in crime. We must provide them with a kind of guide which teaches them how to refuse participation in atrocities and what to avoid. And we must insist time and again that all those responsible for atrocities and spoliation will be ruthlessly punished.

[...] If we desire to transform masses of German enemies into actual or potential allies, we must at least make some attempt to remove their fears. This makes necessary a consideration of the problems of war aims. I should like to summarize very briefly my ideas:

(1) We should not talk about new orders, European federations, world federations, and similar grandiose plans. Most people in Europe are sick and tired of hearing these all-comprehensive and therefore necessarily vague promises.

---

5. I.e., members of the Prussian landowning nobility.

(2) We should not promise that the United Nations will install a world government or a European government, that we shall make a revolution or prevent a revolution, or that we want to educate the Germans in a new democratic spirit. [...]

(3) We must adopt a very simple principle of International morality, namely that we cannot impose upon the German people a principle that we ourselves do not accept. That applies especially to the problem of the partition of Germany. The Germans fear partition and each plan for Germany's partition which is discussed in our press is eagerly used to increase fear of the future (see for instance, Stuttgarter NS Kurier, April 14).[6] We take it for granted that England and America should be unified states, the expression of the will of a unified people and we would violently oppose any idea for the partition of our countries. We should repudiate officially a partition of Germany, though we should insist that the declaration of frontiers is a quite different matter.

(4) All these statements tend to culminate in the Atlantic Charter[7] which, in Article II, establishes the principle that no territorial changes "that do not accord with the freely expressed wishes of the peoples concerned" should be enacted. Article III respects the right of all peoples to choose the form of government. Though the Atlantic Charter has been attacked and ridiculed, it still remains, in spite of its vagueness, the only adequate plan for domestic political life and for international organization.

It is, indeed, nothing but the reformulation of Woodrow Wilson's Fourteen points, and is felt as such by the European people. Critics of the Atlantic Charter point out that the ideology which lies at its bottom, is utterly bankrupt. In 1918, it is true, the European masses welcomed Wilson as a new messiah. It was Wilson's New Freedom and Wilson's Fourteen Points which were able to keep [Bolshevism] out of Europe. We have thus to learn from the experience of 1918 to 1919 and to pose the question why the Wilsonian ideology collapsed in Europe. Three reasons are responsible for it:

(a) The withdrawal of America from the League of Nations and her refusal to implement non-aggression pacts. [...][8]

(b) The aid and comfort given by the European ruling classes to German reaction and the subtle sabotage that these ruling classes carried out against German democracy.

(c) The most important element, however, still remains the fact that the German counter-revolution composed of Army leadership, big business,

---

6. During the mid-years of the war there had been all sorts of schemes for breaking up Germany into small states. The term used at the time was "dismemberment."

7. This charter was set up when Churchill and Roosevelt met in Newfoundland between August 9 and 12, 1941.

8. Illegible passage.

East Elbian Junkers, and high civil servants, established itself in power on the way the German revolution broke out.

The Atlantic Charter can be made again a reality under three conditions.

(a) We must present to the European people a definite commitment of the United States that she will not revert into an isolationist policy but will fulfill her international obligations if a new League of Nations should be established.
(b) We must give definite assurances that foreign governments will not strengthen anti-revolutionary trends in Germany and will not support conservative groups in their fight aginst a rejuvenated German democracy.
(c) We must, above all, make a clear and unambiguous declaration that if a revolution should break out in Germany [...], if the German people should finally decide to eliminate the seedbed of imperialism, militarism and [feudalism], no foreign government will stop them.

These demands for a new offensive against Germany are primarily negative in character. I repeat that it is my belief that the liberation of Europe from Nazi controls must be the aim of the German peoples themselves. The task of the United Nations is exclusively to inflict so heavily a military defeat on Germany that the power of the German military machine is completely broken and that the belief in the [...][9] superiority of Nazi strength is finally exterminated.

---

9. Illegible word.

Document 13 · 3 August 1943

Memorandum from Irving H. Sherman (OSS Counterintelligence Branch) to Hugh R. Wilson (OSS Planning Group)[1]: Proposal for the Establishment of a Committee of German Exiles

SECRET

Save Germany Group
(Restorierung des Vaterlandes Gruppe)

Any attempt to influence the German people requires a special kind of approach in view of the methodical orderliness of the German Mind. The German is always "German". His history has disciplined him to do as he is told and, consequently, he is an unusually good citizen. He is sentimental, but not emotional, and any attempt to influence him must proceed on highly logical lines.

Approaches to him can be infinitely more successful if they are made by Germans. We must not forget the laborious steps which the National Socialists went through in 1933 to get German citizenship for Hitler.[2] The fact that he was not a German was a mental hurdle for many Germans, which the National Socialists knew had to be overcome.

The National Socialist Government was something which the average German could accept, even though there were many aspects of National Socialism

---

1. NA, RG 226, Entry 144, Box 15, Folder P[lanning] G[roup] #41. Hugh R. Wilson was one of the Germany experts in the OSS. In 1944, he advocated the idea of political separation of Germany into several parts. He argued, however, that separation should not be forced upon the Germans by the Allies, but be created by a voluntary act of the Germans themselves. Wilson discussed these plans not only with Americans but also with German planners for civil affairs in Great Britain. His suggestions invariably reached the desk of the President.

2. In February 1932, Hitler was formally made a government official of the German State of Braunschweig.

which the average German accepted only with reluctance. It was "legally" constituted, it operated within the framework of the law, and often went to absurd extremes to make "legal" its actions. As long as things went well on balance, the German was not too unhappy, but now that things have seriously gone wrong for him, he can be made receptive to suggestions for radical conduct.

The German is not easily converted to disloyalty to his Government. An invitation from the enemy to join a particular course of action, would encounter serious obstacles in the German mind, but an appeal from *free Germans* urging the same course of action, would find much more sympathetic reception. In this case, the German is working with Germans, and that is something he can logically accept.

Unfortunately, the Russians announced a "National Committee of Free Germans"[3] while the thoughts herein indicated were being developed, but whereas some of the benefits of surprise may be lessened, there are still many essential advantages between what the Russians have done and what is here proposed.

I urge serious considerations be given to the formation of a Save Germany Group, made up of eight or ten outstanding German refugees. I would prefer it be called a "Group" rather than a "Committee", to distinguish it from the French and Russian Committees recently formed.[4] "Save Germany" would portray to the Germans that disaster is impending.

This Group should be constituted by the outstanding representatives available in each particular category of German society, so that any German can find in this Group a representation for what he would like to find. There should be no Jews represented in this Group. The Group should be made up of a prominent Catholic, a Protestant, Deutsch Nationale [German National Conservative], Social Democrat, Communist, with representation, perhaps, for one or two other groups, if suitable representatives can be found. We should select the most outstanding refugees available in these categories, in the light of the influence their names are likely to carry with the Germans and the extent to which they are likely to lend themselves for our purposes.

An indivudual like Dr. Gruening [Brüning],[5] for instance, is useless for this type of project. He will not do all that we ask of him, and for what he would be prepared to do, he will undoubtledy want a quid pro quo in the way of commitments and promises. Our Group should be made up of best names available of people to whom we need make no serious promises and who will cooperate solely on the basis of a common desire to overthrow National Socialism.

---

3. See in particular document [14].

4. I.e., the Free Germany Committee and the League of German Officers in Moscow, and the Comité Allemagne Libre pour l'Ouest (CALPO) in France.

5. Former Reich Chancellor Heinrich Brüning (1930–1932) had emigrated to the U.S. and was living and teaching at Harvard University.

This Group will not be a Government-in-exile. It will be clearly indicated that it makes no pretense of being the basis for any future Government. This Group will be the mouthpiece for important MO [Morale Operations] work. It is probable that collateral opportunities would result for SI [Secret Intelligence] and SO [Special Operations].

A tentative list of suggested candidates, and alternatives, follows. These individuals are all in either the United States or Canada. It might well be that certain refugees in England might be better suited than some here suggested, and this possibility is being explored:

1. Hermann Rauschning—President Danzig Senate—Ex-Nazi
   Dr. F. Wilhelm Sollmann—Minister of Interior under Stresemann.
2. Freiherr Wolfgang von & zu Putlitz—German Foreign Office
   Hans Von Hentig
3. Dr. Hans Simons—Son of President of Reichsgerichtshof
   Kurt Riezler
4. Dr. Carl Spiecker—Catholic
   Annette Kolb—Catholic
5. Dr. Paul Tillich—Protestant
6. Max Brauer—Mayor of Altona—Prominent Social Democrat
   Thomas Mann
7. Dr. Horst Baerensprung—Reichsbanner—Police President of Magdeburg
8. Oskar Maria Graf—Communist
   Heinrich Mann—Communist

Document 14 · 6 August 1943

Memorandum from James Grafton Rogers[1]
(OSS Planning Group) to the Joint Chiefs of Staff:
Manifesto to the German People by the
Moscow National Committee of Free Germany[2]

SECRET

Memorandum for the Joint U.S. Chiefs of Staff

Subject: Manifesto to German People by Moscow National Committee of Free Germany

Statement of Problem

1. To advise the Joint Chiefs of Staff of the psychological and political implications of the manifesto recently issued by the Moscow National Committee of Free Germany. [...]

Facts Bearing on the Problem

2. The Manifesto. a. On 21 July 1943, "Pravda" (the official Communist Party organ in Moscow) published a manifesto to the German people issued by the National Committee of Free Germany, which had "organized itself" in Moscow at

---

1. NA, RG 226, Entry 144, Box 15, Folder 100. A friend of Secretary of War Henry Stimson and General George C. Marshall, James Grafton Rogers was an influential, conservative member of the OSS.

2. For other OSS estimates and for discussions on the Free Germany Committee see documents [15], [29], [38] and [90].

meetings on 12 and 13 July.[3] (Copy attached as published in the N.Y. "Daily Worker" on 22 July 1943). This manifesto called for immediate action of Germans at home and of the German army to overthrow the Hitler Government, to cease military operations, to recall the German troops to the Reich's frontiers, and to embark on peace negotiations, renouncing all conquests. It proposed for Germany, now faced with collapse, a strong democratic state on equal footing with other nations and the restoration of property and of civil rights.

b. The manifesto purports to be signed by thirty-three German refugees and prisoners, including Communist leaders, former Reichstag Communist deputies, and soldiers.

c. The manifesto has been widely circulated and supported by the Soviet press and radio and represents official Soviet policy, emanating from a source which may be supported or repudiated.

3. *Analysis of Soviet Intentions.* The manifesto seems to reflect confidence in Russia's military and political strength in the present situation and her determination to provoke at least a limited revolution in Germany before any peace negotiations. It could serve equally well as cover for a separate peace between the Soviets and a militarist regime in Germany or for a far-reaching program of eventual invasion and Bolshevization. On the other hand, the fact that the Soviet government has allowed the Free German Committee to be set up and has given it support in the Russian press without consulting the other United Nations does not necessarily mean that Russia is determined at all costs to continue a lone wolf policy in regard to Germany. Whatever the intentions of the Soviet government, the manifesto may have far-reaching implications which are analyzed below.

4. *Psychological Warfare Implications.* a. The psychological implications of the manifesto may be stated as follows:

(1) From the Point of View of the U.S.S.R. As an instrument of psychological warfare in furtherance of the Soviet military program, the manifesto aims to create a situation in Germany which will assist in the overthrow of the Hitler Government and will thus place Germany in a position where peace terms acceptable to the Soviet Government can be negotiated.

(2) From the Point of View of the United States and Great Britain. While the manifesto is aimed primarily at the overthrow of the Hitler Government and at the building of a "strong democratic" Germany on the pattern of Soviet Russia, such action is to be attained under conditions opposed to the present views and pronouncements of the United States and Great Britain, particularly those pertaining to an "unconditional surrender". While this manifesto calls for the cessation of mil-

---

3. The Free Germany Committee was created following the surrender of the German Sixth Army at Stalingrad. It consisted of German prisoners of war and communist emigrés.

itary operations and the recall of German troops to the German frontier, it does not provide for disarmament or the disbanding of the German military machine. If Germany responds to the manifesto, Russia would be placed in a highly advantageous position relating to peace with Germany, since the terms under the manifesto are more acceptable than those laid down under our "unconditional surrender". It would be possible for Russia to make a peace (or separate peace) under terms and conditions highly advantageous to herself and at least on the surface to Germany as well, while the United States and Great Britain would be left with the alternative of continuing the war or of accepting a negotiated peace with Germany.

5. Political Implications.   a. The political implications of this manifesto are not only far-reaching from the Soviet viewpoint but disturbing from the ideological and political viewpoint of the United States and Great Britain.

b. The manifesto, while undoubtedly aiming at the overthrow of the Hitler Government, at the same time contemplates the setting up within Germany of a government favorable to Moscow. This might result in a communistic Germany, which would scarcely be acceptable to the United States and Great Britain. Further, success of the manifesto might bring about a breakdown of resistance, in which event Russia, with forces on the field, would be in a position to arrange a peace and a German government to its liking.

c. The manifesto represents a major political move. It was probably timed with confidence to coincide with military developments on the Eastern Front and the increased air activity in the West. With Italy about to disintegrate[4] and with the approach of winter on the Eastern Front, it is not out of the question for Germany to seek a way out of the war. The United States and Great Britain offer "unconditional surrender" with no assurance of protection against the urge for vengeance on the part of the people of occupied countries. In comparison, the Moscow manifesto offers on its face value many advantages.

d. Complete political unity does not exist between the Soviet Union and the other United Nations, and political differences arising out of the manifesto may lead to a dangerous situation between these countries. The possible dangers to our military and political strategy are such that a re-examination of our American political position as it relates to the manifesto is indicated.

e. The action of the Soviet government creates a favorable opportunity for German psychological warfare to exploit political disunity among the Allies, to increase British and American suspicion of Russia and vice versa. Any premature or hasty steps on our part to protect ourselves against the possibly adverse consequences of Soviet policy might aggravate the situation and result finally in the failure or at least postponement of our main European war objective—total victory over Germany.

---

4. After the overthrow and arrest of Mussolini in late July, the new Italian government under Marshal Badoglio had entered into secret negotiations with the Western Allies on 3 August 1943.

6. [...]

Conclusions

7. A careful study of the psychological and political effects of this manifesto leads
to the following conclusions:

a. As an instrument of psychological warfare the manifesto may have great
value in assisting in the overthrow of the Hitler Government. In view of
this, nothing should be done to minimize this effect.

b. The manifesto may denote an indication to seek a separate peace with
Germany.

c. Present Soviet policy towards post-war political development in Germany
as reflected in the manifesto is dangerous in its implications in that it might
result in a government opposed to the political and idealistic principles for
which we are fighting. Our political position will be greatly enhanced as our
military forces arrive on the continent of Europe.

d. That our future actions should continue to use all psychological warfare
and military pressure toward the overthrow of the Hitler Government and
the total defeat of Germany.

e. That if a joint Anglo-American-Soviet policy is not established, we must be
prepared at the psychological time to present to Germany conditions which
will offset the Russian proposals in the armistice and the peace.

> **For the OSS Planning Group**
> *James Grafton Rogers*
> **Chairman**

Document 15 · 11 August 1943

Memorandum from John C. Wiley
(OSS Foreign Nationalities Branch)[1]
to President Franklin D. Roosevelt:
Comments on the Moscow Manifesto
to Germany[2]

SECRET

Memorandum

Comments on the Moscow Manifesto to Germany

... [3]

The manifesto and Soviet complaints about the lack of a second front require analysis.

Although the Soviet Union is suffering grievously from a war unparalleled in casualties and destruction, the Soviet military situation is at this moment peculiarly favorable. Soviet complaints over the second front, therefore, do not stem from the same dire need for military succor that existed a year ago.

The manifesto and its timing are, of course, primarily political. It is the opening gambit for a peace move. Our "failure" to open a second front could provide

---

1. Roosevelt Library, Hyde Park, F. D. Roosevelt Papers. President's Secretary's Files, Box 167. The Foreign Nationalities Branch (FNB) had been set up in 1941 to report upon foreign politics as they unfold in the United States in connection with foreign nationality groups. It had been William J. Donovan's intention to place the work in the hands of two personalities with a long diplomatic experience John Wiley and DeWitt C. Poole. In December 1941, Roosevelt gave his "OK" to the FNB outfit.

2. This memorandum was one of the very few OSS papers that was sent to the President not through William J. Donovan or his deputy, G. Edward Buxton, but through one of the OSS division leaders. In his covering letter Wiley asked Roosevelt to "forgive me for trying to inflict it [the memorandum] on you." He also stressed that he had professional experience "in Germany and Eastern Europe, including Moscow."

3. The omitted passage deals predominantly with British policy toward the Soviet Union and with Soviet policy as a continuation of traditional Russian policy.

the alibi. The peace proposition conveyed to the Germans by the manifesto is an alternative to "unconditional surrender" that might be more seductive to many Germans. We, with "unconditional surrender", do not even give Germany an assurance of protection from the vengeance of the conquered peoples, an assurance that is implicit in the Soviet proposal.

Field Marshal Kutuzov, who was Commander-in-Chief against Napoleon, is once again a national hero in Russia; a new Soviet decoration is named after him. He discovered in October, 1812, that it was better not to crush Napoleon since Russia's ally, England, would, he thought, be the only one to gain. His idea was simple, that Napoleon had learned his lesson; he would never again be a danger to Russia, and if he could reform his legions in France, he might then be able to cope with the British from whose iniquities Russia so long had suffered.

Marshal Stalin, like Marshal Kutuzov, may now think that Hitler will never again be a danger to Russia; that the Germans might be useful in curbing the iniquities of the English (and of the Americans, too), and that a *Moscow*-Berlin Axis might be the answer to the Kremlin's prayer (with, of course, the center of balance heavily in the East).

If Germany makes a deal with Moscow and withdraws to her frontiers, it must be noted that the Reich would be deprived of Rumanian oil, Balkan minerals and foodstuffs and would be completely encircled. Germany would then be subject to the full force of Soviet pressure. In other words, from the moment that such an agreement was carried out, Moscow could always exact anything desired of Berlin unless we and the British rushed to the aid of the Reich, which is unthinkable at this time.

A *Moscow*-Berlin Axis, notwithstanding war-weariness, would be more formidable than the Berlin-Rome alignment ever was.

As a counter-poise, the British Isles would be inadequate. Our position would become unfavorable.

Soviet political planning is both daring and prudent. The Kremlin is as yet committed to nothing. The Free German trial balloon could be quietly abandoned, or the Free German Committee, and other committees, too, could become the spearhead of the new Europe.

American Policy—

American policy in this war is difficult to formulate. This is largely because it is so very simple. It is not adhesive to popular appeal or even understanding. This derives from the negative fact that the United States was in grave danger and was attacked. We did not go to war; war came to us.

[...]

At present, we face the dangerous paradox of having our political authority on the Continent of Europe diminish while our military strength is notably ascendant. Attack from the air and the destruction of great German cities are wounding Germany. Now, only Russia has land armies to retrieve the fallen game.

Our position, namely, concentration on the military task of winning the war, must be re-interpreted politically. The Russians are not yet irrevocably committed to a line of policy; neither are the Germans. The British can be influenced if we adopt a strong and positive line. We have vast strength. If exerted politically, it can still save the United States from fighting a great and costly war merely to have achieved the intolerable end of permanent mobilization.

In this war both Germany and Russia have produced great military surprises. We must be fully prepared against political surprises equally enormous. If such a surprise should be a union of Russian imperialism with Comintern revolutionary technique, joined with German military and economic competence, the result would be difficult to handle. Russian-German collaboration is not as fantastic as it sounds. Its roots go back to Bismarck, even to Frederick the Great. After Rapallo[4] and again after the Ribbentrop-Molotov agreement,[5] there was effective German-Russian collaboration. Each country now has a military elite, each a great bureaucracy, industry is managerial, and proletarianization is no stranger to the Reich; moreover, Western democracy is more incompatible with the Soviet system than that of another totalitarian state. Thus, elements of affinity already exist between them. The hatreds of war in Europe pass quickly into history. Rapallo came soon after Brest Litovsk.[6]

Suggested Lines of Action:

(1) Formulate a clear-cut, long-term policy, comprising maximum and minimum peace aims.
(2) Press the British into alignment.
(3) Avert a situation where we might be impelled to "outbid" the Russians, or where Germany could play one ally off against the other.
(4) Limit the doctrine of "unconditional surrender" to "Hitlerite Germany". No matter how undesirable, it is made necessary by the fact that Mr. Stalin has already done this.
(5) Expedite the setting up of a second front in as great force as possible—but in the Balkans, where it could best influence both the course of the war, diplomatic relations with the Kremlin, and the peace to come. True, a Balkan front is difficult; perhaps it is impossible. If so, we must, of course, give up the project, but if it is merely very difficult but not impossible, we must by all means set up the Balkan front.[7] An invasion of France and the Lowlands would give us no political authority in central and eastern Europe. Only a successful Anglo-American invasion of southeastern Europe can give us a real voice in the eventual peace settlement. To err on

---

4. The Rapallo Treaty of 16 April 1922 was a special agreement between Germany and the Soviet Union in which all World War I financial liabilities between the two powers were cancelled.

5. 23 August 1939.

6. This is a reference to the Peace Treaty between the then victorious Germans and the Soviet Union on 3 March 1918 at Brest-Litovsk. The Versailles Treaty, however, cancelled the foregoing arrangements.

7. This alternative to a massive invasion in Normandy, France, was favored by Churchill.

the side of supposed caution in reaching the historic decision on what to do now might store up the gravest dangers for the future.

(6) Keep Germany oriented to the West and prevent her turning East.

(7) Leave nothing undone to reassure the Kremlin of continuing Anglo-American support, political and economic, in a peace without conquest.

Such lines of action, if promptly, skilfully, and resolutely pursued, will save a situation which is rapidly turning bad. It is wrong to underestimate our strength or to overestimate that of our enemies and allies. We can and must win both the war and the peace.

Document 16 · 19 August 1943

Telegram from Allen W. Dulles (OSS Bern) to OSS Washington: Thoughts for Political Warfare[1]

SECRET

TOR: 8/19/43 9:00 pm

623–627, inclusive. Thus far in this war, our political warfare has lagged behind our military warfare. To vitalize our psychological warfare, can we not do something during or after the Quebec Conference[2] in the way of appealing to the masses in the Axis countries? I am aware of the fact that the terms of unconditional surrender must not and will not be altered, but Axis propagandists [have] distorted this into synonymity with the oppression of the common man and the enslavement of peoples in the capitulated countries, etc. Could not Allied leaders emphasize that while surrender is admissive of complete military defeat, it actually will inaugurate a new life for the oppressed in Axis and Axis-controlled countries; that it means the end of the war, the end of bombing raids, the end of the Gestapo; the resumption of labor's right to organize for its own protection; of the people's

---

1. NA, RG 226, Entry 134, Box 339, Folder 1817.

2. 17 to 24 August 1943.

right to choose their own government, to exercise the right of free speech, to have old age pensions, social security, currency stabilization (in the sense of putting a firm foundation beneath world values and thereby protecting workers' savings). These are the things that the enslaved peoples of Europe are interested in today—not future nation boundaries. If we take concerted measures in both the psychological and military fields of warfare, we *can* crack Germany and end the war this year. This is [not] mere wishful thinking; it is the opinion of tough military critics here and the consensus of calm persons who have watched and are watching the situation in Germany, and in the Satellite and occupied countries. Germany is a fighter who has been knocked down a couple of times. She can go for several more rounds if we let her get her breath. If we hit her with the hardest military and political punch we have, we can bring about the collapse.

Document 17 · 31 August 1943

Memorandum by the OSS Morale Operations Branch in London: Suggestions for a German Underground Plan[1]

SECRET

The Hamilton Plan[2] and the Organization of the German Underground

Discussions of the Hamilton Plan by European Theater personnel of MO [Morale Operations Branch] have resulted in:

---

1. NA, RG 226, Entry 139, Box 175, Folder 2316. The plan was offered in this somewhat tentative form for panel discussion by representatives of all OSS branches.

2. Apparently the plan was named after Dr. James Hamilton, a psychologist who worked for the OSS Morale Operations Branch. Besides Hamilton, several members of the MO European desk, including Lt. McGranahan, Mr. Seger and Mrs. Taylor contributed to the plan.

(a) General approval of the plan by MO, in its original form, as a PW [Psychological Warfare] operation of limited scope (with modifications affecting the form of the Document suggested in the Plan, and the wording of the Oath to be inscribed thereon);

(b) The suggestion, developed more fully below, that the time has perhaps come to tackle the problem of organizing anti-Nazi forces in Germany into a cohesive, determined, revolutionary Underground.

The Hamilton Plan in its original form (but incorporating the changes suggested by MO) is referred to below as the Minor Project, while the organization of an integrated and active German Underground is referred to as the Major Project.

It was the opinion of MO representatives that further discussion of both projects should be held with representatives of other branches, since obviously the implementation and activation of the Major Project would be the task not of MO alone, but of all branches of OSS. The following outline of MO's deliberations is therefore offered as a basis for a conference with representatives of other branches.

1. The Minor Project

The Hamilton Plan in its original form may be briefly outlined as a plan "for mobilizing an opposition movement within Germany" based on the circulation in Germany of reports that Germans who have been passively opposed to the Nazis in the past are now banding together in groups of three, four, or five, to sign a Document attesting this opposition and committing them to a program of active resistance to the Nazi Government. It is assumed that the *report* of such a movement would have the effect of *creating* it, that the rumored groups would soon have a very real existence. The signing of a Document would have both a ritualistic and a practical significance; it would tend to confirm and intensify the individual's sense of opposition to the Nazis, by associating him with others sharing his point of view. And the Document itself, signed and dated before the defeat of the Nazis, would be evidence that the signers were partners in victory, thus securing preferential treatment for them as right-minded Germans. The Hamilton Plan emphasizes the importance which Germans signing the Document would be likely to attach to it as a form of insurance. For this reason, the Plan states, the Document "will have to be definitely and validly dated, so as to prevent Nazi opportunists from signing (it) after defeat and forging an earlier date." The Hamilton Plan therefore suggests that the Document take the form of a dated sheet from a current newspaper "upon which signatures and commitments are inscribed." For further details of the Plan, its implementation and activation, reference is made to the plan itself, which is attached in its original form to these notes. [...]

Approving the Hamilton Plan as a PW operation of limited scope, MO representatives made the following suggestions:

(a) That the "Oath" on the Document be strongly worded committing the signers to active resistance to the Nazis.

(b) That this oath be inscribed not on a dated sheet from a current newspaper since old newspapers would presumably be available to Nazi opportunists for the forging of documents at a later date), but on a postcard, addressed by one member of a group to another, and incorporating the name of a third (eventually a fourth or fifth) member in an otherwise innocent communication.

To illustrate: Hans, Heinz and Hermann mutually declare their opposition to the Nazis and agree to execute a Document. To certify that this Document was indeed executed on a date prior to an anticipated Nazi collapse, Hans addresses a card to Heinz: "The beer here is first rate. Hermann and I send greetings." The card is mailed, receives a date (postmark), and is delivered. Hans, Heinz and Hermann reconvene and execute upon this dated card their oath of opposition to the Nazis, adding their signatures. Thus, with the unwitting assistance of the postal authorities, they are their own witnesses to the fact that the Document was executed on or immediately after a given date.

In further discussion of the postcard idea, it was proposed that oppositional groups be encouraged to increase by cell division. Hans, Heinz and Hermann have executed a Document; this document is retained by Hans; both Heinz and Hermann must now form oppositional cells of their own; Heinz therefore induces Hugo and Heinrich to execute a Document with him, which he retains; and so on ad infinitum. If the movement were to take this cell structure, each member would be in possession of a Document bearing the signatures of two other members, while his own signature would appear on two documents. The gain in organizational cohesiveness would be somewhat offset by loss of security. But the plan in any form envisages the eventual amalgamation of the groups executing documents, so undue importance need not be attached to this point.

In MO discussions of this modification of the plan, the point was made that by adopting the cell pattern for the movement, the use of the dated postcards would be obviated. Documents could be dated by signatories and the validity of the dates on a series of documents would be attested by their chronological order. Thus Hans, Heinz and Hermann execute and date their Document on September 15; Heinz then persuades Hugo and Heinrich to join the movement, and their Document is executed and dated September 19. Hugo in turn creates a cell with the aid of X and Y, and their document is dated September 22. There would be no prescribed physical form for the documents in this case, but only a prescribed text for the oath. This prescribed text might read as follows:

For Freedom, Peace and Human Dignity:

We a group of patriotic Germans, condemn the Nazi system of tyranny and war which has brought such terrible suffering upon the German people. We pledge ourselves from now on to do everything conceivable to hasten the downfall of the Nazi system, and make Germany a peaceful, free and decent land.

Name. . . . .
Name. . . . .
Name. . . . .
Members of the (Widerstandsbruederschaft or Hamburger Bewegung)

[…]³
It will be observed from this oath that a name—Widerstandsbruederschaft (Resistance Fraternity) or Hamburger Bewegung (Hamburg ~~Government~~ *Movement)*—has been proposed for the movement. The first is an MO suggestion, in the highest degree tentative; the second stems from the Hamilton Plan. In the Hamilton Plan we read: "Any movement which represents or requires the concerted thoughts and actions of a large number of people requires a name." Appendix 5 to the Plan continues: "The name of the movement should emphasize its indigenous source," and suggests that if the Plan were launched immediately, the name Hamburger Bewegung, implying that the movement originated in that much bombed city, might be particularly effective. There is certainly a point here, for recent SI [Secret Intelligence] reports have referred to evidence of increased underground activity in Hamburg.

MO further suggests that a symbol be adopted for the movement. The psychological importance and the practical *[…]*⁴ of such a symbol (which, as the movement it represented gained headway, would appear chalked on walls and pavements, and used to deface the Swastika) is obvious and need not be supported by argument. It would naturally be essential to avoid using any symbol which, like the three arrows of the Iron Front of Weimar Republic days, might already carry a special significance in Germany. The symbol proposed by MO, three interlocking circles […]⁵ has been investigated by R&A, which reports that it has no knowledge of its previous use by any German political, religious or social organization.

2. The Major Project

The Hamilton Plan may fairly be called a minor project only so long as it is thought of as a limited action against enemy morale, instigated by rumor and black radio, resulting in the formation of small, isolated oppositional groups throughout Germany. These groups might indulge in individual acts of passive resistance and minor sabotage, but they could not take on the character of a movement unless communications were established among them, a development which the Hamilton Plan in its original form leaves largely to chance. However, by imposing a cell structure on the movement from the start, an important step would be taken toward the creation of a large-scale resistance movement. Further steps in the same direction might include:

---

3. The omitted passage gives a German translation of the prescribed text.
4. Insertion of illegible, handwritten word.
5. The original document shows a drawing in this place.

1. Securing the collaboration of German political leaders and trade unionists outside of Germany, mainly for the purpose of getting at their constituents at home.
2. Securing the collaboration of any underground organization which may already exist in Germany.
3. Securing the collaboration of underground organizations in occupied countries.
4. Securing the collaboration of foreign labor in Germany.
5. Establishing communications with the movement through channels opened by 1–4.
6. Suggesting a program of action (strikes, sabotage, etc.).
7. Suggesting a positive ideology for the movement. (This is a consideration of prime importance.)

A number of these steps call for some discussion.

In connection with (1) it is safe to assume that a great many members of the outlawed political parties and trade unions of Weimar Republic days, never Nazis at heart, are now, after four years of war, more violently opposed than ever to the Nazi regime. One means of reaching this large but scattered and politically heterogeneous section of the German people, would be through its representatives outside of Germany:

a. The Conservatives.   Large numbers of Germans, formerly members of the conservative Deutschnationalepartei [Deutschnationale Volkspartei, DNVP] or the conservative-liberal Deutsche Volkspartei (Stresemann), are known to be anti-Nazi and should by all means, if they can be reached, be embraced in the movement envisaged by the Major Project. Contact with them might be established through Gottfried R. Treviranus, former Frei-Konservativ [sic] minister of the Bruening Cabinet, now residing in Canada.[6]

b. The Liberals.   Two groups of liberals are important—those of the Stresemann school of thought, and those who formed the German Democratic Party (Demokratische Staatspartei). The Democratic Party formerly had its own association of democratic trade unions. Contacts with these groups might be made through Dr. Paul Schwarz, former German Consul General in New York, now residing in New York, and Dr. Gustav Stolper, former editor of the Deutsche Volkswirt ["German Economist"] and member of the Reichstag, also residing in New York at this time.

c. The Centrists (Catholics).   It would be most important to secure the collaboration of this group. Aside from the fact that the Center Party had its own Catholic

---

6. Although Treviranus had attained Canadian citizenship in early 1943, he was by August 1943 permanently residing in the U.S.

trade unions with a large membership, hundreds of thousands of its adherents have put up a valiant fight against the Nazis, and some of its "Gesellenvereine" [journeyman societies] have for years been engaged in underground activities. The person to contact would be Dr. Werner Thormann, a former leading functionary and editor of the Center party, now residing in New York, working with the Biographical Branch of OSS.[7]

d. The Social Democrats and Free Trade Unionists. Considering the fact that the Social Democratic Party [SPD] formerly had more than one million members in Germany, and the Free Trade Unions between 4 and 5 million members, and in view too of the fact that these groups have been engaged in underground activities off and on throughout the years, they would seem to be, like the Catholics, of the greatest importance to a genuine underground movement. Contacts with them might be sought through more than one person, and abroad as well as in the U.S. In England the German trade union representative, recognized as such by the British Trade Union Congress, is Hans Gottfurcht; in Stockholm he is Fritz Tarnow, former member of the Reichstag and President of the Carpenter's Union. In the U.S. contact could be made through Richard Hansen, now working with the OSS, who conducted underground activities for years, first from Schleswig-Holstein[8] and later from Denmark;[9] and through Gustav Ferl, now residing in Indianapolis, who for seven years, until 1940, was the Liaison Secretary of the German SPD-underground in Belgium.

The question as to whether or not anti-Nazis in Germany, especially those over 40 years of age, are likely still to be thinking in terms of their former party or trade union affiliation may be answered by referring to the amazing occurrence in Milan the day following Mussolini's fall from power,[10] when representatives of five of the pre-Fascist parties, which had been outlawed for twenty-one years, assembled spontaneously in the former Fascist headquarters to constitute a point around which a politically revived Italian people could and probably will rally. Is it not reasonable to suppose that many Germans in a like manner still cling to pre-Nazi political faiths and loyalties, and that these Germans are precisely the ones most likely to form the nucleus of a large-scale Underground movement?

There is an additional reason for approaching anti-Nazis on the basis of their former party or trade union affiliation. While it may be assumed that anti-Nazis in Germany are united today in their contempt [sic] for an opposition to the Nazi

---

7. The OSS Biographical Records project (later Biographical Records Section) had been been founded in mid-1943 by Emmy C. Rado, Ann Stewart, Dr. Thormann and Dr. Kempner. In their New York City office, Rado and her staff collected among other things information on anti-Nazis (white lists), Nazis (black lists), and neutrals (grey lists) in Germany.

8. Northernmost state of Germany.

9. From 1933 to 1940. After the German occupation of Denmark, Hansen emigrated to Sweden and, in mid-1941, to the United States.

10. 25 July 1943.

regime, and that former party lines are no longer of any importance politically, they may still be of great importance personally. Any underground activity, no matter how guardedly carried on, is so extremely dangerous that as a rule only those associate in it who have known one another through long years of membership in the same organization. For this reason, it might be found necessary, and would certainly prove expedient, to approach representatives of the various parties and trade unions seperately. The principal groups are all represented abroad.

As for (2), it would seem that little specific information is available on the subject of existing underground movements in Germany. Various SI and R&A [Research and Analysis] reports hint at the possibility that foci of resistance have developed or are developing there, and a comprehensive inquiry into the matter is suggested. (See SI Dissemination A 9962, on reports of secret trade union meetings in Hamburg, Munich and Essen and other resistance activity among German workers. See also SI Dissemination A-10087a reporting the discovery in Berlin of an alleged plot in which high postal authorities were involved.)[11] It is clear that if small resistance movements are in fact springing up in Germany, full advantage would have to be taken of them in implementing the Major Project.

It is in connection with (2) that (3) and (4) are important, for contact with resistance movements in Germany obviously could most easily be made through underground movements in occupied countries, with which OSS presumably already has relations, and through the use, as undercover agents, of foreign workers drafted for German industry.[12] The extent to which SI and SO contacts with the underground in France, Belgium, Holland, Denmark, Norway can be employed for an MO operation of the sort envisaged in the Major Project (in its initial phase) is something which a conference of branch representatives might well clarify. It is the understanding of MO that R&A is engaged, or will soon engage, in a study of the situation of the foreign worker in Germany, with a view to suggesting PW operations aimed at these workers, or through them at the German people, as well as methods by which such operations might be carried on.

The most important point of all, (7), must now be considered. The ultimate effectiveness of the Hamilton Plan, as either Minor Project or Major Project, would depend in large measure on adding a positive appeal to the merely negative of anti-Nazi sentiments. An example of such a positive appeal is familiar now in the famous Manifesto of the Free Germany Committee formed in Soviet Russia.[13] For a number of reasons, this Manifesto is likely to make a strong impression not only on Communist elements in Germany, but on all Germans opposed in their hearts to the Nazi regime.

No issue of foreign policy in Germany has ever aroused greater, more widespread interest, or stirred Germans more deeply, than the issue of German-

---

11. Not printed.
12. See documents [23] and [84].
13. See in particular document [15].

Russian relations.[14] Even long before World War I this issue provoked a political tempest, when Wilhelm II cancelled the German-Russian "Reassurance Treaty" (Rueckversicherungsvertrag) which Bismarck had concluded.[15] And all through the years of the Weimar Republic there were bitter conflicts between those Germans who oriented themselves toward the Eastern world, that is to say, toward Russia. The dividing line on this issue did not run between economic, social and political groups but cut through all of them. (However, the German army was always pro-Russian, irrespective of the Soviet dictatorship. Thus General von Seeckt, in organizing the black as well as the white Reichswehr was able, during the years 1924–1929, to insure the training of German pilots, illegal under the Treaty of Versailles, by allegedly helping the Russian army to train theirs. A considerable part of the German industrialists were also Russian-minded, despite the anti-capitalist attitude of the Russian dictatorship. On the other hand, a large section of the German labor movement—including a large part of the Social Democrat party [sic], the Catholic Centre [sic] party, of the Free as well as the Christian Trade Unions—was definitely oriented toward the democratic West.)

Utilizing this split in German public opinion the Russian Free Germany Committee appeals to all pro-Russian Germans, even including some sections of the Nazi party. The Manifesto represents the only positive approach to the German people and the German army made so far:

a. It refrains from quoting "unconditional surrender" as a condition for peace.
b. It offers an amnesty to all Nazis who repent and join the Free Germany Committee.
c. It says nothing at all about German disarmament, but implies that Germany will be permitted to have an army of her own afterwards.
d. It appeals to nationalist as well as democratic tendencies by referring to the German (or Prussian) liberation war of 1813—quoting, for example, Theodor Koerner, who was also quoted in the manifesto issued by the Munich students in the Fall of 1942.[16]

Thus the "Free Germany Committee" constitutes a strong appeal to German anti-Nazis, and the question arises whether or not an underground movement

---

14. This section of the paper was considered by several members of the MO Branch to represent "research"; it was feared by them that such a passage might irritate the analysts of R&A. There is no documentation of the outcome of this discussion.

15. The Rückversicherungsvertrag of 1887 was cancelled by Emperor Wilhelm II only three years after its conclusion.

16. This is a reference to the "White Rose" (Weiße Rose) resistance group at Munich University whose members were Alexander Schmorell, Christoph Probst, Willi Graf, Hans and Sophie Scholl as well as Professor Kurt Huber. The actual phrasing of one of their leaflets was: "Students! The German people are looking at us! They expect us to break the Nazi terrors with spiritual force just as Napoleon was broken in 1813." For other references to this movement see documents [21], [22] and [32]. All members of the White Rose group were executed on 22 February 1943.

inspired according to the Hamilton Plan can look to something more than merely being recognized as anti-Nazi and aligned in support of the U.S. and Britain in their warfare against the German army and the Nazi system. As long as we have no pronounced policy with regard to the future status of Germany it will be difficult to compete with the Free Germany Committee influence within the German underground. If the "Free Germany Committee" had not appeared on the horizon at this time, merely a negative anti-Nazi movement might have been successfully fostered. For the overwhelming desire of anti-Nazi Germans is to get rid of the Nazi system as soon and as completely as possible. Now, however, such an underground movement will have to answer to the questions put to it by the adherents of that strange combination of former Communist Reichstag deputies and the grandson of the Iron Chancellor Bismar[c]k,[17] and a simple statement of opposition to the Nazis will not be enough.

(Attention is here called to the proposal of Irving Sherman of the New York Office for the formation of a Save Germany Group [...])[18]

We encounter here the difficulty that the high policy of the United Nations with regard to the "conditions" of Unconditional Surrender is still undeclared. But various signs—most striking among them President Roosevelt's remarks in his recent Lend-Lease letter to the Congress—indicate that while no specific discussion of these "conditions" is permissable in either white or black propaganda,[19] it will perhaps not be forbidden to this propaganda to suggest to the German nation that its future, following total defeat in the war, will be less grim than Dr. Goebbels pictures it. SI cable 623 from Bern, dated August 19, 1943,[20] is an eloquent plea for a positive line of this sort. Using it as a basis, MO has devised the following appeal, to be used in implementing the Hamilton Plan in its initial phases. The appeal is presumed, like the movement itself, to have originated inside Germany:

Germans!
Use your heads!
You have been told that "unconditional surrender" means annihilation.
It does not!
Unconditional Surrender means
The end of the war
The end of bombings
The end of hunger
The end of the black shirt terror

---

17. This is a reference to Heinrich Graf von Einsiedel, a leading member of the German Officer's League in Moscow.

18. Document [13].

19. I.e., open propaganda and propaganda concealing its origins.

20. Document [16].

The return of peace
The return of freedom
The return of security
The return of plenty
It is not peace that means annihilation, it is War that means it, for the Nazi criminals, unworthy of the blood of the great German nation, are determined to sacrifice you to the last man on the altar of their lust for power.
Disown the criminals who have dishonored and are destroying you!

[...]21

To sum up:

MO representatives feel that the time has come to organize a large-scale resistance movement in Germany.

It proposes that the Hamilton Plan in a modified form be adopted as a basis for this operation.

It proposes that by means of the various channels suggested above (German political and trade union groups, existing underground movements in and outside of Germany, foreign labor) a resistance movement be brought into being, equipped from the outset with a positive ideology: "Unconditional Surrender" is a military requirement and must be met—but Germans need not fear that unconditional surrender means national suicide—it means, in fact, an end to the war, the liberation of the German people from its worst enemy, the Nazi regime, the opening of the road to national political and social rehabilitation, the return of the rights of self-determination and self-government, of labor to organize, of the people to reestablish their security.

It proposes that this movement, once under way, be controlled as far as possible by the same means used for its incitement—through the collaboration of German political and labor groups both within and without Germany—and by such other means as may suggest themselves.

It concludes with the admission that complete control of any large-scale resistance movement which may be created within Germany will prove impossible. If successful, the Movement will be found to develop its own program and its own leaders, and to be amenable to outside influence only insofar as it requires outside assistance for the realization of its aims.

...22

---

21. The omitted passage gives a German translation of the prescribed text.

22. Attached to this paper are the following appendices: I The Hamilton Plan as originally presented: Project for mobilizing an opposition movement within Germany; II Psychological Vulnerability of the Target Group; III The Document: Discussion and Details; IV Communications; V Terminology; VI Schedule; VII Post-Invasion Uses of the Movement.

Document 18 · 8 September 1943

Report from Lanning Macfarland (OSS Istanbul) to OSS Washington: Founding of a Free German Movement in the Service of the Western Allies[1]

Report Concerning the Foundation of a Free German Movement in the Service of the Allied War Effort

Source: Cereus [Archibald Coleman]

Subsource: Dogwood [Alfred Schwarz]

Germany's military defeats on all fronts, the crushing weight of the Allied air offensive, the overwhelming war potential of the United Nations, and the recent collapse of the Fascist ideological front,[2] have combined to rouse and strengthen the latent forces of opposition in Germany and to produce a psychological situation, in which well-planned guidance and assistance, both military and propagandistic, afforded to the anti-Nazi groups may well suffice to burst the "Fortress of Europe" open from within, and save men and material during the final assault.

A thorough study of the problem in the light of our knowledge of the German mind, and of the information which we have been able to accumulate through

---

1. NA, RG 226, Entry 190, Box 72, Folder 14. This is one of the many reports furnished by the Dogwood-Cereus circle, which channeled OSS operations from Turkey into Europe. "Dogwood," Czech engineer Alfred Schwarz and "Cereus," journalist Archibald Coleman, established secret connections to four Nazi-dominated countries—Austria, Germany, Hungary and Bulgaria. They were the liaison between Helmuth James Graf von Moltke and the OSS in Washington. See in particular documents [25] and [32]. The Dogwood outfit was terminated on 31 July 1944 after its penetration by the Nazis had become known. For a second "Dogwood" report on the "Free German Movement" see document [26]. Through his contacts with Turkish government circles, "Dogwood" had prevented the handing over of German exiles to the Nazis ever since 1933. Although this report was authored jointly by several German exiles in Turkey, Hans Wilbrandt's particular imprint is recognizable.

2. On the same day (8 September 1943), General Eisenhower announced the armistice with the new Italian Government.

our close and continuous contact with the German underground movement, regarding the state of German morale and the psychological factors potent in Germany today, have all given us the conviction that the solution of this task, is in the formation of a German Democratic movement, which will co-ordinate and lead the forces of opposition, both in Germany and abroad, in the closest possible collaboration with the Allies.

Interviews and conferences preparatory to the creation of such an organ of the German opposition, at the outset with the sole end of creating an instrument of our political and military intelligence, have been in progress at our department in charge of Central-European intelligence for some considerable time. In August, 1943, they led to the foundation of the *"German Freedom Movement" (Deutscher Freiheitsbund-DFB)* which, by its programme, personnel, and intellectual equipment far outreaching the specific province originally envisaged for it, seems in a position to give us the results we need both for the guidance of strategic and tactical operations, and for the enlightened planning of the peace with Germany. We are convinced that the psychological anticlimax at the conclusion of this War, when the terrible strain of bombs and Gestapo terror will snap, will bring political disorientation, and make the German mind a prey to various aberrations, as in the period from 1918 to 1921. But it will also be accessible, as it was then, to the strong appeal of reason and sanity; and it is by stimulating such rallying and steadying tendencies that the victorious nations can do much to prevent the radicalization of Germany and thus safeguard and make fruitful their victory. The German problem is only one facet of the broader problems of European civilization, but it is the central facet; it can be settled only within a European frame in which the German people is not merely an object of world policy, but a partner in carrying out that policy. The DFB, well-supported, may, beyond its function as a military instrument, become the most valuable ally of the United Nations in incorporating Germany within such a world policy, whatever shape it might take.

The DFB is an organization of Germans who have united to work for the liberation of Germany and her reconstruction on democratic lines, in close co-operation with the Allies in the common struggle against Hitlerism. The DFB is led by a number of men (cf. enclosed list under I) who have occupied leading positions in the political, economic and intellectual life of democratic Germany, without being associated in German minds with the era of misery and political strife that made the first German republic unpopular. They possess valuable contacts with like-minded men inside Germany, with circles of the German Wehrmacht and all sectors of German economic life, on the Employer as well as on the Labour side. As men who have been active in pre-Nazi politics they have maintained connections to a number of leaders and exponents of the former democratic parties and of the Labour Unions, all of whom are willing to collaborate toward the common goal the more readily, as working within the framework of a German democratic movement, they are not exposed to the discredit inevitably attaching to mere instruments of a foreign power.

The Draft Programme of the DFB as laid down by its leaders is encl. as II. The Movement does not address political demands to the Allies, nor does it expect from them any pledges relating to the future. On the other hand, it works exclusively in the interest of the democratic Germany of the future, to be built in cordial co-operation with the United Nations along the lines of the liberal and secure world order that constitutes the common aim of free men. It recognized that for the achievement of this goal the whole-hearted collaboration of free and democratic Germans in all fields of military and political warfare against Hitlerism is an essential condition, and it is fully prepared to give its unconditional help in this.

The immense tasks of the Movement from the point of view of furthering the Allied war effort are the following:

1. To enlist the all-out co-operation of Germans prominent in Production, Transport, and Armed Forces for the purposes of Allied military and industrial intelligence. The fact that the DFB operates in a neutral country on the margin of Axis-held Europe predestinates it for such a function;

2. To form and co-ordinate underground fighting organizations based on the active remains of the old democratic parties, to engage in a) passive resistance, b) open organized resistance at a given time and place;

3. To direct Allied propaganda addressed to Germany by providing abundant propaganda material for the ideological warfare against Nazism, and from their insight in the German mind and their deep personal concern in the issues at stake evolve and drive home the convincing arguments, explosive ideas, and stirring formulas that will never be found by non-Germans, however sound be their judgments of the German psychological make-up, and their German accents. According to abundant evidence from German sources, Allied propaganda to Germany is still failing to "put it across"—not least among the reasons for this is the evident "Cui bono" of the Allied propaganda effort;

4. To create a staff of reliable free Germans destined to be the political core of the re-born democratic Germany, and carry its ideas of liberty, supremacy of law, and political tolerance into the masses, thus providing a timely and sorely needed counterweight to the Radicalism of both Right and Left.

The document enclosed under IV represents an attempt to define our ideas concerning the form which the co-operation of the DFB with Your Department of Central-European Intelligence should take in order to realize all the potential value of such a collaboration for the conduct of the War and the planning of the Peace.

A preliminary list of some of the Free German personages in America who should be contacted by the DFB is enclosed under V.

The documents enclosed under III are propaganda pamphlets in the German original and in translation, which the DFB propose to use in its broadcast and other propaganda.

The German Freedom Movement

The German Freedom Movement comprises Germans of various professions, denominations, and political associations, who have united to collaborate for the liberation and reconstruction of Germany. The movement is entirely independent of any political agency, working exclusively and singly on behalf of Germany.

What Is to Be Done?

Fundamental Thoughts and Draft Programme of the German Freedom Movement. National Socialism is doomed. It will not survive the War it has started and lost. There will be a hard fall—and what is to fall, had better be pushed over. A swift death-blow might save hundreds of thousands who otherwise would be senselessly sacrificed. The destruction of the guilty is not worth further discussion. Mussolini has toppled; Hitler will topple after. The two worthies were one, "for better, for worse". Now it is "worse" for them—the cup of shame and suffering is full. Hitler must die, that Germany may live. *But what is to come after?*

That national defeat is not followed by days of jubilation, everyone realizes. Whoever has seen Hamburg and Cologne, Dusseldorf [Düsseldorf] and the Ruhr, the North Sea coast, Mannheim and Nuremberg, knows that our impoverishment is even more awful than in 1918. *The longer the destruction of the Hitler gang is delayed, the more of our national capital will be destroyed*, the more cities and factories, railroads and dams will be wrecked by aerial bombardment, the more war cripples and war orphans will have to be cared for, the more surely will the funds of our National and private insurance and our savings banks vanish in the bottomless abyss that has already swallowed ninety thousand million RM [Reichsmark] previous to 1939, and several hundred thousand million RM since. The whole extent of the destruction of human and material capital will not become evident to the German people, until together with the guilty scoundrels the smoke-screens of Propaganda and the stultifying Press censorship have been cleared away.

What Will the Peace Be Like?

The victors, not the vanquished, lay down the terms of peace—this rule is without exception in history. We must be prepared for hard conditions in any case. If Hitler does not fall until foreign armies have marched into Germany, a dictated peace will be unavoidable. If, on the other hand we have overthrown the Nazi regime before, unprompted and unaided, our voice will at least be heard. *Only a Germany led by sincere democrats can be a partner in any negotiations.* We must attempt to salvage the unity of the Reich, and the right to govern ourselves. Then we must start rebuilding from the ruins as well as our weakness will permit. No miracles from Heaven will come to our aid. Our own insight and our own toil alone can help us.

The dream of World Domination by the People of Overlords has vanished for good. *The German nation can continue to exist only at peace with the other nations and in honest cooperation with them.* Anyone associated with the Nazi Regime would encounter the most profound distrust in the world. But all efforts of decent new men at the head of Germany's foreign policy will also be doomed to failure, unless they are backed up throughout by the steady and sincere will of the people to support their aims. The inheritance of the Nazis in foreign policy is a pile of ruins. To build up world confidence anew it will cost decades of untiring effort. *The new foreign policy can only begin with a self-education by the German people.* A nation lacking all external means of power can bring to bear only the power of its good will. Internal squabbles would reduce us to complete impotence abroad. Secret rearmament leagues, secret arms stores, "Black Reichswehr"[3] and the rest of it will not be tolerated by the victors. *But the point is that we ourselves must not tolerate them!* We must become a peaceful nation not by outside compulsion, but from our own sincere wish. In this way alone can the wounds be healed which Hitler and his henchmen and hangmen have inflicted upon the world.

Within our country, too, after 10 years of Nazidom we find little but ruins. Millions of men capable of work are dead, millions are crippled, millions of women are worn out, the entire nation is undernourished, hundreds of cities are crushed, thousands of factories destroyed. *To get bread, clothing and housing is the most urgent task of the coming years:* it will take nearly all our strength. For generations we shall be steeped in poverty. The reconstruction of our economy will require decades of sacrifice. We must not listen to prophets of Utopia, who promise to spirit away poverty. Again: only our own insight and our own toil can help us! *Privileged classes will have no place in impoverished Germany.* There will be no more unearned increments. The squires on the large estates of the East must disappear: the squires of share packets must disappear. *We need no rich people—we need only working people.* Cripples, orphans, invalids, old people we must care for; those capable of work however will have to work.

On the land we need peasants who walk behind the plough, not Lords of the Manor. *The soil of the landed gentry must be divided up, promptly and thoroughly.* The new settlers will start the humble and hard way; we have no well-groomed farms to offer them. In the neighbourhood of the industrial cities we shall have to do our best to provide land for professional gardners and vegetable farmers in order to increase food production; it will be difficult to purchase food abroad until our export industries have been rebuilt. *The peasant will need help toward the regeneration of his ruined livestock:* high grain prices we cannot honestly promise him. The romantic, nonsensical experiment of privileged "hereditary farmers"[4] will disappear; the soil must be free to pass without hindrance into the

---

3. This illegal and secret partisan army existed in the early years of the Weimar Republic comprising up to 20,000 members in 1923.

4. This is a reference to the so-called Reichserbhofgesetz of 29 September 1933. Under this law, people became hereditary farmers if they could prove their "Aryan" ancestorship as far back as 1800.

nads [hands?] of the most efficient farmer. The care of the forests belongs to the State or to the organs of local government. The Raiffeisen cooperative societies[5] remain the basis of agricultural credit; for marketing purposes they will collaborate with the cooperative stores of the cities. *The raising of bread and meat prices through duties must stop*; then the artificially inflated prices of land will be lowered for the benefit of all.

To rebuild our shattered cities will take many years. Here, too, we shall have to avoid the mistakes of the past. We shall not restore dank yards, airless tenement blocks, or historical slums. A nation that is to regain at long last physical and moral health, needs healthy housing as urgently as its daily bread. The rule of Block Wardens is over. The small house—be it ever so modest—shall be the home of the German child!

In the *manufacturing trades* we need a balanced co-existence of large and small units. Iron and steel, turbines and locomotives can only be produced by large plants; hammers and tongues, tin articles and plumbing belong to the small tradesman. Hitler promised the small manufacturer mountains of gold; but nobody has trampled down the small independent existences more ruthlessly than he. The noble lords of coal and steel, on the other hand, were the friends and financiers of the Nazis—they know best, why! These accounts, too, will have to be squared. *Our national economy needs efficient technicians and businessmen for all its organs of production and distribution: it does not need tycoons.* New forms must needs [sic] be found for the property rights in concerns that have outgrown the manageable shape of family concerns in which the owner himself takes a hand. The State, organs of Local Government, and co-operative societies will in future be invested with such rights of ownership. The independent productive functions of the co-operative societies will grow in importance as time goes on, while *the heavily indebted heavy industries will have to be taken over by the state straight away*. We shall not be in a position to do without the experienced owner-manager in the finishing industries; Utopian experiments in this field would be damaging to the common weal. Income tax will be clamped down hard and regularly on excessive profits, and rigorous inheritance taxes will put a stop once and for all to the accumulation of new giant fortunes. We can do without the moneyed aristocracy—but good workers and good savers we need in millions!

Whoever is directing a productive unit on behalf of the community conscientiously and successfully, shall participate in profits; *but individual enrichment must never and nowhere be the self-justifying economic motive.* An equal chance for vocational training must be vouchsafed to everybody; free competition will elevate the gifted and industrious. A moderate inheritance shall pass tax-free from

---

5. German agricultural cooperatives established by Friedrich Wilhelm Raiffeisen in the middle of the nineteenth century.

parents to their children; but we need a definite limit for inherited property. By widening our Social Insurance into a comprehensive national insurance scheme we shall be in a position to safeguard all honest working men and women against a penurious old age. There will be no room in impoverished Germany for the idle Rich; "Mastermen" to finance a new Nazi Party or Party bosses shamelessly amassing fortunes in the midst of general misery must never arise again.

All Executive Power Must Issue from the People! "Statthalter", "Gauleiter", "Reichsführer"[6] and suchlike irresponsible potentates are not needed in the new Germany. Free *Self*-Government alone can rebuild what the tyranny of "Führers" has wantonly destroyed. *The political foundation of the new Germany will be the self-governing municipal and rural communities.* Local Self-Government in every free nation provides the best training for democratic self-government in the State. Only those who have worked unselfishly in some field—no matter which—of local self-government, may become representatives of the people in the Reich Parliament; the era of Rasping Big Noises in mass meetings who end by seizing power must never return. *The Reich needs small electoral districts*, where every candidate can be scrutinized. Universal, equal, free, and secret franchise is the fundamental pre-requisite of liberty in politics.

The finances of the self-governing bodies and of the Reich should be subject to a never-failing control by Parliament and a free press.

National Socialism has degraded the People to the "Masses", good only for parades before the bosses and for the field of honour. Their conditions of life and work were determined by the arbitrary will of bureaucrats and "trustees"; all liberty of organization and bargaining was destroyed. *Now we shall build up the professional unions anew,* create new wage agreements, evolve for ourselves and gradually improve a new Labour Code and a new National Insurance. *We shall be poor—but we shall be nobody's serfs.*

Every State needs Administration and Jurisdiction. *But the administration should be the nation's servant, not its master, and the judges must administrate the law as made by the representatives of the people itself.* We need a police, but not a Gestapo. We need State servants, but not tyrants without responsibility or control. *Misplaced officials must disappear just as surely as anyone incapable of holding his own in his profession: the impartial judge, however, must be irremovable.* No free people can tolerate the disgrace of arbitrary arrests without judge or jury; no free nation can look on while its citizens are manhandled without trial or sentence, because their race, their religious faith, or their political convictions displease some potentates. We have had enough, far more than enough, of the doctrines exalted in Germany and all Europe under the name of "New Order", and put into practice with axe and rope! *The new Germany needs only the order of liberty and law!* Without Freedom of the Press and Freedom of Speech in the Parliaments of

---

6. Nazi terms for German regional leaders.

the State, and the self-governing bodies none of the people's fundamental rights can be made secure.

Our Civil Service Needs a Thorough Clean-Up. There was a time when the careful selection and meticulous discharge of duty of the German official was our pride and our fame; how little has remained of that, too, under the Hitler gang! Thousands of officials, teachers, and judges were arbitrarily deposed; the process was termed "restitution of professional officialdom". These old State servants will now return to their posts; for proved partisans of liberty and law, such like they, are particularly welcome and necessary for administrative reconstruction. For the rest, every official will be called to account for his actions and omissions during Hitlerism; the honest and decent among them will have to fear nothing from this reckoning, the dishonest and corrupt will have to fear all. Those who have enriched themselves unjustly, or worse, have stained their hands with blood— whether at home or abroad—must and will find their just punishment. The clean-up will be inexorable; only a thoroughly purged Germany can regain her inner health and the respect of the other nations. The press, too, must be purged of all venal scribes of the infamous regime, and the universities of all "teachers" of youth who owe their office to the Party, not to their scientific achievement. Whoever has taken an active part in Nazi swindling or Nazi terror in any form or manner whatsoever, must vanish from public life forever; every member of the Nazi Party will have to render account of all changes in his financial situation since 1933. During the whole process Justice and Equity will be the sole judges; *we do not want Nazi methods with the sign reversed in the new Germany*. For that reason all mere camp-followers of the guilty party shall be spared; ruthlessly though we shall descend upon the convicted criminal, we shall observe as rigorously the principle that stupidity is not an actionable offence. We want a thorough purge, but not blind revenge!

In the practice of law an immense pile of arbitrary "laws" and decrees will have to be cleared away. The removal of this rubble will be the most urgent task of the first Reich Parliament; the old officials and judges deposed by the Nazi Regime will give us their expert help in this. In constitutional law and the practice of the courts we shall constantly have to gather up the threads cut in 1933; a wholesale resurrection of the past, on the other hand, we do not desire; nor could we enforce it if we did. In this as in many other things we must learn from the mistakes of the past. We do not need more laws, but better and more popular laws; not more bureaucracy, but far, far more free self-government than hitherto. Compulsory ideological education by Nazi methods and for Nazi purposes will never be allowed again; but self-education in citizenship we need like our daily bread. *Without freedom of thought and worship, and freedom of the press, a free national and public life is an impossibility*.

We have all suffered during the awful years of Nazi tyranny. But after the thorough clean-up we will let by-gones be by-gones, devoting all our strength to the work of reconstruction. In this we shall be guided by diverse ideals, and thus evolve different political parties. Every sound nation needs conservative as well as progressive forces; their peaceful rivalry is a symptom of a wholesome national development. *Yet few large parties are better than many small ones*: here is another opportunity for learning from past mistakes, and from the experience of all free nations. "Capitalism" or "Socialism"—these will be the warring alternatives with us as well as in the victor countries. One party will rightly argue that there has never been liberty without private property; another party will contend, just as rightly, that the social reforms of recent generations would never have become a reality without the constant criticism of the Socialists. *As long as the ideals are free, and their controversies unhindered*, spiritual strife will bear valuable fruit; compromises between conflicting aims are neither foolish nor shameful, but simply indispensable in a free and great nation.

In the sphere of Religion the same holds true. *Parents must be at liberty to educate their children in their own faith—and the churches and denominations must vie with each other in positive achievements.* Collaboration is always possible, where there is liberty and goodwill. *We shall not ask anyone about his grandmother:* whoever is ready to co-operate in Germany's reconstruction will be welcome. Let us beware only of doctrinaires who have ready-made patent solutions for every problem up their sleeves; they are just as dangerous as those permanently embittered men who know no other thought but that of revenge and retribution.

In the outside world respect for the German people has struck an all-time low. Not because we were defeated—our armies have fought gallantly, and any State may lose a war. No—it is the appalling crimes against the civilian population of the occupied countries which have brought disgrace on our name, the shootings of hostages, slaughter of Jews, the burning of entire townships, the starving of helpless old people and children in invaded Greece, all the horrible deeds that were perpetrated in the name of the German people, often without its complete knowledge, but always by the orders of German potentates, carried out by Germans upon whom thus fell part of the guilt. These atrocities will not be soon forgotten by the nations that suffered them; decades will pass before our people will be forgiven. Every single German who will go abroad in future years will be touched by this curse, and our foreign policy for decades to come will labour under it. Only a resolute reform, resulting, after the indispensable clean-up, in an education of youth in a radically different spirity [sic], will gradually effect a change for the better. *Moral regeneration is no less essential for us than economic and political reconstruction.* How often during the last decade has our people had to listen to the phrase that Hitler has "restored its honour"! In reality no politician in the millenium of German history has heaped more terrible disgrace upon Germany's honour than the creator of the concentration camps and "People's Courts", the organizer of the synagogue fires, the tearer of non-aggression pacts, long before he ever soiled the prostrate lands of Europe with his bloody footprints. We must not close our eyes before this guilt: *There must be a fundamental change in the education of our children and grand-children.* Only under this condition the fair-minded and far-seeing men of whom there is no lack among our present enemies will be able and willing to collaborate with the new Germany. But without such collaboration there will be no recovery for our country, and no peace for Europe.

There is reason to hope that after this war there will be no repetition of the foolish "reparations" of the Versailles Treaty of 1919; it seems that the lesson of that period has been learnt in other countries. But contributions of labour towards the reconstruction of the devastated war areas will probably be demanded from us, and the looted machines, libraries, and works of art must obviously be returned. *For the work of reconstruction abroad members of the guilty party will have first priority;* this will at last provide them with an opportunity for useful work. The fortunes of the convicted war criminals as well as all other profiteers, which have been tucked away abroad, shall be devoted by us to the work of reconstruction abroad.

All internal reconstruction will for years be handicapped by the universal impoverishment. *We shall have to work harder and live more modestly than we did in the years of reconstruction after the First World War.* The overwhelming extent of capital annihilation since 1939 will only gradually come to be realized by the majority of Germans. In 1919, after all, our country was not destroyed when we returned from the front, and the number of war victims was smaller by millions than in 1943, let alone in 1944. *The sooner we pull out the Nazi weed by the roots, the more senseless sacrifices we can yet prevent.*

Altogether there are sad perspectives opening before our people at the close of Hitler tyranny and Nazi horrors. We must face them unflinchingly, and let all future action be guided by their injunctions. There are still left to us the soil of our mother country, our capacity for hard work and our technical skill. Practically nothing will remain of the fortunes of the formerly well-to-do, and even our Social Insurance, with all its funds sunk in worthless Reich bonds, will emerge from the catastrophe entirely destitute. *The longer we hesitate to round up the Hitler gang, the more awful grows the depletion of our nation's human and material resources. Let us rise up at last and become masters of our own destiny!* The gangsters who have led us into the abyss are not interested in the future of the German people. They know that they have forfeited their heads, and think only of saving their own miserable skins. Their days are numbered, together with those of the war they wantonly unleashed. Let them perish as quickly as possible! But Germany shall live, the German people must not and shall not perish! What do the differences of class, denomination, and political ideal signify, which used to separate us to our detriment in the past, in view of the common task of saving our country and our nation! *Let us save Germany by removing Hitler and his gang swiftly and thoroughly!*

The new Germany will certainly be no paradise. Decades of poverty and abnegation lie before us. Who really has the German people's welfare at heart, must not keep it in the dark about that. We shall have to keep order at home in order to prevent needless disturbance of the work of reconstruction. Those who want decent work, shall get it; they will get it, too, for the extent of destruction is sufficient, and the inevitable transitional difficulties can be overcome in a few months if all give their full help. Luxury and debaucheries will not be features of the new Germany—Karinhall, Schwanenwerder, and Berchtesgaden[7] will not find new barons, and the edifices of a costly megalomania in Berlin, Nuremberg, and Munich will remain but as warning ruins. But what do material possessions signify compared with the happiness of being free again, and able to work in peace for our children? Let us shake off the past decade's unholy intoxication with blood and power in resolute self-composure and self-purification!

As long as there is work for a nation, there is hope!
German Freedom Movement

Launching and Structural Outlines of DFB

I. Foundation and Publicity of the DFB in the U.S.A.

For the realization of the entire project it is necessary to found the DFB without delay in the United States;

a) because only after the foundation of the Movement in the U.S. all Germans in neutral countries will be free to join the Movement and work for it without being prosecuted for illegal political activity, as they inevitably would be if the Movement were organized in a neutral country;

b) because the foundation of the Movement in the U.S. gives the Movement added authority in neutral countries, making it easier for it to carry its appeal into the Reich and call into being a strong underground organization in Germany itself, which would be but the German branch of the DFB.

The fact of the DFB's existence should be publicized by press and radio, as well as by the publication of the draft programme in existence, and specific mention should be made of the extensive connections already established with Free Germans in neutral countries and with members of the opposition in Germany. The names should also be given of the prominent German emigrants at present living in the States who will be called upon to join the Movement. A preliminary list of names of such personages has been furnished by the DFB, and is appended as Document V.

---

7. Names of residences of leading Nazis. Karinhall was Göring's private estate (named after his wife Karin). Berchtesgaden was a resort used not only by Hitler but also by Speer, Bormann and others.

II. Direction of the Movement

The central direction of the various branches of the DFB would be at Istanbul, and remain closely coordinated with our Department. The DFB's Central Office would have three Departments in Istanbul.

1. Department of Military Intelligence
2. Department of German Underground Organization
3. Department of Propaganda

Department 4, working on post-war problems, would be directed in the U.S. There would also have to be a separate Propaganda Department in the U.S., which in the interest of a consistent and centrally planned propaganda line would coordinate its broadcasting and other propaganda material with the Department 3 at Istanbul.

The structure and functions of Departments 1 and 2 of the DFB at Istanbul will be defined and worked out during further special conferences with the competent members of the DFB, and the Departments built up forthwith. Department 3 of the DFB has elaborated a working programme concerning broadcast propaganda, which is under consideration at our Department and will be forwarded in its final shape without delay. The working programme of Department 4 would have to be outlined by our Department in collaboration with the leading men of the DFB here and subject to the approval of the competent U.S. Government Departments.

20 short propaganda broadcasts have already been prepared up to date. [...] It is contemplated to include the DFB broadcasts in the programme of the Algiers or Tunis stations at first three times a week, on Tuesdays, Thursdays and Saturdays, later, if it is found advisable, regularly every day. The programme had perhaps best be called "Deutschland spricht zu Deutschland" ("Germany calling Germany"), and announced as the voice of the German Freedom Movement.

III. Financing of the DFB

The initial expense of organizing the Movement will continue to fall upon our Department, until as a result of the official founding of the DFB in America the Movement has acquired a stock of contributing members and a sufficient income to give the German departmental officers freedom of movement and immunity from the odium of being in the pay of a foreign power. The DFB departments directly working for our Intelligence and the Allied war effort will be financed by us to the extent to which they are engaged in such activity.

[Document IV]

Personal Particulars of Some Members of the German Freedom Movement (DFB)

Kessler, Prof. Dr. Gerhard, 60 years old, Professor of Economics at Istanbul University. *Democrat.* 1912–1927 Professor at Jena University; 1927–1933 Professor at Leipzig University. Former collaborator of the celebrated deputy and political writer Friedrich Naumann. Democratic Reichstag candidate for Saxony in March, 1933, and author of the last book against Hitlerism to be published in Germany, "Kampf und Aufbau". Was immediately deposed in 1933, and has been in Turkey ever since.

Rüstow, Prof. Dr. Alexander, 55 years old, Professor of Economics at Istanbul University. *Liberal.* When in Germany, scientific correspondent of the Verein Deutscher Maschinenbauanstalten, author of numerous publications. In Turkey since 1933.

Reuter, Prof. Ernst, 54 years old, Professor of Local Government Science at the School of Political Studies at Ankara. *Social Democrat.* 1926–1931 member of the Central Municipal Council of the City of Berlin in charge of Communications, 1931–1933 Mayor of Magdeburg. Member of the German Reichstag. In Turkey since 1935, where for four years he held an appointment as economic adviser to the Turkish Ministry of Economics.

Willebrandt [Wilbrandt], Dr. Hans, 40 years old, businessman at Istanbul, *Social Democrat.* Until 1930 in the services of the Economic Research Department of the Trade Unions, Co-operative Societies, and the German Social Democrat Party. After 1930 held an appointment with the Central Co-operative Funds Administration of Prussia (Zentral-Genossenschaftskasse). In Turkey since 1935, first as Adviser on Co-operative Agriculture to the Ministry of Economics, later in the Istanbul export and import business.

Preliminary List of German Organizations and Personages in U.S.A. to Be Approached by the DFB

Association of Free Germans, Inc., New York City, headed by the former Prussian Minister of the Interior, Albert Grzesinski.

Prominent members of this association, which seems to pursue ideals and aims kindred to those of the DFB, are among others:

Fr. Stampfer former member of the German Reichstag, Chief Editor of the leading Socialist paper "Vorwärts."

M. Brauer Mayor of Altona.

Dr. Bärensprung Former Police President of Magdeburg.

Gerhard Seeger [Seger] former member of the German Reichstag.

Georg Bernhard Chief Editor of the Vossische Zeitung, etc, etc.

Dr. Gerhard Colm University teacher.

Dr. Simons formerly a highly placed Civil Servant; son of the former President of the Supreme Court.

Dr. Wolfers formerly Director of the Berlin School of Political Science (Hochschule für Politik), now teacher at an American University.

Dr. Staudinger former member of the German Reichstag for the Social Democratic Party.

Hermann Rauschning Prominent anti-Nazi, author of "The Revolution of Nihilism", "Conversations with Hitler", etc., etc.

Thomas Mann would be of paramount importance for any movement appealing to *all Germans*.

Document 19a · 9 September 1943

Report by the British War Cabinet's Joint Intelligence Sub-Committee[1]: Probabilities of a German Collapse[2]

SECRET

[...]

Probabilities of a German Collapse

Report by the Joint Intelligence Sub-Committee

1. In the late summer of 1918 the Allies were studying, as we study today, the impact on Germany of great reverses of fortune. The records of that period show that the Allied estimate of Germany's power and will to continue the struggle was then very wide off the mark. On the 13th August, 1918, Mr. Lloyd George and

---

1. NA, RG 165, ABC 381 Germany (29 January 43), Sec 1-A. J.I.C. (43) 367 Final.
2. For U.S. intelligence estimates see documents [19b] and [19c].

General Smuts told the Imperial War Cabinet that they did not think we should be able to force a decision in 1919. On the same day Ludendorff told the German High Command that it was no longer possible to force the enemy to sue for peace by offensive action, that the defensive alone could hardly achieve that object, and that the termination of the war would have to be brought about by diplomacy.

2. A study of the evidence available to the Allies at the time shows that they did not lack the material from which to form a correct appreciation. They failed to do so because they attached too much importance to intelligence of a purely military character, and too little to political and economic intelligence, which is necessarily more indefinite. The experience of 1918 emphasizes the danger of letting the enemy's apparent military strength blind us to fundamental weaknesses in his position as a whole.

3. A comparative study of the evidence available in 1918 and in 1943 shows many striking similarities. [...][3] There are, it is true, big differences between the Germany of 1918 and the Germany of 1943, but we do not think that these differences are so fundamental as to invalidate the comparison and the conclusions which flow from it.

4. In the late summer of 1918, Germany's military resources were still formidable and her Army was still fighting with discipline and determination. As a result of military reverses and the defeat of her U-boat campaign, Germany and her Allies had lost the initiative and had been thrown on the defensive in all theatres of war. Germany had passed the peak in production and had virtually exhausted her reserves of manpower. On the other hand, the resources of the Allies as a whole, backed by the immense productive capacity of the United States, were increasing rapidly. Accordingly Germany had been forced to abandon any hope of regaining the initiative and was faced with the prospect of holding out during the winter only to resume the campaign in the following spring with the odds still more heavily against her. In all these respects the German situation is similar today.

5. It had then as now, become increasingly difficult to disguise the true state of affairs from the country as a whole. The people having lost all faith in victory, were becoming increasingly unwilling to support the strain imposed by food shortages and mounting casualties. Today the food position in Germany is not so serious but the heavy casualties, particularly on the Russian Front, and the shattering effect of Allied air raids have produced a similar, and perhaps even greater, sense of hopelessness and loss of morale.

6. By the late summer of 1918 all [of] Germany's allies had realized that the end was near, and Germany, unable in face of her own difficulties any longer to give them adequate military or material support, could not prevent their defection as soon as opportunity offered. There is abundant evidence that Germany's European Allies take a similar view today and that they are again only waiting [for] the first opportunity to get out of the war. One has already done so.[4]

---

3. A document that shows some of these similarities is attached to this document but not printed.
4. I.e., Italy.

7. In these circumstances the German High Command in 1918 recognized the inevitability of eventual defeat and the futility of continuing the struggle. We believe that a similar feeling that Germany has lost all hope of winning the war, and that further fighting can only lead to useless bloodshed and destruction, is prevalent in Germany today and that it is shared even by some of the military leaders.

8. If it were not that the political situation in Germany today is very different from that of 1918, we should unhesitatingly predict that Germany would sue for an armistice before the end of the year. Up till the beginning of the last war, the German people enjoyed a reasonable degree of liberty of speech and action and, despite wartime restrictions, in 1918 vestiges of independence and free institutions remained. Today the Nazi regime has had ten years in which to destroy all trace of democratic ideas and institutions and has during this period been training the nation to endure great suffering. Police and party control over all phases of the life of the country is very much more effective than anything that existed in 1918 and has so far proved strong enough to make impossible any kind of organized opposition. Moreover Germany today is faced with the demand for unconditional surrender to the United Nations, including Russia, instead of with President Wilson's comparatively mild 14 points. Finally the fear of retribution, particularly among the leaders, is this time far greater.

9. Despite these differences, important as they are, we must be prepared for a situation where further military reverses, the Allied air offensive and the defection of Germany's allies produce even this year a crisis. Those responsible for directing the war will themselves cease to believe that any plan which they can make will avert defeat or even secure a compromise peace; those responsible for production and civil administration will recognise that they can no longer deal effectively with their problems. Awareness of this would quickly spread. In these circumstances the cohesion and resolution of the central government would be weakened and some change of regime might be brought about to prepare the way for an armistice. The request for an armistice would in the first instance probably be made either to Great Britain and America or to Russia rather than to the United Nations as a whole. Although there is no general today with the prestige of a Hindenburg or Ludendorff, a group to intervene in this way might be found from among those generals who are not too deeply committed to the Nazi regime, but even they may fail to concert action before complete disintegration has set in. These generals might act in concert with influential civilians and use them as a medium for approaching the Allies.

10. In assessing the likelihood of such a situation arising, great weight must again attach to the view taken by Germany's allies. As in 1918, they are probably in a better position than we are to appreciate how near Germany is to collapse. It is of the greatest significance that at the present time Germany's European Allies without exception are convinced that her defeat is inevitable and not far distant; so much so that those that remain are all anxiously exploring possibilities of deserting the skipping ship. There is equally good evidence that Japanese observers in Europe regard Germany's position with grave apprehension. Finally the

European Neutrals who should also be in a good position to judge, are convinced that Germany has lost the war and most of them are adjusting their policy accordingly.

11. A study of the picture as a whole leads us inevitably to the conclusion that Germany is, if anything, in a worse position today than she was at the same period in 1918. Once again, if military factors alone were taken into account, our appreciation would be that the German army, despite declining morale and fighting efficiency, would be able to fight on for a considerable time. But the war will not be decided purely by military factors. The end will come when we have broken Germany's will to continue the struggle. In this the demoralisation of the home front, economic difficulties and the political shock of the defection of her allies will play their part no less surely than the defeat of Germany's armies in the field. If therefore the Allies can take advantage of Germany's declining strength and press home attacks by land and sea; maintain and even intensify their air offensive; exploit the instability of South-east Europe; and pursue a vigorous political and propaganda campaign, we may see the defection of the rest of Germany's European Allies and, even before the end of this year, convince the German people and military leaders that a continuation of the war is more to be feared than the consequences of inevitable defeat. With the German people no longer willing to endure useless bloodshed and destruction, and the military leaders convinced of the futility of resistance there might be, as in Italy, some sudden change of regime to prepare the way for a request for an armistice.

(Signed)

V. Cavendish-Bentinck
E. G.N. Rushbrooke
F. F. Inglis
S. G. Menzies
J. M. Kirkman (for D.M.I.
[Director, Military Intelligence])
C. G. Vickers
Cabinet War Room Annexe,
S.W.1.
9th September, 1943

Document 19b · 21 September 1943

Report by the OSS Research and Analysis Branch: Possible Patterns of German Collapse[1]

SECRET

Possible Patterns of German Collapse

1. Introduction: The Pattern of 1918

It will be useful to preface this analysis of present prospects facing Germany with a brief survey of the pattern of collapse in 1918.

The breakdown of resistance in 1918 was in the first instance a military phenomenon, though its course and outcome were determined by the social, economic, and political structure of the German nation as a whole. The high command recognized as early as August 13 that the war was definitely lost. The defection of German allies, which began in September, merely hastened the process of defeat. In October, after a few inept and futile peace feelers, the high command was forced to ask for armistice terms.

[...]

Why did power fall into the hands of a democratic parliamentary coalition? The reason is twofold: both the prevailing temper of the German people and the existing organizational structure of political life favored this outcome. On the one hand, the German people were sick of the war with its appalling bloodshed and undernourishment; and they were for the most part under the influence of a democratic ideology. On the other hand, there were in existence well-organized democratic parties which were in a position to represent the wishes of the people for peace and constitutional

---

1. NA, RG 59, R&A 1483. This document was authored jointly by German exiles and former members of the New School for Social Research (and of the so-called Frankfurt School) Herbert Marcuse, Felix Gilbert and Franz L. Neumann; all of them had been analysts in the Central European Division of R&A since the end of 1942. Evidently, historian Felix Gilbert wrote the passages dealing with the events of World War I.

reform. No other serious contenders for power existed. The conservatives were compromised by their reactionary policies and the revolutionary parties were sectarian.

The situation in the summer of 1918 can be summarized in the following way. The German people had had their fill of war and autocracy; they had never tried democracy, and believed in its possibilities. When defeat became certain, the high command lost power which shifted almost automatically to the non-revolutionary democratic parties.

2. Possible Patterns of Collapse in 1944

I. The Difference Between 1918 and Today. In its military and economic aspects the present position of Germany offers both parallels and contrasts to that of 1918. But on the political side there is hardly anything in common between now and then.

Military defeat for Germany seems just as certain now as it must have in the summer of 1918. But her enemies are still a long way from the homeland at present; there is more defensive space in which to maneuver now than there was in 1918. This relative advantage is partly offset by the vastly greater importance of air war today, which reaches into the heart of the Reich. The people are better fed than they were in 1918, but again air raids are an offsetting factor. War weariness must be felt on a scale at least comparable to 1918. Thus in 1943 a war-weary German people is faced with defeat, perhaps less immediately but no less certainly than in 1918.

Politically, however, the situation today is utterly different from 1918. The Nazi dictatorship is entirely different from the military dictatorship of the last war: unlike the latter it is a totalitarian dictatorship used in the sense that society has been completely pulverized into its individual atoms which are then organized and manipulated from the top down, not from the bottom up. No voluntary organizations—except the churches—are left above ground; any attempt to form them or to express discontent is met with ruthless terror.

It is, of course, true that there has been close agreement as to aims between the Nazis and Germany's traditional ruling groups, and the former have increasingly penetrated into the latter, so that many big industrialists and some generals today were upstart Nazi politicians a few years ago. But the process of integrating the Nazis into the ruling class is a long way from complete; the group still has a separate and recognizable identity. As long as the regime was enjoying successes this separateness was not particularly important, and it even had its advantages. The Nazi movement provided a social escalator for the recruitment of talent from the lower middle class; in the event of complete merger with the ruling groups the old hardening of class lines would set in again. But in times of adversity, the distinctive position occupied by the Nazi governing clique has a special importance which it is [sic] essential to understand. In the eyes of people all over the world, both inside and outside Germany, the Nazi leadership, including those industrialists, bankers, civil servants and generals who have openly sided with it, bear the responsibility for the war and all that it has brought with it. As long as things were going well for Germany, this meant disapproval from outside and approval from within. But now that things are going badly and Germany is faced with the prospect of defeat, the Nazi group is becoming the object of nearly universal popular detestation. They are the one group which can have no hope of salvaging anything from the approaching debacle. And this means, as a matter of course, that whatever their services to Germany's ruling class may have been in the past they are rapidly becoming a liability and a menace at the present time.

If the Nazis nevertheless remain in power the reasons are easy to understand. So long as the system of totalitarian control over every aspect of German life remains intact, there is no possibility for a popular opposition to crystallize. And the army leaders, who are the only ones having disposition of sufficiently powerful force to challenge the Nazi position, would run the risk of annihilation if they should attempt an ouster move. The Nazis have, especially in the Gestapo and the SS, forces with which to fight back. If an open conflict should develop, the door would be open to revolt from within and invasion from without. Clearly the army leaders and the industrialists, with whom they would undoubtedly be allied, must act with extreme caution in any plan to kick the Nazis out, and it may even be that they will be permanently paralysed by the dilemma facing them.

In 1918 the absence of totalitarian controls and the presence of political parties made the transfer of political power relatively simple and bloodless. No such conditions exist today.

In addition to the organizational aspect of the problem, there are other differences between the popular opposition of 1918 and the potential popular opposition of today. Then, workers, liberals, and Catholics were under the influence of democratic ideology; it seems unlikely that this will be so a second time. The Weimar Republic was in itself a bitter experience for many of the masses. The working class and what remains of the lower middle class is likely to emerge from this war in a "never-again" frame of mind. It is, of course, possible that the German people will be too exhausted and battered to play an active role for some time after the close of hostilities, but when their influence is felt again it will probably be much more revolutionary than the democratic opposition of 1918.

Further political differences between 1918 and 1943, in the sense of differences in outlook and motivation among various classes of the population, are traceable to the different character of the opposition coalitions then and now. In 1918 it was France, England, and the United States, countries with essentially similar social structures, which were all fighting for the same straightforward goal: to stop Germany's drive for greatly increased world political and economic power, and to weaken Germany so that she would not soon be in a position to try again. Today it is England, the United States, and Soviet Russia. England and the United States, again similarly constituted and similarly motivated, are working with socialist Russia for a common immediate military aim. But Russia may have more far-reaching goals than checking Germany's renewed drive for world conquest: she may be looking forward to the social and economic reconstruction of Germany. Alongside an immediate community of interest, there may thus be a long-run diversity of interest between the two major parts of the anti-German coalition. This fact naturally has powerful repercussions inside Germany. The same factors were present in Germany after the Russian revolution in 1917–18, but because of the greater attractive power of democratic ideology and the weakness of the young Soviet republic they were not yet of a decisive importance.

So far as the Nazis are concerned there is not much difference between Germany's eastern and western enemies, a fact which finds formal expression in the Anglo-Russian alliance binding the two parties not to enter into negotiations with the "Hitlerite government."

For army leaders and industrialists, however, the situation is different. They would certainly like to be on the winning side against Britain and the United States, but they are not sentimentalists and will hardly be inclined to fight to the death in a losing cause. As between the western powers and Russia from the economic and social angle, they must necessarily prefer the former, and since victory is out of the question, they may work for the defeat which is least dangerous to their own material interests, a defeat which will permit the preservation of private capitalism. The army leaders and industrialists may therefore try to ensure the dominance of Anglo-American over Russian influence in the reconstruction of Europe. This may give them a chance to play the role of junior partner to British and American businessmen in the rehabilitation of world economy. This objective does not exclude the possibility that these interests can try to cooperate politically with the U.S.S.R. in order to improve their bargaining position.

For the potential popular opposition in Germany, the character of the enemy coalition is also likely to have a profound significance. If the United States and Britain continue to show themselves hostile to or fearful of popular forces, it is possible that, despite undoubted anti-Russian feelings in the middle and lower classes, a German popular movement may be strongly pro-Russian in its orientation. The reason is very simple: that the Russians have nothing to fear and everything to gain from the fullest possible development of a radical popular movement.

To sum up: today the political situation in Germany is radically different from 1918. A smooth transfer of political power from a totalitarian dictatorship to an organized political opposition is out of the question because the very essence of totalitarian dictatorship is the absence of organized opposition. And as long as the totalitarian controls remain intact the army must hesitate to intervene for fear of precipitating a crisis which would involve the disruption of both home and fighting fronts. It is in this setting that we must attempt to trace the possible courses of German collapse.

II. Pattern of Collapse. a. Against this background, the following possibilities of collapse may be envisaged.

If the United Nations remain united—that is, if Germany's political warfare aimed at splitting them and at concluding a negotiated peace with either Russia or the Western Powers is unsuccessful, the following alternative courses will remain open.

1. The Nazi leadership may determine to retain control to the very end. [...]
2. The Nazi leadership, realizing that the game is lost, may resort to a shadow government. [...]
3. A Conservative anti-Nazi government composed of generals, industrialists, and high civil servants may be established in opposition to the Nazis, possibly by a coup d'etat. Such a coup d'etat will lead to the arrest of Hitler and other Nazi leaders; it may rescind the anti-Jewish legislation; restore the freedom of the churches and invite persons like Dr. Kass [Kaas],[2] the last parliamentary leader of the Catholic Centre party, and Niemoeller to enter the government.

In this way, the political opposition in Germany would be split. Large masses of the people who are merely war-weary will be satisfied with any kind of government that ends the war and restores some kind of dignity. The stability of such government will, however, depend entirely upon the attitude of the United Nations.

For [sic] there is no question that revolutionary movements will arise again, even though they may lack mass support from peasants, middle class and even that of sections of the workers. The conservative government will certainly be unable to cope even with this revolutionary trend. The controls, primarily of a Nazi character, will have then broken down and fanatic Nazis and the SS in especial [sic] may join the revolutionary forces.

Military occupation in such a situation will face the most difficult problem: to side with the conservative government; to side with the revolutionary forces; not to recognize either. Non-recognition of the revolutionary force implies, however, fighting against them.

b. *If the United Nations are split, the following possible courses of collapse may be envisaged.*

The split in the United Nations cannot be utilized by the Nazis themselves. Russia and the Western Powers are committed not to deal with a Nazi government. If the Nazis want to profit from disunity they must ostensibly disappear. The Nazis may determine to stay (see a–1),[3] but this may be considered unlikely, because of the determined opposition of the traditional ruling group.

1. A camouflaged Nazi government may be instituted by the Nazis. [...]
2. The Nazi shadow government may then be set up to deal with the Western Powers. [...]
3. A coup d'etat may, however, be staged by the traditional ruling classes if the probability of a separate peace with either Russia or the Western Powers appears likely.

---

2. Monsignore Ludwig Kaas had been living in the Vatican since 1933.
3. Part a-1 of summary found at the end of this document [19b].

A genuine conservative government to deal with Anglo-America will have considerable popular support in its initial phase. It will retain this support as long as the material conditions of Germany have not deteriorated. If this happens (and it is likely to happen) the strong undercurrent of hatred of Anglo-American imperialism will merge with the anti-capitalist sentiments, and the support which the opposition will undoubtedly receive from Russia will merge into a powerful revolutionary movement with a strong national-bolshevist flavor. Military government will, under these circumstances, be extremely precarious.

A genuine conservative government to deal with Russia will have powerful support from the officer corps, considerable support from parts of German industry and strong popular support. This popular support will be readily forthcoming because the fear of Russia will be relieved and the left wing labor groups will realize that while Russia's support of such government will be merely an expedient of a temporary nature, a conservative pro-Anglo-American government will be there to stay because of Anglo-American support.

The Possibilities of a Revolution

There is, of course, always present the possibility of a revolution in Germany regardless of the unity or disunity of the United Nations.

1918 has taught us, however, that a revolution directed against a system of control not broadly based socially and in which the autonomous political and social organizations were still intact must be hopeless until the control system itself was already in a state of decomposition. The Bolshevik Revolution had demonstrated that it is only possible to overthrow a government that does not exercise efficiently the means of coercion and social control.

The situation in Germany is, however, much more unfavorable to a revolution than was the case in 1918. The Nazis have learned from 1918. The nearer military defeat comes, the stronger the controls become. Moreover, the traditional ruling classes are much more afraid of a revolution in 1944 than they were in 1918. They could—and did, then—successfully rely on the trade unions to prevent the transformation of a political and constitutional upheaval into a social revolution. Without the trade unions and the Social Democratic party, 1918 might have given birth to a Socialist revolution.

This bulwark no longer exists. A revolution today will certainly take a much more radical turn than it did in 1918. The traditional ruling class will, for this reason, stick to the Nazi party in its attempt to ward off a revolution, pinning their hopes on a coup d'etat and on support from all or some of the United Nations.

The objective conditions thus do not favor a revolution. The subjective aspects, however, show an extremely ambivalent character. The atomization of German society has confined articulate opposition to small sectarial groups, probably localized and thus without national cohesion and organization. On the other hand, the mood of the essential part of the workers and of many intellectuals, farmers and middle class men is certainly much more radical than ever before in German history.

Can one expect the small revolutionary groups in Germany to assume political leadership of the discontent masses prior to Germany's military defeat or the removal of the Nazi party rule under the above-mentioned conditions? The answer is no. Strong as the longing of the masses and the determination of the underground groups may be, the controls are too tight. The revolutionary groups can play an active role only if a non-Nazi government (indigenous military dictatorship, etc.) exists.

To sum up:

a. *If the United Nations are united:*
   1. The Nazis determine to stay to the very end.
      Consequences: Utter internal collapse.
      Scorched earth policy by the Nazis.
      External threats.
      Social convulsions.
      No indigenous political movement powerful enough.
      A real possibility.
   2. A Nazi shadow government.
      Consequence: The SS goes underground.
      Revolutionary movements toward democratic socialism.
      The importance of timing of military occupation.
      A real possibility.
   3. A conservative coup d'etat.
      Consequence: Greater stability.
      Revolutionary movements with smaller mass basis.
      A possibility.
b. *The United Nations are split:*
   1. The Nazis determine to stay.
      Consequence: see a.- 1.
      Little possibility.
   2. A Nazi shadow government to deal with Russia.
      Consequence: Considerable support from sectors of the traditional ruling classes and masses.
      Unlikely to be accepted by Russia.
   3. A Nazi shadow government to deal with the Western Powers.
      Consequence: Support from the traditional ruling classes.
      Partial initial mass support.
      Later, intensified revolutionary movement.
      Unlikely to be accepted
   4. A coup d'etat conservative government to deal with the Western Powers.
      Consequence: Considerable initial popular support.
      Growth of revolutionary movement with deterioration of social and economic conditions.
      Real possibility.

5. A coup d'etat conservative government to deal with Russia.
   Consequence: Considerable popular support; transition into Socialist government with Russia's support.
   Real possibility.
c. *The Possibility of a Revolution apart from the alternatives under a. and b.*
   No real possibility.

Document 19c · 21 October 1943

Memorandum from the U.S. Joint Intelligence Committee to the Joint Chiefs of Staff: Probabilities of a German Collapse[1]

SECRET

Probabilities of a German Collapse

The Problem

1. To consider the British Joint Intelligence Subcommittee paper J.I.C. (43) 367 (Final), London 9 September 1943 "Probabilities of a German Collapse,"[2] circulated by the U.S. J.I.C. as J.I.C. 112/1, 23 September 1943, and to formulate our own views on the subject.

Summary and Conclusions

2. While we agree in general with specific statements appearing in the British paper we feel that on the whole it presents a more optimistic view of the imminence of German collapse than is justified by the evidence available to us.

3. Although we agree that a comparative study of the evidence available in 1918 and today is instructive, we believe that because of the great differences in many

---

1. NA, RG 165, ABC 381, Germany Sec 1-B. J.I.C. 112/2.
2. Document [19a].

fundamental features between the situations then and now, only conclusions of a very general and speculative nature can at present be safely drawn from such a study.

4. As to salient factors in the present situation: Due largely to the apparent lack of unity among Germany's enemies, we doubt whether the present situation appears as hopeless to the German military leaders as did the situation which confronted them in 1918 after the Battle of Amiens. Principally because of the effectiveness of the present organization of Germany in repressing political expression, and the present fear of the consequences of surrender, morale on the home front in our opinion would today have to become much worse than in 1918 in order to produce an internal crisis leading to the termination of German resistance. We doubt whether morale on the home front is now as bad as in September 1918. We believe that the morale of the German ground forces is still considerably better than it was at any time in 1918 after 8 August. The growing shortage of military manpower, as in 1918", and the German inferiority in air strength, the latter far more serious than in 1918, are in our opinion the most disadvantageous features of the present German position. The food situation, so serious in 1918, is today very much better, but that improvement may be offset by the far heavier scale of air attack.

5. We estimate that, in terms of the further deterioration which will have to occur before resistance terminates, the overall German situation is still considerably better than it was at any time in 1918 after the Battle of Amiens on 8 August.

6. We do not believe that the defection of Germany's allies or their desire to get out of the war can be accepted as an indication that German surrender is necessarily imminent.

7. We conclude that an increase in the degree of unity shown by the United Nations, further military reverses, the continuation of the Allied air offensive, and the defection of Germany's allies might even within the next three months or so produce a crisis which would lead shortly thereafter to the termination of German resistance; but we estimate that the odds are considerably against its occurrence at so early a date. We do not now feel justified in going beyond that point in estimating the probable date of termination of German resistance.

... [3]

15. Unconditional surrender by the Nazi leaders is scarcely conceivable in any circumstances, but if an increasing desire for peace and a willingness to submit to the terms imposed by the United Nations become sufficiently widespread, the Nazi leaders will eventually find themselves unable to control the situation. We shall not attempt to predict the changes of leadership and other events which will then occur or the manner in which they will take place, but it

---

3. The omitted passage contains a more detailed statement of the British views outlined above.

seems extremely unlikely that the transition to a leadership willing and able to accede to the terms imposed by the United Nations will occur as smoothly, as quickly, and with as little disorder as in 1918. German resistance might, however, collapse during the transition period before the latter point had been reached.

Our present intelligence does not indicate that the Nazi leaders are likely to lose their control of Germany in the near future, unless possibly to representatives of the army officers and the big industrialists. While such a change of leadership might mark the beginning of the end so far as German resistance is concerned, the end might not be reached until further changes of leadership had occurred. ...[4]

Document 20 · 21 September 1943

Telegram from Allen W. Dulles (OSS Bern) to OSS Director William J. Donovan: Nuclei of the German Opposition[1]

SECRET

TOR:9/21/43 8:30 pm

#763–767. [...] As yet there is no coordinated opposition other than the following nuclei with whom we are developing every possible contact: (1) Certain Protestant and Catholic church circles. (2) Labor elements which are both unorganized and isolated. (3) Communists. (4) Special departments of the government. (5) Various Army circles. The work of these groups is hidden and all of them lack coordination. If a change were to come it would most likely come from the top much as it did in Italy although at the present everyone here agrees that an attempt to organize would only bring about ruthless supression.

The conflicting plans are favored by the opposing groups but when a crisis is reached and some feel this is not too distant, the attitude of the military leaders

---

4. The omitted passage deals with the internal situation of Germany after 1916, touching upon such points as the food situation, casualties, arms and manpower shortages.

1. NA, RG 226, Entry 134, Box 340, Folder 1819.

will probably influence the decision. One of these plans is the Western solution which entails opening the doors to the Anglo Saxon occupation forces; the other plan the Eastern solution, that is, by approach to Russia.[2] At present, the military attitude is not clarified, but the Gestapo tends to favor the Eastern solution. [...]

Document 21 · 25 September 1943

Memorandum by Willy Brandt[1] (Stockholm): Opposition Movements in Germany

SECRET

Oppositional Movements in Germany

The question of which forces are active in the German opposition steadily becomes of great importance. Every serious attempt to answer this question is, however, met with great difficulties. It is very difficult to obtain a complete picture. On important points detailed information is lacking and one must therefore be content with pointing out the main tendency.

The more or less organized opposition in Germany—in this connection we completely disregard general discontent and criticism—comprises three main groups: the military opposition, the opposition of the church together with some conservative and liberal groups, and the labor opposition. The position of the youth must be discussed as a special problem. The establishment of the National Committee of Free Germany[2] and similar efforts in England and America have also rendered the question of German emigrants of current interest.

---

2. See document [5].

1. NA, RG 226, Entry 100, FNB-INT-13 GE-928. At the time, German exile journalist Willy Brandt who was later to become Chancellor of the Federal Republic of Germany, was a naturalized Norwegian citizen. Both the OSS and the U.S. Minister to Sweden, Herschel V. Johnson, believed him to be deeply anti-Nazi and anti-Quisling. Brandt was attached to the Norwegian Press Bureau in Stockholm. Also, he was Secretary of the German Social Democratic Party in Sweden. For a later Brandt report on the German oppositional forces see document [40].

2. The original version "German National Committee in Moscow" was replaced by a handwritten correction.

The relationship between the party and the *Wehrmacht* has for a long time been the object of serious misjudgements. Up to the very last the Nazis have helped to spread false reports concerning the dissention between the party administration and the generals. This has been part of their work to confuse people abroad.

It must first of all be stated that there is no uniform German officers' corps. The officers of the national defense (*Reichswehr*) are today in minority, but also among these a great many were pro-Nazi. They despised Hitler and the other Nazi upstarts. In the main they agreed, however, with the Nazis, even though they did not agree with them that the end justifies the means. But they did approve the end: rearmament and Hitler's imperialistic program. And to begin with Hitler's political strategy proved to be successful in spite of the scruples and warnings of many of the old officers.

The opposition from Wehrmacht quarters grew in earnest when Hitler's strategy of prestige led to fatal consequences. The party rule in the occupied countries and in Germany itself and the increased influence of Gestapo and SS also caused much discontent on the part of many of the officers. The generals continuously tried to prevent Himmler from being placed in charge of the Ministry of the Interior.

The opposition to the "party" and Führer's Headquarters is today considered good form in many German messes and similar places. Practically all responsible military chiefs and a considerable part of the officers' corps, very likely the majority, realize that Germany has lost the war. When asked how it will be possible to win the war, even Nazi officers answer that a miracle must happen. The prospect of a German defeat has widened the gulf between the party and the Wehrmacht. This will, at the same time, be an obstructive factor when it comes to taking active steps.

As has already been indicated, a great many German officers still loyally support the Nazi Government, a factor which should still be borne in mind. The others fear the consequences of a German defeat—external consequences in the form of the very severe claims which they expect the United Nations to place on Germany, and internal consequences in the form of chaos and social revolution. Many officers also say that it would be sheer madness to relieve Hitler and his people from the responsibility for the final military breakdown.

The German generals have the reputation of being very poor politicians. In the course of the last few years, several attempts to form an organized political opposition to Hitler have been crushed by the Gestapo.[3] Nor may it today be forgotten that a rebellion by the generals may be crushed before it reaches a head. Waffen SS and the ordinary SS have one million men, equipped with the best weapons and especially trained for civil war. Contrary to the Italian militia, the SS is certain to fight. The German Fascism will not collapse in the same way the Italian did.

---

3. Altogether almost 40 attempts on Hitler's life took place.

The German military leaders are also far less independent than the Italian military leaders. There is no German King who would be able to play the same role as Victor Emanuel.[4] The German officers have sworn faith to Hitler. Nor is there in Germany any person to whom it would be natural to act the part of Badoglio. Halder and Manstein have been mentioned, but you may rest assured that they themselves do not know anything about it.[5] In reality the highest chiefs hold themselves in the background. The fate of von Fritsch and Reichenau frightens them.[6] The weight of the organized military opposition lies with the staff officers. The opposition as a whole lacks detailed organization and a uniform will.

On the other hand, it cannot be denied that there are "Italian" tendencies also in Germany. The breakdown of Fascism has meant a loss of prestige to the Nazi Party. Public opinion is on the whole marked by dissatisfaction with the party. The generals have obtained somewhat freer hands in making purely military decisions. The German retreat on the East Front has thus been carried out without any interference to speak of from the headquarters of the Fuhrer. Also in other fields the military administration has succeeded in obtaining a somewhat more independent position. The Wehrmacht has taken over certain social functions which were previously handled by functionaries of the party. The foreign service of the Wehrmacht has been extended. The situation as a whole is marked by the fact that party bureaucracy is losing influence. SS advances but not at the cost of the Wehrmacht. One may speak about a kind of polarization of the forces.

Even if the German generals realize that the war is lost, there is little reason to believe that they will in the near future take action which would cause Hitler's fall. It is known that such plans exist, but it is to be doubted that they will ever be carried out. In addition to the arguments already mentioned above, it must be emphasized that many Germany [sic] officers are of the opinion that they will obtain better terms of peace and capitulation by postponing the final settlement. They hope that the actual or imagined dissentions between the United Nations will become more acute and that Germany will be able to take advantage of this situation. Many also believe that the conflict between the Allies may give Germany a chance to obtain a separate peace, either with Russia or with the Western Powers.

---

4. King Victor Emanuel had assisted in bringing about the downfall of Mussolini. See also documents [19b] and [24a].

5. As a matter of fact, General Halder had already been dismissed in December 1942 because of disagreement with Hitler's decisions concerning Stalingrad. After the 20th of July plot, he only narrowly escaped execution. Von Manstein, however, could never be convinced by the German Resistance (in particular Beck and von Tresckow) to join the opposition.

6. General Werner Freiherr von Fritsch, the Commander in Chief of the Wehrmacht (1935 to 1938), had never disguised his contempt for the Nazi Party and the SS. With the help of Reinhard Heydrich's Security Services faked charges were concocted against von Fritsch. In February 1938 he was made to resign, and on 22 September 1939 he sought and found death in Praga near Warsaw, Poland. Field Marshal Walter von Reichenau had been killed in action on the Eastern Front in January 1942.

One has the impression that the revolutionary generals are of the opinion that they should not go to action until such a possibility of obtaining separate peace exists. They certainly realize that Hitler does not wish to obtain peace with either the Western Powers or the Soviet Union.

For the most part mention is only made of the German's hope for a separate settlement with the Russians. But there are also a great many German officers who would prefer to come to an agreement with the Western Powers. Some of them assume that Churchill and Roosevelt are not in earnest when they declare that they are going to crush the German militarism in the same way as they will crush Nazism. That part of the officers' corps which still hopes to come to speaking terms with the British and Americans is in contact with industrial circles and other groups which belong to the conservative opposition and the German Church front.

Today the movement among the German military who are inclined to make an agreement with the Russians is of great interest. Ever since the years immediately following the last World War there has been a National-Bolshevik fraction [sic] among the German officers. This group has also connections within the Nazi Party. Still more important is, however, the former Reichswehr school since it was based upon intimate military collaboration with the Soviet Union.[7] There are further a great many officers who do not belong to any definite fraction [sic], but who, in spite of the fact that they regard Communism as an internal enemy of the country, are interested in an agreement with the Soviet Union, as they believe that Germany will in that way obtain more favorable terms of peace. To some people this is equivalent to establishing a foundation for preparations to take revenge on the Western Powers.

The declarations made by Stalin[8] have, of course, become known in Germany, and it is reasonable that officers' circles have above all seized that statement that the Soviet Union does not intend to annihilate the German State or any military force in Germany. The German Moscow Committee, including some well-known officers as members, has made a certain impression among the German military. There is also reason to assume that the new German officers' association in Russia, headed by some of the Stalingrad generals, will be an encouragement to those circles within the German officers' corps which aim at making peace with Russia.[9]

It may, however, be stated that only a minority of the German officers are at all interested in these questions. But an active minority may also play a decisive role. In this connection the plans of the highest military have the greatest interest. Some weeks ago it was reported from Germany that the leading generals had

---

7. This is a reference to secret German-Soviet military collaboration in the 1920s.

8. In particular his Order of the Day of 23 February 1942 in which he distinguished between the "Hitler-Clique" and the German population.

9. See also documents [31] and [57].

decided to undertake a systematic retreat on the East Front, as they realized that such a retreat was one of the essential conditions for their being able to come to an agreement with the Russian Government.

There is reason to believe that certain circles within the Nazi Party will support a policy aiming at peace and collaboration with the Soviet Union. Some support of the masses will probably also be obtained, as it will certainly be possible to revive at least some of the Communist influence among the Ger-man labor. On the other hand, it must be realized that anti-Bolshevism still is an important factor in Germany. Moreover, the liberal and the conservative opposition as well as large parts of the latent labor opposition sympathize with the Western Powers. The fear of getting under a new dictatorship is also very prominent among many German oppositionists. Regarded from the point of view of the internal German conditions there are many things that argue against the possibility that the movement which aims at a "Russian" solution will actually win out. A decisive factor will, however, be the form the collaboration between the Western Powers and the Soviet Union will take in the near future. At the same time, there is no use to close one's eyes to the fact that Russia may to an increasing extent be the power among the United Nations which will give Germany guarantees for a future independent national existence.

When the position of the Wehrmacht is discussed, the mistake is often made of paying attention only to the officers' corps and on the whole of not asking what is going on among the *soldiers.* Many reports state that the morale among the German troops is steadily deteriorating. In this connection there is reason to point out an essential difference between the spirit on the German home front and in the occupied countries on one side and that on the East Front on the other side. However remarkable it may sound, it is still a fact that the disintegration process has developed to a greater extent in the western and northern occupied territories than on the East Front. This is above all due to the fact that the fantastic sacrifices and hardships in Russia have created a strong feeling of solidarity, which in itself is not identical with any positive attitude toward the Nazi Government. This spirit may be compared to that which arose in the trenches on the West Front during the last World War. The strain is so great that the soldiers have no time to discuss political matters. Many of them become apathetic. At the same time they have a feeling that they have obligations toward their fellow soldiers. Just as during a natural calamity, everyone must help each other. This situation has also on the whole created a good relationship between officers and soldiers. The contrary may be said about relations between Waffen SS and the regular units of the Wehrmacht. Every now and then an encounter between ordinary soldiers and SS men is reported.

It is known with certainty that small illegal groups have been formed among the German soldiers in several places. It is generally former members of labor organizations who in this way keep together and discuss certain questions concerning the future. Illegal pamphlets are also being circulated among the German soldiers to a greater extent than previously, and not only as a result of Allied propaganda. This activity is at present confined to very limited circles and concerns only a very small percentage of the German soldiers. Such groups may, however, play a very important role in a critical situation. They may be able to form the basis for the election of delegates among the soldiers, soldiers' counselors or whatever they will be called. Just because there are still a good many Nazi officers, it is not very probable that it will be possible to maintain discipline within the Wehrmacht on the same basis as previously. The radical forces among the soldiers which today represent only a small minority but which in a critical situation may be expected to obtain mass support, will not be satisfied with attacking the Nazi officers. They will most certainly raise the question of the responsibility of the Wehrmacht administration and Prussian militarism for Nazism and the war. This does not prevent that a great many officers—especially front officers—even in the future may be accepted as leaders. That which will follow upon the breakdown of Nazism and an evident military defeat is, however, a democratic revolution, or in any case an upheaval with strong revolutionary democratic tendencies. In such a revolution the attitude of the masses, in this connection the spontaneous reaction of the ordinary soldiers, plays an important part. That is the reason why it is not very likely that the Wehrmacht will be able to form the basis for a new administration in Germany.

Discontent and defeatism are beginning to prevail also within the Nazi Party. It is very likely that in connection with the breakdown quite a number of oppositional Nazi groups will appear, but there is little reason to believe that they will play any noteworthy role. The Strasser group[10] and similar circles who maintain the "pure" National Socialist program have in reality very few adherents, and people in Germany will probably not favor a reformed Nazi Party replacing Hitler. The party rule will be hated and many members are now interested in taking steps for their retreat so that they will escape punishment. Local agents and functionaries behave more politely. Judges who have earlier been notorious for their pro-Nazi attitude are now making efforts to display a kind of humane attitude. The party weariness is discussed at internal party meetings all over the country, and it is characteristic that Himmler has found it necessary to issue an order to the effect that all party members must wear the party sign.

An oppositional group which plays a certain role is formed by disappointed idealistic nationalists. They have a certain influence among the students and among other intellectuals.

There is furthermore a strong discontent within the civil party bureaucracy and among Nazi officials, because they are more and more being pushed aside by SS. But this discontent is not of any importance. The "conservative" Nazi opposition which expresses the worries of industrial circles is more serious. Göring may to a certain degree be regarded as an exponent of the right wing of the Nazi Party

---

10. I.e., the break-away Union of Revolutionary National Socialists known as the Black Front, founded by Otto Strasser in 1930.

with good connections within economic life, the Wehrmacht and the administration. Some people therefore believe that Göring might play the part of a German Badoglio. Let us hope that he will not be accepted by any of the United Nations. In Germany it must be taken into consideration what [that?] not only has Göring known how to maintain a strong position in the above-mentioned groups, but that he is also more popular than the other Nazi leaders. But the fact cannot be denied that he is violently compromised among those sections of the people which will make a move when the interior disintegration begins in earnest. The rumors that a triumvirate consisting of Göring, Keitel and Donitz [Doenitz][11] should already have been formed have proved to be untrue. As for Keitel it should be remembered that he is the least independent of the German field marshals.

The active Nazis realize that the only thing they can do is to fight together with Himmler and SS and share their fate. It cannot be emphasized strongly enough that Himmler's power and terror apparatus stands unshaken and that SS will fight stubbornly, if not to the last man, at least for a very long time. In spite of this, the situation in Germany has now become such that surprising changes may take place. The capitulation of Italy, the bomb raids on Hamburg, Berlin, et cetera,[12] and the retreat in the East have caused confusion in the highest German administrative circles. Since 1933 there have not at any time been so many intrigues and disturbances. There is the possibility that it [sic] will suddenly fail and that the various factions will oppose each other. But a policy can, of course, not be based upon such an eventuality.

Of late the *Church opposition* has increased again. This is the most widespread and best organized opposition in Germany. Socially it reflects above all the discontent among the rural population. Church circles have, however, also contact with oppositional groups within the officers' corps, industry, the universities, et cetera. In spite of many restrictions it is easier for the clergy to establish and maintain contacts than for other people. Contact committees have recently been formed at several places in Germany. The Church has a decisive influence in these committees, in which there are not only conservatives and liberals but also representatives of the former trade union people, Social Democrats and Communists. The whole thing is, however, loosely organized and it is not possible to say anything definite about the influence which such more or less self-appointed contact committees will have when the collapse occurs. On the other hand, developments in Italy during the period between the fall of Mussolini and the capitulation show that former parties possess a considerable traditional power. In a similar manner as in Italy, this power in Germany is engaged in preparing a coalition between the

---

11. Reich Field Marshall Hermann Göring was Commander in Chief of the Luftwaffe. General Field Marshal Wilhelm Keitel was Chief of Staff of the Supreme Command of the Armed Forces; Grand Admiral Karl Doenitz was Commander in Chief of the German Navy.

12. In March 1943, the Royal Air Force Bomber Command mounted 10 major attacks on targets in Germany, dropping more than 8,000 tons of bombs. Berlin as well as the Ruhr district were heavily hit. Air raids on Hamburg were carried out between 24 and 30 July 1943.

democratic groups which shall be able to step forth immediately after the collapse.

Most important is the Catholic Church. It is, however, by no means a united oppositional factor. Since 1933 the Church as such has been rather submissive, and at the bishops' meeting at Fulda in the summer of 1940, the wing that supported the Nazi war won. Quite a large part of the clergy also supports Nazism. Many other clergymen have, however, taken a firm stand and the Catholic Church services and processions have constantly gathered many people, not always because people had become so much more religious, but because this was the only legal possibility to protest against Nazism. Today the attitude of the Catholic Church is represented by such oppositional elements as Cardinal Faulhaber and Bishop Calen [Galen].[13]

The Protestant Church is much less uniform than the Catholic Church. The larger part of it supports Nazism. But even here many oppositional elements are also to be found. The role of Niemoller [Niemöller] is often overestimated. He is mainly a symbol. The circles which are represented by Bishop Wurm of Württemberg, the oldest of the German bishops, are of greater importance. The contact between the organized oppositional elements within the Catholic and Protestant Churches has been extended and there exists today a kind of common administration for the German Church Front.

As has already been mentioned, it is easier for the Church than for other groups to keep in contact with the various towns and districts, and especially where Southern Germany is concerned, it may well be assumed that there will be a well-built organizational apparatus which may be taken over by the Catholic central [center] party. This will be of great importance in a situation when the entire Nazi administration is dissolved. The Church opposition will on the whole play an important part in the revolution in Germany. On the other hand, it is obvious that it will not be possible to avoid a considerable differentiation of just this opposition. The social problems will cause dissension, and the fact is that some of the most active anti-Nazis, for instance in the Catholic Church, are simultaneously the most conservative ones with regard to the solution of social problems.

The *conservative* as well as the *liberal* opposition are connected with church circles. There is, however, no united opposition on the part of former conservatives, and the liberal elements had already long before 1933 got into a destructive process of disintegration. A certain activity may, however, be noticed within these circles.

The conservative opposition is mainly based upon industrial circles and other representatives of economic life. The situation is, however, that a large part of industry has from the beginning supported Nazism. Even though many regret this, it is difficult for them to change their minds. The fear of social revolution is

---

13. Michael von Faulhaber and Clemens Graf August von Galen were Cardinal Archbishops of Munich and of Münster, respectively.

also prevalent. Nevertheless, one often hears that people in industry and business circles meet to discuss which attitude they should take when the collapse occurs and during the following occupation. In many places relations between employers and employees have improved and the Nazis complain of passive resistance on the part of some of the industrial leaders. Any active efforts may hardly be expected from this side. Many men in German economic life hope for an American occupation as the comparatively least evil.

The middle class in the cities was earlier the main social supporter of Nazis. Today these people are among the most dissatisfied. However, no great political activity can be expected from this group either. Their social importance has also been considerably reduced as a consequence of the measures taken by the Nazi Government.

A factor of great importance is that the opposition has increased among the intellectuals and among the so-called technical intelligentsia. This group does not play the same intentionally oppositional role in Germany as in Italy, but the oppositional trend which may be noted, may form the basis of an extensive reorganization. The criticism against Nazism is strongly pronounced among the young intellectuals, and there is today not a single university in Germany where there are not illegal groups. The political attitudes of these groups differ very much, but liberal and democratic tendencies may be noted at many places. The occurrences at the Munchen [München] University some months ago had a symptomatic significance.[14] Among the technical intelligentsia there are strong inclinations for a planned economy on a democratic basis. The majority of the intellectuals who have broken with Nazism refrain from active political work. They concentrate on their profession and consider that they cannot do anything for or against the cause since great political and military problems are concerned. When one considers the problems connected with the formation of a democratic administration during the occupation of Germany, it is, however, important to know that a large part of the German intellectuals and technicians may be used.

In this connection some remarks on German *youth* may be appropriate. In Italy it proved that the most active opposition was based upon young people who on the whole had no experience of their own from the time before Fascism. When Mussolini was overthrown the youth was seen to participate in the spontaneous uprising in the North Italian industrial districts and at other places. In Germany it is not so simple. But neither in this country has the entire youth been poisoned by Nazism. Those who participated in the Nazi movement in the years preceding 1933 are the most dangerous ones. A large part of the youth who has since been passed through the Nazi school, the Hitler Youth, the Labor Service, et cetera, has to a large extent become non-political. This forms a poor start for the restoration of a democratic society, but it is, however, a little more favorable than if the Nazis

---

14. At Munich University, the "White Rose" Resistance Circle had produced leaflets calling for German youth to rise against the Nazis. See also document [17].

had succeeded in winning in earnest the broad masses of the young generation. Among the best groups of youth that have grown up during the last few years, considerable scepticism is prevalent. People who have been in touch with young German soldiers report that their minds are occupied with the fact that the present government has forced them into an existence of professional soldiers; that they have never received any training in a trade; and that they do not know what they are going to do after the war. 15 and 16-year-old boys who were evacuated from Hamburg after the heavy bombardments, report that there were very few real Nazis in their school. It may be recalled in this connection that already in 1938 the Nazis felt obliged to proclaim that the "generation fight" in Germany was ended. The young generation had achieved its aim. There was no longer time for any opposition of the youth against existing institutions.

The young generation in Germany is thus not a uniform pro-Nazi reserve. On the contrary, it may be expected that quite large parts of the youth will take an active part in the revolutionary process which will follow after the collapse. On the other hand, it is clear that more than half of the youth will have disappeared when peace comes. In the spring of 1943 it was estimated that half of the five million soldiers between the ages of 17 and 25 had been killed. Another million soldiers were so seriously wounded that they were incapable of continued military service.

In connection with a valuation of the feelings within the middle classes, it may be appropriate to say a few words also about the endeavors of the *monarchistic groups*. Several reports from Germany indicate that there is a certain mass-inclination in favor of a monarchist solution after the war within the middle class and among the rural population. This is especially true when older people are concerned. They combine "the good old times" with the kingdom and the empire. Endeavors aiming at a restoration of the monarchy may also count on support from certain industrial circles. It is a generally known fact that the majority of the officers of the Reichswehr favor a monarchy. Nor will the Church have any objections against a monarchist solution. This is especially true where the Protestant Church is concerned.

Up to now it has generally been assumed that the members of the House of Hohenzollern[15] had been compromised to such an extent that they could not possibly play any important role. It has, however, lately been rumored that a certain amount of activity is being displayed in order to prepare the way for the ex-Crown Prince. It is maintained that higher circles within the Catholic Church take a sympathetic attitude toward these plans, as they reckon that this would involve a stabilization of conditions and a concentration of the elements that regard it as their main task to prevent radical social revolution. It has also been reported that work is being done in Bavaria and in other parts of Germany for the benefit of earlier dynasties. The importance of the activity of these circles should, however, not be overestimated. Large parts of the German people, not least among labor, will reject a monarchist solution as they would interpret such a solution as an

---

15. Ruling dynasty of Brandenburg-Prussia (1415–1918) and of Imperial Germany (1871–1918).

expression for a reactionary post-war policy. The monarchist tendencies are bound to come in conflict with the forces which aim at a democratic revolution.

That part of the German opposition which is often underestimated in spite of the fact that it will probably be of the greatest importance, is the *labor opposition*. The German *labor* movement has certainly made many mistakes, but it has, however, contrary to all other parties, never collaborated with Nazism. This fact will be of great significance when people will look for a new political orientation. Another fact is that representatives of the labor movement have been the most active persons to carry on illegal political activity and that the nucleus of the former members of the trade unions at the work places have not at any time after 1933 joined the Nazis.

The illegal political activity emanating from the former labor parties was steadily hit by new blows from the Gestapo during the years between 1933 and 1939. The war made the work still more difficult. The illegal groups to a considerable extent rely on young people, especially trade union people of younger years. Many of them were drafted. The connections with the points of support abroad were cut off. The military victories of Hitler had a paralyzing effect. The illegal activity reached its lowest point in 1940. Since then it has made new progress, even if on a very small scale. From the most different parts of Germany it is recorded that small illegal Social Democratic, Communistic or "coalition Socialistic" circles are active. Some of them spread illegal papers or news bulletins, while others confine themselves to preparing their future political contribution and extend the network of political agents. It happens that groups within a certain district are in contact with each other, but on the other hand, there is generally no collaboration between illegal circles existing in the same place. The work is to a great extent carried out by women. In the course of the last year it has been possible to state that illegal groups in Germany have made efforts to resume contact with comrades at the front.

It is impossible to get an idea of the total extent and structure of the illegal movement. There is every reason not to overrate the extent of the work which is carried on. Thus it should not be counted upon that the illegal groups which exist today might immediately form the basis of new political parties. As already mentioned, the groups are isolated from one another. Nor have they any common ideology. The process which will be necessary in order that new political parties take form will show many chaotic signs. The young members of the illegal circles are also unknown. On many occasions they will on the whole not be able to act with the authority which is a condition for their being accepted by the broader masses. On the other hand, even the smallest circles have, of course, a certain importance, especially when it comes to the intellectual settlement of the problems which the German opposition will have to face as a consequence of a military collapse.

The organized illegal activity is not the only, nor perhaps the most important form of the labor opposition. The main importance lies with the work places. Even if the workers have been moved back and forth and even if many of them have been drafted for military service, a rather large part of the older skilled workers are still at their old jobs. At many work places there is thus a nucleus of former representatives of the trade unions and of the enterprises. These people have not played any active part under Nazism, nor have they become Nazis. The workers have to a great extent turned to these former representatives for advice, and in the course of the war the management of the enterprise has also in many places negotiated with the former representatives, and not with the functionaries of the labor front. It may be assumed that the old staff of representatives of labor may form the basis of a new trade union movement in Germany, and it is known that certain preparations are being made along this line. The representatives of labor may, however, also play an important political role. The breakdown of Nazism will be connected with confusion in many different fields within the administration. In this chaos the work places will form natural units. At the different work places delegates selected by elections will assume the administrative functions and various tasks which are combined with the supply of foodstuffs and other commodities. To an occupation power it would seem natural to utilize this organized element in the German chaos.

Reports which have every now and then been published concerning strikes at German works have in almost all cases proved to lack foundation. No revolutionary sentiments prevail at the work places. Many of the workers have become apathetic. The long working hours also contribute in having a paralyzing effect. Most decisive are, however, those examples which show that Gestapo and SS do not hesitate to use any means when it is a question of crushing opposition within labor. In addition to this there are the complicated conditions which are a consequence of the transfer of foreign workers to German industries. Many works are completely dominated by foreign workers. The tension between these and the German workers was to begin with rather high. Moreover, there was much dissension among the various groups of foreign labor. Lately it has, however, been reported from various places, not least from important big industries, that relations between German and foreign labor have improved considerably.[16] A contributory factor is that the foreigners have learned a good deal of German and can now tell the Germans what is actually going on in the occupied countries. In some cases illegal groups comprising both German and foreign labor have even been formed. Such contacts will, however, not prevent the most serious frictions from appearing the same day the war is over. The foreign workers are already today discussing how they will organize themselves in order to provide the transportation means which they can get hold of in order to get home as quickly as possible. A closer contact between German and foreign labor will, however, enable a regulation of relations so that they do not result in actual disorganization. The German trade union delegates do not support strikes and similar measures. They are of the opinion that it is impossible to carry out a strike as long as the Nazi terror system stands unshaken. To strike under the Nazi regime is equivalent to shaking the

---

16. For OSS considerations and plans to exploit the situation of foreign labor in Germany see document [23].

foundation of the regime. Some acts of sabotage are, however, carried out by active groups. The main principle of the oppositional labor is to work slowly. It may seem that this is to do too little, but it is not the intention of this report to give judgement as to what is right or wrong. We confine ourselves to describing the actual situation. Neither is the passive opposition at the work places without some significance from a point of view of war economy. A labor productivity reduced only by one percent means that Germany loses more than one billion crowns a year.

It is not possible to state anything definite about the proportion in strength between the various political tendencies within the labor movement. One is, however, often inclined to exaggerate the power of the Communist movement. The Nazis have often deliberately given false reports in order to frighten the people abroad. The latest thing was that a Swedish journalist was made to believe that 65 percent of German labor was Communist. This is certainly not true. The large masses of German labor today do not belong to any party. Many of them are instinctively opponents, but without adhering to any particular political tendency. A great many of the younger elements among the active opponents are drifting toward the Communist movement. The Social Democrats, however, still maintain a strong position among the delegates of labor at the work places. Some believe that the proportion between Communists and Social Democrats at the places of work is probably 50:50. It is possible that this is correct—apart from Southern Germany where the Catholics have a certain influence among labor and where there also earlier existed independent Catholic trade unions—but it should also be noticed that there is a strong tendency in the direction of obtaining a confederation among labor. Especially young workers who are engaged in oppositional activity are often heard stating that they do not want to return either to Social Democracy or Communism. The tendency appearing from a series of reports to the effect that not even former Communists want any dictatorial government after the war is still more important. Among other things, people who have lived in Hamburg, formerly one of the main centers of the Communist Party in Germany, confirm these reports. There seems to be an inclination for a radical democratic policy with a socialistic tendency. Moreover, claims for the creation of a united labor party will certainly also be raised. Whether this can be realized depends not only upon German conditions but not least also upon the policy of the Soviet Union.

The problem which naturally occupies the minds of the non-Nazi workers in Germany is: what will become of Germany after the war? One has the impression that the national feelings are of considerably less importance among workmen than many people believe. It is also realized that, even if a radical change of regime is carried out, Germany will be forced to assume extraordinary obligations in connection with the European reconstruction. On the other hand, it must be reckoned that German labor will oppose a dismemberment of Germany[17] and

---

17. See document [12].

that its delegates will refuse to conduct a policy which might stamp them as agents for foreign powers. All sensible anti-Nazis in Germany realize, however, that a rational collaboration with the occupied powers [sic] must be established. In order that the collaboration be rational, it will be of importance that, beside the military authorities, there will also on the Allied side be civil representatives, not least trade union people, for whom it will be easier to come on speaking terms with the German organizations.

Labor in Germany will also be among those that want the most radical settlement with Nazism and the groups which have helped Nazism to come into power and thereby prepare this war. It goes without saying that such a settlement will also strike Prussian militarism. First of all the German opposition is interested in securing certain democratic liberties and rights, such as freedom of organization, freedom of gathering, freedom of the press—always with exemption for the Nazis—, freedom of religion, et cetera. What is then naturally occupying their minds is how it will be possible to supply the population with foodstuffs and what steps may be taken in order to keep people employed and lead the soldiers back to as normal an occupation as possible. It seems necessary to "take over" a large part of the system of planned economy of the Nazi State in order to solve these tasks. There would otherwise only be confusion. It is, however, important to see to it that reliable people take over the administration and the control. As to this and other tasks no dissension in principle need arise between German Democrats and Allied Nations. The German opposition is, however, steadily pointing out how important it would be if the Allied Nations should give clear information as to the policy they intend to follow with regard to the defeated countries. Such desires are expressed above all by those elements who agree that German militarism must be destroyed together with Nazism, as they realize that this is one of the most essential conditions for the establishment of a German democracy. That part of the German opposition which is based upon a solid democratic foundation and which desires intimate collaboration with the great democracies is naturally interested in learning whether it is on the whole going to be accepted as an ally when it comes to the reconstruction after the war.

Summing up, it may be stated that the German opposition has its main support among labor, part of the intelligentsia and the Church, especially insofar as it represents the dissatisfied part of the rural population. In addition there is the opposition within the officers' corps and the activity which may be expected to be developed by the common soldiers when they return home from the fronts. Even if the disintegration of the military morale has reached the most advanced state in the occupied countries, it is most likely that the soldiers who will pour back from the East Front will play the most important role. They are the most numerous and the ones who are most closely welded together.

Geographically the Catholic opposition has, as is well known, its strongest support in Southern Germany. The labor opposition is strongest in Northwestern Germany (the Hanseatic cities, et cetera), in Berlin, the Ruhr district, Saxony and Silesia. Unfortunately, it cannot be avoided that the intensified bombardment of German industries also hits those districts where the latent and partly organized opposition has reached the most advanced state. It should be emphasized that not even after the heavy bomb raids, for instance against Hamburg, have the Nazis succeeded in obtaining popular approval of their propaganda of hatred against the Western Powers. Wide circles of the population in the very districts suffering the most from the bombardments do not regard the English and Americans as their enemies.

Although it may be stated that there is opposition within all the groups and districts which have been mentioned, no illusions should be entertained as to the striking power of this opposition. The present regime can still without difficulty control the domestic oppositional elements and render them harmless. The only group which under the present regime might be able to settle accounts with the Gestapo and SS is the army. Such action by the military will probably not occur, but if it should it would very likely fail on account of inadequate preparations and lack of cooperation. There remains then another eventuality: that the internal administration will be dissolved as a result of extended air raids. Trends in this direction could be noticed after the bombardments of Hamburg and Berlin in July and August. Aside from these eventualities, one comes to the conclusion after sober consideration that the oppositional elements in Germany will not emerge in earnest until the military defeat is an irrefutable fact, when the regime will be dissolved by overwhelming pressure from the outside.

How are then conditons among the German emigrants and what influence may they have upon developments in Germany [?]

The Russian revolution in 1917 was decisively influenced by Russian emigrants. German emigration will certainly not play the same role. But it should be wrong to disregard it as one of the factors which may be determining for Germany's future policy. The internal German opposition lacks intellectual leaders, people who can carry on German democratic traditions and who have knowledge of international conditions. The small illegal groups have had very limited possibilities to form an opinion of developments in the world. Yet it is not known how many of the former agents escape alive from the prisons and the concentration camps. Some of those who get out will be broken down and the others have for many years been cut off from all contact with the outside world. The restoration of a democratic community in Germany will depend upon international conditions. Refugees who have learned about the conditions in the country where they have stayed will be able to act as intermediaries between their fellow countrymen and the conquerors or the occupation powers.[18]

German emigrants are not united. The defeat in 1933 and the difficult material conditions in a number of the countries of refuge have had demoralizing effects. Some of the emigrants have been assimilated in the countries of refuge. Especially the main part of the Jewish intelligentsia who fled from Germany may not be

---

18. See also document [17].

expected to return. During the period of the people's front, collaboration was started between German Democrats, Social Democrats and Communists. This collaboration stopped after the German-Russian pact.[19] In the country where the coalition efforts were most advanced—France—part of the German emigrants succumbed after the occupation in 1940. The rest escaped to America. Today German emigration has four main centers: England, America, Russia and Sweden. It comprises three main groups: the trade union-socialistic, and the Communist and Bourgeois wings.

The German Social Democrats maintain the remainders of their party administration in London, with Hans Vogel and Erich Ollenhauer at the head. Among the more well-known German Social Democrats in America, there are Friedrich Stampfer and Albert Grzesinski. There is also a large Social Democratic group in Sweden. A number of former social democratic members of the German Parliament are living in that country, in America and in Switzerland. Beside the former Social Democracy, there are also a few oppositional socialistic groups which are, however, based upon democratic pinciples. The most important among these groups are the German SAP [Sozialistische Arbeiterpartei],[20] counting among its members such men as [Jacob] Walcher in the United States and [August] Enderle in Sweden,[21] and the so-called "Neu-Beginnen" group under the leadership of Paul Hagen (U.S.A.)[22] and Paul Sering (England). For a long time efforts have been made to unite the various German Social Democrats and other democratic Socialists. There has been established in London a Socialistic federation where the oppositional groups are represented beside the Social Democratic Party administration. A group which has not joined this federation is the one which is headed by Kurt Geyer [Curt Theodor Geyer] and Walter Loeb and which is most closely connected to the Vansittart circle.[23] Unity concerning close collaboration between the German democratic Socialists has been reached also in Sweden. This coalition has been supported by the international labor group consisting of democratic Socialists in Stockholm.

It may be assumed that the main part of the democratic Socialist emigrants will endeavor to form a Democratic-Socialistic Coalition Party. Especially in the course of the last year, detailed investigations concerning various problems connected with the reconstruction in Germany have been started. The main tendency is a radical democratic policy which, it is considered, must necessarily include

---

19. I.e., the Hitler-Stalin pact of 28 August 1939.

20. The Sozialistische Arbeiterpartei [Socialist Worker's Party], formerly a leftist faction within Germany's Social Democratic Party (SPD) had split off from them in 1930/1931.

21. August Enderle, a friend of Willy Brandt, had established in March 1937 a regional section of the International Transport Federation (ITF) in Stockholm. For the collaboration between the ITF and the OSS see document [33].

22. See document [1].

23. A minority of German exiles supported the germanophobic doctrine represented by Robert G. Vansittart, Chief Adviser in British foreign affairs; this attitude became known as "Vansittartism."

essential socialistic measures. As to foreign policy there is [sic], no doubt, within German emigration circles certain nationalistic tendencies, but on the whole it may be said that the democratic Socialist wing aims at a sincere peace policy within the framework of a European federation and international law. Many of the German Socialists realize that only by many years of persistent and honest work can they convince the other nations that Germany has really undergone a serious change.

The activity of the German trade unions is influenced by the democratic Socialists. The main leadership rests with Fritz Tarnow (Sweden). Communists and others are, however, included in the trade union groups both in Sweden and in England. The German trade union people are of the opinion that a uniform labor federation should be established after the war. The Communists assert that they do not intend to reestablish separate trade unions. The main problem is, thus, whether it will be possible to come to an agreement with the representatives of the Catholic trade union movement. In a discussion as to how the German trade union movement is to be restored, two principal points of view arise. Some people are of the opinion that the restoration must be started by small illegal groups at the work places. Others maintain that a provisional central management should as soon as possible take over as much as possible of the organization apparatus of the labor front,[24] but, of course, not its personnel. It is not impossible to come to a synthesis between these two opinions. Everyone will understand how important it would be if a provisional trade union central [center] could be reestablished already at an early date. Much chaos could then be avoided. The trade unions would also then be able to collaborate with the occupation powers when such important problems as the supply of foodstuffs and the conversion of the industrial and agricultural production are concerned.

The German Communists have a great number of their representatives in Russia. Little is known about their activity and their plans for the future. The leader of the party, Wilhelm Pieck, participates, together with former Communist members of the German Parliament and intellectuals who sympathize with the Communist Party, in the German National Committee which was formed in Moscow in the summer [of] 1943.[25] As for the rest, the committee consists of German officers and soldiers who represent prisoners of war in Russia. The German National Committee carries on an extensive propaganda activity comprising broadcasts, leaflets and papers. The propaganda is not marked by particularly Communist views. The broadcasts have rather a nationalistic character. They are also in the first place intended to influence the officers in Germany. The aims of the program of the committee are among other things that the private property right be respected and restored and that amnesty be given Nazis who break

---

24. I.e., the Deutsche Arbeitsfront (DAF, German Labor Front), formed by the Nazis after the dissolution of the trade unions.

25. See also document [100].

with Hitler before the collapse. It is also implied that the power of the military shall not be displaced. There are among non-Communist Germans abroad many who believe that the propaganda carried on by the Moscow committee may play a certain role in influencing certain circles in Germany, but simultaneously they stress that the program of the committee is not suitable as a coalition basis.

It is known that the German Communists in Russia display a rather extensive activity in the camps for prisoners of war. There is reason to believe that groups are being formed which will play an important role in the case of a possible restoration of the Communist Party in Germany.

Attempts to establish a free German committee in connection with the Moscow committee have recently been made in England. The work in that country is led by Wilhelm Koenen, former Communist member of the German Parliament, and other Communist representatives. Adele Schreiber, a former Social Democratic lady member of the German Parliament, and Professor August Weber, a member of Parliament who belonged to the German Democratic Party (the State Party) [Deutsche Staatspartei] support this initiative. At present the committee movement in England does not, however, seem to be able to unite the main part of the Social Democratic and bourgeoise [sic] Democratic Germans who live there. In Mexico there is a free German committee which is led by Paul Merker, the former trade union leader of the Communist Party. In the United States a great number of the radical German intellectuals have been persuaded to give their support to the Moscow committee. In Sweden the German Communists were interned until only a short time ago. They are now publishing the weekly paper *Information* which carries on propaganda on the line of the Moscow committee, but there seems to be no foundation for establishing a German committee in Stockholm.

Attempts were made at an early date of the war by the German bourgeoisie to establish a German committee with its seat in Canada. This attempt failed, however. The intention was that among others Otto Strasser, Rauschning, Treviranus and Wilhelm Sollmann, the Christian Social Democratic member of the German Parliament, should belong to this committee. The importance of Otto Strasser has long been overrated abroad. He has very few connections and little prospect of playing any important role in Germany after the collapse of Nazism. The same may be said about Rauschning. Little is known about Treviranus. He may have connections with certain oppositional industrial circles in Germany. Some bourgeois Democrats, with among others Professor Georg Bernhard, have formed a smaller German committee[26] together with some of the Social Democrats in the United States. Among the intellectuals Thomas Mann occupies a special position. It was first believed that he had decided not to return to Germany. But his recent

---

26. I.e., the German-American Council for the Liberation of Germany from Nazism, otherwise known as the Association of Free Germans.

statements indicate the contrary, and some people believe that he might become president in a democratic Germany.

The German Church opposition has some representatives abroad, but they work very cautiously and do not collaborate with the rest of the emigrants. The most prominent representative of the Catholic Central Party, Dr. Bruning [Brüning], is a professor in the United States. Bruning has connections with leading American circles[27] and many people believe that he is selected to play an important part in Germany after the war.[28] No official statements have been made by Bruning, nor has he sought contact with other emigrant circles. It must also be expected that Bruning would meet considerable opposition, as, at least in labor circles, his period as State Chancellor is regarded as a step on the road toward Hitler's assumption of power.

Many reports from Germany are to the effect that the foreign radio propaganda plays a very important role. This is also confirmed by a number of penitentiary and death sentences. The Social Democrats and the bourgeois Democrats regret that they are not allowed to participate to any extent to speak of in the radio propaganda to Germany. They point out that Russia is following entirely different lines than the Western Powers. In this connection it is also mentioned that it ought to be in the interest of the Western Powers to carry on an active information work among the German prisoners of war and that, in this field, they ought to be able to collaborate with qualified and reliable people among the refugees. Anyway, it should be realized that the radio will play a still more important role when the collapse of Germany really occurs. When the German administration collapses and all kinds of local organizations will act independently of each other, a determined influence through the foreign radio may become a stabilizing and uniting factor.

---

27. Among Heinrich Brüning's acquaintances and friends were not only numerous collegues at Harvard University and German exiles such as Paul Tillich and Prince Odo von Württemberg but also people like George S. Messersmith, Assistant Secretary of State, A. Roland Elliot, Executive Secretary of the Student Division of the YMCA, New York, and Edward C. Carter, Secretary General of the Institute of Pacific Relations.

28. In June 1944, Brüning was approached by a German resistance circle to return to Germany. See document [44].

Document 22 · 27 September 1943

Report by the OSS Research and Analysis Branch: The Underground Movement in Germany[1]

SECRET

The Underground Movement in Germany

I. Introduction

It is possible to make a chronological division of the history of the German Underground. The period of 1933–1939 is marked by the attempt of the strongest political parties, the Social Democrats and the Communists, to maintain an underground on a national or mass scale. But as these attempts at mass underground movements were beaten by the activity of the Terror, it became clear that national or mass organizations were impossible. From about 1935 to 1939, therefore, attempts were made to provide a more effective organization in the form of small elite groups or cadres in the locality with no contact with each other except through responsible leaders. Alongside the party undergrounds there existed as well trade union undergrounds, suspicious of party activity, and concerned primarily with the utilization of trade union methods in combatting the exploitation of the workers through the German Labour Front [Deutsche Arbeitsfront, DAF]. Thus for this earlier period the underground has been essentially a labor underground, engaged in a desperate fight with the instruments of terror for mere survival, and aiming only to work within the framework of existing Nazi institutions. In this period the Nazis could gradually weaken, but not destroy the underground in each of the political, economic, social and religious oppositional groups.

After an initial further decline the underground has experienced some revival and expansion since the outbreak of war (1939–43). The German conquest of

---

1. NA, RG 59, R&A No. 992.

areas into which the leaders of outlawed parties and organizations had escaped who had maintained contacts within Germany, not only deprived the German underground of support from the outside, but also supplied the Gestapo with additional information with which to crush the illegal opposition in Germany. Contacts with the outside world were almost completely cut off. At the same time the German-Soviet pact[2] may be supposed to have exercised a discouraging effect upon Socialist undergrounds in Germany. With the removal of this check in 1941, and the beginnings of a reversal in the fortunes of war, the general conditions were established for a gradual deterioration of morale leading to the strengthening and enlargement of the underground. The incorporation of police units into the Wehrmacht has weakened the police forces at home. The exploitation of the workers, male and female, industrial and agricultural, in the interests of total war, has necessitated some relaxation in controls, in order to win their acquiescence. The compound of fear, despair, exasperation and suffering wrought by the privations inflicted by a strained war economy, by continual bombings, and by military reverses, produce in some of those not totally exhausted a desire for some tangible means to end it all which [sic] fortifies underground resistance. Of all this the recent appointment of Himmler as Minister of the Interior[3] is a token.
…[4]

III. The Underground Since the War (1939–1943)

It is clear that the pattern for underground organizations remains fundamentally the same for this period. The predominant underground is the labor underground, Social Democratic, Communist and Trade Union, all of which may be said to have been strengthened in the past two years, as a result of general conditions referred to in the *Introduction*, and possibly, in more recent months as a result of the dissolution of the Comintern [Communist International].[5]

It is to be assumed also that these undergrounds are to a large extent responsible for the open resistance of German labor to the measures of its Nazi overlords and for what sabotage that has taken place. The actual number of underground organizations has increased. For some there is little more than a name or a vague reference. Information, however, concerning others, makes it clear that it is not impossible that women, foreign workers and prisoners of war may become an important part of underground activity. Moreover, the underground has definitely spread to the army and the party, and war weariness has led to an illegal peace movement.

---

2. I.e., the Soviet-German Nonaggression Pact of 23 August 1939.

3. In August 1943.

4. The omitted paragraph deals with the underground movement before the war.

5. The Comintern, founded in 1919, had been dissolved by orders of the Moscow government in May 1943.

A. Vague and Unidentifiable References to Undergrounds.

1. The report (January, 1943) that the leader of a non-Communist underground with cells scattered throughout Germany[6] came to Stuttgart to address an audience of 125, including members of the middle class and clergy, after having met similar groups in Bavaria.
2. The report (June 25, 1943) of the trial at Strasbourg on June 5 of Alsatians leading an anti-Nazi organization extending into France and Germany.
3. What is called *The Cultural Progress Organization*, and described simply as an anti-Hitler movement […] is still alive.
4. One PW's brother was executed in September, 19?? [sic] for attempting to organize a secret anti-Hitler movement. […][7]
5. A group of left-wing sportsmen has engaged in [anti]-Nazi activities and specialized in the distribution of leaflets. In March, 1942, some 250 of them were arrested, among them Sperling, German lightweight wrestling champion and Zeelenbinden, German heavyweight wrestler.[8]

B. Women and the Underground. A single reference of this kind comes from a PW who reports the formation of a secret organization based upon the resistance of women to total mobilization and engaged in placing stickers on walls. They changed fatal for total in the public slogans: "Total mobilization calls on you, too, for sacrifice". […]

C. Underground Demands for Peace. What is called the German Peace Movement (Deutsche Friedensbewegung) was founded in western Germany and was reported by a PW to have held a Peace Conference in January, 194[2]. It may be the same as, or associated with the National Catholic German Peace Movement which is credited with the organization of the demonstrations of students in the University of Munich,[9] and the publication of leaflets.

D. Conservative Student Underground. The Fighting League of Student Youth (*Kampfbund Studentischer Jugend*) described by a PW as a rather nationalist and conservative organization centering around the University of Berlin.

E. Conservative Military-Industrialist-Junker Underground. An officer PW belonged to an anti-Nazi military organization which had been growing for sev-

---

6. The name of this leader is not given in the OSS secret intelligence reports.

7. This is a reference to 14 South German Communists, among them Georg Lechleiter, who were executed in September 1942 in Stuttgart.

8. *See special report of the Central European Section: Report on Prisoners of War Interrogations—Opposition to the Nazis.*

9. I.e., the White Rose resistance circle. See also documents [17] and [21].

eral years. It is headed by a general of high rank who is calculated to act as an interim leader until such a figure as von Neurath could organize a government.[10] Outside of the military it has a following of diplomats, Junkers, big industralists, and even a few of the Gestapo. It is anti-Communist and wants a united non-Nazi Germany. The fact that no discipline can be exercised over its members and that it has lost many of its officer members to the Eastern front has limited its growth. Regular recruiting of non-military members was undertaken and attempts were made to atomize the whole organization into cells of fifty members. Publishers were associated in the movement. It is expected that military members called to the front can carry on the work there. Within the *Wehrmacht*, attempts have been made, for the most part by Austrians, to organize oppositional groups and a pamphlet urging the formation of Soldiers' Committees has been distributed among German forces in France.

F. The Party Underground: Storm Troop Friends (SA Freunde). This party underground has been in existence since 1940 and is composed largely of party members who have become dissatisfied with the leadership of the party and the general trend of events in Germany. It seeks to gather all disgruntled individuals within the SA to work against the regime. It contains economists, engineers and gold party medal holders.
    ... [11]

G. The Labor Undergrounds. If the German worker had not been won over by the Nazis before the outbreak of the war, if his feeling for class solidarity had not given way to the *Volksgemeinschaft* [people's community] or the *Betriebsgemein-schaft* [work community] before this date, then it could hardly be shown that this has happened since. As the war drew off all but the older workers and the very young into the Wehrmacht, women, proletarianized members of the lower middle class, and foreign workers have come to take their place. The measures of total mobilization have embittered large numbers of the women and middle class and it is well recognized that the foreigners are a potential vanguard of an army of occupation. Women and foreign workers have been a source of strength rather than weakness to the solidarity of the workers in the factories. In spite, therefore, of the rigid set of industrial, party and police controls set up in the factories, the

---

10. Konstantin von Neurath, the former foreign minister, had been relieved of his office in connection with the so-called Fritsch crisis of February 1938. Although at some points he had favored the removal of Hitler, von Neurath remained in various official positions until the end of the war. Konstantin von Neurath was never a driving force in the conspiracy against Hilter. During the last months of the war, however, his son (Alexander Konstantin von Neurath) was involved in the secret surrender negotiations with Allen W. Dulles and General Karl Wolff in Switzerland and northern Italy. See documents [91], [93] and [94].

11. In the omitted paragraph the different sections of the SA Freunde are described.

workers in some instances have known how to protect themselves against excessive exploitation within the framework of Nazified [sic] industry.[12] … [13]

1. *Sabotage and Other Subversive Activity.* Foreign workers are known to have engaged in sabotage in the Kiel shipyards; Italian workers in the Merck Chemical Works at Darmstadt, and French and Russian workers on the German railroads are reported to have changed destination cards so frequently that new control systems have had to be set up. Russian workers have committed sabotage in the Leuna works in Merseburg. Acts of sabotage on the part of German workers are reported at several metal works near Frankfurt/M., at the Bavarian Motor Works at Munich, at the Mauser Werke at Rottweil on the Neckar,[14] at Düsseldorf, and on the canals. Hamburg appears to be an active center for sabotage. Workers from the Dralle glycerin factory have been shot for it, and it has been reported on the wharves of Blohm and Voss, in the harbor, and at the Hannover Station. At the beginning of April workers on their way to early shifts are said to have stopped to celebrate the raising of a red flag on the St. Michael's Kirche.

Subversive slogans and leaflets have become, especially in the last eighteen months, more abundant. The Social Democrats have revived their old ones associating the Nazis inevitably with war. "Rather the old-time unemployment and fifteen marks a week dole than war." They appear scribbled in pencil on walls of corridors and lavatories. Stickers are numerous and illegal leaflets are distributed even within factories (The Auto-Union Factory at Zwickau). In Munich 17 persons from southern Germany were sentenced who had been accused of having printed and distributed during 1942–43 leaflets exhorting the population to commit acts of sabotage against the armament industry. The leaders of the group were women residents of Munich, others came from Stuttgart, Freiburg and Ulm. In the first week of May, 1943, leaflets stamped "Hunger" and "Don't be a Hitler slave" were distributed at night in the streets of Leipzig by cyclists. Since the fall of Mussolini pamphlets appear to have become more frequent, the latest one calling for a halt. "Stop it! There's only one way to save ourselves. Stop the war! Stop working in factories! Stop it!" Social Democrats in Switzerland even believe that the time is ripe for inducing a general strike in Germany.

[…]

2. *Continuation of the Social Democratic and Socialist Underground.* a. There have been meetings of Sudeten Social Democrats which were limited, however, to discussions of future plans.

b. Members of the Social Democratic Party founded in 1938 the *Sozialistische Arbeiter Jugend* [Social Democratic Youth Movement].

---

12. *See the special report of the Central European Section on Labor Morals.*

13. The omitted passage lists individual acts of industrial sabotage.

14. In reality, the Mauser Werke were located in Oberndorf on the Neckar; Rottweil was the location of a branch of IG Farben (the so-called Pulvermühle).

c. A *Demokratischer Schutzbund* [Democratic Protection Association] was founded in September, 1939, at Bremen by a young worker formerly active in the illegal Reich[s]banner[15] at Bremen after he had been released from prison and the concentration camp. Its members were former members of the Social Democratic Party and young recruits from the *Sozialistische Arbeiter Jugend*. The organization attained a maximum of some ninety groups in and outside Bremen, composed of three or four individuals whose only contact was with each other. Contacts between the groups were maintained by the leader, and names and addresses were never written down. This strength was gradually reduced by call-up. The activities of the league are limited to propaganda of a general anti-Nazi and anti-war kind. The members talk in their places of employment, among their friends, in shopping queues and trams. Emphasis is placed also upon the proper education of children in the home in an anti-Nazi direction. The League is reported to have sent one of its members outside Germany to establish contacts with the British Intelligence and this member is supposedly responsible for much of the sabotage on German ships in occupied countries.[16] Beyond current propaganda the League hopes to be able to assure that when once democracy is established in New Germany it will not be supplanted by another totalitarian government.

d. It has been reported (March, 1943) that former leaders of the Social Democratic Party, including Franz Kuenstler [Künstler], former chairman of the Party in Berlin and Max Westphal, the leader of the Social Democratic Youth Movement, were rounded up and executed as possible leaders of revolt.[17]

e. In Essen, on May 3, 1943, 63 workers who participated in an illegal meeting to celebrate the first of May were arrested and held for trial before the People's Court, and indicted for having arranged an illegal socialistic meeting. Eleven belonged to free trade unions before 1933.

f. An ISK (*Internationale[r] Sozialistische[r] Kampfbund*) report of October, 1942, referring to a connecting network with good groups in many of the important factories, and especially in the Rhineland and the Ruhr.[18]

3. Continuations of the Communist Underground. a. *Anti-Faschistische Aktion* [Anti-fascist action] has not been liquidated.

b. The workers of Berlin have founded a Communist Youth International (*Kommunistische Jugend Internationale*).

c. A young Berlin machinist and trade unionist was asked by the Bezirksleiter [district leader] of the Communist Party to transform a small discussion group of

---

15. The Reichsbanner, a paramilitary Social Democratic Party formation, had been dissolved in 1933.

16. This is probably a reference to Erich Prenzel, who after his release from prison contacted Waldemar Pötzsch, a German trade unionist living in Antwerp, Belgium. The OSS was not aware that Prenzel was a double agent working for German intelligence.

17. Franz Künstler had been sent to several concentration camps; he died in the late summer of 1942.

18. In 1928, a radical faction had been expelled from the German Socialist Party. The banished members thereafter formed their own organization, the Internationaler Sozialistischer Kampfbund.

which he was a member into a unit of the *Roter Frontkämpferbund*.[19] The request was refused because of the fear that the Communist Party had been infiltrated by too many Nazi spies. The discussion group preferred to meet alone.

d. The arrest and sentence to death of fourteen persons at Mannheim (May 19, 1942) for trying to set up a Communist organization in Mannheim and circulating hectographed illegal newspapers;[20] the report that in October and November 1942 a great number of workers were imprisoned for "illegal Communist activities"; the report (April, 1943) that illegal Communist groups were becoming stronger and that their clandestine meetings were seldom discovered; the report from a worker that eighty out of one hundred and fifty workers in a Baltic port were Communist in sympathy and had some kind of secret organization. Indeed, there seems to be some evidence for the growing strength of German Communism among German workers.

[...]

4. *Continuation of the Trade Union Underground.* a. The secret meeting of German trade union leaders is reported for April 13, 1942, which approved an appeal to the German workers. From Swedish Trade Union Circles is reported a secret meeting of German trade union representatives in Berlin on April 30th of this year, the first convention of this kind since the outbreak of the war.[21]

b. A report (June, 1942) of an excellently built-up underground trade [union] movement in the large plants, especially among the metal workers. The underground representatives are said to be directed by an Executive Committee for the whole factory, consisting of former shop stewards and trade union functionaries who collect dues and subscription funds. The activities of the group are limited to internal factory struggles.

c. The International Federation of Transport Workers (IFTU) has undoubtedly maintained connection with the illegal underground of German railroad workers and seamen. The organization of railroad workers formed by Hans Jahn (see above) is indeed recorded as the best possible means for contacting the German underground movement. 170 out of the original 280 members of his organization are still active in various areas, have been trained in underground work and understand the methods of clandestine underground activity. [...] The Joint Council of the International Federation of Transport workers, Miner and Metal Workers broadcasts regularly from London to the workers in Germany and occupied countries. On April 3, 1943, J. H. Oldenbroek, the successor to the late Edo Fimmen as secretary of the IFTU, promised in the name of the combined membership of the more than five million workers of the three internationals spread

---

19. The Communist Red Front organization.

20. The arrest took place in February 1942; the oppositionals were sentenced to death on 15 May 1942 (not on May 19).

21. This message stemmed from German exile trade unionist Fritz Tarnow.

over thirty-six different countries before the war, that "we pledge every possible moral and financial support to those who form underground trade union groups in the occupied and axis countries alike."

The period since the war is then marked by an increase in the strength of the underground which remains essentially labor. What remains of the Social Democratic underground is not any too clear. [...] In addition to party organizations per se there has evidently been some effort on the part of the Communists to bring together all oppositional groups in Germany into a common front (The Rhineland Conference—Dec. 1942). There is no reason to believe that the trade union undergrounds have not participated in this revival. But the striking conclusion to be drawn from the evidence is the expansion of the underground into other than labor circles. A conservative, national, anti-Nazi and anti-Communist group seeking to combat common front Communist activities has joined together groups from the army, industry, agriculture, the civil service (diplomats) and even some of the Gestapo. Conservatism in student circles has taken underground form in the *Kampfbund Studentischer Jugend* [Student Youth Action Group]. The desire for peace attracts all groups in *Deutsche Friedens Bewegung* [German Peace Movement], and a continuation of Catholic opposition can be seen in the National Catholic German Peace Movement.[22] Women have engaged in minor subversive activity, and the underground has finally reached disaffected groups within the Party in *SA Freunde*[23] which incorporates intellectuals (engineers and economists) as well as old party members.

At the same time that the underground has revived and expanded it has also enlarged its activities. While the fight for existence continues, and it maintains its reportorial functions, it can dare to engage in bolder forms of action. It can lead the struggle of the worker within the framework of German labor controls, organize strikes, and cooperate in escape. It can organize mass protests in the form of processions and demonstrations. It can hold conferences of its leaders, and representative conferences of its members. It can go beyond anti-Nazi talk in home, factory and in public groups and publicize slogans of its own; it can prepare, publish and distribute stickers and pamphlets. It can even engage in acts of terrorism and sabotage and conduct clandestine radio stations. Thus it aids in the building up of a secret public opinion. Moreover, it can occasionally dare to plan for a more distant future.

It is well, however, not to exaggerate. This is not to say that the destruction of the regime by any underground is immediately at hand, or that a social revolution impends. It is not possible to speak of any national or mass underground, or for that matter of any organized regional one except it be, perhaps, in Austria. The individual undergrounds are still atomized into small groups within the city, the town and

---

22. *For some evidence on the opposition of religious groups since the war, see the special report of the Central European Section on* The Christian Opposition in Germany. [No copy of this report could be found in the National Archives in Washington, D.C.]

23. An association of members of the Nazi Storm Division (Sturmabteilung, SA).

the factory. But there are at least signs of a change. Conservative and Communist circles are aiming to consolidate larger groups of the opposition to the Nazis. [...]

It remains to be said that within a totalitarian state the strength of an underground movement does not depend upon numbers. Totalitarianism and a widespread underground are a contradiction in terms. Its strength depends at the moment upon the intelligence and character of those few who have survived, and upon their plans for activizing [sic] the great amount of disaffection present in all classes of German society, a disaffection which is growing enormously as the German people begin to realize the impasse into which they have been led. Deprived for the most part of the support which, before the war, came to these undergrounds from exile parent organizations, it remains for the United Nations to find means to substitute for these, and make efforts to cooperate with the German leaders in a coordination and further activization [sic] of the underground that is left. That amounts in the main to the promotion of the labor underground. After all the opposition in military, industrialist, Junker, and bureaucratic circles relies in the last analysis upon the coup d'etat rather than the powerful underground for the seizure of power. The opposition in religious and lower middle class circles may, with important exceptions, be assumed to have not gone much further than the private discussion group. The peasant, though restive and often hostile, is hard to budge. There remain the workers. They, however, are caught between their devotion to the class and the national struggle, and the resistance is therefore partial rather than total. They are, moreover, obsessed by the fear of what the consequences of defeat and the destruction of the regime will bring for them. This fear can be attacked only by an intelligent political warfare, which by offering some alternative to the chaos, civil war or even national annihilation which, in case of defeat, many expect, may hope to transform a partial into a total resistance. Even as it is the record is a tribute to human endurance and courage, and the revelation of a great hope. Faced with the sharpened instruments of Terror, the underground needs, in addition to its own growing strength, a guidance and a support which offer some reward to the endurance and the courage, and give some substance to the hope.

Document 23 · 30 September 1943

Report by the OSS Research and Analysis Branch: The Foreign Laborer in Germany as an MO Target[1]

SECRET

The Foreign Laborer in Germany as an MO Target

...[2]

9. Significance for PW [Psychological Warfare] Operations

PW should be aware of the following distinctions, national, occupational, and regional—in their operations with foreign labor in Germany:

1. Distinctions according to nationality
   The nationalities best suited for Allied PW operations are:
   Danes
   French
   Belgians
   Dutch
   Czechs
   Skilled workers are found primarily in these nationality groups. The skilled worker offers an excellent opening for PW operation. There are two reasons for this:

---

1. NA, RG 59, R&A 1243.

2. In the first few chapters of this lengthy report, R&A discusses the number of foreign laborers in Germany, the geographical distribution of the various national groups, and their distribution in terms of occupation. Furthermore, reactions of the German population and control measures by the Nazis are analyzed.

a) it is the skilled worker who has most opportunity for sabotage.

b) it is the skilled worker who possesses the best political trade union education.

The French group may have now approximately 1,000,000 including those P/Ws whose status has been commuted to that of civilian workers.[3] It is advisable to eliminate from consideration Poles, Rumanians, Slovaks and Thuringians [sic] and to concentrate on the above nationality groups.

2. Occupational Distinctions

Potentially, the most fruitful industrial branches are:

Mining

Metal Industry

Building Construction

Transportation

Dockworkers and Seamen

In the first place the largest number of skilled workers are employed in these occupations.

In the second place it is these industries which contribute the really tight spots in German industry.

3. Regional Distinctions

The regions best suited for PW operations are:

The Northern Parts

The Northern and Northwestern industries

The Rhenish Westphalian industrial region

The Berlin area

The Wiener Neustadt and Linz

Saxony

Apart from the accessibility of some of these regions, all regions mentioned above had a high degree of unionisation in the Weimar Republic (Rhineland, Westphalia are Socialist and Catholic). They are centers of heavy shipping and metal and steel processing industries. Stuttgart and Schweinfurt are, of course, as important as the seat of the ball bearing industry. Stuttgart, besides, has considerable motor vehicle industry.[4]

4. Suggested Operations: General Remarks

The positive opportunities of exploiting the situation of foreign labor in Germany point in two directions. On the one hand, the presence of foreign workers in Germany presents the opportunity of fanning *antagonism* between foreign

---

3. See S.I. [Secret Intelligence] document A 11542. R. Castagnet, chief French labor organizer, states that owing "to commutation of war prisoners into free workers" the number of civilian workers had reached 810,000 in April 1943, about 20% of all male Frenchmen between 15 and 45 years were now in Germany. The above figures of 1,000,000 has been estimated on the basis of a discussion with Louis Franck of the Western European Section.

4. I.e., the factories of Mercedes Benz and Porsche.

workers and Germans and of using foreign workers as disruptive agents in Nazi society. On the other hand, it is possible to use the large number of foreign workers to promote an attitude of *friendship and cooperation* (a) with the German population in general, (b) with those groups in Germany (workers, peasants, women, underground, etc.) which may be won over for subversive activities against the Nazi regime. Both possibilities offer numerous opportunities for direct action. They are, of course, not mutually exclusive for PW operations.

The former method (fanning antagonism) is clearly the most obvious. It is reported that the Russians are already using it to great advantage. They are propagandizing German troops on the Eastern front with the threat which foreign workers present to German homes, jobs, and families. Unfortunately, this method also aids the Nazi policy of estranging Germans and foreigners, thereby retaining more effective control over both.

The second method (friendship and cooperation between Germans and foreign workers) is obviously more difficult, but may promise greater and more lasting results. It might not only lead to winning German labor support for the foreign laborers' campaign of slow-down and sabotage, thus perhaps contributing to a reactivisation of German labor in general, but it might also provide a valuable basis for European cooperation in the post-war period.[5]

5. Method I: Antagonism and Frictions

The presence of foreign workers opens numerous possibilities. The actual operations, however, must distinguish between various targets which must be approached differently.

First, the *foreign workers* themselves.

(i) Campaign of sabotage and slowdown in factories and farms may be continued. A new field has been opened up by the air war over Germany and offers many opportunities for sabotage action during and after raids.

(ii) Usefull skills may be concealed, and thus force a larger number of German skilled workers (mostly elderly men with Socialist background and leanings) to remain in factories instead of being released to the army.

(iii) Infiltration of Allied news and propaganda. This can be used not only for the "enlightenment" of the home front as to German military misfortunes in general, but may also increase anxieties by spreading specific reports concerning the fate of German soldiers in Allied hands.

(iv) Foreign workers provide excellent material for spreading rumors regarding all possible subjects (especially at the present, rumors regarding Party activities and personnel, frictions and conflicts within elite groups, prospects of victory, and effect of air raids).

(v) Fifth column activities may be further encouraged (espionage, etc.)

---

5. *For a more detailed discussion of these two attitudes toward foreign labor see OSS Special Report "Foreign Workers in Germany: Significance for P/W," pp. 9–10.* [Not printed].

Secondly there are the ways in which the *German soldiers* may be approached with regard to the presence of foreign workers at home.

(i)   Anxieties may be increased over the intrusion of foreigners into domestic life (relations to wives and children).[6] Also, it may prove effective to reiterate the idea that foreigners are only called upon to *work,* Germans to *die.*

(ii) Soldiers are directly concerned about unreliability of the industrial and military products manufactured by foreign workers.

(iii) Soldiers may also be aroused to special resentment over slowdowns and acts of industrial sabotage by foreign workers because this brings about a drop in the pro- duction of war material—a drop which may be decisive in the final military situation.

Thirdly, *German workers* may be reached by PW operations on the following grounds:

(i) insecurity in factory operations due to acts of sabotage,

(ii) frustration of their military effort because of sabotage and slowdowns by foreigners,

(iii) guilt feelings about the inferior position of foreign workers with equal skills.

These points also offer opportunities for addressing that part of the *German public* (women, youth, etc.) which comes in contact with foreign workers.

7. Method (II): Cooperation and Friendly Relations

The targets, in the very nature of this method (cooperation being the chief aim) cannot be so clearly distinguished as under the "antagonistic". It should be repeated, however, that as far as the effect of PW operations is concerned, the two methods are not mutually exclusive.

The principal aim of this method is to promote an understanding between *German people* and *foreign workers* in order to produce techniques and conditions which can be used against the Nazi regime.

This may effect the relationship between *foreign workers* and *German workers* in the following ways:

(i) German workers may be drawn into the campaign of slowdowns and sabo- tage.

(ii) German workers may learn about opposition methods as practiced by for- eign workers both in their own country and in the Reich.

(iii) Contacts between the politically-conscious leadership of the two groups may be encouraged and broadened.

----

6. In 1994, the OSS Morale Operations Branch started large-scale propaganda operations along these lines. There were leaflets created, for instance, which gave the impression of German women having sexual relations with foreign workers. German front-line soldiers were the target of this cam- paign.

(iv) Workers' underground groups may be strengthened through these same channels, if cooperation between foreign and German workers can be established.

(v) Foreign workers offer the best means of spreading Allied pro-labor propaganda guaranteeing German workers old rights and privileges without Nazi terror.

(vi) Foreign and German workers may learn to distinguish between unreliable labor groups and labor leaders. This would prove valuable for post-war reconstruction of the German labor movement.

The relationship with the *German public* in general is affected in similar ways:

(i) Foreign workers are on-the-spot witnesses for those guilty and those not guilty in the Nazi system.

(ii) Foreign workers offer perhaps the most effective channels for positive pro-Allied propaganda concerning post-war Germany. Their influence could be highly effective because the German public attitude toward foreign workers and prisoners of war is largely determined by deep-seated fears about post-war retribution.

Document 24a · 5 and 6 October 1943

Report by OSS Agent Theodore A. Morde: Conversations with German Ambassador Franz von Papen in Turkey[1]

SECRET

Meeting No. 1—October 5, 1943[2]

**The Following Notes Were Written
Immediately After the Meetings:**

I opened the meeting by adressing von Papen as "Mr. Ambassador." I explained that I had come on a highly secret and important mission from the United States for the sole purpose of seeing him. I mentioned that last week I had been in Algiers for whatever inference he might derive from that fact; that I had travelled thousands of miles by plane and that my presence in Istanbul was an absolute secret; that I had not yet registered with the Turks nor had I reported to the American Embassy. This pleased him very much. "Good," he said.

I then said bluntly that I was not an intelligence agent,[3] that this interview was no trick, and that I came to him in complete good faith. I said that I wanted to speak openly, honestly and frankly and I wanted him to trust me implicitly. He then asked me if I would tell him just who I was, and I replied that I wished to do so. I told him that because of the delicate nature of this mission I carried no credentials other than my passport, which I showed him. He noted the page which

---

1. Roosevelt Library, Hyde Park, F. D. Roosevelt Papers. President's Secretary's Files, Box 153 [formerly 167], Folder OSS/Donovan, 1941–1943. Another version of this report was edited by OSS agent Archibald Frederick Coleman some thirty years after the war in the journal *Metro: The Magazine of Southeastern Virginia*. Coleman claims to be in possession of the original notes by Theodore Morde. While Coleman's story seems very likely, the editors nevertheless decided to print this version as it was the one that eventually reached the President's desk.

2. The first meeting took place at the German Embassy in Istanbul, Turkey.

3. This false statement is missing in Coleman's version of the Morde Report. It is likely to be a later addition by the OSS which should lend more credibility to the document.

states "the bearer is Assistant to the American Minister["], etc. to Egypt and asked if I had spent much time in the Middle East. I replied yes, approximately a year and a half, and explained that I had served in that capacity in my job as Ass't, later Chief, of the OWI [Office of War Information] there.[4] He read my name aloud and pronounced it with a heavy German accent as "Mord-a," and he referred to me throughout the interview from then on as "Mr. Morda." I told him that I was now travelling under the disguise of a correspondent and showed him my pass; he exclaimed with satisfaction when he saw my fingerprints on the pass, and said he was completely satisfied that I was who I represented myself to be, and that he was pleased with my frankness and apparent honesty and open and above board manner. He said that he was very glad I had come and that he, frankly, too, wanted to meet me; that the very fact that he had told Rustow [Rüstow] and Posth[5] that he would grant the interview proved how interested he was in what I might have to say. He then relaxed completely, smiled, offered me another cigarette, lighted it, and gave every evidence that he no longer entertained any suspicions about me. Knowing that he had expressed to Rustow a fear that I might be an intelligence agent, I repeated again that I definitely was not one, that I knew nothing about intelligence and that I was there solely to talk with him and present a plan for his consideration; that I came as a trusted messenger for persons I could not identify to him. I even pointed out to him that obviously the fact I was not a person of renown, and was a young man in appearance, aided me to come to him inconspicuously and without risk of suspicion and he agreed emphatically, seemingly with renewed confidence in me. It was plain to see he now looked on me as a typical American, the out-and-out type with nothing to hide and willing to place his cards on the table.

I then explained to him that I had with me a highly confidential paper which outlined something in which he might be very interested; I warned him beforehand that what he read on that paper in no way represented the official views of the U.S. government; that the actual paper itself had been a plain piece of paper with no letterhead or any type of official marking.

I said that the message on the paper had merely been typed and that there was nothing on it to prove it came from any official U.S. gov't source or any other source; that if its contents were divulged no proof could ever be offered as to its source, and that he had only my word to vouch for whether it represented anyone's true opinions or not. I said that *I* had not written it, but that I was here to find out if he might be interested *if* the aims and details expressed in that document could be worked out.

---

4. I.e., in Cairo.

5. German exile Alexander Rüstow (OSS code name "Magnolia"), a vigorous anti-Nazi, was in close contact with the OSS and at the same time well acquainted with the von Papen family. Johannes Posth, the Director of the German Orient Bank, served as a liaison between Rüstow and von Papen. Posth was, however, not to know anything about the involvement of the OSS. On German emigrant activities in Turkey see document [18].

I then gave him a magnifying glass and a tiny film—an actual photograph of the paper—and after much difficulty he was able to read it by holding the lens some four inches away from the film. He was tremendously affected. It seemed to me that tears were very close to his eyes. He sat back and closed his eyes for a minute and then whatever reserve he had felt up to that moment broke.

He began to talk. He asked me if there could be any hope that what he had read might be true. He said the time had come when the war must stop. He said that he prayed that a just peace would come soon, and that all this horrible bloodshed would stop. He said hundreds of thousands of Germans were homeless, with no place to go, because of Allied bombings. He said all Europe was threatened with Communism. He seemed then to catch himself, and immediately I began to talk myself.

I told him that I and every American, like him, wanted this war to stop. But, I said, the war will never stop and the bombings will never stop and the suffering will never end until Hitler and Nazi Totalitarianism have been expelled from Germany. As I said that, he nodded, as in confirmation. Watching his face closely, I said that the average American had no hatred for the German people, but that they did hate Hitler. That *I* hated Hitler. I hated what he had done to Germany, to its culture, its art, its very life. As I said this, I tried to say it with every ounce of sincerity I could. I said it again, and I could feel him respond; several times he nodded in agreement, and his eyes never left mine.

I said that there *was* a chance of peace for Germany, a just peace, a peace that would not again be based on terms like those in the Versailles treaty, but I said Americans felt, and America felt, that it was now up to the Germans to clean their own house, to GET RID of Hitler, and Goebbels, and Goering and Himmler and the rest of the criminals who had brought Germany to the state she was now in. Not once did he interrupt while I impressed on him our hatred for Hitler.

I then told him in a quiet tone that I knew Germany and loved Germany; that many Americans knew and loved his country and some day hoped to live in peace with Germany; that our aim was peace not for just another twenty or thirty years, but a hundred, even two hundred years. He said he, too, knew America, that he had many friends in America and had never wanted to feel any hatred towards America. But he said, our bombs are instilling in the Germans a hatred toward Americans that had never been there before; that he hoped they could be stopped before this hatred got deep, that up to the present the Germans mainly blamed the British.

He then said our propaganda was wrong, that Americans seem to think *all Germans are Nazis. That, he said, was not true.* He said that if Americans only hated the Nazis, they should offer some hope to the Germans who were NOT Nazis; that now the Germans are afraid that they will all be included in the revenge that had been promised to them by us and the British.[6]

---

6. Obviously von Papen referred to the Casablanca Conference of January 1943 where Roosevelt and Churchill had proclaimed that the only terms the Allies would accept from their enemies were those of *unconditional surrender*.

I told him we knew very well that not all Germans were Nazis, and that was why I had come to him. I said that it was commonly believed in America that he hated Hitler and the Nazis; that it was believed that he was one of the few great statesmen left in Germany and that if anyone could lead the Germans out of the mess they were in, he alone was the man. He was pleased at this. Then he said in an apologetic tone that books and the cinema and rumor had painted him in colors that were not true, always stressing mainly what he did as a captain in World War 1 [sic]. He asked me if I could possibly believe he, as a *captain*, could really have done all the things he was accused of doing.[7]

He said people gave him credit for too many black deeds that in the first place, he had never been in a position of authority to perform, as a mere captain. He said such wild things had been written and said about him that he had not even taken the trouble to issue a denial, that he felt it was beneath him to try to refute irresponsible journalists. He said in the last war his position had been different and after all, whatever he did, he did in behalf of his country, as any American would do in behalf of the U.S.A. He said if he had been able to remain in power as Chancellor that this war would never have come about. He said that surely anyone who knew his career as a leader in Germany did not need to be told how he objected to Hitler's rise to power. "Unfortunately", he said, "Hindenburg was too old and he was not able to take the strong measures needed. "[sic] And then," he continued, "came Scheichler [Schleicher]. As a result, I found it necessary to continue to serve Germany as best as I was permitted.["]8

I said: "But, sir, you are the one man who can re-form a new Germany. You are respected, not only in your own country but throughout the world, as one who has Germany's interests foremost in your heart." While he made no comment to this, it was obviously what he wanted to hear. I told him that he, with the possibility of again becoming the leader of a postwar Germany, now had the opportunity to hasten that day; that what America wanted was the immediate elimination of Hitler, either his capture or death. I said I wanted to make myself perfectly clear; that if some way could be found whereby he could help achieve that objective, America was prepared to help in many different ways. I told him that if Hitler should suddenly be flown by plane out of Germany to a spot under American control, like Iceland, or No[rth] Africa; or even No[rthern] Ireland, a reaction might set in in the U.S. such as was occasioned when Mussolini was suddenly removed from the Italian scene. I hammered this home. I said "You have seen how America welcomed Italy as a new ally and how just her treatment of Italy has been since she surrendered." I said Italy will again be a great nation in the world. I

---

7. Having served during World War I as a Military Attaché in Mexico and Washington, D.C., von Papen was expelled from the United States on 3 December 1915 for organizing sabotage activities.

8. In reality, von Papen had been involved in persuading the increasingly senile President von Hindenburg to remove General Kurt von Schleicher as the last Chancellor of the Weimar Republic. Schleicher, for his part, had been largely responsible for bringing Chancellor Franz von Papen down in a web of intrigue. Schleicher had been killed by the Nazis during the so-called Röhm-Putsch in July 1934.

pointed out how hatred for the Italians largely dissipated in the U.S. and England once the baloon had been pricked and the main object of their hatred, Mussolini, no longer figured in the picture.[9]

I told him that the same thing not only might but probably would happen in the U.S. once Hitler were out. He asked me what would happen to Hitler, if such a thing should happen as, for instance, Hitler should be delivered into the hands of the Americans. I said I had no idea, but that I thought, as in the case of Hess, he would probably be treated as a prisoner of war in accordance with his former rank as head of a state, and confined in a safe place away from mob violence until such time as he could be accorded justice and tried by a court to be established after the war.[10] He then made a strange remark: he said there was a great fear in Germany over the prospect of the many leading figures being unjustly tried by a postwar court comprised of representatives of the United Nations; that it was only just that these leaders be tried by German courts, that German justice formerly had always been correct and fair. I asked him if he thought that the Nazis would have permitted American or British courts to try Roosevelt or Churchill if they had won the war. He did not reply.

I again made it very clear to him that if he knew of any possible way to hasten the fall of Hitler, he could count on every assistance from America. He [I?] asked him if he fully understood what I was implying, and he replied he did, but that obviously at that moment he was not able to give me any sort of answer.

At least three times he brought up the matter of our demand for unconditional surrender, and nothing less than that. He said that this was being pounded into the minds of the Germans and that perhaps even those who might care to hasten the peace were afraid to do so in the face of that prospect. I told him that from my knowledge of America and its leaders, he could count on hearing our demand for unconditional surrender to the very day our army marched into Germany; that this did not mean that there was no hope for Germany, far from it. That America and our great President, Mr. Roosevelt, knew that a lasting peace could not be achieved without Germany once again assuming her place in the lineup [sic] of the United Nations and the democracies. *But* that it would have to be a new type of Germany, and one with which we could enter into economical negotiations honorably and with complete trust.

He asked me if I thought America planned to keep a standing army in Germany after the war, if America planned to police Europe. I told him again that I had no idea, that that [sic] it was believed, and I believed, that definitely, yes, America would maintain an army in Germany for a long period, long enough surely to insure that a lasting peace was hastened and to guard against any anarchy that

---

9. On 12 September 1943, however, Mussolini had been liberated by German troops and put at the head of the north Italian Republica Sociale Italiana.

10. On 10 May 1941, Rudolf Hess, the deputy leader of the Nazi Party, had secretly left Germany on a solo flight to Scotland. After a parachute landing, he was imprisoned and treated as a prisoner of war. At the Nuremberg trials in 1946 he was sentenced to life imprisonment.

might break out. It is my definite impression that this was exactly what he hoped and wanted to hear.

He asked me if I thought Mr. Roosevelt would care to deal with him, personally. I said that was something I naturally could not answer, that it was conceivable everything in the future, as far as the President was concerned, and insofar as he himself was concerned, depended on what he did in our favor to help bring the war to a quick conclusion by ridding Germany of its present government. I said, "Mr. Roosevelt is a great statesman, the leading statesman in the world today." He replied: "Yes, he is a great man." He then said he doubted if Churchill would ever want to deal with him. "I got along very well with Chamberlain," he said, "but Churchill and Chamberlain are two different types of men."

He then referred again to the bombing of Germany, which he characterized as "horrible". He said we could not hope to gain by this means. He said that only 10 per cent of Germany's war production has been affected by the bombing. He said "it was the innocent people who are suffering today."

He said he would like to talk for a minute about Italy. "Why," he asked, "did you insist on unconditional surrender from Italy?" I said I thought that should be apparent. He said it was a great mistake. He said if we had been content merely to make Italy a non-belligerent neutral, Germany would have withdrawn her forces from Italy and not attempted to defend it. He said, as it was, Germany was compelled to resist in Italy. I told him that any choice other than demanding unconditional surrender would have been ridiculous, from a military standpoint; that we needed Italy's airbases from which to bomb both Germany and Occupied Europe; and further, that we knew we would soon have all of Italy and that Germany had never tasted an onslaught of bombing such as she would soon have to face once we had all of Italy in our possession. I said it seemed so needless to continue this terrible waste of Germany's and our own men, when the conclusion of this war could be speeded if only he could aid in bringing about the collapse of the Nazis.

He said that the people of Germany believed, and perhaps rightly that the war was forced on them, and yet they alone stood in the way of Communism from sweeping Europe. He said that the Germans could not understand why the democracies were not awake to that danger. I said that he knew America well enough to know that Americans had no sympathy for Communism, as such. He said our bombings of cities like Hamburg was doing more to spread Communism in Europe that [than?] anything else, not only in Europe, *but in Germany itself.*[11]

He asked what I thought the coming Moscow conference[12] was for. I told him I had not the slightest idea but that it presumably was to reaffirm our friendship with Russia, to plan further military moves that would lead to the defeat of Germany, and possibly even to sign documents attesting to that fact. He said he

---

11. For a different estimate of the effects of Allied bombardments on Hamburg and other German cities see Willy Brandt's memorandum of 25 September 1943, document [21].

12. I.e., the Moscow Foreign Ministers' Conference of 19 to 30 October 1943.

thought we and the British were blind, and that any documents signed would be worth just what the Russian-German treaty was worth. And then he threw in a warning that some day we in America and England may wake up to find that the Nazis have signed a separate peace with Russia, and then where will we be? He said he had just finished reading Davies' book about Russia,[13] that Davies had become a Russo-phile and that he was dangerous to America for that reason.

He concluded the interview by asking me if he could meet me again after having a chance to think over what we had been discussing, and suggested a meeting in two days. I told him I must leave in two days and requested that he arrange a meeting for tomorrow. He agreed and said he would arrange that we meet on an island in the Marmera [Marmara], Krinkipe, where our mutual contact, Pesth [Posth], had a house. He said that he would sail to the island in his own boat to avoid being followed.

As we rose to leave, he took me by the arm and said: "You cannot realize how seriously affected I am by this talk with you. A man in my position has a great weight to carry and many troubles. I will think of what you have said to me and will try to give you an answer to take back with you to America."

He said there had been several attempts on his life and that it was very dangerous for both of us to meet. He asked me to be careful, and never permit a word of our conference to reach anyone except President Roosevelt, whom he trusted.

I asked him about the car which was stationed near the front gate of the embassy. He said the car had men in it whose job was to protect him, and that if I had made an attempt against his life, they had orders to shoot me. But he told me I had nothing to worry about.

As we were about to shake hands and part, he again took my arm and pulled me over to a large map on the wall. "Look at that great space," he said, indicating Russia, "think what industrial havoc they can do, and what they can do to all Europe."

With that, he grasped my hand very firmly, smiled and said he would look forward to our meeting tomorrow, at which time he would return my magnifying glass and try to give me a message to take back to America.

He then opened the door, and I stepped into the hall, again trying to appear very German. He said a few words in German to Rustow, who joined me in stiff bows to him, as we made our exit.

Our return to the same waiting taxi, and subsequent ride back to Istanbul was without comment on my part or Rustow's, and without incident. The interview with Von Papen [sic] lasted an hour and five minutes.

---

13. Joseph Edward Davies, *Mission to Moscow: A Record of Confidential Dispatches to the State Department, Official and Personal Correspondence, Current Diary and Journal Entries, Including Notes and Comment up to October 1941* (New York: Simon and Schuster) 1941.

Meeting No. 2—October 6th, 1943[14]

The Following Notes Were Written
Immediately After the Meeting:

My second meeting with Von Papen [sic] lasted an hour and a half and differed from the first meeting in that Von Papen [sic] was eager to talk and spoke freely, without hesitation, and apparently with complete confidence in me. He opened the conversation by telling me that he had devoted many hours of thought to what we had discussed yesterday and had prepared some notes, which he showed me, consisting of three pages in his own handwriting. He said he would not give these to me, since I likewise had not given him anything in writing attesting to our meeting, but that I was free to take any notes myself on what he had to say, with one reservation: *That I was to show them to no one other than the President.* He said his message to me this afternoon was for the President, that he wanted me to see him, and explain to him just what he, Von Papen, felt and what he proposed.

He dealt first with the points brought up in the film which I gave him yesterday. He also asked if he might retain the film and I told him, certainly. He returned my magnifying glass which he borrowed yesterday.

He said he wanted to stress that he was "first and foremost, a German patriot." That his life had been devoted to his country and that his country, not his government, came first.

Re paragraph 1 of the outline I gave him, he said the word "dominate" was wrong—that the real Germany that represented the German people did not want to "dominate" Europe; that tradition and history showed that Germany had never wanted to "dominate" Europe, politically.

He said he thoroughly approved of a Federation of the European states in the post war world, and as a German, he felt Germany should be permitted a role of leadership in the economics of Europe. But, he said, there should also exist a fair economical understanding between all the states, which should be considered as more important than anything political; that a Federated government of Europe should have time to give proof that a mutual understanding existed economically, and that later should come any discussion of political disputes or treaties.

He said he felt Austria was and is German and must remain German, that the people of Austria would so choose if given a chance to decide by themselves. That Austria never again should be placed in the hands of the Hapsburgs.[15] He made a gesture as if dismissing the Hapsburgs as not worth considering.

---

14. This second meeting took place at the summer house of Johannes Posth on Krinkipo Island, Sea of Marmara, Turkey.

15. The Habsburger, i.e., the Austrian monarchy.

He said that the Sudetanland [Sudetenland] part of Chech territory should have autonomy, as after Munich.[16]

Regarding Poland, he said he believed the frontiers of 1914 should be restored, that the "hated" corridor should be eliminated; that Poland should be given an outlet to the sea near Liebaw; but that the province of Posen should be given back to Germany to which it had belonged.

He said he felt there should be no trouble arranging a peace with France, which should be restored to the French intact. As for Alsace-Lorraine, he felt that some arrangement could easily be effected with France whereby perhaps a division could be made, possibly based on a just plebiscite.[17]

He said he felt the Ukraine was needed by the new Europe as a "food larder", that the Ukraine should perhaps be made an independent state, allied by common treaty with Europe, but definitely with Europe and not with Russia, or under any Asiatic influence. That the Ukraine should be independent and merely serve the purpose of a granary to feed Europe's populations, all countries on a fair and equal basis.

He said that in the postwar Europe, there should be no fight for markets. He said that there should also be no fight between Germany and America, or Germany and Britain for markets ... that Germany needed our products (citing automobiles) and we needed hers, as chemical products, photographic apparatus, etc.

Re the paragraph in the outline dealing with Japan, he dismissed Japan with an expressive wave of his hand, saying Germany had no interest whatever in Japan.

He said the postwar oil situation was important to Germany; that he hoped it might be possible for Germany to get a concession in the Pacific area now under Japanese control, and perhaps also a concession in the Pacific that would serve Germany as a source of supply for at least a minimum quantity of rubber; but he said that the question of colonies should not stand in the way of peace, and that Germany, under a new government, would be prepared to let a just peace conference decide her need in that respect.

He said his interest and that of other leaders of Germany, who were not Nazis and did not approve of the Nazis, was to safeguard the economical, and to whatever extent possible, the political *existence* of the *German people*, certainly *not the present government of the German people, for the German people could not be included in that government.*

He then turned to a general discussion of other subjects, on which he made the following remarks:

---

16. During the Munich Conference of 29 to 30 September 1938, Neville Chamberlain and Edouard Daladier had conceded to Hitler the seizure of the Sudetenland.

17. The provinces of Alsace and Lorraine had been an age-old bone of contention between France and Germany; annexed by Germany in 1871, they were returned to France after World War I.

Again referring to a Federation of European states, Von Papen said he sincerely believed this was not only possible, but, from Germany's standpoint, desirable. That he would like to see the capital in Berlin, of course, but this was not essential; that representation in the Federation should be according to population, on some such lines as our House of Representatives. He repeated again that Germany, the pre-Hitler Germany and the post-war Germany, had no wish to "dominate".

He said he himself knew, and that it was known by the German people, that they had no hope of winning the war; further, that even the Nazis knew it. He warned that the Nazis were still capable of tricks, and suggested it was even possible that when Russia reached the point of invading German territory, some "Red" general might try to pull a coup d'etat and, salvaging what he could of the German army, make a deal with the Russians and go over to their side in order to share in the Communist sweep of Europe. He said this *"could"* happen one day! That that was why we must have an immediate peace, as soon as it could be arranged, to forestall such a catastrophe, that would not only cause ruin to the German people and Europe, but also to America's and England's aims and desires for a lasting peace.

He said "success breeds success" and that already some Nazi leaders are gazing admiringly on what Communism had been able to do for Russia, and that they even admired Communism in many respects and felt that it might even be a better system than their own, and worth imitating. He said that Germany was now in the position that Russia was [in] when the war between Russia and Germany began.

Von Papen again said that our bombings of Germany were doing more to spread Communism inside of Germany than anything else . . . that hundreds of thousands of people are homeless; that in their condition of despair, they were already turning to Communism as their "hope;" that they were saying to each other: "it works." When I mentioned that Hamburg had been a communistic center in Germany before the war, he agreed and said "Look at Hamburg as an example of that." He said Hamburg is completely ruined and the destruction is "terrible", as is the suffering. He begged that we stop this horrible bombing, that it was not necessary for us to win the war, that our leaders should realize that they were doing more harm than good. He then went on, temporarily loosing control of his feelings, and said that [the] German people were not behind the Nazis, that they were beginning to feel that the Allies must be even worse than the Nazis, if they continued this ruthless bombing. That we had a real chance to do good propaganda by showing that our hatred of the Nazis was not directed at the German people themselves. That our radio and our press should not include the German people and the Nazis as one, that they should refrain from so doing in order to inspire a hope in the German people when they so badly need it.

Von Papen said with every show of sincerity that the war must stop; pounding the table hard, he said that homeless people who were without hope and who were suffering deeply, could only mean inevitable anarchy in Europe; that the working classes who were hit most were a people who could easily follow the communistic banner later.

Again referring to the future peace, he said he hoped America and Britain would keep an armed force in Europe for a long enough period to guard against anarchy and to preserve law and order, but that he personally doubted if the democracies could ever be convinced of the necessity of doing this. He said also that he hoped peace terms would permit Germany to maintain some army to keep guard on her east wall against the Russians; that such a guard would have to be maintained to save Europe, and that Germany wanted to do this as her share, and to protect herself.

He said he feared, and most of all, the German people feared another Versailles treaty with its 14 points.[18] He bitterly condemned the Versailles treaty and said it was only because of its unfair terms that the German people had ever been swayed to fall in line behind Hitler. That up to the time that Hitler came to power, Germany had tried to be a model nation, under his leadership and that of von Hindenburg. That they had tried, but failed, because the German people were deprived of what they considered their rights and were easily won over by Hitler when he promised to regain them for them.

Once when von Papen was talking about the Nazis, he smiled broadly and said there were many people in Germany who called them "animals," including his family! (His family were with him, waiting for him on their boat while he talked to me). He told me he had told them he had to "discuss some business matters."

He said the German people were NOT behind the Nazis, as we in America seemed to feel; that they would gladly expel them if given a chance, and would welcome a new government, if this new government could give them any hope of releasing them from the stress to which they were now submitted.

Von Papen said another mistake Americans made was to put Nazis and Prussians in the same category. That a Prussian officer learns to be a gentleman, to love his family, learns honor and discipline, and learns to live as a "poor man," *and not try to get rich, like the Nazis!* He said we were making a "grave mistake" to class them together.

Once our conversation touched on Turkey, and he said Turkey would never enter the war on the German side, that that fact was recognized even by the Nazis, and that Turkey had never been on the German side.

He said that Germany even though she was lead by misguided leaders, had succeeded in staving off Communism, and that he had heard that the British referred to Germany's eastern army as a British Expeditionary Force. I said that I had

---

18. On Wilson's 14 points see also documents [3], [12] and [19a].

heard it said in America it was a question of "dog eat dog," and said "if you'll excuse me" and he laughed heartily.

He said the chief fear of the German people was that Germany would be carved into little states; he admitted, when I pointed it out, that the Italian people had fared well at the hands of the Allies, but said it would have been better from a propaganda standpoint if we had told them before that their fate would not be severe, as then they could have weakened Mussolini easily from within; that Badoglio's coup d'etat was easier than the Italian people had ever expected it would be.

I then told him again that my visit would be a complete failure if he could not give me a message to take back to America that would show some way whereby he and Germany were anxious to end this war by an act of their own from within. I said only one thing would ever satisfy the American people, and that was for Hitler to be forcibly ejected from Germany, along with his cohorts, and if possible delivered into the hands of the American people. I told him that the whole war psychology of the American people would be greatly affected if some day a plane landed in Iceland or No[rth] Africa with Hitler, and perhaps Goering, Himmler and Goebbels on it, signifying the removal from the German scene of the top Nazis. That *only* by their removal could America ever consider discussing a peace with Germany. I told him bluntly that I was there to ask that he bring this about.

He replied very gravely that this was asking a great deal of him. That he realized it was a job that had to be done by the German people themselves. That it had to be done from within and could not be done from without. He said, too, not to forget that there *were* many Hitler supporters, especially among the youth, and that his death or removal would have a great and questionable effect on them. That "changing horses in mid-stream" was not easy, and was especially delicate in time of war.

Finally he said that to overthrow Hitler would be difficult, but he thought it could be done. He said this most thoughtfully, and seriously.

But, he said, for him to stir revolt in Germany and for him to convince "his friends" that the time had come to throw out Hitler and the Nazis, he must have something to "offer" to those friends, something definite and "solid" and based on a sacred understanding. He asked me directly: "If there were to be a new government in Germany, would America and Britain be willing to make peace?" I said I couldn't say, but I thought it all depended on the government formed, and more than that, depended on the Nazi leaders, including Hitler, being delivered into actual Allied hands. That unless this were done, there would always be a suspicion in America and England that Hitler and the others were in hiding somewhere, and that they might be living, even if they were reported dead ... that their physical persons must be in the hands of the Allies before any such story would be believed.

I asked him directly if he personally were ready to aid the Allies in getting rid of Hitler. He said that depended on whether President Roosevelt was prepared to offer him a promise of peace that would be attractive enough to "his friends" to support him in that effort. He said he *must* be able to give them an incentive, something concrete that promised a future for Germany that would not be as harsh as unconditional surrender with all its harsh implications. I said, suppose that can be arranged, will you *then* do your utmost to get rid of Hitler and the Nazis? He replied very simply, yes.

He said that he had the highest respect for the President, and knew he could trust him to live up to his word. That if I, or some other envoy of the President could supply him with proof that we meant what we said in holding out a hope for Germany's future, he would then take steps to bring about what we desired, i.e., a new government in Germany, and a complete ousting of the Nazis.

He said he wanted me to tell the President that he, von Papen himself, was too old for personal aspirations, but that he would be honored to be in charge of the new government of Germany, and that he was looked up to by the German people and trusted as a leader. That he, however, would be willing to aid whatever new government was chosen, regardless whether he personally led it.

I asked him if he would be willing to meet the President, supposing that that could be arranged, or if he would be willing to meet one of our highest leaders, and he said he would be *most* willing, if it could be arranged, but that it would be very difficult. That his life was constantly in danger, and three attempts had been made already. He then asked me if I thought it might be possible for him to meet Mr. Hull when he returned from the Moscow conference. Then he seemed to think this over, and said no, he felt Mr. Hull was too conspicuous, but that if he were coming to Turkey, he thought it might be arranged, if I would help.

I told him we were prepared to help him get rid of Hitler in any way he suggested. He said he recognized that no one could help them inside Germany, that they must do it themselves.

I then proposed that if I were to meet him again in—say—a month or five weeks, with a definite assurance from the President along the lines he wanted, would he fulfill his part and effect this change of government in Germany. He said that he would leave for Germany during my absence in the states [sic], or in any case, would get in touch with his "people" and return to Turkey with a definite plan of action to accomplish what he and we mutually desired. He said: "Tell your President that I will leave to contact my people in Germany. Tell him that I must have something definite to offer them. Tell him that I will do my best and that I believe we will have success."

I told him, if he would do that, I felt my mission had been a success. He smiled and shook hands warmly and said again he must ask my complete confidence as any disclosure of our conversation to anyone other than the President might lead to his death. He said that he trusted me, and that I must be very careful, and that in return I could trust him without reservation not to disclose to anyone what had taken place between us. He said he hoped to meet me again in four or five weeks.

Document 24b · 26 October 1943

Memorandum from Robert E. Sherwood (OWI Overseas Director) to President Franklin D. Roosevelt: Veto Against the Morde-Papen Plan[1]

[SECRET]

Memorandum for the President [...]

Last week a young man named Theodore Morde came to see me. Pa Watson[2] had referred him to me. Morde had previously been with my outfit, first under the Coordinator of Information and then with OWI [Office of War Information], and had been in our Cairo office.[3] Several months ago he decided he wanted to resign from OWI and join the Cairo office of the *Reader's Digest*.[4] We agreed to let him go as he had been making a certain amount of trouble.

The story he brought back last week was an amazing one: He said that under the sponsorship of General Pat [Patrick] Hurley[5] he had been to Istanbul and had had two interviews with Von Papen [sic], in which he discussed a possible deal for the overthrow of Hitler and the Nazi party.

---

1. Roosevelt Library, Hyde Park, F. D. Roosevelt Papers. President's Secretary's Files, Box 153 [formerly 167], Folder OSS/Donovan, 1941–1943.

2. General Edwin M. 'Pa' Watson was Secretary to President Roosevelt.

3. Morde had served as Acting Director of OWI in the Middle Eastern Theater.

4. In reality, the *Reader's Digest* position was a cover for Theodore Morde's employment with the OSS. In April 1943, OSS Colonel Gustave B. Guenther had recommended Morde to Donovan as special agent to Lanning Macfarland, the OSS Station Chief in Turkey.

5. In January 1943, President Roosevelt had appointed Hurley as his "personal representative in the Near and Middle East."

Knowing Morde, I was a bit leary of this—and subsequently I have heard from our Cairo office that General Hurley disclaims all responsibility for it and, in effect, denounces Morde.

I am going to make a full report of this to the Acting Secretary of State[6] with the suggestion that Morde should not again be given a passport to leave this country.

But, in my opinion, the really important part of the whole story lies in the activities abroad of the *Reader's Digest*. They are now printing a large edition in Africa in English for distribution among our troops. Morde told me that this edition is going to be greatly expanded and extended for our troops all through North Africa, Sicily and Italy.

As you know, the *Reader's Digest* has become more and more bitter and partisan in its attacks on this Administration. In its world-wide circulation it is, in effect, undoing the work that my outfit is constantly trying to do overseas. They seem to be able to get plenty of paper for their expanded editions in places where we are hard-put-to-it to get paper for such essentials as airplane leaflets.

It is my suggestion that, in view of Morde's dangerous activities, there might be some way to prevent the issuance of any more passports to men who are going overseas in war-time solely for the purpose of increasing the circulation of the *Reader's Digest*, particularly among our own American troops.

Robert Sherwood

---

6. Adolf A. Berle. See also document [24d].

Document 24c · 29 October 1943

Memorandum from OSS Director William J. Donovan to President Franklin D. Roosevelt: Support for the Morde-Papen Plan[1]

SECRET

Memorandum for the President

I beg you to read this[2] carefully. It contains an idea that your skill and imagination could develop.

I don't pretend to suggest what price should be paid by our government for the hoped-for result.

If the plan went through, and *if* the culprits were delivered and fittingly tried and executed, and *if* unconditional surrender resulted, it would strengthen your position morally at the peace table.

Russian propaganda is evidently directed to this very purpose.

This paper is presented by Theodore A. Morde, representative of the *Reader's Digest* in Cairo. He worked originally for the COI [Coordinator of Information] and then for OWI [Office of War Information]. He subsequently became assistant to Alex [Alexander C.] Kirk in Cairo.[3] He resigned to take the *Reader's Digest* job and meet the person concerned.[4]

This agent presented his plan to only two persons: Brigadier General Patrick Hurley, when he was in Cairo as personal representative of the President, and Colonel Guenther, in charge of OSS in the Middle East. Both were sworn to secrecy, and neither knows the outcome of the plan or meetings. Both considered

---

1. Roosevelt Library, Hyde Park, F. D. Roosevelt Papers. President's Secretary's Files, Box 153 [formerly 167] Folder OSS/Donovan 1941–1943.

2. Documents [24a].

3. Kirk, who had been Ambassador in Berlin until October 1940, was Minister to Egypt.

4. In reality, Theodore Morde was an OSS agent. See document [24b].

the plan feasible. General Hurley expressed a desire to go to Turkey with this agent to assist in the plan, but did not do so, apparently because his orders did not permit him to participate. Colonel Guenther, while neither he nor OSS officially sponsored the action or plan of this agent, gave every assistance to this agent in matters of transportation and contacts.

This agent finally succeeded in establishing personal contact with von Papen after gaining the confidence of one Alexander Rustow [Rüstow], an anti-Hitler German, now a university professor in Turkey. Rustow in turn contacted von Papen's closest friend, a Herr Posth, head of the Deutsche Orient Bank in Istanbul, who arranged the actual meetings with von Papen.

William J. Donovan
Director

Document 24d · 10 November 1943

Memorandum from Adolf A. Berle, Assistant Secretary of State, to President Franklin D. Roosevelt: Denial of a Passport to Theodore A. Morde[1]

Memorandum for Miss Tully

I return herewith secret memoranda to the President from Mr. Robert Sherwood and from General William Donovan[2] relative to Theodore Morde.

I discussed these memoranda with the President this afternoon in the car going to the airport and he approves the denial of a passport to Mr Morde. In view of this discussion, I am not sending any formal reply other than this.

[...]

---

1. Roosevelt Library, Hyde Park, F. D. Roosevelt Papers. President's Secretary's Files, Box 153 [formerly 167] Folder OSS/Donovan 1941–1943.
2. Documents [24b] and [24c].

Document 25 · 27 October 1943

Report from "Dogwood" [Alfred Schwarz, OSS Istanbul] to OSS Washington: OSS Channel to the German High Command[1]

SECRET

Report on the Consolidation of our Connections to the German High Command[2]

A senior officer in the War Production Department (Wehrwirtschaftsamt) of the OKW[3] (Camelia),[4] with whom we are in contact through our German collaborators[5] here has declared his readiness to prepare the way for a far-reaching development of relations between the German High Command and our General Staff, provided

a. that he is informed about the principles that guide the American attitude and political intentions towards post-war Germany,
b. that he is given assurance that the fact of his collaboration with our Department will be brought to the knowledge of the highest Allied authorities, and
c. that all possible security measures are taken and the strictest secrecy is observed.

---

1. NA, RG 226, Entry 92, Box 591, Folder 5.
2. OSS connections through the Dogwood-Cereus circle in Turkey. See document [18].
3. Oberkommando der Wehrmacht (Supreme Command of the Armed Forces).
4. Helmuth James Graf von Moltke. An expert in international law, Moltke served as legal advisor to the Abwehr, the German Military Intelligence Organization in the OKW, led by Admiral Wilhelm Canaris. The Abwehr was basically a counterintelligence organization, yet it also performed secret intelligence and sabotage functions. Since 1935 the Abwehr had grown from small beginnings to a large agency with some 13,000 members, thus having approximately the same size as the OSS.
5. Alexander Rüstow and Hans Wilbrandt. See document [32].

Being a personal friend of the former American Ambassador in Berlin, Alexander Kirk, he proposed that a meeting should be arranged between them at Istanbul,[6] during which the basis of a working agreement concerning full co-operation could be agreed upon.

We propose that the mission be entrusted to a special envoy, who should be known to our German collaborators here as an authorized spokesman of the USA Government, and who should be sent here with a letter of recommendation from Mr. Alexander Kirk to Camelia, and, apart from that, with a special message from one of the supreme political or military authorities of the USA. This message should invite the collaboration of the anti-Nazi members of the OKW and Wehrmacht, lay down the outlines of the Allied attitude toward post-Nazi Germany, and contain the assurance that Germany will be given an undisturbed opportunity to adopt a democratic form of government.

The last point should be stressed in view of the fear of Bolshevism in German conservative circles. Finally the message should authorize the responsible heads of our Department to maintain the connection and conduct the negotiations.

An invitation to Camelia to come to Turkey, stating that Mr. Kirk would be here in the second half of November, has already been despatched in consultation with our German collaborators in the confident expectation that Camelia's wishes will be adequately met by the despatch of a plenipotentiary introduced by a letter from Mr. Kirk.

The suggested steps should be prepared as soon as possible, as every delay will evidently prejudice the success of the scheme. The outlines of a plan of collaboration are being prepared.[7]

---

6. Alexander Kirk meanwhile held the post of U.S. Minister in Cairo.

7. For Moltke's visit to Turkey in December 1943 and his contacts with German emigrants and members of the OSS, see documents [31] and [32].

Document 26 · 3 November 1943

Report from Lanning Macfarland (OSS Istanbul) to OSS Washington: "Free German Movement" Under Anglo-American Auspices[1]

SECRET

Germany: Political: The Case for a "Free German Movement" Under Anglo-American Auspices, Restated with Reference to the Moscow Committee "Free Germany"

[Source]: Dogwood

In Intelligence contacts with Free Germans we constantly come up against the fact that whole-hearted collaboration is unobtainable unless the protagonists of Anti-Nazism are given solid grounds to hope that their contribution will benefit not only the annihilation of Nazism, but also the survival and recognition of the free democratic Germany they are devoting their lives to realize. In this connection we refer to our reports Nr. 6 (Sept. 8) and Nr. 94 (Oct. 27).[2] This hindrance becomes increasingly more cumbersome as the volume of potential adherents of the anti-Nazi movement is growing to include more and more influential figures inside Germany, and as our contacts for intelligence purposes expand and open up great possibilities.

We cannot overstate the urgency of achieving *before the possible interruption of ordinary means of communication* with Germany in connection with a new Balkan front, an intelligence penetration so deep, wide, and technically fool-proof that the interruption, when it comes, will be irrelevant for us. We can get the unreserved collaboration we need for this purpose from Germans high up in Wehr-

---

1. NA, RG 226, Entry 92, Box 591, Folder 5.
2. Documents [18] and [25].

macht and in German economy whom we have contacted. But these German patriots will make their contribution, which would be invaluable to us at the pre-'sent juncture, only for a democratic Germany, not as agents of Allied intelligence. The creation of a German Freedom Movement would be for these people a suffi-cient guarantee that their contribution will be put on record as made in the name of a free Germany *belligerent against Hitler.*

The foundation in Moscow of the "National Committee 'Free Germany'"[3] gives the argument for a similar, but more competent and comprehensive organization under Anglo-American leadership additional stimulus and urgency. Inside Ger-many, two causes have been responsible for the absence of a general movement of resistance:

1) a meticulously organized terror unexampled in history.
2) a general apathy bred by the conviction that surrender will entail the dis-ruption and annihilation of Germany, even if she gets rid of Hitlerism and her ancient liberalism emerges triumphant.

The Anglo-Saxon powers have as yet done nothing decisive to dispel this fear. To make things worse, the Soviet Union has confused the issue by sponsoring the *German National Committee "Free Germany"* which has attracted some notice among sections of the German army and general public, but which with its pres-ent ill-assorted personnel, vague programme, and ambiguous political character could and should never become the nucleus of a democratic Germany. If the Anglo-American powers jointly intend to create such a nucleus and secure the War and post-War advantages which an organized and reliable league of German democrats and liberals can offer, an analysis of the Moscow committee must be made, and a definite stand taken on the strength of this analysis.

On the basis of reports on the effect of the Moscow committee in Germany and abroad, among exponents of the Nazi party and Wehrmacht and among tried democrats of the German opposition outside Germany, we have compiled the present notes in order to clarify the issue.

For short-term appeal to Germany the Moscow committee has the following advantages over a new committee sponsored by the Western Powers:

a) It has been founded earlier (July 1943). Having been for a time the only German organization enjoying the support of an Allied Government, it may have attracted temporarily some sections of the German opposition that would rather have joined a less fortuitously assembled body of tried democrats, if it had existed then;
b) It consists of men who know Hitler's Germany in its present physical and psychological state, having only recently left it. They have fought in this

---

3. See in particular documents [14] and [15].

War, though for a cause they now profess to disdain, and have not been in emigration. This may be an asset from the point of view of mass psychology;

c) It does not talk of unconditional surrender, but on the contrary emphasizes the need for salvaging the army to secure an "honourable peace" on "tolerable terms";

d) It can draw for its staff and personnel upon a large body of non-emigrant Germans, as the Russian army holds the greatest contingent of German prisoners.

Some of these advantages for short-term popularity are obvious and grave disadvantages from the point of view of a real democratic reform of Germany. It is seen from an examination of the Moscow committee's paper "Freies Deutschland" that most of its leading men have not really come to an understanding of the meaning of Fascism, but are merely angry at its ruinous consequences for Germany. They have fought for Hitler and carried out his orders for years, voicing no opposition, while all was going well. There is a strong impression that in their pronouncements only lip-service is paid to democratic ideals. It appears from photographs in their paper that they have not abolished Nazi uniforms, medals, or symbols. In the dozen or so issue[s] of the paper one can find little evidence of a realization by these men of Germany's share in the guilt of Nazism, and a consequent determination to see Germany thoroughly reformed.

There are other grave objections to the Moscow committee, some of them relating to the striking prominence given to members of the Prussian nobility, and the sinister emphasis placed upon the "preservation of a strong and unperverted Wehrmacht", others upon the suspicions necessarily raised in some quarters by Russia's toleration of such utterances. Although there are strong grounds for thinking that the Soviet Government has created the German National Committee as a reply to the creation by the Nazi Government of a so-called Free Russian Army under General Vlasov[4] it was immediately suspected in some quarters that Russia was considering the partial preservation of a German army as an instrument to be used in possible future controversies with Britain and America. The triple aspect presented to the World by the Moscow committee evidently prejudices the Moscow committee's chance of becoming representative of anything in particular. It is a body professing democratic aims, sponsored by communists, and presided over by "Junkers". Such a Cerberus may be opposed, or supported, by almost anyone on almost any grounds. It would nevertheless be a mistake to set up a "counter-committee" without reference to the Moscow body. Such a step would certainly be interpreted as a sign of discord in the Allied camp, and exploited by German propaganda; on the other hand, to leave the Moscow

---

4. In December 1942, General Vlasov, a prisoner of war and patriotic Russian, had formed the Smolensk Committee to organize Russian opponents of Stalin. This committee was supported by the Germans.

committee in sole charge is equally undesirable for the stated reasons. The best
solution would lie in the creation of a Free German Committee having the support of the Anglo-Saxon powers without appearing as their mere instrument,
having its operational base in [a] neutral country, and being *unequivocal and
homogeneous in its personnel and programme*. It would have to include democratic
and liberal emigrants of tried sincerity and intellectual equipment, as well as carefully picked officers and men from the American and English prisoner camps.
The manifold advantages of rallying the positive forces of the German nation *now*
have been previously stated (cf. references given at the head of this report).[5] This
committee would not be open to the various suspicions and objections raised in
German and Allied minds by the strange composition and tone of the Moscow
committee; it would establish contact with the latter and absorb or overshadow it.
It alone would be in a position to make an important contribution to the Allied
war effort by collaboration in the province of Intelligence and Inner Front; and it
would be an infinitely better equipped and safer trustee of the United Nations for
the collection and political direction of the existing German opposition after the
War, having by then established relations of confidence and collaboration with
the Allied authorities.

Document 27 · 8 November 1943

Telegram from Allen W. Dulles (OSS Bern)
to OSS Washington: An Estimate
of the German Opposition Against Hitler[1]

SECRET

1018 through # 1020 [...]

Organized opposition does not exist in Germany. Gestapo terror effectively
prevents their organization. Oppositional groups exist and some of them are
known to each other, and are linked together by members who belong to more

---

5. The copy kept by the OSS in their Central File does not contain such references. The original
report is missing in the National Archives. See, however, document [18].

1. NA, RG 226, Entry 134, Box 341, Folder 1821.

than one group. The former leaders of German parties who are still in the country are not very important. Many are too old, and a great number of others have died. Still others are in concentration camps or under surveillance of Gestapo. Possibly the young men, who have belonged to secret opposition groups for a long time, and who are unknown to the outside world, will step forward. Both Catholic and Protestant clergymen oppose the Nazis, but are at present unable to act. After the Nazis have been liquidated, the clergy should play an important part.

Of the 75 percent or more Germans opposed to the Nazi regime, there are only 2 groups who could possibly initiate practical action. These are the labor and military groups. As an example of this point of view, the generals could remove Hitler and the Nazi regime by using the armed men at their disposal. Labor can start sabotage in industrial plants, transportation lines etc. [in order to] obstruct the war effort.

Hence, propaganda should be directed together with other attempts towards teaching sabotage to workmen and encouraging action by hesitating generals.

[...]

Document 28 · 23 November 1943

Telegram from Allen W. Dulles
(OSS Bern) to OSS Washington:
Opposition of the German Churches[1]

SECRET

TOR 11/24/43 1:15 am

[...]

The following Catholic leaders in Bern are in contact with the Catholic Movement within the Reich: Dr. von Galen, the Bishop of Münster's brother,[2] Dr. Josef Wirth, who used to be Chancellor;[3] Professor Muckermann;[4] and Professor Frederick [Friedrich] Dessauer, who used to be a member of the Center party in the Reichstag from Frankfurt. We are maintaining either direct or indirect contact with all of the above Catholic leaders. An additional detailed memorandum is being prepared for our use by Father Maydieu. We also have a list of about 40 names of people who are playing important parts in the Catholic Movement in the Reich at present. As occasion allows, we will send these names to you.

Both Protestant and Catholic clergy are organized in *Bekenntniskirche*,[5] and the majority of them are strongly opposed to the Nazi regime. Remarkable courage is being exhibited by certain parsons and priests. Quite a few of these clergymen are

---

1. NA, RG 226, Entry 134, Box 341, Folder 1821. The information had been given to Allen W. Dulles by French Father Maydieu during the latter's brief visit to Bern on 23 November 1943. Maydieu took a particular interest in preparing for the resumption of intellectual life after the war wishing to reaffirm the brotherhood of Catholics in all nations of the world. In the United States, the information was not only passed on to all major branches of the OSS, but also to Dominican priest Delos, a French emigré.

2. For Bishop von Galen see documents [21], [28], [65] and [70c].

3. Joseph Wirth of the Catholic Center (Zentrum) party had been German Chancellor in 1921/1922.

4. Friedrich Joseph Muckermann was one of the first informants who got in touch with Allen W. Dulles in Switzerland. Having lived in both occupied and unoccupied France, he kept Dulles informed about the morale of the French population. He was also an important link to the Vatican.

5. In reality, the Bekennende Kirche (Confessional Church) was a Protestant, not a Catholic opposition movement. Next to this movement existed the Nazi-supported Deutsche Christen movement.

being held in concentration camps. However, because of terror they are kept from directly opposing the Nazis, and the majority of them are not political conspirators.

As soon as the Nazi regime has collapsed, they will assume active roles in aiding the construction of a new state based on Democratic and Christian ideals. The Protestants as well as the Catholics have in many cases demonstrated exceptional courage, but as a result of the quasi-protection afforded by the Vatican[6] and their more closely interwoven organization, the Catholic Clergy have been better able to protect themselves against the inroads of Nazism.

---

6. On the basis of the Concordate concluded in 1933 between the Vatican and the Hitler government

Document 29 · 26 November 1943

Report by the OSS Research and Analysis Branch: "Free Germany": An Experiment in Political Warfare[1]

SECRET

"Free Germany": An Experiment in Political Warfare[2]

In spite of the success of the political warfare conducted by Woodrow Wilson against Germany in 1918, the Allies in this war have made on the whole vague and perfunctory use of political appeals as a weapon against Hitler.[3] This timidity has sprung in part from a candid recognition that the Nazi terror has almost entirely eliminated widespread popular discontent as a political factor. It has sprung also from an indecision over the proper direction of allied post-war policy toward Germany. The single major attempt to resolve these dilemmas has been undertaken by the Free Germany Committee of Moscow.[4] The Committee has addressed its appeals much less to the masses than to those sectors of the ruling

---

1. NA, RG 59, R&A 1593.

2. Based on memoranda from the OSS Research and Analysis Branch and the Federal Communications Commission.

3. Like Allen W. Dulles, the analysts of R&A believed that Wilson's propaganda campaign during World War I had been generally successful. In contrast, Franklin D. Roosevelt always favored a less positive attitude toward Germany. Clearly, the American President was the architect of the "Unconditional Surrender" policy as proclaimed at the Casablanca Conference early in 1943. On 1 April 1944, he even pointed out in a memorandum to the Secretary of State: "Italy surrendered unconditionally but was at the same time given many privileges. This should be so in the event of the surrender of Bulgaria or Rumania or Finland. Lee surrendered unconditionally to Grant but immediately Grant told him that his officers should take their horses home for the Spring plowing. That is the spirit I want to see abroad—but it does not apply to Germany. Germany understands only one kind of language."

4. For earlier assessments of the Free Germany Committee see documents [14], [15], [17], [21] and [26].

class likely to be interested in and capable of overthrowing Hitler; and it has kept its program for post-war Germany in terms so general that they exclude only the extremes of Vansittartism and appeasement.[5] The fact that the country carrying out the campaign is probably the one least likely to be believed by Germans should not obscure the degree to which, as psychological warfare, Free Germany propaganda is carefully designed and skillfully executed.

A. Antecedents of Free Germany

The Free Germany campaign, while basically to be considered a military expedient, reflects an adaptation to the German situation of the political reorientation which the Soviet Union itself has undergone. The experience of the interlude between the wars, when nationalist Fascism dealt international Communism a series of defeats on successive European battlegrounds, taught the Communists that they had underestimated the vitality of national loyalties. In 1939 Stalin made a tacit confession of the stubbornness of nationalism as a political fact, when he renounced the necessity of world revolution, even as a safeguard for the Soviet Union, and expounded the doctrine of the co-existence of systems. The experience of war brought the conclusive demonstration of the potency of patriotic appeals, even in the Soviet Union itself, and Communist parties everywhere have been instructed to plug nationalism almost to the exclusion of class solidarity and workers revolution.

While the content of the Free Germany campaign was thus shaped by Stalinist policies, the employment of the Committee as the instrument probably originated in the ineffectiveness of Moscow's regular German language broadcasts. The twenty-five programs beamed westward daily from Moscow were always limited in their influence by the fact that the speakers were either Russians or German Communists. Even when they carefully avoided Communist slogans, they were bound to arouse German suspicion and resistance.

Knowing how successfully the German home front was immunized against the USSR, Soviet propagandists doubtless cast about for more effective methods of disrupting the German war effort. The chief problem was to find non-Communist Germans who would cooperate and to set up an organization for them. The first tentative move was made on 8 October 1941, when the "First Conference of German Prisoner-of-War Privates and Noncommissioned Officers in the Soviet Union" was held at "Camp No. 58."

The election of Walter Ulbricht, former Communist member of the Reichstag, as president of the Conference indicated that exiled German Communists residing in the USSR were taking a leading part in organizing the war prisoners. [...] The manifesto issued by the conference was addressed particularly to "workers, peasants, the lower middle classes, and those engaged in intellectual pursuits."

---

5. I.e., extremely anti- and pro-German attitudes, respectively. On Vansittartism see document [21].

This first experiment in reaching the Germans was thus an attempt to appeal to German opposition groups along the recognized lines of a Communist front organization. Its feebleness probably accounts for the failure of the Free Germany Committee even to refer to it.
... [6]

C. The German Officers Union
[...]

The establishment of the Officers Union represented a turning point in the activities of the Committee. The efforts were thereafter addressed more often to the armed forces than to any other German group. High-ranking officers, anxious to salvage as much as possible from a defeat which seemed steadily more inevitable, appear to have become increasingly interested in using Soviet facilities to advance their own aims. Since generals served best the political warfare purposes for which the Committee was established, they immediately were allowed a leading part in its operations.

D. Free Germany Broadcasts
Higher officers and other non-Communists thus seem to have taken an increasingly greater part in the Free Germany broadcasts. Of the 179 talks monitored by the FCC [Federal Communications Commission] between 22 July and 15 October, 101 were delivered by identified speakers; of these, 47 were given by officers, 16 by enlisted men, 17 by members of the clergy, and only 17 by German Communists. There is no internal evidence that the 78 unidentified talks were predominantly prepared by Communists.

About 90 percent of the broadcast time is spent on hammering home to the German people the blackness of their military and political position. [...] If, however, the war is soon stopped on the Committee's terms, the German people are promised an independent, democratic and truly national government, civil rights, and a free economy based on middle-class rights, trade unions, private property, and social legislation.

Though considerably more specific than a program of unconditional surrender, the Committee's platform has been left to a great extent in rhetorical and ambiguous terms. The phrasing is apparently designed to offend as few Germans as possible. In spite of the strictures against racism in the Free Germany manifesto, for example, condemnations of Nazi anti-semitism are exceedingly rare.

The target of the campaign has shifted almost completely from the veteran anti-Nazi underground organizations to Germans who have just recently lost faith in Hitler's leadership. While the Committee has recognized workers as the

---

6. The omitted passage deals with the history and the formation of the Free Germany Committee.

largest single economic group, its gestures toward them are tempered by the warning that they cannot expect to impose their own special interests on the rest of the public, and by affirmation of freedom of commerce and the restoration of property to the rightful owners. The attack on the great trusts renews the appeal to the lower middle and working classes which Hitler found so useful in the years before 1933. Yet the Committee is far from closing the door to fairly drastic change. The explicit statement that the future German democracy "will have nothing in common with the helpless Weimar regime," as well as the exhortation to organized "fighting groups at the enterprises, in the villages, in the labor camps, in the universities" contain definite revolutionary implications, imprecise enough to appeal to Communists, Social Democrats, and left-wing Nazis alike.

E. Unconditional Surrender

The fundamental strength of the Manifesto lies in the fact that it offers these varied groups among the German people the prospect of national survival and independence *if* the Nazi regime is destroyed and the war concluded soon enough. It thereby seeks to counter the powerful Nazi argument that Germany must fight to the end because all Germans are in the same boat and defeat will mean national annihilation.

The gap between the Committee's appeal and the Casablanca pledge[7] gave rise in some quarters to the suspicion that the Committee was set up as the instrumentality for a separate peace. Actually warnings to the German people not to hope for a separate peace have appeared with enough regularity to suggest that the Committee at an early stage issued a directive to include them. But "unconditional surrender" itself is not mentioned; and, since it has always been a compromise peace with the Hitlerite leadership that was excluded, German listeners have been left to believe that a non-Hitlerite government might succeed in negotiating an armistice.

[...]

F. Purpose of the Free Germany Committee

The question remains whether the Free Germany Committee is simply a device of political warfare designed to hasten German collapse or whether it contains some intimation of Russian plans for the future of Germany.

In the first place, the possibility of using the Free Germany Committee as the contact point for separate peace negotiations, if it ever existed in force, has now been eliminated by the Moscow agreements.[8]

---

7. I.e., the policy of unconditional surrender.

8. This is a reference to the Foreign Minister's Conference held at Moscow in late October and early November 1943 where the Allies had agreed upon ruling out separate peace negotiations with the Germans.

Much of the Committee's program, moreover, is inconsistent with declared Soviet intentions. Stalin has repeatedly stated—and the Soviet Press has echoed him—that the Hitlerite state and army must be destroyed and Germany brought to unconditional surrender. While saying that it is impossible to destroy Germany as such and that it would be foolish to deny Germany an army, Stalin has never indicated that he wishes the German state to be strong or the *Wehrmacht* to be kept even relatively intact.

It is undoubtedly significant that the Soviet Government has scrupulously avoided public approval of any aspect of the Free Germany program beyond the overthrow of Hitlerism and the return home of the army [...]. The Soviet press has, in the main, emphasized and acclaimed only the disruptive part of the Free Germany campaign—the instigation of army and civil resistance to the war effort.

Yet, while the USSR is at this point chiefly interested in bringing to bear every possible tactic which will weaken Germany, the Free Germany movement cannot be dismissed as a mere technical device of psychological warfare. It is designed according to current Stalinist specifications and it has an inevitable political import, just as any war measure which involves organization and propaganda must have.

It may be assumed that Russia's first prerequisite for the post-Hitler government is that it shall be pro-Soviet in foreign policy and "democratic" in internal policy. The question of the extent to which it must have socialist tendencies in internal policy remains obscure. Stalin's doctrine of the co-existence of systems eliminates the dogmatic necessity for a socialist Germany; and the USSR has only permitted the expression, not urged the adoption, of even the moderate reforms envisaged by the Free Germany Committee.

But it would appear that the USSR, however nationalist in its own orientation, still has more to gain from a leftist than from a rightist Europe. Though the Soviet Union's stake in the *status quo* has increased considerably since 1918, it would nevertheless appear inclined to favor a certain further leftward movement in all European countries save its own, and particularly in Germany.

Yet, it is clear that the Himmler terror has rendered it most unlikely that Hitler will be overthrown by a worker's revolution. In this case, the obvious Soviet strategy is to encourage groups in the German ruling class which are powerful enough to overthrow Hitler but not powerful enough to set up a lasting government of their own. One such group is very likely the Army leaders, who will be able to stay in power only by finding some base in the civil population. The Manifesto, by ruling out the Nazis and the business leaders, thereby compels a leftward drift on the part of the military in search of support. Confident that the Army leaders do not constitute a class capable of governing Germany by themselves, the Russians can safely use them as tools against Hitler. Once in power, the generals must either share civil authority with some at least broadly nationalist and probably leftist group or else be thrown by them.

The Free Germany strategy thus presumes that an Army *putsch* against Hitler is the shortest path to social revolution. Whether the USSR will insist on social revolution is another question; it would seem at present most unlikely that it will do so, since it can profitably gamble on the drift of events, or even on the possibility of world order without world socialism.

The Free Germany Committee must thus be regarded, not as a clear indication of Soviet policy toward Germany (though it inescapably reflects certain intentions inherent in present Soviet strategy), but as a clear indication of an alternative the USSR is prepared to follow if the western democracies try to make some arrangement for Germany not acceptable to the USSR. In the interim the Committee will doubtless be kept alive as an implicit warning to Britain and the United States not to forget Russia in drawing up the post-war world.

[...]

Document 30 · December 1943

Memorandum from Willem Visser't Hooft
(World Council of Churches, Geneva)
to Allen W. Dulles (OSS Bern)[1]:
The Situation of the Protestant Church in Germany

CONFIDENTIAL

The Situation of the Protestant Church in Germany

1. The Heritage of the Church Conflict

The conflict between the Protestant Church and National Socialism is in reality a conglomeration of three conflicts. The first to appear was the one between the "German Christians" (who desired to bring the church in line with National Socialist doctrine as well as National Socialist forms of organization) and the Confession Church [Confessional Church; *Bekennende Kirche*] (which took its stand on the historic confessions). But since the state intervened in this conflict by imposing "German Christian" leaders on the church, there arose a conflict between the Confession Church and the State which became increasingly acute as the State became more openly totalitarian and anti-Christian. The question of the right attitude to the State led again to a controversy inside the Confession Church between the moderates (Bishop Marahrens and several other bishops of regional churches) who tried to avoid an open break with the government, and the radicals (the "Dahlem" group, until his imprisonment led by Pastor Niemöller), who rejected all opportunistic considerations and fought for the full freedom of the Church. This last group had

---

1. NA, RG 226, Entry 190, Box 27, Folder 99. This is one of a series of reports on the German church situation that Willem Visser't Hooft, Secretary General of the World Council of Churches in Geneva, forwarded to Allen W. Dulles on the latter's request. Like his brother John Foster Dulles, who was a leading member of the American Federal Council of the Churches of Christ, Allen was interested in strengthening the religious element in a post-war world, both as a stabilizing factor for the morale of the German people, and as a stronghold against Bolshevism.

formed a "Provisional Church Government", which through its "brotherhood councils" attempted to give spiritual leadership to the "confessional" parishes.

By 1939, the situation was as follows. The various attempts to transform the whole church into an instrument of National Socialist propaganda had failed because of the strong opposition of both the radical and moderate wings of the Confession Church. But (with the exception of the regional churches of Bavaria, Wurttemberg, and Hanover) the churches had come to be governed by German Christian leaders or administrators who followed the instructions of the Ministry of Ecclesiastical Affairs. Through various measures (imprisonment, dismissals, "confessional" theological seminaries forbidden, etc.) the state had succeeded in weakening the Provisional Church Government to such an extent, that it could only function intermittently and in a clandestine manner.[2] At the same time, the gulf between the moderates and the radicals had become very deep since the first had under state-pressure publicly criticized the former for their attitude at the time of the Munich crisis.[3] By this time the situation was therefore that, while the State had not succeeded in using the church for its ideological purposes, it had certainly succeeded in its alternative policy of dividing and weakening the church.

At the same time, the State had increasingly ousted the church from public life. Whenever churchmen, individually or collectively, expressed their mind on actions of the state, immediate reprisals were taken. And all activities undertaken with the purpose to extend the influence of the church, particularly public evangelism and youth work, had been gradually forbidden.

2. Did the Church Conflict Continue During the War?

For the sake of both interior and foreign propaganda, the authorities tried to give the impression in the early stage of the war that the church conflict belonged to the past. But in fact, the conflict continued in somewhat less visible form. No frontal attacks were made on the church as a whole, but through a great variety of measures and interventions its public position was further weakened. Thus a considerable number of pastors were forbidden to speak or to travel. Leading personalities of the Provisional Church Government were imprisoned. Religious instruction in the schools was severely curtailed and in many cases abolished. Practically the whole religious press was suppressed. The publication and sale of religious books was severely restricted. The sending of religious literature to soldiers was forbidden, etc.

---

2. In 1937, the Seminaries of the Confessional Church were declared illegal. Under difficult circumstances Protestant theologian Dietrich Bonhoeffer, a member of the Kreisau resistance circle around Count von Moltke, continued his educational work at Finkenwalde near Stettin. The College was, however, smashed twice by the Gestapo.

3. In september 1938, the Munich conference had transferred the Czech province Sudetenland to Germany.

During the war years little anti-Christian and anti-church propaganda has been carried on among the general public. But the propaganda against Christianity and the church within the party organizations has become more outspoken and violent than ever. In fact, the old idea of using the church was given up and replaced by the conception that it should be allowed to die out. For this reason in some areas (Warthegau) experiments were made with a policy which would make it practically impossible for the church to gain new members.

Thus during these last four years the conflict between church and state had become the dominating one. And the two other conflicts, the one between "German Christians" and "Confessionals", and the other between "moderates" and "radicals", have lost much of their importance.

The present position of the groups within the church is as follows:

The *"German Christians"* have ceased to exert any considerable influence, though some of them still hold leading positions (Thuringia). As it becomes increasingly clear that there can be no peace between National Socialism and Christianity, their compromise position becomes untenable and they are attacked, both by radical Nazis and by confessional churchmen.

The group of *"moderates"* has been split. Some, like Bishop Marahrens, collaborate closely with the Ministry of Ecclesiastical Affairs, and have at different occasions accepted to make public declarations which echo the official government view (though they seem in some cases to have refused to speak when they were invited to do so). Others, such as Bishop Wurm of Wurttemberg, have come to take an increasingly independent attitude in relation to government and party and have gone out of their way to create a common front of all groups which stand for a church with a message and life of its own.

Thus a concentration of forces has taken place under the leadership of Bishop Wurm in which the regional churches of Bavaria and Wurttemberg, the Provisional Church Government of the Confessional Church, and the Brotherhood Councils all take part. The common platform has been defined in thirteen theses concerning the mission and task of the church which have met with a very wide response. These theses affirm that the only criterion of the Church's message and life is the Bible and reject all interference from the outside. They underline that the church has the right and duty to proclaim its message publicly as the Word of God for the people and the State. This body of churchmen which represents the truly vital elements of protestantism of Germany, is now planning actively for the future and will no doubt take the leadership of the whole Protestant Church when the National Socialist state breaks down.

3. Losses and Gains

As a result of the conflict which has now lasted almost ten years, the church has lost considerable ground in the life of the nation. Its evangelistic and educational work has been largely destroyed, so that large masses of youth grew up under pagan rather than Christian influence. Since three-fourths of the pastors are mobilized for the army or other services and since the theological faculties are almost empty, the problem of providing leadership to the parishes has become almost insoluble. Moreover, the suppression of the religious press and conferences has isolated the parishes from each other. Since the National Socialist ideology has an absolute monopoly in public life and the church is not allowed to have any say in the affairs of state and nation, the voice of the church is practically not heard outside the walls of the church buildings.

But there are gains as well. The conflict has led to a very real deepening of consecration on the part of loyal churchmen. The parishes have a stronger sense of solidarity. Laymen take over responsibilities such as they never carried before. New forms of personal evangelism have been worked out which reach many outside the church. And so the church has opportunities to shape what is often called a "secret public opinion".

And, perhaps most important of all, the fact that a considerable section of the church has proved to be a bulwark, almost the only bulwark, against the penetrating influence of National Socialist ideology, has made a deep impression on all circles who are for different reasons antagonistic to National Socialism. The church is today taken seriously in intellectual, political, and social circles which considered it formerly as an antiquated institution. Thus one finds that, while many have left the church during these years, others have returned to it. Church attendance has increased in many places. At special church meetings which deal with fundamental problems, an attendance of one to three thousand persons is not exceptional. In other words, the result of the years of struggle is that, both with regard to its *effective* membership and to its *effective* place in the nation, the church is stronger today than it was ten years ago. It was characteristic for the old situation that it had a nominal place in the life of the nation to which it was not really entitled because of its inner weakness. It is characteristic for the present situation that, while it has almost no official influence, its real strength is considerable.

4. Has the Church Only Fought for Its Own Freedom?

It has been stated at different occasions and by persons of considerable authority that the great weakness in the German church situation is that the church only fights for its own independence and does not resist state and party in their violation of justice and of the basic rights of men. But this opinion is not wholly justified.

It is true that the main issue in the church conflict has been the freedom of the church to proclaim its own message and to order its own life. Especially during the early years of the struggle, a very large group of churchmen have taken the position that the church has no right to interfere in the political sphere and many have even gone so far as to welcome the political and social achievements of National Socialism, while condemning its policy toward the church.

Moreover, opportunities for the church to make its voice heard in public affairs had become almost non-existent. In war-time public criticism of the government was immediately construed as treason against the national cause. The result was that especially during the war church leaders have not offered *public* and *general* resistance to the policies of National Socialism, outside the realm of church life.

But this does not mean that the church has been altogether silent concerning the grave moral issues which have arisen in national life. Direct and indirect protests have been made at different occasions. For obvious reasons only few of these have become known to the general public in and outside Germany.

Thus there have been definite protests against the persecution of the Jews, both through sermons and letters addressed by church leaders to the government. In this connection it should also be reported that a number of pastors and Christian laymen have tried to save Jews by helping them to hide or escape, and some have been sent to concentration camp because of this. Again, strong protests have been made against the practice of euthanasia. If it is remembered what risks the men have taken who have made them, and what prices some of them have paid, these protests will be seen in their true significance.[4]

Nor should it be forgotten that the open resistance of the church against the application of totalitarianism in the sphere of the spiritual life has in fact taken on considerable political relevance. In a totalitarian situation resistance on any point becomes a political factor. The church has demonstrated that National Socialism is not all powerful and cannot overcome spiritual forces for which men are willing to risk their lives. It is a living reminder to the nation that there exist forces which have deeper roots and greater permanence than National Socialism and that resistance against the official ideology is not impossible.

The German Protestant Church has certainly not spoken out as it ought to have spoken out. But it is only fair to acknowledge that it has been among the very few forces which have maintained their integrity in the struggle with totalitarianism and that it has been a bulwark against the total victory of totalitarianism.

5. Changing Political Attitudes

In the church itself the experiences of the years of struggle have led many to a revision of their former political attitude. While a few years ago the tendency towards an absolute separation between religion and politics and towards concentration on the purely spiritual task of the church was very strong, there has since developed an insight into the close connection between ideology and politics. Even today there are still many in the German Church whose conviction is almost wholly other-worldly and who take the "pseudo-Lutheran" position that the state alone has the first and last word in the realm of politics. Their attitude has been well described as "religious schizophrenia", for they keep their religion and their political life in watertight compartments. But their attitude is no longer represen-

---

4. In 1941, Bishop Wurm of Stuttgart had protested against the murder of mentally disabled people by the Nazis; two years later he also condemned the persecution of the Jews.

tative for the most active leadership of the church. The conviction that the church has a message concerning right and wrong in public affairs and that the future of the nation depends on its willingness to listen to that message, is growing. The manifestation of what unrestrained and irresponsible power means in practice has forced many to understand that the church must accept its responsibility in public life and clearly proclaim the validity of Christian norms for the state and the government.

It can be said that the great majority of active church members have no longer any doubts as to the anti-Christian character of the present regime. Many just accept this fact as a burden which they must bear. But a not incommensurable number of individual churchmen have drawn the conclusion that it is their duty to work for the overthrow of that regime. In the circles of the resistance movement in Germany one often finds convinced Christians at the centre. Several have been imprisoned for participation in illegal activities. It is by no means merely because of forbidden ecclesiastical activities that the Gestapo has a very special interest in the doings of churchmen. Unfortunately it is at present not possible to give a full account of all that goes on in this realm. But we have reason to say that the place of Christians in the resistance movement is much greater than one would expect in view of the church's past political passivity and its present numerical weakness.

6. The Place of the Church in Post-War Germany

What will be the place of the church in post-war Germany? We can only attempt to answer that question by mentioning certain significant trends of thought and life which seem to point to the future. It remains, however, quite possible that out of the turmoil which totalitarian government, total war, and total defeat will have produced in Germany there will grow up forces and situations quite different from those which have already become more or less visible today.

There are many signs which show that the church in Germany enters upon a time of unprecedented opportunity. This is so because large circles of the German people are discovering (and many more will probably discover) the emptiness of the official ideology. The religious "vacuum" demands to be filled. People who have lost all that seemed to make life worth living; soldiers who have gone through the unspeakable horror of the Eastern War; civilians who have lost their family, their jobs, their property, and become "proletarianized"; and all those who have lost at the same time their political faith—either become desperate nihilists or … turn to a substantial religion. Already young people from the party organizations who are tired of the monotonous party propaganda come to the church to find something more satisfying. Then again, the many who have come to oppose National Socialism on political and social grounds begin to realize that in the world of today political attitudes can only stand the strain if they are rooted in spiritual convictions. And finally, there is the new prestige which the church has gained because it has proved "tougher" than all other institutions and has been willing to pay a high price for its independence.

Thus it is not unlikely that the position of the church in post-war Germany will be far stronger than it has been in the years before the war or before National Socialism came on the scene. In fact, leading churchmen wonder whether the main problem of the church in the immediate post-war era will not be, that it will be too popular and that political and social forces will attempt to exploit its prestige for their particular purposes. If Germany gets an new regime which is favourable to the church, there is a certain danger of a sudden return to an "official Christianity".

It remains, of course, tragically true that large masses of Germany, particularly of the younger generation, have become almost completely paganized. And it is likely that many of these will not find their way back to the church, but rather move towards some sort of nihilism. Thus Germany, which has always been a country of extremes, will probably present the picture of a country with a strong Christian and a strong anti-Christian movement. This would, of course, be doubly true if Communism would get the upperhand in Germany.

What will be the attitude of the church in social matters? On the basis of the convictions which find expression in church circles today, it may be expected that Christian leaders will stand for a solution of the social problem which avoids the anarchy of capitalistic liberalism and which avoids the regimentation of full-fledged control by the state. It is on this basis that churchmen and labour leaders who used to be miles apart in their social conceptions are now preparing the future together. It is also significant that the "Malvern Report" produced by Church of England leaders with its critique of capitalism and with its insistence on social security has met with a considerable response in these circles.[5]

In this connection it must, however, be added that there is among the Christians of Germany a very deep rooted horror of Communism, which they consider as a wholly destructive force. If, therefore, the masses of labour would turn to Communism, either in a German or a Russian form, it is quite possible that the church would become the bulwark of the anti-Communistic forces. Thus the church, which would fight Communism on spiritual grounds, would be lined up with those who defend the old order for purely material reasons and it would lose its present opportunity to win back the masses of labour. It must, therefore, be hoped that the German church will not be put in a position in which it will have to choose between reactionary capitalism and revolutionary Communism.

And what do Christians in Germany hope for in the political realm? It would seem that the consensus of opinion is that the first step must be to create a law-abiding state. After the decade of violation of justice and utter arbitrariness, law

---

5. In January 1941, Archbishop William Temple of York convoked a Church of England Conference in Malvern. The conclusions of this conference came to form the basis of the war and peace aims debate that ensued in Britain in the course of 1941. The Malvern report included the demand for social justice as the foundation of a future order, and it also called for the unification of Europe as a "co-operative commonwealth."

must once more become the arbiter between the citizens and the state as well as between the citizens themselves. Power must once more be made subject to definite criteria of justice and be used in a responsible manner. But this does not mean that they desire the return of parliamentary democracy. Most Christians feel that to introduce full-fledged political democracy in the present situation would be to create chaos. A government with strong authority accepting the limits imposed by Christian standards and by the rights of the citizens seems to them the only possible one for the post-war period. This form of government should, however, in their conception, be combined with far-reaching decentralization, so that the various regions may again develop their particular traditions and arrive at a considerable degree of autonomy. It is perhaps not generally recognized that the regional churches are almost the only remaining bearers of these regional traditions and that they are, therefore, the natural advocates of this most necessary policy of decentralization.

7. The Place of the German Church in the Post-War World

The attitude of the German Protestant Church toward the other churches and toward the international situation will, of course, largely depend on the developments in the near future. We can, however, distinguish the following elements which will at least be part of the whole picture.

One of the most remarkable aspects of the church situation during this war is certainly that, in spite of terrific pressure, relations have continued to exist between church leaders in Germany and those in other countries. Here again the full story cannot now be told, but this much can be said that through prisoners of war work and the help given to "orphaned" missions, through information and visits, the consciousness of common membership in the Church Universal has remained real on both sides. It may be added that with the exception of certain utterances of the "official" church council the message of the church has remained largely free from war hysteria and the propaganda of hatred. The typical war-time sermon has remained on a high Christian level.

The situation in this respect may change now that the terrific bombardments create the impression that the allied nations are also using totalitarian methods of warfare and that there is deep and general indignation about these methods in church circles as elsewhere. But the most influential church leaders are aware of this danger and raise a warning voice against the growing hatred. When after the Hamburg bombardments[6] the "official" church administration (which collaborates with the government) advocated the "unreserved determination to fight the war without the slightest sentimentality" there was an immediate reaction from responsible church leaders in which it was said that the bombardments are to lead

---

6. In July 1943.

to repentance for the many sins which the German nation has committed or has allowed to be committed without opposition, and that the Christians are involved in this suffering because they have not with sufficient frankness and unanimity called injustice by its true name.

There is then in the church, and not only in the church, a readiness to recognize guilt. And there is a readiness to meet Christians of other countries on the basis of a common recognition of guilt. But from the standpoint of the German church it will have to be definitely a *common* recognition and not a unilateral condemnation of the German nation alone. For while Christians in Germany are to a large extent aware of the fact that their nation bears a crushing responsibility for the catastrophic happenings of these last years, they are convinced that the other nations by their sins of omission and commission have also greatly contributed to the creation of the international chaos. In this connection it should also be remembered that practically nobody outside the party is sufficiently informed concerning the nature and extent of the horrible crimes which have been committed against defenceless people in the occupied territories.

The degree of readiness to collaborate with the churches of other countries will largely depend on the attitude which these churches will take toward the German Church and to the German nation. If that attitude would be one of sentimental reconciliation which takes the responsibility of the German Church less seriously than the German Church takes it itself, the process of inner change which now goes on in that church will not be helped but hindered. If, on the other hand, the other churches take a merely condemning attitude, no basis for collaboration can be found. A repentant sinner whose repentance is not taken seriously, is not liberated from his sin, but a repentant sinner who meets with a pharizaic attitude may well become a hardened sinner.

The post-war German Church will no doubt eliminate those of its leaders who have not resisted or even helped National Socialism in its attempt to subordinate the church to its aims and will give places of influence to men who have stood for the independence of the church.

The attitude of these leaders in international problems will depend very largely on the way in which Germany will be treated at the time of the Armistice and of peace-making. If Germany is allowed to do its own house-cleaning, these men will be among the most trustworthy and active supporters of a complete overhauling of national life. But if the process of cleaning will be carried out under foreign auspices and leadership, they will probably not collaborate in it. In any case, it is not to be expected that any of them will show readiness to act directly or indirectly as an agent of a foreign power which would treat Germany as a vassal

---

7. These ideas had been developed by members of the Kreisau resistance circle around Count Helmuth von Moltke.

state. But it may be expected that they will collaborate in a solution of the German problem which, while curtailing German political and military power, allows the German people to have its own place among the other nations.

In Christian circles who are actively preparing for the future, the conception of the future international order is that of a European Federation, in which frontiers would gradually cease to have political and economic significance, but in which cultural and national traditions would be safeguarded. These same circles are sceptical about plans to revive a world-wide League of Nations which is not based on and rooted in regional collaboration. Their hope is, that Europe may rediscover its fundamental unity in the Christian faith, and that the Federation to be formed will be strong enough to oppose any possible tendencies to form governments of a totalitarian or anti-Christian character.[7]

In view of their deep rooted fear of Bolshevism and also of Panslavism, these circles look to the Western powers for leadership in showing a way out of the present chaos. They are disappointed that so little definite hope has been held out concerning a radical approach to European social and international problems. It may, however, be expected that when such an approach is made, they will be ready to act as its advocates in Germany.

Document 31 · Second Half of December 1943

Herman Plan. Exposé on the Readiness of a Powerful German Group to Assist Allied Military Operations Against Nazi Germany[1]

TOP SECRET

Exposé on the Readiness of a Powerful German Group to Prepare and Assist Allied Military Operations Against Nazi Germany

Note: This exposé defines the attitude and plans of an extremely influential group of the German opposition inside Germany on the subject of hastening the victory of the Allies and the abolition of Nazism. It has been prepared on the basis of frequent and searching conversations and discussions with a leading representative of this group about the political future of a free democratic Germany cleansed radically of Nazism, and about the maximum contribution that can be made immediately by determined German patriots toward making this Germany a secure reality.

The exposé is to reproduce clearly and concisely the views and intentions of this group of responsible democratic Germans within Germany.

Background and Standing of the German Oppositional Group

Apart from the Nazi Party hierarchy and its subordinate organs and functionaries, there are left in Germany two elements vested with political power: the offi-

---

1. NA, RG 226, Entry 180, A 3304, Roll 68; second (probably later) version NA, RG 226, Entry 190, M 1642 frames 377–386; Heideking/Mauch, Herman-Dossier, pp. 588–591. German version: van Roon, Neuordnung, pp. 582–586; Moltke/Balfour/Frisby, Anwalt der Zukunft, pp. 264–268. Date inferred from internal evidence. The plan must have been written after Moltke's departure from Turkey on 16 December 1943; on 29 December, Alfred Schwarz was in possession of the plan. See document [32].

cers corps of the Wehrmacht, and the upper ranks of the Civil Service, which, in their ministerial grades at least, represent a fairly closely-knit network of officials interconnected by personal acquaintance, official association, often long-standing friendship. Within the overlapping spheres of high officialdom and professional army circles, three categories of people can be distinguished:

1) Politically non-descript specialists who are absorbed altogether in their service duties, being either too vague or too cautious to express their views or engage in political activity. They constitute the majority, especially among the professional officers.
2) Confirmed National Socialists.
3) Decided and conscious opponents of Nazism.

The third category is again divided in two wings, of which one favours an "Eastern" pro-Russian orientation, the other a "Western", pro-Anglo-Saxon trend. The former is considerably stronger than the latter, particularly in the Wehrmacht; in Luftwaffe circles it rules supreme. The driving force behind the Eastern wing is the strong and traditional conviction of a community of interests between the two mutually complementary powers, Germany and Russia, which led to the historical cooperation between Prussia and the Russian monarchy, and between the German republic and Soviet Russia in the Rapallo period (1924),[2] when the Reichswehr and the Red Army concluded a far-reaching understanding regarding military collaboration and reciprocal training facilities. Historical bonds of this character are reinforced by the deep impression wrought by the power and resilience of the Red Army and the competence of its command. Among the Eastern wing the foundation of the German Officers' League at Moscow[3] has evoked a powerful echo, the more so, as the leaders of the league are recognized in the Wehrmacht as officers of outstanding ability and personal integrity (by the standards of their caste). This group has for a long time been in direct communication, including regular wireless contact, with the Soviet Government, until a breach of security on the Russian side led to the arrest and execution of many high-placed officers and civil servants early in 1943.[4]

The Western group of the opposition, though numerically weaker, is represented by many key men in the military and civil service hierarchies, including

---

2. The German version gives the correct year 1922.

3. The German Officers' League (Bund deutscher Offiziere; BDO) had been founded in Moscow in September 1943. Under its leader, General Walther von Seydlitz-Kurzbach, it called for the overthrow of the Hitler regime and the retreat of the German armies to the original Reich borders of 1937. See also document [29].

4. This is a reference to the so-called Red Orchestra (Rote Kapelle) resistance circle around Harro Schultze-Boysen and Arvid Harnack. The organization was crushed by the Nazis not in early 1943 but in late 1942. The Red Orchestra outfit was basically Communist, and worked in close cooperation with a Soviet espionage network. The aim of this organization was to convey military intelligence to the Russians.

officers of all ranks, and key members of the OKW. Furthermore it is in close touch with the Catholic bishops, the Protestant Confessional Church, leading circles of the former labour unions and workmen's organizations, as well as influential men of industry and intellectuals. It is this group which is seeking to establish a practical basis for effectual collaboration with the Anglo-Saxon Allies.

Conditions of Collaboration with the Allies

The following are the future material factors and present political arguments which form the logical prerequisites of a successful collaboration between this Western Group of the German democratic opposition and the Allies.

1) Unequivocal military defeat and occupation of Germany is regarded by the members of the group as a moral and political necessity for the future of the nation.

2) The Group is convinced of the justification of the Allied demand for unconditional surrender, and realizes the untimeliness of any discussion of peace terms before this surrender has been accomplished. Their Anglo-Saxon sympathies result from a conviction of the fundamental unity of aims regarding the future organization of human relations which exists between them and the responsible statesmen on the Allied side, and the realization that in view of the natural convergence of interests between post-Nazi Germany and the other democratic nations there must of necessity result a fruitful collaboration between them. The democratic Germans see in this unity of purpose a far safer guarantee of a status of equality and dignity after the War than any formal assurances by the Allies at the present time could give them, provided any such assurances were forthcoming.

3) An important condition for the success of the plan outlined in the following points is the continuance of an unbroken Eastern front, and simultaneously its approach to within a menacing proximity of the German borders, such as the line from *Tilsit* to *Lemberg*.[5] Such a situation would justify before the national consciousness radical decisions in the West as the only means of forestalling the overpowering threat from the East.

4) The Group is ready to realize a planned military cooperation with the Allies on the largest possible scale, provided that exploitation of the military information, resources, and authority at the Group's disposal is combined with an all-out military effort by the Allies in such a manner as to make prompt and decisive success on a broad front a practical certainty. This victory over Hitler, followed by Allied occupation of all Germany in the shortest possible time, would at one stroke so transform the political situation as to set free the real voice of Germany, which would acclaim the action of the Group as a bold act of true patriotism,

---

5. A line approximately marking the far eastern borders of Prussia.

comparable to the Tauroggen Convention concluded by the Prussian General Yorck with the Russians 1812.[6]

5) Should, however, the invasion of Western Europe be embarked upon the same style as the attack upon the Italian mainland, any assistance by the Group would not only fail to settle the issue of the War, but would in addition help to create a new "stab-in-the-back" legend,[7] as well as compromise before the nation, and render ineffectual for the future, the patriots who made the attempt. There is no doubt that half-measures would damage the cause rather than promote it, and the Group is not prepared to lend a hand in any collaboration with limited aims.

6) If it is decided to create the second front in the West by an unsparing all-out effort, and follow it up with overwhelming force to the goal of total occupation of Germany, the Group is ready to support the Allied effort with all its strength and all the important resources at its disposal. To this end it would after proper agreement and preparation be ready to despatch a high officer to a specified Allied territory by plane as their fully empowered, informed, and equipped plenipotentiary charged with coordinating the plans of collaboration with the Allied High Command.

7) The readiness of a sufficient number of intact units of the Wehrmacht to follow up the orders given under the Group's operational plan, and cooperate with the Allies, could only be counted upon with a sufficient degree of certainty if the above conditions are fulfilled. Otherwise there would be a grave danger that the orders and operations agreed upon by the commanders and staffs belonging to the Group would at the decisive moment fail to materialize for lack of support, or be executed only with great friction.

8) The Group would see to it that simultaneously with the Allied landing a provisional anti-Nazi Government would be formed which would take over all non-military tasks resulting from the collaboration with the Allies and the political upheaval that would accompany it. The composition of this provisional Government would be determined in advance.

9) The Group, which comprises personages belonging to the most diverse liberal and democratic parties and schools of thought, regards the possibility of a bolshevization of Germany through the rise of a national communism as the deadliest imminent danger to Germany and the European family of nations. It is determined to counter this threat by all possible means, and to prevent, in particular, the conclusion of the War through the victory of the Red Army, followed by a Russian occupation of Germany before the arrival of the Anglo-Saxon armies. On

---

6. This is a reference to the so-called Tauroggen Convention of December 1812 when General Hans David von Yorck signed a neutrality agreement with the Russians without being commissioned by the King of Prussia. This understanding implied Prussian-Russian military cooperation; at the same time it sparked Prussia's uprising against Napoleon Bonaparte.

7. During the Weimar period nationalist circles in Germany had fomented the belief that Germany had not been defeated in the field but rather by internal forces such as the Social Democrats. This legendary belief was generally referred to as *Dolchstoßlegende* (stab-in-the-back legend).

the other hand, no cleft must be allowed to develop between the future democratic Government and the masses of German labour. A non-Communist democratic home policy will only be possible in conjunction with a whole-hearted policy of collaboration with Russia, designed to eliminate all hostility or friction with that power. In this way it should be sought not to antagonize the strong pro-Russian circles in Germany, but to rally them in a common constructive effort and win them over. Finally, what must be avoided at all cost is the development of a situation which would lay a democratic Government open to the reproach of placing foreign interests above national concerns, and unify against this Government the forces of nationalism, communism, and Russophily.

10) The envisaged democratic Government, in order to steal the thunder of left radicalism, should operate at home with a very strong left wing, and lean heavily on the Social Democrats and organized labour, even, if necessary, seek the cooperation of personally unimpeachable independent Communists.

11) The initial HQ [Headquarter] of the democratic counter-Government would under the postulated circumstances best be South Germany, perhaps Austria. It would be advisable not to subject the civilian population of this territorial basis to indiscriminate air attack, since experience teaches that bombed-out populations are exhausted and absorbed by the effort of providing for their bare survival and subsistence that they are out of play as far as revolutionary action is concerned.

Document 32 · 29 December 1943

Letter from OSS Agent "Dogwood" [Alfred Schwarz,[1] OSS Istanbul] to U.S. Military Attaché General Richard D. Tindall (Ankara)[2]: Plea for the Support of Helmuth James Graf von Moltke's Peace Initiative

TOP SECRET

Sir,

This is to introduce the enclosed memorandum,[3] which has been prepared by Herman's friends[4] who conducted the negotiations between Herman and myself during his recent stay,[5] and who know intimately, and share, his plans and political aims. In this memorandum they wish to give a concise statement of the background, motives, and potential value to the Allies, as well as to democratic postwar Germany and the rest of the World, of the influential group of which Herman is the authorized emissary. It has been prepared in the light of the recent conversations held indirectly between Herman and myself, and between yourself and Herman, and may serve as an explanatory comment to Herman's letter to Kirk,[6] which is also appended, and which is not fully intelligible without such a brief on the facts.

---

1. NA, RG 226, Entry 190, Microfilm 1462, Roll 52, Frames 314–319; Heideking/Mauch, Herman-Dossier, pp. 585–588. Name of author deduced by conjecture. See also documents [18] and [39].

2. General Tindall was Military Attaché attached to the U.S. Legation at Ankara. According to a directive by OSS Director Donovan of April 1943, all peace feelers by Axis representatives had to be reported through diplomatic channels to the State Department.

3. Document [31].

4. Alexander Rüstow and Hans Wilbrandt.

5. Moltke stayed in Istanbul from 11 to 16 December 1943; he had also visited Istanbul between 5 and 10 July 1943. The official reason for his visit was German shipping interests in Turkey.

6. Not printed. In December 1943, Moltke had written a letter to Ambassador Kirk in Cairo with whom he wished to meet in order to discuss the overtures of the German opposition.

I think it may be useful at this point to sketch briefly the manner in which contact was sought and established, and the reservations on the German side which prompted them to proceed as they did. Herman has been sent abroad as the emissary of a number of German anti-Nazi staff officers and high official[s] (associated loosely with other liberal elements and exponents of Labour), who are determined to work together for the defeat of the Nazi regime as the only way to save Germany from complete annihilation. They are daily risking their lives and the lives of their families in the effort to widen and consolidate their organization, which in view of the key positions held by most of their members in the GS [General Staff], the Army and Civil administration commands tremendous executive power when acting by a preconcerted plan. Herman has been chosen for the mission of contacting the Anglo-Saxon Allies because of his excellent personal relations to high-placed Allied politicians and prominent press people, who know and are able to appreciate his background and associations, save him elaborate credentials, and in whose absolute discretion he can have confidence. Among his trusted friends are Alexander Kirk,[7] Field Marshall Smuts,[8] and Dorothy Thompson.[9] His extreme caution is easily understood if it is realized that during previous overtures through official Allied channels several flagrant breaches of security occured which jeopardized the entire organization and caused the execution of an important member for high treason.[10] I know the details of these occurences, and fully appreciate the refusal of the Group to deal with anyone but persons of tried discretion, who are known to them or recommended by their trusted friends. The Group is fully aware that their trusted Allied contacts are not necessarily in a position to make decisions or discuss terms; but they are confident that they will be able not only to put them through to the authorities who are competent to handle their momentous proposals, but also to impress forcibly upon these authorities the fact that several hundred of the most valuable war and peace allies of the Anglo-Saxon powers left in key positions in Germany have their

---

7. Before Hitler's declaration of war on the United States in December 1941, Moltke had had several secret meetings with ambassador Kirk and his successor, George F. Kennan, in Berlin.

8. See document [83a].

9. Moltke and Dorothy Thompson had met each other for the first time in 1934 in Vienna. In her 1942 radio broadcasts to Germany (called "Listen, Hans"), Dorothy Thompson encouraged the German opposition, and especially her friend Helmuth James von Moltke to openly oppose the Nazi regime. "Hans," the addressee, was no other than Helmuth James von Moltke. In a letter of 23 December 1953, to Mother Mary Alice Gallin, OSU, Dorothy Thompson confirmed that the "broadcasts [...] were peculiarly directed to this one person, in anticipation that they would appeal to many others of similar mind."

10. The person referred to cannot be clearly identified, as several members of the opposition had been executed by the end of 1943. Among them were members of the White Rose (Weiße Rose) and Red Orchestra opposition groups as well as German diplomat Rudolf von Scheliha.

heads in the noose along with their families, and that a happy-go-lucky attitude in dealing with the matter is inappropriate.

As it turned out, it unfortunately proved impossible to secure for Herman safe passage to Cairo within the time at his disposal, let alone arrange for a meeting here with responsible Allied personages introduced by Alexander Kirk or another of Herman's trusted acquaintances. I myself could from the nature of my position, and in the absence of specific powers or credentials, not be an officially acceptable Allied negotiator; but at least I succeeded in conducting informal indirect discussions with him through our common friends, dissuading him from breaking off all contact and inducing him to agree to a meeting with you (as a personage of official standing and personal competence and integrity) which would serve to legitimize the contact.

I now wish to state my own personal attitude in this vitally important matter. At this time, when plans for the decisive attack against Germany are probably near completion, there is no time to be lost in fully informing President Roosevelt, General Marshall, and General Donovan, Chief of the IS [Intelligence Service],[11] avoiding the delay entailed in normal official procedure. Written reports are quite inadequate to the occasion. A conference should be arranged with at least one of these personages during which the full extent and moment of the proposed scheme may be fully reported upon, and all arrangements for a decisive meeting with the German plenipotentiaries not later than January 1944 may be made. I cannot state emphatically enough my conviction that absolutely no effort should be spared to bring the scheme to fruition in the shortest possible time. No limited intelligence effort and no scheme of partial assistance by German staff members can offer even a remotely comparable chance of ending the War in the West at one stroke, and save perhaps many hundred thousand lives. I believe that no one who is informed of this unique chance, which we have been hard at work to help to materialize, can shoulder the responsibility for not having done all in his power to forward this knowledge with all possible caution and despatch to the supreme authorities in charge of the conduct of the War. Far-reaching parallel schemes involving the cooperation of Germany's present Allies are far advanced[12] and may be combined with the present project to heighten its prospects of success.

I am preparing an account of the scheme in a covering report[13] on the enclosed memorandum[14] and on Herman's letter to Alexander Kirk, but we are not decided

---

11. I.e., the OSS.

12. For the Dogwood-Cereus-Circle, see in particular document [18].

13. Not printed.

14. Document [31].

where best to direct this report. I am probably correct in assuming that you, Sir, will be reporting on the matter on your own account, enclosing the same documents. Since the matter brooks no delay or confusion of competences, I hope you will agree with me that the official steps we take in this matter had best be coordinated. To this end, I should greatly welcome an opportunity to meet you personally, or failing this, to have your written advice on how to proceed.[15]

I am, Sir,
Your obedient Servant

15. For the reaction of OSS Washington to the Herman Plan, see documents [37a], [37b] and [37c].

1944

Document 33 · 8 January 1944

Report of the OSS Labor Branch: Ongoing Projects[1]

Washington Labor Section

The Washington Staff including men on temporary assignments with title or brief description of duties is as follows:

Major Arthur J. Goldberg: Head of Labor Section

Carl Devoe: Executive Officer

Thomas S. Wilson: Area Officer for Labor Desk ETO [European Theater of Operations], Sweden and Far East

Mortimer B. Wolf (on temporary duty): Area Officer for Labor Desk NATO [North Atlantic Theater of Operations]

Daniel Margolies (on temporary duty): Area Officer for Labor Desk METO [Mediterranean Theater of Operations] and Lisbon

Lt. Al Suarez (on temporary duty): Recruiting Officer

One of the principal jobs undertaken by the Washington staff since Major Goldberg's overseas survey and return[2] has been a comprehensive recruiting program to provide agent personnel and radio operat[ors] for the various projects in the several theaters. Specifically the goals set have been as follows:

50 German recruits for NATO to service Faust "A" Project

50 German recruits for ETO to service Faust "B" Project[3]

---

1. U.S. Army Military Archives, Carlisle Barracks, PA, William J. Donovan Papers, Box 67A, File 273.

2. In 1942 and 1943, Goldberg had been the head of the OSS Labor Desk in London.

3. The OSS Faust Project is discussed later in this document.

15 Greek recruits for METO to service Pericles Project[4]

15 Yugoslavs for METO to service TUNIC Project[5]

Specific purposes of these projects are more particularly described in the respective Theater reports.

In addition to the recruiting done locally and in New York, four recruiting missions were arranged through Colonel Conelly on each of which an officer attached to the Labor Section was present and personally interviewed all of the recruits finally accepted. The following is the statistical summary of the results of the recruiting program:

Number of men interviewed (approx.): 750

Total men now attached to Labor Section and in training 20

Total men whose transfer has been requested but who have not yet reported for duty 25

Total men trained and awaiting transportation 7

Total men en route 2

Total men awaiting TCA [Training Corps Assignment] 1

Labor Desk Area Officers are responsible for reports and communications by cable and pouch to and from the field. They also coordinate the activities between the field offices and Washington.

Ship Observer Project

Operations

The Ship Observer Project which was set up to obtain military, economic and psychological information concerning both enemy and neutral territory by interviewing specially selected seamen has been particularly useful with respect to port defenses, troop movements, ship movements, port facilities and security and considerable information of X–2 value.[6] In addition a great deal of information regarding underground movements and publication rationing, availability of

---

4. The OSS Pericles Project was intended to establish organized communications between the OSS and the Greek EAM (National Liberation Front). As the EAM was a left-wing dominated group, there had been no direct communications with the United States.

5. Similar in its scope to the Pericles Project, the Tunic Project was to be directed from an advance base at Bari, Italy. Its object was to establish contacts with the Yugoslav resistance.

6. The work of X–2 (Counterintelligence Branch of the OSS) included, besides spy-catching, the penetration of enemy intelligence services and disinformation.

food, black markets, morale, etc. has been supplied. The information almost always covers port cities, although in some cases the informants have been familiar with inland conditions as well. Many of the foreign informants have formerly worked in industrial plants in occupied countries and were familiar with the details of such plants.

Over the year and one-half of operation of this project, close contacts have been made with hundreds of seamen in the Merchant Marines of all countries touching American ports. These unpaid contacts are constantly on the alert for material useful in the war effort.

During the past months, many specific projects have been developed. Among the more important of these has been the work of this project in recruiting seamen of foreign nationalities as agents for work in their occupied homelands.

It has also been possible to secure through returning seamen innumerable documents, newspapers, underground publications, and various types of negative intelligence. Discussions regarding the possible assistance of the project have been held with Commander Morgan and Commander Pratt as a result of which information of this type has been turned over [to] the negative intelligence unit. [...]

Labor Desk in London

Operations

(1) General. During the past three months the Labor Desk has maintained and developed its previously established contacts and through its enlarged staff has succeeded in creating new sources of information. The Labor Desk is working in close conjunction with British SOE [Special Operations Executive] and French BRAL [Bureau de Recherches d'Action à Londres] as well as other governmental information services.

Besides the above mentioned contacts the Labor Desk has strengthened its ties with ITF [International Transport Federation], CGT [Conféderation Générale du Travail], British Labor Unions and the refugee representatives of labor groups from various continental countries.

(2) ITF. Besides its regular flow of intelligence from the majority of continental countries, the ITF has placed at the service of the Labor Desk valuable organizers and leaders who are attempting to increase the number of underground contacts on the Continent. Through the efforts of the ITF the services of Hans Jahn, organizer of the German Railway Union,[7] and Fano of the Italian Railway Workers

---

7. German exile Hans Jahn was also one of the most important informants of German emigrant Toni Sender. Sender was a former social democratic member of the Reichstag, who had organized an OSS-sponsored European Labor Project in the United States.

Union have been put at the disposal of the Labor Desk which arranged their transportation to North Africa and to Italy, where they are now engaged in contacting the railroad workers of Italy and German railroad workers who are not in Italy. […]

(3) The Three-Way Fund. Throughout this period the payments under the Three-Way Fund have been continued. Both Guigui, official CGT representative in London, and Laurent, CGT officer in Paris who had charge of the distribution of the fund, have recently acknowledged by letter the great benefit French resistance has received from payment of this subvention.

The French labor groups have been responsible for part of the material which OSS receives from French intelligence sources and in this respect the Three-Way Fund has proved extremely helpful.

Plans for the active cooperation of CGT with the invading forces on and after D Day have been worked out in detail with CGT representatives in London. Preliminary instructions have been transmitted to the representatives of CGT in the 17 organizational districts into which France has been divided. These representatives are carrying out these instructions from the London Labor Desk and are preparing to comp[ly] with further demands of the Desk.

(4) Mission Varlin. This is a plan conceived as a joint American and British operation working through the machinery and with the active cooperation of CGT. The United States is represented by the Labor Desk of OSS, the British by SOE, and the French by BRAL and the CGT.

The object of the Mission is briefly as follows:

Through its existing underground machinery of CGT under the direction of its Paris Committee [we] will seek to expand and improve its channels of communication with French workers in Germany who at present are organized in Stalags.[8] They will seek to achieve a maximum penetration of the Stalags so as to bring all trustworthy Frenchmen in Germany within their network. Through this work it is hoped to create a network of information which will extend throughout Germany. The attempt is being made from Great Britian and from the Swiss border.

Two French bodies recruited by OSS Labor Desk in North Africa have been transported to England by the Labor Section and have received training through BRAL and CGT for the past month and a half. When the training of the bodies had been completed, SOE arranged a Reception Committee which was to meet the bodies in France during the month of December. Unfortunately the weather was so bad that the attempt to send the men into France was abandoned until the

---

8. I.e., labor camps.

January moon period. It is expected that the project will be in actual operation some time during January 1944.

(5) Faust B. Plans have been arranged for the reception and training of the recruits from the United States for the Faust B project. The object of this project is to contact reliable German underground labor groups and thus create a network of informants throughout Germany. [...] Due to the feeling of expectancy caused by the imminence of the opening of the second front, the London Labor Desk is urging the prompt transportation of recruits now in the United States over to Great Britain so that they may be on hand for use at the time of the invasion.

In conjunction with this project the Labor Desk in London has been collecting information regarding materials and documents needed for the use of our agents in enemy countries. This information is also being forwarded to Washington.

The Labor Section in Washington now has 17 recruits for the Faust Projects in advanced stages of training. The Faust recruits will complete their SI-SO [Secret Intelligence-Special Operations] training on January 21,[9] and in response to urgent requests recently received, ten of them will be shipped to the London Labor Desk.

[...]

Labor Desk in North Africa

Operations

During the past two months several of the plans discussed with General Donovan in North Africa have been put into effect by the Labor Desk in NATO. The operations have been handicapped by a number of factors, including shortages of instructor and staff personnel, insufficiency of training facilities, difficulties of transportation and unavailability of necessary equipment. These obstacles are being remedie[d] but the process is slow and the conditions of work remain adverse. Nevertheless, considerable progress has been made in carrying past plans into operational stages as well as in blueprinting and making painstaking preparations for future operations.

The activities in NATO are briefly summarized below under the various project titles that have been assigned:

(1) "Heine" Project[10]: This project was suggested by General Donovan while in Algiers during the past summer. In essence, it consists of sending officials of the strongly organized International Transport Workers Federation into northern Italy for promoting resistance among the railroad workers there and spreading

---

9. Since September 1943, OSS agents in the Labor Branch had not only been trained in intelligence gathering but also in the conduct of special and subversive operations.

10. This project was named after Hans Heine, a German exile who collaborated with the OSS in London.

dissatisfaction among the German railroad workers themselves. Two officials of the ITF spent a number of weeks in Algiers training agent personnel for this penetration. At present they are both at our advance base in Bari, one having arrived at the end of November and the other at the end of December. They immediately established contact with emissaries coming through the German lines. One of them who speaks Italian fluently has studied the Italian situation itself at first hand and also acquired information from government representatives interested in labor problems. It appears that although the Northern Italian railway workers have a functioning organization of considerable strength which we shall be able to use, there is considerable difficulty at the moment in establishing contact with Italian railway workers in northern Italy since a great many of their leaders were shot or went underground after the fall of Mussolini. Hence, at the moment there is no evidence or accurate information about personalities in the north of Italy. Our agents are making every possible attempt to reestablish contacts with this group.

(2) "Stork" Project: This project contemplates agent penetration of Austria and Germany by infiltration from Partisan-held territory. Mr. Van Arkel is currently in Bari[11] where he has concluded the necessary arrangements with the Partisan representatives for a personal trip into Partisan territory for the conclusion of final arrangements with high elements of the Partisan command. The Bari office communicates directly from Algiers, with an alternative tie-in to Corsica. It is probable that a courier through the Partisans can be arranged; if not, other means will be found. Arrangements have been made for parachuting in additional supplies. There is a map tie-in with Algiers and their grid system can give any spot with precision. All arrangements have been completed for reproducing almost any German documents. It is intended that on the trip mentioned above Mr. Van Arkel will be accompanied by at least four qualified agents, who will remain in Yugoslavia when he returns to Italy, and by his Executive Officer Captain Govers, who will likewise remain at the Yugoslav base; the goal of the trip is some location as close as possible to the Headquarters of one of the Partisan Corps and as close as possible to the territory selected for operations.

The project has suffered no doubt by a temporary setback as a result of military action taken by the Germans, who have occupied one of the islands on which it was proposed to land, and were sighted by rescue planes off another. Other points will now have to be selected.

(3) "Redbird" Project: The Redbird Project is intended to make effective contact with a comprehensive Austrian political group called "Free Austria" by means of sending in a WT [wireless] operator. The original contact was established through Istanbul when a representative of this group, himself in the radio business, contacted one of the OSS representatives and plans were made to send in a

---

11. Gerhard van Arkel had established a Labor Desk in Algiers and was working as OSS labor representative in Bern.

radio transmitter. However, this bogged down in the middle and so far there is only an unverified guess that the radio transmitter was stalled in transit in Sofia. Accordingly, Algiers Labor Desk was contracted by Bari and, after a project to parachute a transmitter in to the group was shelved, it was decided to pursue the same objective through the Bari advance office of the Algiers Labor Desk. The Labor Desk representative now in Bari has selected a man suitable for the job. The project is marking time while doubts as to his availability are cleared up.

(4) "Sparrow" Project: The Sparrow Project is intended to effect physical contact with extremely high-placed Hungarian officials with whom the Bern office has long been in relatively intimate association.[12] It is intended to convey an OSS Labor Section representative of sufficiently high rank through Partisan territory to a rendezvous agreed upon with a Hungarian General with whom conversations are to be held.[13] Arrangements are now in process for selecting the appropriate officer.

(5) "Faust" Project: The training and recruiting of German and French-speaking personnel, both for penetration teams and for use in various capacities with the invasion army, has been carried forward in NATO. [...] The recruiting efforts in this country have been pushed vigorously. Four agent recruits are on their way to join the 17 already in NATO.

...[14]

Labor Desk in Sweden

Operations

The representative of the Labor Desk arrived in Stockholm during the early part of June 1943.[15]

On June 21 we received our first report and periodically thereafter on the average of at least every two weeks we received further reports covering his activities. His accomplishments in brief during his operations were as follows:

(1) He made contact with the leading figures of the international trade unions and the Swedish trade unions and in this connection established a working relationship with the head of the ITF in Stockholm.[16] The transport reports which have heretofore been made available to us through the ITF are still being provided through these same channels.

---

12. The most important contact was Lieutenant Colonel Otto von Hatz, the Hungarian military attaché in Turkey.

13. The ultimate goal of the project, the withdrawal of Hungary from the war, never came about. Yet, the OSS was able to gather Hungarian intelligence from within the Nazi empire.

14. The omitted paragraphs deal with labor projects in Greece and Yugoslavia.

15. This is a reference to Mr. Dorfmann who together with Miss Traugott was in charge of labor matters in the Stockholm outpost of the OSS.

16. This is a reference to Charles Lindley.

(2) He made contact with and was engaged in perfecting projects for penetrating Germany in collaboration with the leading German trade unionists in exile in Sweden.[17] Through these same sources he was receiving reports from recent emigres from enemy territory with whom those refugee elements were in contact.

(3) He was likewise in touch with the responsible leaders of Hungarian, Polish, Norwegian and Austrian refugee trade unionist groups.

(4) In his contact with the Swedish Seamen's Union he operated the Swedish end of our Ship Observer Project, interviewing selected seamen of the Swedish boats which stopped at enemy ports.

(5) Through the trade union contacts and the refugee elements, channels of communication were being perfected through which information concerning conditions in Germany and German-occupied countries was received in the form of (a) chain letters in innocuous code, [18] and (b) spot reports from travellers, seamen, and people crossing the border illegally.[19]

(6) Mr. Victor Sjaholm, the Railway Labor Executives Association representative who went to Sweden worked very closely with our representative for the purpose of developing contacts with the railway workers of enemy and enemy-occupied countries by means of Sweden and with the help of the Swedish railway workers group. Although his original mission has been completed, he has been asked by the American Legation to remain there to assist them in matters in which they are concerned.

Plans were being formulated for physical penetration from Sweden when all activity and all active operations were suspended in the latter part of October 1943 when, on a trip to London, our representative met with a fatal accident.
...[20]

Bern

From time to time the Labor Desk has communicated to our Bern representative[21] the names of various figures formerly active in trade union circles many of whom were thought would be of aid to him because of previous underground experience and contacts leading into enemy territory. Bern has indicated in many cables that these persons have been and are extremely helpful to him and are collaborating with him in definite projects for penetrating Austria, Hungary and

---

17. This was in particular August Enderle, a member of the Sozialistische Arbeiterpartei [SAP, Socialist Workers Party], who was very close to Willy Brandt, the SPD Secretary.

18. According to former members of the International Transport Workers Federation [ITF], these anti-Nazi letters were usually concealed as Deutsche Bank correspondence, carried over the Swedish border by seamen and mailed within Germany to Deutsche Bank customers.

19. These interviews were systematically initiated and carried out by August Enderle for the ITF.

20. The omitted passage deals with organizational details and with operations of the labor desk in Lisbon.

21. I.e., Gerhard (Gary) van Arkel.

Germany. One of these projects is about to be activated having progressed to the point of arranging a rendezvous. The Labor Section through its Bari, London and Algiers representatives is keeping in close touch with developments in Bern with a view to coordinating the activities of the Labor Section and its field offices with Bern.

Document 34 · 27 January 1944

Telegram from Allen W. Dulles (OSS Bern) to OSS Washington: Report on an Opposition Group Called "Breakers"[1]

TOR:28/1/44

#1888–9. The German oppositional group, called Breakers,[2] is composed of various intellectuals from certain military and Government circles. They have loose organization among themselves. Luke's surname is John [Otto John] and [we] have been given to understand that he is one of 659's [Canaris's] men for Spain and Portugal,[3] intended especially for Anglo-Saxon contacts. [...] You may be interested to know that for the most part, Breakers maintain their foreign contacts and communications through 659 organization[4] and both our 512 [Hans Bernd Gisevius] and Gorter [Eduard Waetjen] act as intermediaries here in Bern.[5] (Note from 110 [Allen Dulles]: I quite understand that you may doubt the foregoing statement but I am convinced of its accuracy after examining the situation for a period of months.)

---

1. NA, RG 226, Entry 146, Box 235, Folder 3296.

2. OSS code name given by Allen W. Dulles.

3. Otto John's position as a legal adviser for the Lufthansa served him as cover for work with the Abwehr, the German Military Intelligence headed by Admiral Canaris.

4. I.e., the Abwehr.

5. Beginning in early 1943, Hans Bernd Gisevius, at one time official of the Gestapo and the Reichsinnenministerium (Ministry of the Interior) and in 1943 a prominent member of the anti-Nazi resistance, had established close working contacts with Allen W. Dulles in Bern. When it became more and more difficult in the course of 1943 to shuttle between Germany and Switzerland, Eduard Waetjen took over Gisevius' job as a courier. At that time, lawyer Waetjen, an Abwehr man, was stationed in Zurich under the cover of a member of the German Consulate.

For a number of reasons, I have not talked with Zulu [British intelligence] about the Breaker's situation at this particular time, and pending further developments I recommend that you also refrain from doing so on the basis of information in my messages.

Document 35 · 27 January 1944

Telegram from Allen W. Dulles (OSS Bern) to OSS Washington: Political Orientation of the "Breakers" Movement[1]

SECRET

TOR: 1/28/44 6:40 am

#1890–3. To Carib and Jackpot, with reference to your #1051. We have at the present time, by means of Gorter [Eduard Waetjen],[2] secured a line to Breakers which we think can be used now for staying in close touch with events. Since any slight break would be disastrous, no constructive purpose would be served by cabling particulars. The Breakers contain 3 tendencies, on the whole, i.e., evolutionary, revolutionary, and military. The 1st of these factions takes the stand that, in the face of history and the people, complete responsibility should be shouldered to the grim conclusion by the leader and his cohorts. In general, the other two groups think that drastic action should be taken to get rid of the leader, and that a new government should be organized before the fighting stops so that it could thereupon join in the negotiations. In spite of these contrary opinions, these groups keep in touch and are very eager to obtain political ammunition from our side. They consider this to be sadly wanting, and they wish it to reinforce their movement at the present time and following the collapse, as well. Western orientation is preferred by the Breakers over Eastern orientation, but they fear that their nation is being directed by events toward the influence of the East. They are in favour of extensive social changes.

---

1. NA, RG 226, Entry 134, Box 228, Folder 1368.
2. See document [34]

Are you able to check, in an extremely judicious manner, the word which we have received that an associate of Gorter, whose name is Luke [Otto John], has been in contact with Bearcat [Willard L. Beaulac] and Rocky [Tony Graham-Meingott]³. It is very likely that this is exceedingly secret. I am informed by Gorter that he and his friends are inclined to doubt the encouragement which Luke has received from Rocky regarding the idea that negotiations would be facilitated by putting the Military in power and changing the government.

I would appreciate hearing of any indication with which you could supply me regarding what you would be interested in achieving via the Breakers, and could be pursued effectively at this time. I do not understand what our policy is and what offers, if any, we could give to any resistance movement.

Document 36 · 4 February 1944

Telegram from Allen W. Dulles (OSS Bern) to OSS Washington: Leading Members of the "Breakers"¹

SECRET

TOR: 2/4/44 9:10 pm

#1965–#1966. To Carib and Jackpot. The names listed below may possibly be of interest with reference to my wires on the subject of Breakers:

1. The socialist leader, Leuschner, previously the Minister of Interior in Hesse.

2. General Oster who was previously 659's [Admiral Canaris's] right-hand man. Some months back, he was taken into custody by the Gestapo but was

---

3. Since 1943, Otto John had been in contact with the American Chargé d' Affaires in Madrid, Willard L. Beaulac. It had been John's idea to use the Madrid connection as a channel for the German resistance (Carl Goerdeler and others) in order to get in touch with the Americans. While Beaulac tried to approach his superiors in the State Department, all his letters remained unanswered. The second contact, with British Intelligence Officer Graham-Meingott, was likewise unsuccessful.

1. NA, RG 226, Entry 138, Box 2.

released.[2] However, he has been kept under watch. I am informed that Keitel has just discharged him officially.[3]

3. The former Mayor [of] Leipzig, Goerdler [Goerdeler]. He is a capable organizer.

The Breakers are inclined to be leftish and I understand that they feel that someone like No. 1 [Leuschner] would be a more acceptable kind of person, if it is assumed that neither the Communists nor the military dominate the transition period.

Document 37a · 28 February 1944

Memorandum from Professor Karl Brandt[1]
to OSS Director William J. Donovan:
Advantages of the Herman Plan

TOP SECRET

Upon your request I am giving hereafter my critical evaluation of the Herman Plan[2] with which I became familiar today after perusal of the document you handed to me.[3] As a background for what follows I want to mention that according to my continuous analysis of the economic situation inside the continental

---

2. Hans Oster, Chief of Staff to Admiral Canaris and a staunch opponent of Hitler, had passed on to the Allies warnings concerning German invasion plans as early as 1939 and 1940. In April 1943 he was temporarily arrested and suspended from office. The Gestapo accused him of shielding an operation to smuggle Jews out of Germany.

3. On 16 December 1943, Field Marshal Wilhelm Keitel, Chief of Staff of the OKW, declared that Oster should have no further contacts with members of the Abwehr.

1. NA, RG 226, Entry 190, M 1462, Roll 52, Frames 333–343. During World War II, German exile Karl Brandt prepared detailed reports on behalf of the Board of Economic Warfare and the OSS. His studies on economic issues and methods of bombing attacks against Germany were much appreciated by William J. Donovan. Some of his reports also went to the OSS Foreign Nationalities Branch.

2. Document [31].

3. Brandt who was living in Stanford, California, happened to be in New York for business reasons on 28 February 1944. He wrote this memorandum within a few hours in the OSS office at Rockefeller Plaza. Unknown to Brandt and the OSS, Moltke had already been arrested in January while preparing for another visit to Istanbul.

fortress I am convinced that the resources at the disposal of the enemy are despite progressive bombing still large enough for carrying on the battle until the fall of 1945 and that, consequently, with the undiminished strength of the enemy's ground forces it is the greatest probability that far in excess of 500,000 American boys will have died in battle before the fortress will fall by military assault only.[4] Moreover, I deem it probable that in that case a prostrate and battered continent may ultimately fall into a definitely pro-Russian orientation.

Nature of the Plan

In my appraisal the plan represents the offer by the most respectable revolutionary group inside Germany, lodged in vital strategic positions, to assist the efforts of the Anglo-American Allies at cracking the fortress from the outside by a judicial and discriminative paralization [paralysation] of resistance from the inside with the exclusive purpose to accomplish thereby Anglo-American occupation leaving Russian forces outside.

The Merits of the Plan

If the Anglo-American forces have to shoot it out with the German Army to the last, there are two major alternative courses of events:

1) If all goes extremely well, the war will end either in the Fall of 1944, or, much more likely, by the Spring or Summer of 1945. However, Western Europe and Germany will in all likelihood be devastated to such an extent that by the immeasurable moral and social erosion and the material destruction alone one of the key positions of the Western World will be lost. It is already perceptible that the incessant bombing and obliteration of metropolitan areas creates huge masses of a proletariat of the bombed-out middle-class and all of labor. Inevitably the population not only in Germany but also adjacent countries will potentially lean toward a Soviet society which offers the immense opportunity for Russia to utilize passively this tendency against Anglo-American interests. What is much worse than this deterioration under the impact of the battering of the Fortress, Himmler's Gestapo, which in due time will reach a strength exceeding 3,000,000 of the most brutal killers the world has ever seen,[5] will inevitably have proceeded to "liquidate" systematically all and every Germans who by their moral stamina and personality could possibly be the nucleus of a rehabilitated future Germany which would fit into the fabric of a strong but peaceful Western World. Thus even

---

4. During World War II the United States lost some 400,000 soldiers in all theaters of war.

5. The Gestapo consisted of 45,000 men. Brandt's number does not include the military wing of the SS, the so-called Waffen-SS.

if the American losses in lives should be relatively small, the Continent would probably be lost when it is won.

2) If, on the other hand, all does not go well with the invasion, one or several huge beachheads with all the troops and material invested will be thrown into the sea with the natural resurgence of the resistance by the German Army. In this case, the war would be protracted, but by gradual deterioration of the material resources and the complete devastation of the substance of all the peole who still own a residual of modest means of livelihood would proceed until the point of the inevitable surrender of the Army. In this slow process the political and social credo of the German people would shift like the cargo on a vessel in a hurricane. All the people who are the victims of the Nazis as well as their active collaborators will under the leadership of their generals (particularly the Russo-phile wing) grab the opportunity of taking revenge against the naturally hated Allies who annihilated all their cities by forming an independent sovereign Soviet Republic with an army and seeking admission as a member in the Soviet Union.

In view of these alternative courses for exclusively military assault the Herman Plan offers to short-circuit the war to the necessary and, namely the defeat of the German Army and the complete military occupation of all of Germany as well as the liberation of all German-occupied territory west of a further advanced Russian front. It sets no conditions but with a cool realism begins with the acceptance of the inevitability of the military defeat, in fact it recognizes the necessity of the defeat of the German Army and the destruction of its power for the sake of a survival of Germany. The authors of the Plan visualize correctly that the vicious circle of the lust for expensive conquest inherent in this institution with its overwhelming potential power and its penetration into the political and economic fields must be broken by its conspicuous defeat.

The real test that this plan does definitely not represent a slick ruse manoeuvered by imperialists in the General Staff or Nazi chieftains lies in the absence of any such military conditions as any plan by Hitler's generals would inevitably try to stipulate. By virtue of this fact alone I give full credence to the genuineness and sincerity of the efforts evidenced by the document I have read.

The Group Behind the Plan

The origin and psychology of this group of whose existence I have been well aware[6] and whose activity toward tangible ends began in the Summer of 1939 dates back toward the years of agony in the latter part of World War I. The members of this group carry on in the tradition of many splendid men, particularly among the young generation of 1914 which fought as soldiers and young officers

---

6. Ever since the 1930s, Brandt had been in touch with oppositional circles in Germany. In 1939/1940, in particular, he had met with German diplomat Adam von Trott zu Solz on American soil. Furthermore, Hamilton Fish Armstrong, the editor of Foreign Affairs, kept him informed about the internal situation in Germany.

in the trenches of the First World War and from the profound and tragic experience derived the conviction of the necessity and the possibility of freeing Germany for the sake of Western civilization from the insane ambitions of the aggressive imperialists in the Army, the heavy industries and among the ranks of the Junkers. Most of them are men of an alert intelligence and a deep understanding of the moral foundation of the West and all of them comprise the English-speaking world most definitely under that concept. Their members are not belonging to any special class, social stratum or profession, but are found among labor leaders as well as the intelligentsia, among conservatives and socialists, Catholics and Protestants, businessmen and civil servants. What unites these people is the thorough grasp of the historical tragedy of their nation and their last desperate effort to prevent at the very risk of their and their entire families' lives the annihilation of all that to them means Germany and the heritage of generations. Since all of them stand ultimately—even those who never attend Church or confess adherence to it—on the ground of Christian ethics and thereby are tied into the West, they also want to prevent that either by trying to avert defeat or after defeat Germany will be absorbed into the Russian orbit. These men are culturally as much at home in England, Holland, Switzerland, Sweden or in general in Western Europe as they are in Germany, while Russia means to them exactly as much as Japan or China does to the people in Iowa. Thus these people have for the last twenty years been widely scattered but genuine parts of the warp and weft of the German nation. The dire peril and real agony of eleven years of tyranny and more than four years of war have screened and sifted them out, hardened them and driven them into subtle clandestine organizations. I am unable to write down a list of names, because I have not had many occasions to lift the veil of their secrecy and do not know any more who among their ranks was lost by death or other changes. In fact, it has always been one of the chief principles of protection within this group that one person never knew more than a few trusted members of the whole group, which I strongly urge to respect because it is the only conceivable way of avoiding the mass liquidation of all of them whenever, by accident or carelessness, or resourcefulness of the Gestapo, some identities are revealed. But I am thoroughly convinced that this highly select and strategically located group is incomparably more worthy of full consideration than any other so-called underground movement, because it is neither tainted with left-wing radical conformism nor with any particle of transformed Nazi ideologies, but in contrast represents, as all democratic groups, people of widely differing shades of political ideas while they are united in the last essential convictions.

Alternatives to the Herman Plan

In an attempt to determine the practical value of the Plan, it is imperative to check on potential alternative courses of action. In trying to review such alternatives, the only one that I can possibly think of would roughly be as follows: The Allies could take the initiative to contact certain members of the German General

Staff who are known to represent merely professional military leadership and thought and of whom one could expect that like Ludendorff in August 1918 they would try to terminate hostilities[7] before or at the moment when the complete deterioration of the battle position of the German Army becomes inevitable. Such negotiations could naturally be started in many places, such as Lisbon, Stockholm or Switzerland[8] or elsewhere at any moment. The weakness would lie in the fact that the only strategy in such talks would consist of using threats and presenting in consecutive stages one ultimatum after the other. In order to make it tempting at all to lay down arms, the Allies would inevitably be bound to offer or to grant upon demand from the German side certain conditions. I venture to imagine the conditions which alone would, in my opinion, persuade any such emissaries of the German General Staff to consider or accept surrender. Such conditions would be the unilateral Anglo-American occupation of all of Germany and the guarantee that Russian armies would be kept by Anglo-American troops as well as written American and British commitment be kept [sic] outside the German borders. Moreover, the German General Staff would want to have a binding commitment that Anglo-American Military Government would under no circumstances abuse its absolute power of policing for a period of "blood-letting", an idea unfortunately so dear to the heart of American columnists, magazine editors (*Fortune!, Life, Time!*) which has been very effectively publicized throughout Germany. It is obvious that any such plan would suffer from the deadly constructive weakness that its very conception involves treachery against our great ally, the Russian people and therefore must remain still-born. On the German side the practically impossible plan has still much greater weaknesses due to the fact that one has to deal with a formally but not truly uniform group in which the Nazi gangsters have too tight a grip on those personalities who could possibly arrive at a sensible agreement with the Allies. Moreover, since military expediency would be the exclusive consideration for accepting surrender the only possible timing would be so late that little would be won for either side.

Discarding this only conceivable alternative as impracticable and non-profitable, the Herman Plan appears so much the more ingenious.

Hence it is my considered opinon that this plan deserves to be given most serious and immediate full consideration for political decision and forthright action:

1. as the only existing and very last chance to soften the Fortress progressively from the inside as the invasion is proceeding from the West,
2. as the only available and valid assurance that the high risk of the loss of hundreds of thousands of American lives and extreme delays of the final decision can be reduced to a bearable limit,

---

7. See also document [19a].

8. I.e., neutral places in Europe. The OSS had outposts in the capitals of Portugal, Sweden and Switzerland.

3. as the only practicable and politically permissable way to keep Russia out of Central Europe,

4. as the exclusive opportunity of having available as the occupation is accomplished a strong and reliable framework of German personnel inside the country which not only guarantees successful operation of military government, but at the same time represents a victorious new leadership in Germany which has defeated the Nazis, broken the German Army and established vital cooperation with the American and British people.

If such consideration as recommended should be given this plan, it is by no means certain yet that its execution will have any real effect upon the course of military events. Being a plan for action, its value of realization must be tested at first thoroughly and with the greatest dispatch. If after that it should still be considered as practicable, everything will nevertheless depend on the competence of carrying it out on the German as well as the Allied side. Thus it is far from a surefire method for successful invasion and requires to be tackled with courage and full realization of the jeopardy and risk to the very end.

If it should ultimately fail the full justification for the undertaking must lie in the fact that the responsible statesmen have done the humanly possible in trying to realize the opportunity for saving their peoples the otherwise inevitable tragic sacrifices.

Recommendations for Procedure

Once the decision has been reached to pursue the plan, it will be necessary to test and get assurance as to the following points.

1) The strength and strategic distribution of the group inside the Fortress.

2) The military resources including all the auxiliary and secondary resources under its reach or command.

It will not be possible nor is it advisable to attempt to obtain complete information concerning 1) and 2) for blueprints, diagrams or to get any records in detail. The contact man should, however, give the correct proportions and range of their forces. If the few key personalities which they reveal should have the proper weight and caliber and deserve the confidence their word must be trusted because it is they who put the lives of a large and immensely valuable group of people at stake at any moment. In fact it is my impression that the quality of not more than two or three leading men should be considered as sufficient guarantee because if it is not, the compilation of any number of names will in reality not add an iota of additional security.

3) the question must be posed how the group contemplates to meet and avert the chief jeopardy to the plan, namely,

a) the collapse of the Eastern German front by weakening of the divisions and the equiment there and the possibly resulting vicious assault by the Russian armies,

b) the collapse of the Eastern German front upon the initiative of the Russophile group inside the General Staff and the officer corps to play the same game as the Herman group but by collaboration with the Russians instead of with the Allies,

c) the sudden simultaneous abandonment of resistance on all fronts, including the Russian one, after a sudden show-down inside the General Staff under the impact of a spontaneous palace revolution.

Not all these questions can possibly be answered to full satisfaction, yet the nature of the answers will indicate how realistic the leaders of the group are or at least if they should not have contemplated such eventualities the questions will force them to close the last holes in their plans.

4) The question should be posed how the group plans to prohibit the sudden liquidation of all potential cooperating men by Himmler.

5) The question should be posed what security measures are contemplated to prohibit the Gestapo from getting behind the agreements of action between the Allied General Staff and the Herman group and the exploitation of such knowledge by the German Army without wholesale arrests of members of the group for the sake of getting more and more information and giving the Herman group more rope.

6) Does the group contemplate and is it determined to eliminate the key figures inside SS or regular Army officer corps or otherwise who jeopardize the entire plan either as prophylaxis or when and if the threat becomes imminent? If they do not, what are the reasons for refraining from premeditating such protective action?

7) What sort of major paralyzing or assisting actions are contemplated? (this question should be posed without any additional suggestive questions in order to check how elaborate and specific the plans of the group have already become.)

Conclusion

Supposed that all these questions should be answered to the satisfaction of our Chiefs of Staff, it would be my recommendation that one should establish without delay secure headquarters for the liaison officers of the group, dispatch to them the necessary liaison officers on our side and start to work out with them the complete strategy for the key actions which the Herman group is committed to engineer and manage inside the Fortress. As the machinery begins to work, it would be advisable to start with certain limited and cautious test actions in various expedient theaters of war which are inconspicuous for the Gestapo but sufficiently clear-cut to find out whether the machine works or, if it does not, to spot the defects. In general, it is my convicton that even if one sets the plan fully into motion, there is no need whatsoever to endanger our military operations by it. I would recommend that no major tactical operation should ever be based completely on the assumption that the Herman group can safely deliver what is committed to it. On the contrary, the invading generals should in all cases operate under the assumption that the assisting Herman group action will fail but should be prepared to exploit in full any opportunity created by the group's action.

Document 37b · 15 March 1944

Memorandum from William L. Langer (OSS Research and Analysis Branch) to OSS Director William J. Donovan: Dangers of the Herman Plan[1]

TOP SECRET

Herman Plan

I read the subject plan and its various attachments[2] in your office yesterday afternoon. Since it raises a number of questions of very wide scope one really ought to have it at hand before attempting any criticism of it. Nevertheless, I should like to set down a few points which occur to me. They are only a few because I think many of the thoughts that would occur to any reader of the plan are very effectively dealt with in the Memorandum from Karl Brandt.

---

1. NA, RG 226, Entry 110, Box 47, Folder 3.

2. The Herman file included Moltke's letter to Kirk as well as various assessments by members of the OSS, among them documents [32] and [37a] by Alfred Schwarz and Karl Brandt. William J. Donovan argued in his memorandum that the integrity of Herman's group should be checked before taking any further steps. Hugh Wilson, a member of the OSS planning group, suggested different American negotiators instead of Alexander Kirk who had refused to communicate with the German opposition. Whitney H. Shepardson, Chief of the OSS Secret Intelligence Branch, gave biographical background information on several members of the Herman group. However, he did not trust Adam von Trott zu Solz. Furthermore, Irving H. Sherman, a leading member of the OSS Counterintelligence Branch, emphasized that the plan should be studied in the light of its possibly being "phony" or a "plant" to split the Allies from Russia.

(1) The ABC of the whole matter would be, of course, to determine the size and nature of the organization in Germany supposedly backing this plan. I have just reread the study made by our staff last December on the "German and Austrian Underground Movements" (R&A #992.1).[3] Members of our staff had not at that time and have not up to the present discovered any evidence to support the contention that there is a fairly large, well organized and influential opposition group such as the Herman Plan suggests. There is some slight evidence for the existence of a basically military opposition organization said to be headed by a general of high rank.[4] This claims to have a following of diplomats, junkers, big industrialists and even a few of the Gestapo. Its orientation is anti-Communist and its main objective a united non-Nazi Germany. Possibly this is the same group supposedly represented by Herman. Personally, I find it extremely difficult to believe that such an opposition organization exists or, if it does, that this opposition is in a sufficiently strong position to give orders and have them carried out. Without entering into a lot of detail, I am still of the opinion that nothing can be done in Germany until the Nazi regime collapses and that no such collapse is probable in the immediate future unless the armies are defeated decisively. It is at least conceivable that under such circumstances an opposition group like the one described might succeed in seizing power though it is also conceivable that the military disintegration may take place piece-meal with various generals making separate arrangements with their enemies.[5]

(2) It goes almost without saying that certain elements or groups in Germany must be thinking in terms of surrender to the British and Americans in order to avoid being overrun by the Bolshevik armies. It is certainly true that for a very long time the upper and middle classes in Germany have been divided between those of western orientation and those of eastern orientation. By and large, I should say that dislike and distrust of Russia outweighed hostility to the Anglo-Saxon world, though recent intelligence would seem to indicate that the middle classes which were the chief supporters of the western orientation have become in a measure Bolshevized through heavy losses by air bombardment. I should rather expect, though, that the larger landholders and the military caste would still lean toward the west rather than toward the east because the west would hold some promise of revival and independent action while the domination of Russia on the continent would mean indefinite subordination to a great military power. My own feeling is that the Anglo-American forces can still count on some measure of sympathy and support and that they could even strengthen their hold if they were able to offer the Germans something more promising than abject and complete surrender.

---

3. Not printed; for an earlier version of this report, see document [22].

4. I.e., General Ludwig Beck.

5. For a similar estimate of the situation by R&A see document [19b].

(3) Coming back to the Herman Plan, it is clear that the main objective of its supporters is to hold a pretty generous line against the Russians in the east and to enlist the British and Americans in the defense of Germany against the Bolsheviks. This is a well-worn theme which by this time has become pretty much hackneyed. It seems to me that it would be a very grave mistake to enter upon any such plan without full knowledge and agreement from the Russians.[6] There is no denying the fact that they are the greatest land power in Europe and that there is nothing either the British or the Americans can do to alter that fact. My own conviction is that the present Russian government is prepared to play ball but is equally prepared and determined to execute a volte-face if the British and Americans do not play fair. In this connection, I am convinced that from every point of view they have much greater possibility of independent action than have the western powers.

(4) I do not believe that the Herman group is strong enough to really make a substantial contribution. As a matter of fact, this group itself states that it can be of no service unless the western powers make an all-out effort which would lead to victory. It may be that after a successful invasion of western Europe a group of this type could emerge and serve a very useful purpose in reducing the length of the campaign and the loss of life, but it seems to me that it would do this in any event and in its own interests so that there is no sense in our obligating ourselves. Certainly it would be a vast mistake for any military commander to count upon such inside aid and to modify his plans accordingly. The whole thing appears to me to involve a great deal of risk for us without any commensurate gain.

(5) My recommendations would be:

a. To keep the wires open and find out as much as possible about the constitution and prospects of this group;
b. To inform the Russian government that we have been approached in this way but do not propose to commit ourselves excepting in agreement with the Allied powers;
c. If agreeable to Russia and Britain, to give such aid and comfort as may be possible to the group with a view to using it later as a nucleus for a post-Nazi government;
d. To lay all military plans as though this group did not exist.

William L. Langer
Director, Branch of Research
and Analysis

---

6. At the Tehran Conference of 28 November to 1 December 1943, the three main Allies had confirmed their pledge not to conclude seperate peace agreements with Germany. Also, they had promised to inform each other about any German peace feelers. Previously on 1 January 1942, on the occasion of the so-called Arcadia Conference between Roosevelt and Churchill in Washington, D.C., the Allies had committed themselves not to make a seperate armistice or peace with the enemy.

Document 37c · 3 April 1944

Memorandum by the OSS Planning Group[1]:
Rejection of the Herman Plan[2]

TOP SECRET

Subject: Herman Plan

1. Papers relating to this plan were considered at a meeting of the Planning Group this morning, 3 April, 1944, together with your draft of a memorandum for the Joint Chiefs of Staff dated 2 April 1944.[3] The Planning Group had the advantage of discussion with Mr. Macfarland in order to clear up with him certain points of fact.

2. Responsive to your request for comment, the following is submitted:

a. The Group feels that if any submission is to be made to the Joint Chiefs of Staff, it is undesirable to make submission in present form, since (a) several of the accompanying papers are not self-explanatory, in some instances containing neither the name of the addressee or the name of the writer; and (b) dates of certain of these attendant papers do not appear. It becomes difficult, therefore, to see these papers in their relationship to each other. Indeed, in spite of the background of the Planning Group, it was necessary to ask Mr. Macfarland to identify several of the papers.

b. The dossier contains a letter addressed to Mr. Kirk, which Mr. Macfarland has stated was signed by Herman.[4] This letter, and various references to Mr. Kirk

---

1. NA, RG 226, Entry 190, M 1462, Roll 52, Frames 391–393; Heideking/Mauch, Herman-Dossier, pp. 621–623. The Planning Group was set up to coordinate OSS covert action operations with those of the military, i.e., that is to say the Joint Chiefs of Staff. Its members were appointed by the Secretary of State, the Army, and the Navy. Four of them, including the Group's chairman, were elected by the Director of the OSS.

2. This memorandum was authored by Whitney H. Shepardson, at the time Acting Chairman of the OSS Planning Group.

3. Not printed. In this draft memorandum Donovan had recommended to inform the Joint Chiefs of Staff about the Herman Plan and to pass the information concerning the contacts in Turkey to the Soviets.

4. Not printed; see also document [32].

in other papers, indicates [sic] very great knowledge on his part of the plan and of discussions connected with it than is the case. Mr. Kirk was personally unwilling to play any part in it and did not wish his name to appear in this matter in any shape or form. To carry out his wishes and to protect him from any possible misunderstandings of his position, by the Department of State and/or by the Joint Chiefs of Staff, it is felt by the Planning Group that every reference of any kind of description to Mr. Kirk should be omitted.

3. It is recommended that the plan be not transmitted to the Joint Chiefs at this time because,

   a. A careful study of the plan indicates that there is no action of a military character which the Joint Chiefs could take upon it.
   b. If the Group should be employed further, or exploited further by OSS, any discussion of this matter might impair such exploitation.
   c. The Planning Group feels, and Mr. Macfarland confirms, that these discussions are tenuous in making the statement of the situation rendered more precise before being brought to the attention of the Joint Chiefs.

4. Note being taken of the fact that the expose and attendant papers are premised upon feelings of the Russians and hostility toward them, and the preparation of plans whereby Germany might be occupied by the "Anglo-Saxons" with the Russians being held away from Germany on a military line, Tilsit-Lene [Tilsit-Lemberg], the Planning Group feels that this paper would be unacceptable to the Russians in the extreme and might cause damage to the group in the hands of the Russians without producing thereby any military benefit.

5. *It is therefore recommended* that Mr. Macfarland be instructed to continue his enterprise on an exploratory and informal basis and that he be given the mission to concentrate upon the possibility of using the Herman connections in some way as to assist the invasion effort without any regard whatsoever for any further consideration such as the future of Europe or the future of Germany. That, in particular, he be instructed to play upon this group as a possible instrument of double agents or in any way coldly calculated to promote the success of the invasion, without any regard whatsoever for the German individuals involved, their safety, personal relations to them, or the ultimate effect upon Germany once the invasion has succeeded. The Group feels that this is a proper and authorized function of OSS which can be carried on without reference either to the Joint Chiefs of Staff or to the Department of State. If successful, these two agencies of government can be notified of results when the job is done.

Whitney Shepardson
Acting Chairman

Document 38 · 6 March 1944

Telegram from Allen W. Dulles (OSS Bern) to OSS Washington: Cooperation with the Free Germany Movement in Switzerland[1]

SECRET

TOR: 3/7/44 9:58 am
Corrected copy: 3/8/44 5:44 pm

#2319–2320. In reference to your #1279. 1. The so-called Swiss Section of the Moscow Committee mimeographs the *Freies Deutschland* [*Free Germany* (newspaper)] secretly here and the publication is circulated to some extent in Germany.[2] In addition, a short time ago 678[3] and I made arrangements to publish a booklet for distribution among soldiers and workers in the Reich through *Freies Deutschland* channels. We thought the booklet was highly valuable for general propaganda purposes. We maintain good liaison with this group through a cut-out and it is a splendid method of distributing surreptitious material to the north.

2. Iris[4] is not familiar with the event, as *Weltwoche*[5] reports it. However, it is not improbable that this took place and we are checking the report. At the close of September, an underground unit of German political emigres in France, whom we are assisting with funds through 394,[6] made arrangements for a jail-break at Castres Prison, in the city of Marseilles. Approximately 40 anti-nazi prisoners, of whom 9 were Germans, escaped. Perhaps this is the affair that was intended by the report. 110 [Allen W. Dulles] is well acquainted with *Weltwoche*'s editor.[7]

---

1. NA, RG 226, Entry 134, Box 341, Folder 1824.
2. See document [29].
3. See document [66].
4. Possibly Dulles's friend Mary Bancroft.
5. A Swiss newspaper printed in Zürich.
6. An OSS agent who was stationed in France, probably René Bertholet.
7. Karl von Schumacher.

Document 39 · 4 April 1944

Memorandum by OSS Istanbul Agents "Dogwood" [Alfred Schwarz] and "Magnolia" [Alexander Rüstow]: Secret Meetings Between German and Allied Emissaries[1]

SECRET

During a conversation which took place on March 3 between Sub-Source[2] and the Head of an important German bank institute (refer[r]ed to as "B" in this report),[3] Sub-Source was told by B, who had been in Switzerland some time before, that two distinct German groups were maintaining contacts with American representatives with a view to reaching an understanding for present and future collaboration between the Allies and the German opposition. Sub-Source credits B with fairly detailed knowledge of the contacts that have taken place, but himself was given only the following information:

1. *Prince Hohenlohe* contacted D. [Dulles] in the American Embassy at Bern.[4] In the course of the conversations D. suggested that the oppositional group represented by Hohenlohe should seek the collaboration of the former Reichsbank President, Schacht, who was regarded by the American side as a suitable candidate for the leadership of a movement of opposition.[5] The German negotiator objected to this idea on the grounds that Schacht had long been without influence or personal following

---

1. NA, RG 226, Entry 92, Box 592, Folder 3.
2. I.e., Alexander Rüstow (Magnolia).
3. This is probably a reference to Johannes Posth of the Deutsche Orient Bank in Istanbul.
4. The Dulles-Hohenlohe conversations (in the documents referred to as Bull-Pauls-talks) took place between January and April 1943. Dulles and Prince Max Ernst zu Hohenlohe-Langenburg were no strangers to each other as they had met before in Vienna in 1916. Although transcripts of these conversations exist, there have been controversies during the Cold War period over the authenticity of the documents, which reflected some pro-Nazi and anti-Semitic leanings on the side of Dulles.
5. There is no proof for this assertion. In the United States, Schacht was generally considered to be a strongly conservative, rather unreliable opponent of Hitler.

and would be no asset to the German opposition. In Schachts's stead the German side put forward the name of a well-known personage from Bremen who was known to the American negotiators and met with their approval. This personage was accordingly approached but was evidently unwilling to enter upon any discussions without official sanction, for he reported to the Party about the possibility of contacting American official personages at Bern and was duly authorized to follow up this possibility. Several meetings seem to have taken place, but could serve no useful purpose under the circumstances.

2. A more promising contact was made by a second oppositional group, which is backed by army circles and not associated with or authorized by the Party in any way.[6] The spokesman of this group was E. [Eduard] Waetjen, managing Director of the Syndikat fuer Aussenhandel G.m.b.H., who is reported to have been chosen for this mission mainly on the strength of his connection with the Rockefeller family (Waetjen's sister by this account is married to a member of the Rockefeller family). The proposals of this group were not made with political agreements or concessions in view, but aimed at military collaboration with the Allies. To provide Waetjen with a permanent motive for journeys to and from Switzerland, he was given a commercial appointment at the German consulate at Bern.[7]

Note[8]: The German group mentioned in para 2 is well known to our Department. Waetjen is a close associate of *Hermann* [sic; Helmuth James Graf von Moltke][9] who worked with him on the scheme of collaboration with the Allies which was last reported upon in our No. 281 of Dec. 30.[10] During several stays in Istanbul Waetjen was in contact with one of our collaborators, who had established our connection with Hermann and is maintaining contact with Hermann's group. The negotiations entered upon in Switzerland by Waetjen may well be conducted on behalf of Hermann's circle. Should this be so, it would be important for the further development of Hermann's scheme through our channel to ascertain whether any such contacts has [sic] actually been made with an American Department in Switzerland, and whether the German group which sought the contact is identical with that represented by Hermann. Similarly, the American Dept. in question would have to be informed of the present status of our negotiations with Hermann, and the form evolved for Hermann's proposals in the course of exchanges to-date. Our channels to Hermann's group are functioning, and a message to Hermann concerning prearranged talks with our Department is being despatched by special courier.[11]

----

6. This group was referred to by Dulles as the "Breakers." See in particular documents [34], [35] and [36].

7. This was a cover for Waetjen's connection with the Abwehr.

8. The following comment was made by OSS Washington.

9. See document [83b].

10. Not printed.

11. Moltke had already been arrested by the Gestapo in January 1944.

It is not impossible that B's journey to Switzerland was undertaken with the knowledge or even on behalf of von Papen in an effort to obtain information about German contacts with the Allies via Switzerland.[12] This is the more probable as B has served as an intermediary on a previous occasion, when Sub-Source approached him on behalf of our Department to deliver to v.P. [von Papen] a message from an American Delegate[13] and bring about a meeting between this American personage and v.P. The message was delivered and the meeting took place.

The purpose of the meeting sponsored by B was to ascertain the attitude of v.P. and his associates in the Reich towards a political scheme put forward by the American delegate. On his return from his recent journey to Germany, B conveyed to our Department the assent in principle of the German associates of v.P. to the proposals laid before them. In the absence of any instructions or authorization to proceed, our Department made no further move in the matter. B took the opportunity of his last conversation with Sub-Source about the response brought back by him and about the new German overtures in Switzerland, to ask Sub-Source whether our Department intended to resume direct contact with the Ambassador, as the time was considered ripe for action. As it is highly likely that after B.'s forthcoming report to v.P. about his German mission our Department will receive a communication of some sort via B. and Sub-Source, our Dept. will require some indication of the official Allied attitude to the exchanges that have taken place to date. It is necessary to add that Sub-Source is fully aware that the character and scope of our Department's functions rule out entirely any political initiatives or engagements.

---

12. On von Papen see documents [24a], [24b] and [24c].
13. I.e., Theodore Morde.

Document 40 · 5 April 1944

Memorandum by Willy Brandt (Stockholm): Forces of the German Revolution[1]

STRICTLY CONFIDENTIAL

[...]

(The following is a summary of the point of view of Willy Brandt, the Secretary of the German Social Democratic organization in Sweden. This report was furnished by John Scott, of *Time*.)[2]

Forces of the German Revolution

It is not yet known whether Germany as a whole will be occupied by the victorious powers or whether it will be divided into Eastern and Western zones, the development of which will depend on the various methods adopted by the occupying power.[3]

It is also possible that defeat will coincide with such exhaustion that constructive social work will be impossible. The collapse of the Nazi regime will also affect administration and national economy.

Despite this, a military collapse will provoke a rising by the mass of the people. Many will try to wipe out the Nazi organization as quickly as possible and many will demand renewed freedom of thought, organization and press. Thus the rising will be democratic but the revolutionary process will go farther. Some groups will

---

1. NA, RG 59, 103.918/2245; NA, RG 226, Entry 16, Box 827, R&A 71446. Brandt's report was submitted to OSS Washington by its Stockholm representative through the Legation's diplomatic pouch. At the same time, the document was forwarded by the American Legation in Stockholm both to the Secretary of State in Washington, D.C., and to the Political Division of the American Embassy in London. For an earlier estimate of the German opposition by Willy Brandt see document [21].

2. According to U.S. Minister Herschel V. Johnson, Brandt had prepared his report for an American newspaperman (obviously Scott) who was going to use it as a basis for an article.

3. Allied negotiations on the issue of the occupation and zonal division of Germany were performed by the European Advisory Commission in London.

want to know what is to be done with those who helped the Nazis to power and supported their policy. One demand will certainly be that the estates of the Junkers be confiscated and either divided up or administered collectively. In dealing with the Prussian military clique, it will be difficult to keep discipline between men and officers. Executives, judges and police will be banished, imprisoned or killed.

A democratic revolution brings social consequences which must be accepted. The part played by heavy industry and high finance for Nazism and war [is] beyond all doubt. To break the power of German capital monopoly, cartels etc., must be collectivized. In Nazi-owned factories workers will themselves take over the management, possible in the name of a State organization which is in the process of being formed. Cooperative control of industry will be the natural consequence of serious anti-Nazi movement and an essential condition for disarmament and effective German help in the reconstruction of Europe.

Will the German revolution be able to produce the right people to carry out radical social reform?

The oppositional elements are the following:

The fighting forces, who alone had power to crush Nazism but didn't, include many younger officers who are beholden to Nazism from their advancement. Opposition here has little to do with democracy. The interpretation given to the Allied disarmament demands will be decisive for the future role of the officers corps, but a government of generals would soon come into conflict with true democratic groups. The spontaneous reaction of soldiers will be an important factor in anti-Nazi revolution. Front solidarity is not the same as solidarity with the Nazis. It is hard to believe that military discipline will stand the strain of military defeat and political collapse.

Just because the connection between the fighting forces and the Party despite all friction is so clear, and because there are so many Nazi officers, the demand for election of representatives will find an echo among the soldiers. It is not impossible that many officers—particularly front officers—will later be accepted as leaders. The opinion held by many that the fighting forces could form the basis of a new German administration is, however, wrong.

Oppositional Nazi groups may appear but will only play a very small role.

Younger Generation. Although Nazi influence on this group is great they don't constitute a unified pro-Nazi reserve, but because German youth has gone direct from Nazi schools, etc., to the army they are unsuitable as the foundation of a democratic society.

When peace comes more than half of Germany's youth will have fallen. By Spring 1943 it was estimated that [out of] 5 milliards [million] soldiers aged between 17–25, 1–1 1/2 million had been killed, 1 million rendered incapable of further fighting. The main problem will be to find them a useful place in society.

Democratic reserves are also to be found among working class youth who have been influenced by their parents and among part of the intelligentsia. A certain support of democratic economic policy may also be expected from the technical intelligentsia.

Church. This opposition, which is the most easily organized, expresses the dissatisfaction of the rural population and the middle classes. Catholic church is the most important although not entirely oppositional. Protestant church [is] also divided and less influential but has some strong men e.g. Niemöller. The Church's extensive organization may play an important role in the collapse of the present administration but support of the Church doesn't mean people want to be governed by priests. The position within the Church group is rather difficult because any anti-Nazis are extremely conservative as regards social questions.

The Conservatives. German conservatism is badly compromised by its alliance with Hitler. Many conservative representatives of Germany's economic life who first supported Nazism have regretted it and are now paralyzed by fear of social revolution. Some advocate a restoration of the monarchy but these will find it difficult to avoid a break with the democratic movement.

Labour. Labour has never cooperated with the Nazis and was the first group to work illegally. Too much hope shouldn't be pinned to this illegal activity as groups are isolated. The main strength of Labour opposition is in factories and plants where there is a nucleus of older skilled workers. Passive resistance in plants [is] not unimportant as a 1 percent reduction in production means a yearly loss of 1 milliard [billion?] crowns to Germany.

There are "natural leaders" in German factories who could form [the] basis for democratic trade unions which would replace the Work Front. In the chaos subsequent to Nazi collapse factories would become natural disciplinary elements. In conjunction with factories certain local administrative functions could be organized to deal with problems of food supply, etc.

Oppositional workers' main interest is to form a free Trade Union movement and a uniform political Labour Party on the basis of a radical democratic-socialistic policy. Whether a "Party of Freedom" can be formed depends greatly on factors which will be decided outside Germany.

In short: German opposition has its main support among the workers and in certain circles of the Church and the intelligentsia. Catholic opposition is strongest in South Germany, Labour opposition in Northwest Germany, Berlin, Ruhr, Sacbayn [Saxony and Bavaria?] and Silesia. It unfortunately cannot be helped that the bombing of German industries hits just those areas where the latent opposition is strongest.

The internal opposition will be short of intellectuals after the war, particularly such as know about international conditions. Returning emigrants will play a bigger role in the Labour movement than in conservative groups.

A new government will be faced with the following tasks:

Firstly. Nazi criminals must be ruthlessly exterminated and all public institutions purged, SS-men, Gestapo etc. interned and put to hard labour. Very doubtful whether this can be done if the police force is allowed to remain armed. The police is Himmler's even though there may be many honest men among them.

Secondly. Freedom of thought, religion, belief, organization and of the press must be reestablished. There will be no elections. Base of a new democracy should be formed to give on the one hand a free Trade union and parallel organization and on the other free parties.

Thirdly. Prevent famine: reorganize industry and prevent mass unemployment. This can only be done by taking over a great part of the Nazi economic control apparatus. Therefore [it is] essential that the administration of the planned economy is in the hands of reliable people and that a satisfactory democratic control can be established. Cooperative production and distribution organizations must here play important part.

Fourthly. Democratization of administration, legal and educational systems, etc. Communal self-administration must be strengthened. Cultural and administrative decentralization must be coordinated with increased centralization in the economic sphere.

The solution of these problems is the starting point for further development in a democratic direction [and?] depends on the Foreign Policy followed by the German revolution and on the attitude adopted towards it abroad.

There will still be nationalistic forces in Germany after defeat. It is to be hoped that sincere German democrats will adhere to a European and international idea and try to win the majority of their people to it. This doesn't mean German democrats will willingly agree to everything proposed from abroad.

No peace will be unfair when compared to what the Nazis have done to other nations, but it will be difficult to frame terms which Germans will regard as fair. The only solution is to bring the German problem into the European picture.

The United Nations and democratic Germans have a common interest in crushing Nazism and reintroducing democracy. Economic problems should also be approached from a rational European and international standpoint.

Document 41 · 21 April 1944

Telegram from Allen W. Dulles
(OSS Bern) to OSS Director William J. Donovan:
The Labor Opposition in Germany[1]

SECRET

TOR: 4/24/44 6:32 pm State Department Paraphrase

#2560. The following information for the OSS from a source which will be revealed in another message has been sent also to London as number 668.[2]

For a considerable period the obstacles cited below have hampered our efforts to set up a liaison with the underground of labor circles within the Reich:

a. Everybody outstanding in labor circles is under special surveillance by the Gestapo.
b. Leaders of labor within the Reich who are opposed to the Nazi regime are not able to get out to non-belligerent countries, even to Switzerland.
c. There is no contact between leaders of labor in the Reich and reliable Germans who can go to Switzerland.

At last contact has been established with an individual thought to be in contact with dominant figures in the underground movement of Socialist labor circles and the following views of theirs are expressed:

While the two movements are entirely separate, both the Communists and the Socialists maintain underground organizations in labor circles within the Reich, with skeleton organizations in the bigger urban communities. For the following reasons the former organization commands a broader influence, is more active and is better organized:

---

1. NA, RG 226, Entry 134, Box 349, Folder 1852.
2. The source cannot be identified. The propositions given are, however, reminiscent of the suggestions passed on to Dulles by German exiles Wilhelm Hoegner and Joseph Wirth in Switzerland.

a. The ideology of the Communists finds a fertile field because Germans by the millions have lost all their material possessions.

b. A central committee of the Communists exists in the Reich to coordinate and direct their activities within the country and to maintain contact with the committee of *Freies Deutschland*[3] in the Soviet capital, from which government support is received. Soviet war prisoners and workers by the millions facilitate this contact with Russia through a Moscow-directed secret organization.[4] The fewness of their German guards is a great aid to them.

c. The Soviet [sic] maintains a steady flow into the Reich of constructive ideas and schemes as a program to provide for the rehabilition of the Reich after the war. Such plans and ideas are being disseminated widely among the masses of the German people through the whispering campaign that the Communists have organized very well.

In contrast to the activities mentioned above there is complete ignorance as to the ultimate objectives and the practical ideas for the future of central Europe maintained by the Allied powers. The leaders of Socialism within the Reich say with emphasis that this uncertainty must be clarified as soon as possible in order to counteract the growing influence of Communism. This tendency toward the ultra-radical has grown stupendously and its momentum is gaining rapidly. If it is not stopped the leaders of German labor are afraid that even if the Allies achieve military victory, the peace will be quickly lost and a new dictatorship may take the place of the present one in central Europe. The adoption of a policy of a constructive nature in dealing with the masses of central Europe is urged as a means of dealing with this very dangerous development. The leaders of labor in the Reich suggest the following policy of a moderate nature for orderly reconstruction in order to attract the German laboring element[5]:

a. Some responsible person in the United States to make an encouraging statement which could be transmitted through the channel mentioned above in confidence to leaders of Socialism within the Reich.

b. Some basic statement with regard to the problem of self-government for Germany in the future as well as some intimation of the extent to which the independent operation of the German's own administration will be permitted by the Allies. Self-government by local communities and regions should be stressed particularly, it is recommended.

---

3. For the Moscow Free Germany Committee see especially document [14].

4. This is most probably a reference to the Communist group under Anton Saefkow, Franz Jacob, and Bernhard Bästlein. Based in Berlin, this Moscow-sponsored group controlled the largest Communist network in Germany. In the German capital alone, there were thirty underground cells in various factories.

5. Although the following suggestions were never taken into consideration by the U.S. government, OSS directed their propaganda toward some of the proposed aims.

It is suggested that the Allies issue a series of statements to the laboring classes within the Reich of an encouraging nature and which would stress the prospect of their collaboration in the reconstuction of Germany. These statements should also extend a welcome to the leaders of Socialism to join in the future government of Germany.

There should be a statement that it is not the intention of the Allies to do as the Nazis have done and set up in the Reich a puppet regime composed of German quislings[6] who will govern the Germans and represent the interests of the Allies. Such an idea is obvious to us but the fact that these German leaders of the opposition request assurance on the point is a good example of the bewilderment in the German mind instilled by the long continued propaganda of the Nazis.

These same leaders of labor offer the suggestion that air raids be focused as nearly as they can be upon industrial and military objectives as the bombing of big urban centers is rapidly making all of central Europe entirely proletarian.

Because of the fact that I believe that these opinions are representative of those of labor leaders who are opposed to the present regime in the Reich and who are basically agreeable to taking sides with us, I hope that these views will be accorded due consideration even if some of them have a naive appearance. Such an impression can be accounted for by the fact that for many years the people of the Reich have been isolated from honest news and have had, instead, vicious propaganda as a result of which even some basic truths have been distorted. Now they must relearn some fundamentals of the simplest nature.

Some statement should be made that the labor element in Germany will be encouraged and allowed to organize their own labor movement along their own lines and with no interference from the anti-labor ideas of the capitalist elements among the Allies.

There should be an active exchange of thought set up between forces of a progressive nature in the Allied nations and the Socialist movement among German labor in order to counteract the close contact that prevails between the Russians and German Communists.

Bombarding Germany with leaflets was ineffective during 1939 when German arms were victorious but now the people are open to such propaganda if the material used is prepared on the basis of the constantly shifting trend in the psychology of the masses of the German people. The best effect would be achieved by not dropping bombs and leaflets simultaneously, and such large numbers of the latter should be dropped as to make their quick removable [removal?] by the Gestapo impossible. To implement the constantly changing psychological point of view of the German people these leaflets should be compiled with assistance of the resistance movement in the Reich.

---

6. I.e., collaborators with the Allies, ironically named after Norwegian Nazi collaborator Vidkun Quisling who was executed in 1945.

Document 42 · 4 May 1944

Minutes of a Meeting of the OSS Planning Group: Propaganda Use of Free Germany Committees[1]

SECRET

1. MO Use of Free Germany Committees

[...]

The memorandum from Lt. Col. Mann to OSS field offices in London, Algiers, and Cairo[2] was read which concerned the success which the Russian Free Germany Committee has had in MO [Morale Operations] campaigns to induce surrender by Germans and which suggested that similar committees might be formed in the areas involved to perform like activities against the German Armies.

The first question raised was whether such an operational plan, which fell within the objectives of special programs for Strategic Services activities, needed to be submitted to the Planning Group. It was noted that the Planning Group had previously requested that operational plans which implemented special programs should be submitted to the planning group whenever possible for its review and suggestions. It was recalled that the question of formation of Free Germany Committees in the U.S. and elsewhere had been a subject of discussion in the Planning Group at the time the Russian Free Germany Committee had been established, and it was believed, therefore, that the present suggestions had rightly been sent to the Planning Group for its opinions.

---

1. NA, RG 226, Entry 144, Box 6, Folder 42. In this 398th meeting of the OSS Planning Group, the following persons were present: Shepard Morgan (Acting Chairman), Maj. Gen. J. P. Smith, USA, Admiral Wm. H. Standley, USN, Vice Adm. Wm. T. Tarrant, USN, Mr. Robert Woods Bliss, John Wiley, Brig. Gen. Lyle H. Miller, USMC, Lt. Col. Wm. S. Culbertson, Lt. Comdr. Kenneth W. Hinks, Dr. Norman Brown and Col. (MI) A. H. Onthank (Secretary).

2. This memorandum of 25 April 1944 is not printed.

Comments on the proposed formation of Free Germany Committees, which would endeavor to influence members of the German military forces to surrender, were in several categories:

a. It appeared that the establishment of such Free Germany Committees might have political significance which would require that they be approved in the high British and American circles.
b. The political ramifications with the Soviet Government over the establishment of such committees might be serious.
c. The use of German prisoners of war for such activities would raise many questions, including the possibility of disregarding the Geneva Convention for treatment of prisoners, the control of prisoners in camps, and the necessity of obtaining high ranking prisoners at present from the British.

It was generally concluded,

a. That the use of prisoners of war to transmit surrender appeals to their previous comrades would, if voluntarily done, be a desirable objective for OSS activities, particularly in view of the fact that such activities had already been used by both the Russians and the Japanese.
b. That voluntary action on the part of German prisoners of war would probably not contravene the Geneva Convention.
c. That such activities, if limited strictly to surrender appeals made by individual German officers, and having no political content, would probably not require consent of high political circles in the U.S. or England.
d. That the comparison of such activities by individual prisoners of war with the activities of the Russian Free Germany Committee was both inexact and unnecessary, and that it tended to confuse the objective desired by MO.

Document 43 · 16 May 1944

Memorandum from OSS Assistant Director
G. Edward Buxton to Secretary of State
Cordell Hull: Overtures by German Generals
and Civilian Opposition
for a Separate Armistice[1]

SECRET

1. Since early 1944 the OSS representative in Bern [Allen Dulles] has been approached periodically by two emissaries[2] of a German group proposing to attempt an overthrow of the Nazi regime. The group includes [Wilhelm] Leuschner, socialist leader and former Minister of Interior in Hesse; [Hans] Oster, a general formerly the right-hand man of [Wilhelm] Canaris, arrested in 1943 by the Gestapo, kept under surveillance after his release, and recently discharged from official functions by [Wilhelm] Keitel; [Carl] Goerd[e]ler, former Mayor of Leipzig; and General [Ludwig] Beck.[3] The last two men have been described by the OSS representative as leaders of the group;[4] it is from them that the two emissaries have brought proposals for negotiation.

2. Early in April the emissaries talked with the OSS representative in Bern, conveying the suggestion of a deal between this German opposition group and the Western Allies. The group expressed their willingness and preparation to attempt ousting Hitler and the Nazis. They stated their belief that the time in which successful action

---

1. NA, RG 226, Entry 146, Box 234, Folder 3294; also in FRUS 1944, I, 510–513; Hoffmann, *The History of the German Resistance*, 747–749. The same document was also forwarded to the President. Another copy reached Fletcher Warren (State Department) through Brigadier-General John Magruder (OSS). The memorandum was based on several cables from Bern, including # 2714–16 of 6 April 1944, # 2718–22 of 7 April 1944, and # 3423–31 of 13 May 1944.

2. Hans Bernd Gisevius and Eduard Waetjen.

3. General Ludwig Beck had retired as Chief of Staff of the German Army in 1938 in protest of Hitler's expansionist politics.

4. Goerdeler and Beck had been correctly identified as the opposition group's leaders as early as April 7.

could be carried out was rapidly shortening. They said they were the only group able to profit by personal approach to Hitler and other Nazi chiefs, and the only one controlling enough arms and enough influence in the *Wehrmacht* to accomplish the purpose of Nazi overthrow. The group stated that the German generals now commanding in the West—particularly [Gerd von] Rundstedt and [Alexander Freiherr von] Falkenhausen—would be ready to cease resistance and aid Allied landings, once the Nazis had been ousted. They thought that similar arrangements might be worked out for the reception of Allied airborne forces at strategic points in Germany. While ready to attempt a coup, the group did not guarantee success.

3. The condition on which the group expressed willingness to act was that they would deal directly with the Western Allies alone after overthrowing the Nazi regime. As precedent for excluding the USSR from all negotiations they cited the recent example of Finland, which they said dealt solely with Moscow.[5] This condition the group based on the conservative character of their membership and supporters. However, the group declared their willingness to cooperate with any leftist elements except the Communists; in February they had described Leuschner as an acceptable type of head for an interim government, assuming that neither the military nor the Communists would dominate during the transition period.[6] The group feared political and ideological sway over Central Europe by Bolshevism, with a mere exchange of Nazi totalitarianism for a totalitarianism of the radical left accompanied by the submergence of democracy and Christian culture. They stated that if capitulation were to be made primarily to the Soviet Union, it would have to be carried out by another group in Germany.

4. The OSS representative expressed to the emissaries his conviction that the United States and Great Britain would not act regarding Germany without the concert of Russia. In commenting on the opposition group's proposal, he expressed skepticism of their capability since Beck and Goerd[e]ler have been so prominently mentioned as potential leaders that the Gestapo must be aware of the situation and is only waiting to crack down until plans have gone farther or because the Gestapo may wish to keep an anchor to westward.

5. In May 1944, approximately one month after the April visit of the emissaries to the OSS representative, they received an oral message by courier from the opposition group. Now mentioned as members were also [Franz] Halder, [Kurt] Zeitzler, [Adolf] Heusinger (chief of operations for Zeitzler), [Friedrich] Olbrecht [Olbricht] (chief of the German Army Administration), Falkenhausen, and Rundstedt. The group was reported ready to help Allied units get into Germany if the Allies agreed that the *Wehrmacht* should continue to hold the Eastern Front.

---

5. As early as January 1944, the Finns had made approaches to the Allies through Washington but had been warned that the Russian price for a separate peace would be high: a return to the 1940 frontier. Finland did not break relations with Germany before September 1944 when it signed a treaty with the Soviet Union whose terms were much as they had been in January.

6. Being neither a radical leftist nor a conservative, Leuschner, who was a trade union leader, seemed the ideal candidate to fill this position.

They proposed in detail: (1) three Allied airborne divisions should land in the Berlin region with the assistance of the local Army commanders, (2) major amphibious landings should be undertaken at or near Bremen and Hamburg, (3) landings in France should follow, although [Erwin] Rommel cannot be counted on for cooperation,[7] (4) reliable German units in the area of Munich would isolate Hitler and other high Nazis in Ober Salzburg [Obersalzberg].[8] The opposition group is reported to feel that Germany has lost the war and that the only chance of avoiding Communism in Germany is to facilitate occupation of as large a section of Europe as possible by American and British forces before collapse on the Eastern Front.[9]

6. The emissaries, who had remained in Switzerland, replied to the courier that discussion of the plan would be unavailing because of the proviso concerning the USSR. Later the group dispatched to them a telegram advising no further action "for the time being". The emissaries think nevertheless that the subject is still open. They have characterized the group's proviso as unrealistic, and regard as the core of the proposal only the plan that American and British forces should become entrenched in Germany before the Russians; they urged that it was entirely a military matter if some of the German generals wish to assist the Allied invasion and try to take over the Nazi regime. The OSS representative reiterated to the emissaries that Great Britain and the United States would adhere to their Russian commitments. In answer to the objection that point (1) of the group's plan (paragraph 5, above [...]) might be regarded by the Allies as a trap, they stated that since they were not military men they could only say that sufficient opportunity for requisite precautions would be presented in the form of direct prior contact with German military authorities. The emissaries said that Zeitzler had been won over by Heusinger and Olbrecht [Olbricht]; they added that he was preoccupied in respect of military matters with the Eastern Front, that he would cooperate in any plan to bring about a systematic liquidation of that front in order to escape the blame for a military disaster there—which he greatly fears.

7. One of the opposition group's emissaries acknowledged his lack of confidence in the political courage of the German generals, on the basis of past experience, and said the Allies might do well to ignore their propositions if there were assurance of early victory and a speedy Allied occupation of Germany. The OSS representative at Bern is convinced of the sincerity of this intermediary, as the result of investigation and of experience with him. The representative is of the

---

7. Although opposed to Hitler, Rommel was not in favor of an assassination attempt as he was afraid the Führer would be turned into a martyr.

8. A fortified area in the Austrian Alps that served Hitler, Goebbels, Göring and Bormann as a recreation center. See also document 51.

9. These propositions had been forwarded to Allen W. Dulles on May 13.

opinion that there are some German generals who wish to liquidate their responsibility in the war by collaborating in the construction of an Anglo-American bulwark against the pressure of the USSR in Europe, and he is convinced that the two emissaries are in contact with such a group. Doubtful that the group would have the determination to act effectively at the appropriate time and sensitive to the problem of Soviet relations in the effectuation of any plan in which the group might participate, he believes that the group's activities may nevertheless be useful to undermine the morale at the top echelon in the *Wehrmacht*.

Document 44 · 1 June 1944

Memorandum by OSS Washington: German Oppositional Overtures to Ex-Chancellor Heinrich Brüning[1]

Overtures by a Representative of a German Socialist, Catholic Center, Intellectual and Military Opposition Group

The OSS representative in the Iberian peninsula,[2] writing from Madrid on May 12, 1944, advises that he has been approached by a certain German[3] who is presumably acting for a group said to be composed of remnants of the German Socialists and Catholic Center Parties, with a goodly smattering of intellectuals.

This German presented to our representative a letter which he had written to Dr. Heinrich Brüning, former Chancellor of Germany, now resident in the United

---

1. NA, RG 226, Entry 146, Box 234, Folder 3294. On 2 June 1944, this report was specially disseminated to Cordell Hull and Fletcher Warren in the State Department, to the President's Map Room, the Joint Chiefs of Staff, Dr. William Langer and Mr. Platt.

2. I.e., H. Gregory Thomas, a businessman and lawyer who was later to become a member of the Free Europe Committee.

3. I.e., Otto John, a member of the resistance and legal adviser of the Lufthansa who acted as liason with the German counterintelligence (Abwehr). See document [34]. Otto John was briefly acquainted with Harry Hopkins, and had also served as an emissary in an earlier German attempt to get in touch with President Roosevelt: In April 1942, he forwarded a message by Prince Louis Ferdinand of Prussia to Roosevelt via the Spanish foreign service. In this message the Prince suggested the elimination of Hitler by leading German generals.

States.[4] At the same time, the author of the letter stated that he was planning to leave for Germany about the middle of May and to return one week later, accompanied by a high German military personage. The latter was reported to be interested in "spilling the works" because of his conviction that, if anything is to be saved from wreck, Hitler must be promptly defeated. The usual fears of Russia's advancing armies make this German and his group highly anxious to contribute to Germany's defeat by invasion from the West and to reach an understanding with the Western Democracies.

The letter to Brüning, referred to above, describes the situation within Germany, and is summarized as follows:

1. Germany faces a prospect of total destruction unless Hitler is removed and the nation cleansed through her own efforts.
2. The Opposition (presumably the group represented by the author of the letter)[5] has consolidated itself to the point of forming a civilian shadow government, with the support of the principal Opposition forces in the Army, which contain many of Brüning's friends and acquaintances.[6]
3. They all count upon Brüning's advice and support, and hope that he will come to Madrid and be associated with this group.

A copy of the letter in question has been submitted to Mr. Breckinridge Long, Assistant Secretary of State, with whom OSS has previously discussed Dr. Brüning. In accordance with Mr. Long's judgement and our own, the Brüning letter will not be delivered.

Further information has been requested of our representative in Madrid as to personalities involved and their connections. He has been instructed to continue his contact in a cautious manner and make no commitments whatsoever.

---

4. At the time, Brüning was teaching Public Administration at Harvard University.

5. John's contacts included resistance members in the Abwehr as well as Carl Goerdeler, Stauffenberg and Adam von Trott.

6. During their travels to the United States in 1937 and 1939/1940, respectively, both Goerdeler and Trott had discussed resistance matters with Brüning.

Document 45 · 12 July 1944

Telegram from Allen W. Dulles (OSS Bern) to OSS Washington: Anticipation of a Dramatic Event in Germany[1]

SECRET

TOR: 7/13/44 1:29

#4085. *Breakers*. To Carib and Jackpot

There is a possibility that a dramatic event may take place up north, if *Breakers* courier is to be trusted. We expect a complete account this evening. However, it is not only possible but probable that any news will be suppressed by violence if necessary. Henceforth 512 [Hans Bernd Gisevius] will be known as Culber [also Luber]. He has gone north for discussions with Tucky [Ludwig Beck] and others. This goes along with your #1782[2] but we believe 800 [Adam von Trott zu Solz] connection was also with *Zulu* [British intelligence]. G [Goerdeler], mentioned in the last sentence of my #4080[3] is in hiding.[4] The Chief of Police in Berlin, Helldorf, will henceforth be designated as Bobcat, and Risler will be the new name for General Fromm.[5]

---

1. NA, RG 226, Entry 99, Box 14, Folder 58a. This report was cabled "for action" to the Secret Intelligence Branch in Washington, and also "for information" to General Donovan, General Magruder, the Secretariat of OSS and the OSS Counterintelligence Branch.

2. Not printed.

3. Not printed.

4. The Gestapo had been hunting for Carl Goerdeler even before the 20th of July plot.

5. Colonel General Fritz Fromm, Commander of the Reserve Army.

Document 46 · 13 July 1944

Memorandum from OSS Director William J. Donovan to President Franklin D. Roosevelt: Russian Policy Toward Germany[1]

SECRET

Memorandum for the President

Russian Policy Toward Germany

The rapid progress which is being made by the Russian Armies in their campaign against Germany[2] raises the question of what Moscow's policy may be toward Germany after final victory.

Reactions on this point which have been expressed lately in Soviet military and diplomatic circles in this country, indicate that it would be a mistake to assume that Moscow's policy toward Germany has already been settled in all its details. On the contrary, it is stressed that certain fundamental problems are constantly being studied in leading Russian circles and will no doubt be subject to changes depending on the course of events in the near future.

A review of some of the principal points which have thus been studied may therefore be of particular interest.

---

1. Roosevelt Library, Hyde Park, F. D. Roosevelt Papers. President's Secretary's Files, Box 171, Folder OSS reports, April 7–July 13, 1944. This memorandum was sent to the President on 13 July 1944. In his covering letter Donovan pointed out that this report summarized a series of conversations between an OSS representative and Soviet Officials in Washington and New York. He stressed that the statements were fully in accord with intelligence from other sources.

2. Simultaneously with the Allied landing in Normandy on 6 June 1944, the Soviet summer offensives had started. These offensives led to the rapid collapse of the Heeresgruppe Mitte (Army Central Front).

As outlined repeatedly in previous reports, Stalin and his followers emphasized in official statements given out during the early stages of the Russian-German war, the necessity of drawing a sharp line between what may be termed "Hitler and his Gang" on the one hand, and the "German people" on the other. During the early part of 1943 Stalin's slogan: "History teaches that Hitlers come and go but the German people and the German State remain"[3] more or less represented the expression of the leading principle governing Moscow's policy toward Germany. Nevertheless, beginning with 1943, and more particularly in 1944, following the successes of the Russian campaign and the liberation of Russian territory, the policy of the Soviets sustained a change worth noting. Moscow now stresses the responsibility of the "German people".

In the fall of 1943, Manuilski, one of the leaders of the Communist Party, plainly stated that: "The Soviet Union will hold the entire German Fascist Army responsible for all destruction and criminal acts which were commited on Russian territory".

On the 26th Anniversary of the Red Army in February 1944, as well as during the official party festivities on the First of May, the slogan adopted called for the extermination of the "German scoundrels", as against "Fascists scoundrels".

It is claimed that whereas leading Foreign Office officials in Moscow, including Molotov, Maisky, Litvinov and others, advocate the necessity of a compromise with Anglo-American policy in regard to Germany, on the ground that radical harshness might alienate favorable public opinion in Great Britain and America, military leaders backed by Party representatives in the liberated regions insist upon an intransigent attitude toward Germany. In this latter connection, it is interesting to mention the fact that Sir Vansittart's proposed post-war policy toward Germany[4] has found many sympathizers in Russia, especially in the Army and Navy, although nothing to this effect has ever been published in the Soviet press. On the other hand, Soviet diplomatic circles claim that Stalin himself is inclined to follow "a middle course". He is reported to be convinced that the punishment of war criminals would give sufficient satisfaction to the Russian people and the Red Army commanders. The Kharkov trial is mentioned as a case in point and is believed to have been staged by way of a preliminary experiment and an indication for the future.[5]

---

3. For the first time, this line of propaganda had been followed by Stalin in his Order of the Day of 23 February 1942 when he stated: "It would be ludicrous to identify Hitler's clique with the German people, with the German state. The experience of history indicates that Hitlers come and go, but the German people and the German state remain." The distinction between "Hitlerite" and "non-Hitlerite" Germans was also an ideological undercurrent in all major Soviet press announcements ever since 1942.

4. I.e., a harsh treatment of the German people.

5. After the prolonged, fierce Battle of Kharkov the capture of this city was celebrated by the Soviet population with great ceremonies. Starting in September 1943, several captured Germans and Russian collaborators were put on trial for wartime atrocities and the systematic extermination of the Slav peoples.

It is the consensus of Soviet opinion in this country, that the foregoing line of action will continue to be followed to meet both domestic and foreign policy issues, and that trials similar to the one which was held in Kharkov may deter the Nazis from committing new crimes on the eve of their final collapse. It is indicated, however, that there is perfect unanimity between Stalin and all Party and Army leaders on the necessity of eradicating every remnant of Germany's military machine and every vestige of Nazi Party organization. It is also safe to say that the elimination of all representatives of the German ruling class, including the big Prussian landowners, industrialists, etc. has been decided upon. This is clearly indicated in the Russian projects dealing with the military occupation of Germany, as well as in the instructions which have been given to the underground movements throughout Europe. Finally, the propaganda broadcasts of the Committee of Free Germany clearly advocate the above post-war policy toward Germany.[6]

From the viewpoint of Russian circles, the issue has a direct bearing on prospects of a German revolution. At the present time, Moscow does not anticipate a collapse of Nazi Germany before Hitler's Army has been completely defeated. The Russians do not look forward to any serious trouble taking place in Germany until the day when either the Red Army or the Allies will be fighting on German territory. In general, official Soviet opinion on a revolutionary movement in Germany is rather reserved at this moment. Moscow is much more familiar with the strength of the anti-Hitler movement in Germany than Allied countries are, and is not inclined to over-estimate the potentialities of this movement, which they consider to be rather weak, scattered and lacking the necessary leadership. Similar considerations apply to the clerical movement. The Church is likewise divided: there does not appear to be any unity among Protestants supporting the Niemoeller group,[7] whereas the Catholic von Gahlen [Galen] group is torn by internal conflicts.[8]

Moscow does not believe that the Church movement in general and the Catholic Church in particular can be expected to play an important part or contribute effective support at the critical moment. Insofar as the big industrialist class is concerned, they are completely in the throes of the Nazi Party. The old Socialist Democratic leaders and the Neo-Communists do exert a certain influence, but they are numerically weak and dread the consequences of a possible defeat for the future of their adherents. Finally, as to the emigrants, they have not shown any initiative, nor have they the means of forming the necessary ties with parties in Germany in order to organize a successful movement.

---

6. See document [29].

7. I.e., the Confessional Church. Martin Niemöller himself had been detained in prisons and a concentration camp since 1937.

8. For a different estimate of the German church opposition see document [21].

The foregoing analytical review, coupled with the experience in Italy, which is closely watched by Moscow as a possible yardstick of what might happen in every liberated Fascist country, has led the Russians to the conclusion that the German collapse, when it comes, may develop in the form of spontaneous, disorganized outbursts, while German society itself may be radically broken up for many years to come.

It may be remembered that Moscow has been experimenting with a project of utilizing certain elements in the German Army for revolutionary purposes. These experiments have been rather disappointing. The "Committee of Free Germany", which was set up not only for propaganda purposes but also with a view to gathering "sound elements around an organized nucleus of anti-Hitlerites", has been seriously handicapped in its activities due to the solid framework of the Nazi Party which it encountered and which is sufficiently powerful to forestall serious mutiny and disintegration. The appeals of the "Committee" have not resulted in any satisfactory reaction among Hitler's Army divisions and consequently the Committee has been shelved for the time being and is only held in reserve.

Soviet circles now express the opinion that a consequential anti-Hitler movement cannot be expected prior to Germany's invasion by the Red Army. Incidentally, strong assistance may be expected from foreign labor now settled in Germany and the twelve million foreign workers and war prisoners may contribute a very important part in the ultimate collapse of the Nazi regime, both from an economic and political viewpoint.[9] The Soviets realizing such potentialities are exerting considerable efforts in spreading propaganda among foreign workers in Germany. This propaganda is conducted by a special committee composed primarily of military specialists.

Analysing the situation from another angle, the mistrust of the Soviets toward German democracy is worth stressing. Conversations with Soviets in this country indicate that Moscow is even suspicious about the German Communist movement. The people in Russia are being reminded that German democracy failed twice during the past twenty-five years[10] and has never been successful in bringing about a revolution in Germany. The motto which has generally been adopted in political circles in Moscow is that: "We should not trust German Communists, Radicals or Liberals before obtaining evidence not only of their efficiency but above all of their sincerity". The Soviets will undoubtedly promote and support such elements which manifest their friendliness toward Soviet Russia, but Moscow expects to proceed very cautiously in this respect. For the time being the consensus of opinion would indicate that it is best not to enter into any commitment with any single group in Germany and to reserve a "free hand" in dealing with any future German Government. Consequently, Stalin does not entertain any idea of Germany turning Communistic. He is, however, believed to favor the

---

9. See documents [23] and [84].
10. I.e., in 1918/1919 and 1933.

development of a Popular Front which would offer Russia greater liberty of movement.

The Russians indicate that a big surprise may be anticipated after Hitler's collapse and that Stalin himself may oppose a communistic set-up in Germany.

Document 47 · 13 July 1944

Telegram from Allen W. Dulles (OSS Bern) to OSS Washington: Oppositional Generals Are Concentrated in the Berlin Area[1]

SECRET

TOR: 7/14/44, 0:58 a.m.

4110–4114. *Breakers.* With reference to our # 4085.[2]

A courier from Breakers,[3] who came here a short time ago, advises that the Soviet victories have given new vigor to the Breakers movement.[4] The success of the Allied landing in Normandy[5] and the local developments reported below have also contributed to the impetus of this movement:

1. Breakers have gained a new member in Risler [General Friedrich Fromm]. He holds a responsible command over the reserve from the Berlin region.

2. The headquarters of the *Oberkommando der Wehrmacht* [Supreme Command of the Armed Forces] have been shifted to Sossen [Zossen] (in the vicinity of Berlin) from East Prussia.[6] As a consequence, it is in the vicinity of

---

1. NA, RG 226, Entry 146, Box 235, Folder 3296.

2. Document [45].

3. I.e., Hans Bernd Gisevius.

4. On 2 July 1944, Soviet troops had liberated the city of Minsk.

5. Following the landing at the Normandy beaches on 6 June 1944 (Operation Overlord), Allied troops had taken the port cities of Cherbourg (30 June) and Caen (9 July).

6. In reality, not the OKW but one of the OKH (Oberkommando des Heeres) camps moved to Zossen in July 1944.

Berlin that Eta [Friedrich Olbricht], Zeta [Kurt Zeitzler] and additional generals who are supposedly in the opposition are chiefly concentrated at this time. [sic].*

*Refer also to the declaration by Prime Minister Churchill yesterday, in which he stated that it would be better if the people of Germany were themselves to oust the Nazi regime.[7] With respect to this, please consult the flash which I am transmitting this evening. I am not making any forecasts regarding prospects of success for the Breakers program, as reported. Without any doubt, the Gestapo is keeping its eye on developments and it is possible that the Gestapo may get rid of the leaders. Moreover, it is quite probable that the military men, whose action is indispensable to the achievement of these ends, will lack the "intestinal fortitude" to act, just as they have earlier. Furthermore, I am not unaware of the strength of the idea that Germany's defeat must be connected with the criminal program of the Fuehrer and the Nazi clique. Nevertheless, the moral consequence of a display of bravery in taking steps toward setting their own affairs to rights would be valuable to Germany's subsequent status in the Europe that will exist after the war. In the face of all this, however, I am of the opinion that we are warranted in issuing now a general declaration regarding Germany along the lines stated in my flash and in the preceding portions of this message.

---

7. On 12 July Churchill had responded to a parliamentary question stating in the House of Commons that he would appreciate moves by the German opposition in the direction of political upheaval. He claimed, however, he had not been able to get in touch with the opposition.

Document 48 · 15 July 1944

Telegram from Allen W. Dulles (OSS Bern)
to OSS Washington: Last Opportunity
for the "Breakers" Movement to Act[1]

SECRET

TOR: 7/16/44 2:03 am

#4111–12. [...] The Breakers group is receiving the cooperation of the Bearcat group,[2] which is composed of a considerable number of anti-Hitler elements working separately from the Gestapo. The next few weeks are believed by Breakers to represent the final opportunity to start action to prove the desire of the German people themselves to overthrow Hitler and his organization and to set up a respectable government. The Soviet threat of invasion of German soil in the eastern sector gives the impetus to this movement. The Breakers group wishes [to] keep as much as possible of the Reich from falling into the hands of the Russians. Consequently Breakers' plan of action would call for an ordered retreat from the West, and the dispatch of all the crack divisions to defend the Eastern front. Luben [Luber][3] has made a trip to the North to take part in the discussions there and hopes that he will be able to convince the generals to wage a final struggle against Nazism.

The following is from 110 [Allen W. Dulles]. A presidential announcement to counter Goebbels' line about the Allies' plans for complete annihilation of the German people would encourage the anti-Nazi groups. Attlee's statement, made recently during a debate in the House of Commons, seems to have made a great impression on German groups.[4]

---

1. NA, RG 226, Entry 146, Box 235, Folder 3296.

2. The anti-Hitler group around the President of the Berlin Police, Count Wolf Heinrich von Helldorf

3. I.e., Hans Bernd Gisevius.

4. On 6 July 1944, in his speech before the House of Commons, Clement Attlee, the leader of the Labour Party, had encouraged the German opposition thereby countering Churchill's earlier statement of 24 May in which the Prime Minister had insisted on "Unconditional Surrender." Attlee pointed out, however, that the German opposition would have to take active steps before the British would consider their cause.

Document 49 · 18 July 1944

Summarizing Report of OSS Washington: Nazi Opposition Group Reports Progress[1]

SECRET

Germany: Nazi Opposition Group Reports Progress

The following, transmitted by the OSS representative in Bern, is a sequel to a report dated 16 May[2] concerning an opposition group in Germany, including some high military figures, which favors peace:

The objectives of this group have received new stimulus from the Soviet gains, the Soviet threat of invading German soil, and the Allied landings in Normandy. The group is receiving cooperation from another group composed of a number of anti-Hitler elements which are described as working independently of the Gestapo. The former group believes that the next few weeks represent the final opportunity to initiate steps to prove the desire of the German people to overthrow Hitler and his organization and to set up a "respectable government". It is the wish of the group that as much of Germany as possible be kept from falling into Soviet hands. The group's proposed plan of action would call for an ordered retreat from the west and the transfer of the best divisions to the defense of the eastern front.

The group also has been encouraged by their alleged acquisition of Colonel-General Fritz Fromm because he has charge of reserves in the Berlin area. [*Washington Comment*: General Fromm, Chief of the Home Command, is in charge of army equipment and commander of replacement training for the army.] According to the group, the OKW [Oberkommando der Wehrmacht][3] has

---

1. NA, RG 226, Entry 21, Box 349, L39970. This report, an R&A summary of two Breakers cables [documents 47 and 48], was forwarded by the OSS to the Secretary of State [Cordell Hull], Fletcher Warren, the Joint Chiefs of Staff and the White House Map Room.

2. Document [43].

3. Supreme Command of the Armed Forces.

shifted its headquarters from East Prussia to a locality near Berlin. The group views this transfer as favorable to its purpose, for General Frederich [Friedrich] Olbricht, Chief of the General Army Office, under General Fromm, and Colonel-General Kurt Zeitzler, Chief of Staff, as well as other generals supposedly in the opposition,[4] are now accessible in the vicinity of Berlin.

Document 50 · 20 July 1944

Telegram from Allen W. Dulles (OSS Bern) to OSS Director William J. Donovan: The Attempt on Hitler's Life[1]

RESTRICTED

Germany

The attempt on Hitler's life is, of course, the outstanding item of news this evening. While this attack and the famous Munich bomb attack[2] are the only two attempts which have received wide public notice, I understand that there have been several other attempts on his life, which were discovered before they came to the point of explosion. The man seems to have a charmed life, but possibly an all-wise Providence is saving him so that he may himself see the complete wreckage of the Germany he has led to destruction. Those in Germany who would like to see a change of regime realize that there is no chance of dealing with him a la Mussolini by leading him off in arrest, and that assassination is the only possibility. As yet we have no reports other than the press and radio. I presume you have

---

4. Although Olbricht was in Berlin and ready to act, Zeitzler would not take part in the plot. He had sought to resign at several occasions after the failure of the German offensive in Soviet Russia. Since July 1 he had been on sick leave, on July 20 he was finally to retire. General Fromm played a very dubious role in the putsch.

1. NA, RG 226, Entry 92, Box 557, Folder 1. This cable was sent via radiotelephone.

2. On 8 November 1939, Hitler had only very narrowly escaped from an assassination attempt by Georg Elser in the Bürgerbräukeller, Munich.

all the news that we have on this—we haven't very much except the names of the various generals and admirals who were wounded.[3]

Here is a report from a good source regarding certain inner political developments in Germany. In the Nazi Party, three persons are now the subject of heavy criticism. The most criticism is being directed against Ribbentrop.[4] They hold him responsible for the fact that Germany, in the days of its great military successes, failed to develop a constructive foreign policy. This attack against Ribbentrop also strikes indirectly at Hitler himself, as in Party circles they realize that Ribbentrop played second fiddle. They feel, however, that Hitler, overwhelmed with a belief in his mission as a military leader, paid too little attention to political matters. Second among the criticized Nazi personalities today is Alfred Rosenberg, who is accused as an impractical doctrinaire, and who has been largely responsible for the antagonism which the Catholic Church has evidenced to the regime. The third man who is under attack is Dr. Ley. He is accused of having failed to bring about any real movement among the masses of the people, and having been unable to prevent the opposition of the working classes to National Socialism.[5] The discontent with these personalities is having some effect upon the position of Hitler, although no direct criticism of him is, of course, permissible. One hears it said, however, that he has fulfilled his historical mission, and behind this lies the vague feeling that he is an obstacle to the introduction of any change in policy which might hold out greater hopes of success. The tendency in Germany today is towards the creation of three all-powerful ministries. One is that of Himmler, who, of course stands next to Hitler in power. He has built up a great security and police ministry, which, of course, to all intents and purposes, includes what is improperly called the Ministry of Justice. Goebbels hopes to form the second great ministry. Recently he has increased in power and influence and now takes place after Himmler. He has in mind forming an expanded political ministry, which would include the direction of foreign policy and all propaganda for home and abroad. Naturally, Ribbentrop is in bitter opposition to any step which would place the Foreign Office under Goebbels, and Hitler has so far not approved Goebbels' plan, as he fears such a concentration of power. The third

---

3. On 20 July at 12:37 p.m., Colonel Claus Schenk Graf von Stauffenberg had placed a bomb under a table in the Führer's Headquarters. When the bomb exploded 5 minutes later, 4 out of 24 people were killed, all the others were wounded. Hitler survived with minor injuries. The OSS representative in Bern was not aware of the fact that the attempt had taken place in the East Prussia Headquarters (the so-called Wolfsschanze). Dulles was not informed about the location before 14 September 1944. Details about the events of 20 July in the Berlin Ministry of War are given in an eyewitness report that reached the OSS in September 1944. See document [67].

4. Foreign Minister Joachim von Ribbentrop.

5. Whereas Rosenberg was the leading Nazi ideologue, Robert Ley headed the German Labor Front.

great ministry would be that of Speer[6] who would put together a war-economic ministry which would combine the economic, labor and food ministries. [...]⁷

Document 51 · 21 July 1944

Telegram from Allen W. Dulles (OSS Bern) to Brigadier General Thomas J. Betts (London)[1]: "Breakers" are Breaking

TOP SECRET

TOR: 22/07/44 6:55

The *Breakers* movement is undoubtedly the movement described in my 4110 and previous *Breakers* messages,[2] and the movement appears to be breaking. It was in accordance with the plan that certain insiders such as *Theta*, our 3432 [General Adolf Heusinger], were among those present when the bomb exploded since the bomb could only be placed when a large number of leading military men were together. *Stauffenberg*[3] was a member of the group and also liaison between the older active officers at GHQ [General Headquarters] and the younger group which was formerly headed by HM [Helmuth James von Moltke] (see our 2307).[4] In addition, *Stauffenberg* was adviser to *Lester* and G [Carl Goerdeler] (referred to

---

6. Since September 1943, Albert Speer had been Minister for Armaments and War Production.

7. The second part of this telegram gives information on the partisan forces in Italy.

1. NA, RG 226, Entry 134, Box 4, Folder 63. Betts was affiliated with the Supreme Headquarters of the Allied Expeditionary Forces as Deputy Assistant Chief of Staff of U.S. Army Counterintelligence (G–2).

2. See documents [25], [34], [35], [36], [45], [47], [48] and [50].

3. See documents [50].

4. On 5 March 1944 OSS Bern had described Helmuth von Moltke as "a man close to Breakers, and adviser to OKW on International Law, who, prior to the war, often visited London." However, Moltke had been in prison since January 1944.

in our 4085[5] and hereafter called *Leper* – sic -). *Luber* [Hans Bernd Gisevius] was mixed up in all this and we are now in close touch here with our 670 [Eduard Waetjen], who is [our] local contact man.

Of course the blood purge will be ruthless. However, the fate of the revolt would appear to depend upon whether the Reserve Army "*Heimatheer*" follows its old leaders, some of whom seem to have been implicated in the plot (see my 4110), or whether it will accept *Himmler* as Commander.

Breakers do not control any adequate radio. This is the most discouraging feature. We have, however, noticed a *Reuter* report stating that the rebels sent out a message, which was interrupted, early this morning from *Frankfurt*.

On careful analysis, moreover, the *Hitler-Goering* statements seem to indicate that the revolt was not stamped out at once. Should the opposition be able to hold out in any part of *Germany*, we might consider measures along the lines outlined below[6]:

1. A Presidential statement (Refer my 4110–14[7] and Flash of July 13th).
2. The Bombing of the *Nazi* stronghold in [the] *Berchtesgaden* area. The psychological effect of such bombing might be considerable, even if the direct military effects were negligible. Moreover, any interruption of communication from the *Berchtesgaden* area with the remainder of *Germany* would be especially effective.[8]
3. In the event of the revolution gaining any headway, some statement to the effect that any *German* town that goes over to the opposition would not be bombed but that *Nazi* strongholds and *Gestapo* centers would be ruthlessly bombed.
4. Large scale leaflet raids.

---

5. Document [29].

6. Dulles's suggestions were passed on by General Donovan to President Roosevelt on 22 July 1944, see document [54].

7. Document [47].

8. The so-called Obersalzberg was an alpine fortress with extensive underground facilities. Dulles seems to have believed that the bomb attack had taken place at the Obersalzberg. During the later parts of the war, the German population was kept uninformed about the Führer's whereabouts and the location of his headquarters. The Obersalzberg was finally bombed and destroyed by the British on 25 April 1945.

Document 52 · 22 July 1944

Report by the OSS Research and Analysis Branch: The Protestant and the Catholic Churches in Germany[1]

CONFIDENTIAL

[…]

The Protestant and the Catholic Churches in Germany

Summary

This Guide recommends that in view of the persecution of Christianity by Nazis, Military Government, in order to win the confidence and support of the German clergy and of German Christians, adopt a positive rather than a negative policy with respect to the Christian Churches. Such a policy is believed to be justified not only by the aims of the United Nations for postwar Germany, but also by the interest of military security. […]

Section I. Analysis of the Problem

1. Introduction[2]

The extent to which Military Government will be obliged to concern itself with the Protestant and Catholic Churches in Germany will be determined by the nature of German collapse.

------

1. NA, RG 59, R&A 1655.22. As part of U.S. post-war planning, this report (R&A 1655.22) was prepared on request of the War Department by the Research and Analysis Branch of the OSS. It was distributed as War Department Pamphlet No. 31–120. Civil Affairs Guides were designed to aid civil affairs officers dealing with problems in liberated areas, each guide being focused upon a specific problem in a particular area. They were not basic collections of factual information, as were the Civil Affairs Handbooks, nor were they to be taken as an order by the civil affairs officers. The guides were rather designed to point the factual information toward the making and execution of plans.

2. *For a fuller treatment of the Catholic and Protestant Churches in Germany see chapter on the Church in Civil Affairs Handbook: Germany.*

a. If, before the occupation of Germany, a national government shall have been set up, with which Military Government is prepared to deal, then religious questions can best be left to such a government, subject to the general directives given Military Government for post-war Germany.

(1) If this government stems from the right, the churches will probably be content with their future prospects.

(2) If it stems from the left, and that left is anticlerical, Military Government may be asked to protect the interests of the churches in case this government is not prepared to guarantee to them the position they occupied under the Weimar Republic.

...[3]

3. Christian Churches and the Nazis

...[4]

It must be emphasized that [...] the Confessional[5] and the Catholic Churches have been the only organizations inside Germany to continue a regular public protest, since 1933, against the Nazis. To be sure these protests have been of a limited character, limited by the traditional practice of both churches not to concern themselve as churches with politics, and by the desire of each not to sever itself too completely from this particular manifestation of German nationalism, or at least from those phases of it which were definitely and genuinely patriotic in even an imperialistic sense. Yet, in view of the penalties imposed upon opposition of any kind, the church should obtain recognition for what it did protest against. Inevitably what protests were made have concerned the refusal to compromise Christian with Nazi belief. The public utterances of the Confessional Synods and of the Fulda Conferences of bishops[6] have, at various times, rejected the anti-Semitism of the Nazis, and their general racial theory: they have repudiated their sterilization and euthanasia practices; they have rejected all notions of Hitler as God and the ideologies of blood, soil, and totalitarianism. They have rejected Nazi definitions of right as to what is useful to the people. They have protested against the confiscation of private property, the institution of concentration camps, and Nazi policies in occupied areas. They have protested against the attempts to crowd them out of public life, the loss of their press, the loss of their youth organizations and schools. This they have done while trying to remain loyal Germans. But in so doing they have expressed the convictions of those Germans who do not associate themselves with National Socialism. They have, therefore, harbored the political opponents of the regime. Nor have the churches confined themselves to protest.

---

3. The omitted passage contains a detailed analysis of the historical background of the church and state relationship from the nineteenth century onward.

4. The omitted passage deals with the different factions within the German churches since 1933.

5. For the Confessional Church (Bekennende Kirche) see document [28].

6. I.e., the annual Protestant and Catholic Church conventions in Germany.

They have acted, within the means available to them under a system of terror, to extend protection to Jews and those threatened with extermination: they have acted to keep themselves intact in however weakened a condition. They have extended their protest to occupied territories, and there protected the victims of Nazi brutality when they could. They have proved, therefore, that they were one group which could not be thoroughly coordinated. They have also participated in modest underground activity, discussions, and plans for the future. They have acted to arouse lay opposition among those subject to their influence, and coordinate their efforts when possible. Under persecution the Catholic and Protestant Churches have exhibited, to a certain extent, an unusual solidarity.

[...]

5. Military Security and the Churches

[...] It is obviously the positive rather than the negative aspect of the relationship between Military Government and the churches which requires attention. It is not to be expected that from the churches will come any underground, subversive, or serious anti-United Nations activity. But it is conceivable that, without the positive support of a program similar to the above, the churches would be in a position to organize a public opinion which, if not hostile, might well be neutral or noncooperative. Through a sympathetic appoach to the churches, Military Government has the opportunity to create a great source of support within the German population and to make an ally of an influential element. [...]

Section II. Recommendations

...[7]

12. Attitude Toward the Confessional Church

In the eyes of Protestant Christians in Germany, the attitude of Military Government toward the problem of religion will be judged in part by its treatment of the Confessional Church. It would seem advisable therefore in choosing German advisors on religious questions to include those who have played a role in this movement, and to consider in problems of personnel that membership in or support of the Confessional Church tends to indicate an anti-Nazi orientation and the likelihood of personal integrity. It is not possible to determine at this point what will be the attitude of these men toward the future of their movement. These men understand probably better than any other group of Protestant pas-

---

7. The omitted passages deal with the postwar role of the German churches, in particular with the elimination of Nazis from leading positions in the ecclesiastical administration, the restoration of civil liberties, and the suspension of Neo-pagan associations.

tors in Germany the dangers inherent in any kind of attachment of the church to the state. It is quite possible therefore that these men will be staunch defenders of the absolute separation of church from state. If so, it may be desirable to accord them facilities for organizing themselves throughout Germany as a completely free church. However, the Confessional Church may prefer to put itself on the basis of equality with the other Protestant Churches and the Catholic dioceses, and organize itself as a separate public law corporation, with the right to collect taxes with state assistance, the right to receive its share of subsidies from the state, and the right to participate in religious instruction in the schools and universities. Or as a third possibility, it may be that the Confessional Church, under the general condition of religious freedom, would prefer to submerge its identity along with the other provincial Protestant Churches, and participate in the reorganization of Protestant Christianity. In any of these circumstances, Military Government need only guarantee to the Confessional Church basic religious freedoms and the exercise of civil liberties.

Document 53 · 22 July 1944

Memorandum from OSS Director William J. Donovan to President Franklin D. Roosevelt[1]: The Situation in Germany

RESTRICTED

Memorandum for the President

Here is a report from our representative in Bern [Allen W. Dulles] received by way of radio-telephone:

Germany

"No very clear picture of the situation in Germany can yet be pieced together from the information reaching here. There is no information as yet from arrivals

---

1. NA, RG 226, Entry 99, Box 14, Folder 58a. On July 23, the same report went to the Secretary of State and to General Marshall.

from Germany, and the radio material is available to you as quickly as it is to us. The developments did not come as a great surprise, except to the extent that there were reasons to doubt whether any high officers of the German Army, who had remained in positions of power after the successive purges, would have the courage to act. As reported to you, many high German officers realized, however, that the time was growing short within which the anti-Nazi forces in Germany could act to rid the country of Hitler and the Gestapo, if this was to be accomplished prior to Germany's collapse. These officers considered that Hitler's military conduct of the war was a catastrophe, and that the only hope of saving anything from the wreckage was to remove Hitler. These persons hoped that they could make some sort of a deal with the West, along the lines of the Italian pattern, and thus be in a better position to restrict the extent of Russian occupation of German territory.

"The evidence seems to indicate that possibly the *Putsch* was staged prematurely, probably because the action of the Gestapo forced the hands of those who were plotting to remove Hitler. Rundstedt's removal[2] and then, more important still, the recent removal of von Falkenhausen in Belgium[3] indicate that the Gestapo was fearful of a military coup. Certain other persons who were probably to participate in the plot were also forced to run to cover before it took place. I do not believe the report circulating here that the story of the attempt on Hitler's life was fabricated or exaggerated in order to justify a thoroughgoing purge of the army. If Hitler desired to make a purge, he would not wait for any such excuse. His statement, and those of Goering and Doenitz[4] are hard to explain on any such theory. These statements would have too disturbing an effect on German morale to have been planted merely for the purpose of facilitating the arrest of certain generals. Further, we had ample advance warning that a plot was in the wind to discredit rumors that it was merely a Gestapo concoction. In fact, I believe that what has just taken place in Germany represents the one and only major attempt during the past eleven years to overthrow the Hitler government. No *Putsch* in Germany is possible without strong military backing. The Gestapo are numerous, determined and ruthless. The SS military formations in Germany could probably be counted on fully by Himmler. To meet these forces, the German generals opposing Hitler would need initially to secure the backing of several OKW [Oberkommando der Wehrmacht; Supreme Command of the Armed Forces] divisions strategically located. Only if they could succeed in seizing and holding for a time certain strategic points could the revolt have any chance of success. As yet, we

---

2. General von Rundstedt's role in the conspiracy against Hitler is obscure. Although he was removed temporarily on 6 July he became President of the "Court of Honours," an institution in charge of the expulsion of suspects from the Wehrmacht.

3. General von Falkenhausen, Commander Belgium and Northern France, had been dismissed on 14 July. At various points, Falkenhausen was on the cabinet's list of the conspiracy.

4. All three, Hitler, Goering and Doenitz, had given radio speeches playing down the importance of the coup. See also document [60].

have no evidence that they have succeeded in this. If they had, it would have seemed likely that certain powerful radio stations would be in the hands of the revolters, and we would be getting news of developments. Apparently, certain Nazi stations are off the air. Whether this means they are being fought over, or whether there are other explanations, we do not know. Whatever may be the result of the *Putsch,* the moral effect on Germany and on the Army will be very serious.

"I do not believe that the Army will for long accept and fight effectively under SS leadership. Of course, certain Nazi-minded generals, such as Rommel[5] and Guderian[6] may be able to hold their troops for a time, I doubt whether von Kluge is an out-and-out Nazi, despite his apparent pledge of loyalty today. He certainly was not such some years ago.[7] While it is too early to indulge in many predictions, I think it is safe to say that even if, as seems to be the case, [the] revolt is being or has been suppressed in a Gestapo purge of leading generals, the Army's morale will receive a severe shock from which, in its critical situation, it will be difficult for it to recover. There is no doubt that there is a real crisis in the High Command, with men like Zeitzler and [Wilhelm] Keitel both apparently involved,[8] and this can hardly be hidden from the men at the front. Further, Army circles have always had great respect for [Ludwig] Beck, and if he has been executed, as reported,[9] this will be a great shock to the rank and file of the OKW officers. It is particularly significant that Hitler apparently found no outstanding general to address to the army the same type of appeal which Goering made to the air force and Doenitz made to the navy, and that he was not able even to give the name of the general from the East front who he stated in his last night's speech was to be second to Guderian, who replaces the diplomatically ill Zeitzler. Outside of the opposition group which was responsible for this *Putsch,* I do not believe that any other group exists in Germany which would have any chance of staging active armed opposition. If this attempt has failed, the Germans will probably have to wait for the complete military collapse of Germany to rid themselves of the Nazis, and the next group to attempt this might be the Com-

---

5. For Rommel, see document 43. On 17 July, General Erwin Rommel had been severely wounded during air raids.

6. Heinz Guderian never took steps to overthrow Hitler although his relationship with the Führer had been rather tense since the fall of 1943. At that time Guderian had been contemplating Hitler's removal as military commander.

7. Since 1942 General [Hans] Günther von Kluge had been in touch with several of the conspirators, and especially with Carl Goerdeler. After the Allied invasion in France he had replaced Rommel as Supreme Commander on the Western Front. While at an earlier stage he was clearly in favor of Hitler's removal, he now remained passive and even sabotaged some of the preparations leading up to the 20th of July plot. For Kluge, see also document [67].

8. General Kurt Zeitzler had been on sick leave since 1 July. General Keitel was not involved in the conspiracy. See document [49].

9. Beck had been forced to commit suicide on 20 July, shortly before midnight.

munists, probably aided by a disorganized returning German army and the foreign workers and prisoners, if there is any lapse of time between the military collapse and the Allied occupation. Certainly what Hitler refers to as the Heimatheer [Home Army] is the only military organization now stationed in Germany which is powerful enough to stage an action against the SS forces, and if Himmler's command of the Heimatheer becomes effective,[10] any possibility of revolt will be largely removed."

William J. Donovan
Director

Document 54 · 22 July 1944

Memorandum from OSS Director William J. Donovan to President Franklin D. Roosevelt: Summarizing Report on the Attempt on Hitler's Life[1]

SECRET

Memorandum for the President

The military coup d'état attempted on 20 July 1944 by strong elements of the German High Command appears to have been the outgrowth of political preparations of at least six months' duration. For your information, I have prepared a factual presentation summarizing the data on this subject which has been cabled to us from our representative in Bern.

Since it is possible to infer from the statements of Hitler and Goering that the rebellion was not put down at once, I have also included certain possible lines of

---

10. Himmler had been appointed Commander of the Home Army on 20 July.

1. NA, RG 226, Entry 99, Box 14, Folder 58a. The same report was forwarded to James C. Dunn of the Department of State.

action suggested for consideration by our Bern representative in the event that the opposition may be able to maintain a stand in any region of Germany.

1. Composition and Aims.

Two emissaries of the conspiring group[2] first approached the OSS representative in Bern in January 1944. The group was then described as composed of various intellectuals from certain military and government circles gathered into a loose organization. The membership was said to be somewhat divided as to a course of action, some holding that Hitler and his cohorts should be made to shoulder all responsibility to the bitter end; while others favored an overthrow of Hitler and the organization of a new government before the fighting stops, which might negotiate peace. The conspiring elements were united in their preference for a western rather than an eastern orientation of German policy. In general, they were characterized by their emissaries as well-educated and influential but not rightist individuals; such characterization may have been designed for Anglo-American consumption. The group as a whole apparently maintained its foreign contacts through the Canaris organization.[3]

The following were said by the emissaries in February and April 1944 to be among the members of the group:

General Ludwig Beck, one of the two leaders of the group, former chief of the German General Staff, who retired "at his own request" in 1938. General Beck, General Fritsch, and General Fromm (mentioned later as a member of this group) dominated the Reichswehr Ministry until 1938.

Carl Friedrich Goerd[e]ler, co-leader of the group, a former Mayor of Leipzig, and one-time Nazi representative to business circles in the United States.[4]

Brigadier-General Hans Oster, former right-hand man to Canaris, who was arrested by the Gestapo in 1943 and later released but kept under surveillance and was officially discharged by Keitel in early 1944.[5]

Colonel-General Franz Ritter von Halder, a strong figure in Catholic circles, anti-Soviet, reported ousted in 1942, although thought under consideration by the Nazis for an important new post in late June 1944.

---

2. Hans Bernd Gisevius and Eduard Waetjen.

3. Admiral Wilhelm Canaris, Head of German Counterintelligence (the Abwehr), had repeatedly sought to establish contacts with British and American intelligence services.

4. Goerdeler had spent almost all of the second half of 1937 in the United States meeting American men of affairs and giving public lectures. Although his distaste for the Nazi regime was evident, Goerdeler was generally regarded as acting on behalf of former Reichsbank president Hjalmar Schacht and other German conservatives. Also, after his resignation as Mayor of Leipzig, Goerdeler had accepted in 1937 an offer by industrialist Robert Bosch for a loose contractual relationship.

5. Oster's release from duty in April 1943 was partly due to several initiatives on behalf of German Jews. The day before this memorandum reached the President, Oster had been caught by the Gestapo.

General Thomas (probably General Georg Thomas, Chief of War Economy and Armaments in the OKW).[6]

Hans Leuschner, socialist leader and former Minister of the Interior in Hesse, a former anti-Nazi who may have made some sort of peace with the Nazis.[7]

In early April the group's emissaries again approached the OSS representative, bearing a declaration said to represent the views of General Beck and Herr Goerd[e]ler. This message stated that, with Germany's position coming to a head and the end of the war in Europe definitely in sight, the group was willing and ready to take steps to oust the Nazis and eliminate Hitler (see report to White House Map Room, dated 12 April 1944[8]). The group claimed to be the only one with personal access to Hitler and other Nazi chiefs, with enough arms to accomplish its purpose, and with enough power in the army to make a *coup* feasible. Such action, however, would be contingent upon assurances from Britain and the United States that, once the Nazis had been overthrown, negotiations would then be carried out solely with the Western Powers and under no circumstances with the USSR. The essential conservatism of the group's planners was stressed, but also its willingness to cooperate with any available elements of the Left except for the Communists. The group expressed its anxiety to keep Central Europe from coming under Soviet domination. If capitulation were to be made primarily to the Soviet Union, the negotiations would have to be carried on by another group. Such Wehrmacht commanders in the West as von Rundstedt and Falkenhausen, the declaration maintained, would be ready to assist Allied landings once the Nazis were removed from power.

To these overtures the OSS representative said little beyond expressing his strong conviction that the United States would never act without previous consultation with the USSR. He reported at that time that he had doubts as to the group's chances of success, since he said that both Beck and Goerd[e]ler had been publicly mentioned as potential leaders of a *coup,* and since it could be taken for granted that the Gestapo was aware of this group. The representative thought that Gestapo had not stepped in either because it planned to wait until the group's plans had been more nearly perfected, or because the Gestapo too wished to have "an anchor in the West".

---

6. General Thomas had been involved in peace efforts in 1939 and in efforts to initiate a coup in 1941. At that time he was in contact with General Ludwig Beck, Carl Goerdeler and Johannes Popitz. Thomas retired in November 1942. He was arrested on 11 October 1944 when his early involvement in the opposition was discovered by the Gestapo.

7. There is no evidence for a pro-Nazi move by Leuschner.

8. Not printed.

In early May the two emissaries forwarded to the OSS representative a further communication from the group. Its membership was said by this time to include important new members: Generals von Rundstedt, Falkenhausen, Heusinger, Zeitzler, and Olbricht (see report to White House Map Room, dated 16 May 1944).[9] These Generals were all reported ready to assist Anglo-American units to enter Germany provided the Western Allies would agree to allow them to continue the war on the eastern front.

A new plan of action was outlined in the May communication. The plan called for the landing of three Allied parachute divisions in the Berlin area with the help of local army commanders; major amphibious landings at or near Bremen and Hamburg; the isolation of Hitler and high Nazi officials in Obersalzberg by trustworthy German units posted in the Munich region; and Allied landings on the French coast, though these in their early stages were thought difficult to plan as Rommel could not be counted upon for cooperation. In the communication the group reaffirmed its belief that Germany had lost the war, that the last hope of preventing the spread of Communism in Germany would be an Anglo-American occupation of the greatest possible portion of the Reich, and that the only means of accomplishing this would be to help the Anglo-American forces to enter Germany before military collapse in the East.

The two emissaries at this time expressed the opinion that the group's proviso with regard to the exclusion of the USSR was unrealistic; they regarded the plan for speedy American and British occupation of Germany as the core of the proposal. One of the emissaries admitted a lack of confidence in the political courage of the German generals, on the basis of past experience, and remarked that the Allies might do well to ignore their propositions if an early victory and speedy occupation of Germany appeared certain. The OSS representative reported his own doubts as to whether the group would possess the necessary determination to act effectively at the appropriate time.

In early July a courier arrived in Bern bearing a communication displaying new confidences in the strength of the group (see report to White House Map Room, dated 18 July 1944).[10] This message reported that the movement had gained new vigor from the Soviet victories in the East, from the Allied landings in the West, and from certain developments in Germany. Colonel-General Fritz Fromm, Chief of the Home Command, who controlled the regular army within Germany, was said to have joined the group. Further strength was said to have been acquired by the alleged transfer of OKW headquarters from East Prussia to a locality near Berlin[11] and the resultant proximity to Berlin of General Olbricht, Chief of the

---

9. Document [43].
10. Document [49].
11. See document [47].

General Army Office, Colonel-General Kurt Zeitzler, Chief of Staff, and other generals supposed to be in the opposition. Cooperation was also claimed from a group of anti-Hitler elements headed by Wolff Graf Helldorf, Berlin chief of police and an old-time Nazi. The message said that the group's plan of action called for an ordered retreat from the West and the dispatch of all crack divisions to defend the eastern front. Efforts would be made to convince the generals to wage a final struggle against Nazism.

On 12 July the OSS representative reported that a dramatic event might take place up north,[12] if the information brought by the group's courier could be trusted, and warned that any news would be suppressed by violence, if necessary. This was the last word received before the news of the attempted *coup*.

2. Nazi Counter-measures.

By the first week in July it became amply clear that the National Socialist Government was aware of impending revolt in high military circles. In his funeral oration for General Dietl (2 July) Hitler extolled those who devoted themselves to the German cause with fanaticism as opposed to the lukewarm supporters of the war effort. On 7 July when the break-through in the East began and the western beachhead loomed as a firmly established threat, Goebbels wrote an editorial in *Das Reich* pointing out that the home front was the critical area in the German war effort and that all power should be given to "the fanatics". This article constituted a marked departure from the earlier propaganda line, which emphasized the participation of *all* Germans in the conduct of the war.

These official statements were harbingers of the Party's intention to seize all power in the state, including that over the military establishment. On 19 July news leaked out to Stockholm that Heinrich Himmler would shortly be named to a post of first importance in the German High Command. Himmler's powers, it was said, would include complete control over all military appointments both in the field and in the Home Command.[13] As this report was received, telephone communications between Stockholm and Berlin were cut (1655, 19 July). The report therefore antedates the *coup* of 20 July.

3. The Coup d'Etat.

To the Army leadership the acquisition of such powers by Himmler clearly would be regarded as the end of their political power, domestic and international, which rested on their control of the armed forces. It may be assumed that the High Command felt its international bargaining strength to lie in its armies in the field.

---

12. Document [45].
13. See also document [53].

This was weakened by enemy action and also by the removal of General von Rundstedt and the presence of Rommel on the Western front. The High Command's domestic strength, on the other hand, resided in General Fromm's home forces. As the armies in the field approached defeat the importance of the home army would increase. Only through control of the home army could Germany's military leadership eliminate the Nazis without exposing itself to social revolution.

It is therefore believed that the proposed appointment of Himmler (subsequently announced in Hitler's speech after the *coup*) precipitated the military conspirators into premature action. The actual attempt upon Hitler's life, hastily organized as it was, had to be made before the appointment of Himmler could take place.[14]

We have just received from the OSS representative in Bern the following dispatch, dated 21 July, containing his estimate of the situation:

"The coup d'etat appears to have been the result of the planning and organization outlined in my earlier communications. It had been intended that certain men in the inner circles of the conspiracy, such as General Heusinger, would be at the meeting when the bomb went off because the only chance for planting the bomb was in conjunction with a conference attended by many of the chief military leaders. One of the members of the group was Stauffenberg who served as liaison between the older officers on active duty at General Headquarters and the younger group, formerly headed by Helmut[h] von Moltke. Stauffenberg, in addition, acted as councellor to Goerd[e]ler.

The outcome of the revolt at present rests with the Reserve Army 'Heimatheer' and their willingness to follow Himmler as their chief or whether they will stick to their old commanders some of whom appear to be involved in the plot. Naturally, the blood purge will be unmerciful.

One of the disheartening facts seems to be that the participants in the revolt do not have adequate radio facilities at their command. However, it has come to our attention that a report from Reuter's states that a message dispatched by the rebels from Frankfurt am Main this morning was interrupted.

However, a thorough perusal of the Goering-Hitler statements would lead to the inference that the rebellion was not put down at once."

4. Suggested Lines of Action.[15]

In the event that the opposition does find it possible to maintain a stand in any region of Germany, it has been suggested by our representative in Bern that the Allied Governments might wish to consider the following possible lines of action:

---

14. Himmler's imminent appointment as Commander of the Home Army had played a certain role, but it had not precipitated the conspirators into premature action. Actually, the bomb attack had been planned for an earlier date and had to be postponed several times.

15. See also document [51].

(1) "Some word from the President to counter Goebbel's line about the Allies' plan for complete annihilation of the German people. This would encourage the anti-Nazi groups.

(2) Air raids on the Nazi stronghold in the region of Berchtesgaden. Although the immediate military effectiveness of such action would be unimportant, it is possible that the psychological reaction would be great. Naturally, any break in the communication channels between the region of Berchtesgaden and the rest of the country would be especially valuable.

(3) Providing the rebellion gains any momentum, some announcement to the effect that any German town which sides with the opposition would not be attacked whereas Gestapo centers and Nazi strongholds would be bombed unsparingly.

(4) Large-scale dissemination of pamphlets from the air."

William J. Donovan
Director

P.S. Since writing the foregoing I have received a further dispatch from Bern which reads as follows:

"Up to 1:00 P.M. today (22 July 1944) the Nazi Legation had not had any news from the Foreign Office, not even the customary "sprach regelung" [Sprachregelung]. This is the Nazi term for instructions on how to lie. There are positive signs that if a revolt did get under way, several Nazi officers at this end would abandon the sinking ship."

W.J.D.

Document 55 · 24 July 1944

Memorandum from Wallace R. Deuel (OSS Washington)[1] to OSS Director William J. Donovan: Current Events in Germany

SECRET

Subject: Current Developments in Germany

1. The following ideas occur to me, on the basis of information thus far available, concerning current developments in Germany:

2. It has been clear from the outset that the generals would try to take Germany out of the war as soon as either one or both of the following things should threaten:

- a. the destruction of the German Army in the sense that the Polish and French Armies were destroyed—that is, their reduction to a state in which they could no longer effectively function;
- b. the approach of Allied armies, and most particularly of the Soviet armies, to German soil.

3. Since the second of these things is now happening, even if the first is not, I am convinced that further attempts will be made from now on to get rid of Hitler and take Germany out of the war, and that these attempts will be made by people much like those who seem to have made (or to be making) the present attempt. It would appear to be impossible to tell, at this distance and on the basis of the information available, what the chances of success are of such attempts.

4. At least this much is clear, though: Hitler is a much tougher individual than the last Kaiser was; there is probably no Doorn, where he could be safe in exile;[2]

---

1. NA, RG 226, Entry 190, Microfilm Roll 52, Frame Numbers 21–22. Deuel was Special Assistant to General Donovan.

2. On the advice of his military advisors, German Emperor Wilhelm II had fled to the neutral Netherlands in November 1918. For other intelligence estimates comparing the German situation in both world wars, see documents [19a], [19b] and [19c].

and, unlike the Kaiser, he has an alternative basis of power—namely, the SS. These factors, obviously will tend to make it much more difficult for the Army to take Germany out of the war now than it was for the Army to do this the last time.

5. The basic purpose of Germany's Russian policy for generations has been, of course, to control Russian raw material, Russian space, and Russian manpower in Germany's interest. Germany's governments have resorted at different times to two methods of achieving this purpose: One, to win control of these factors of Russian power by means of friendship with Russia; two, to accomplish this purpose by conquering Russia. Hitler has now tried both these methods and has failed in both. It seems to me that the generals will now try to make a deal with Russia, since they and Hitler together have failed so catastrophically to conquer the Soviets.

6. The fact that Hitler and Göring have told their own people that there was a plot among high-ranking generals must surely have a shattering effect, in time, on the morale of the troops. It would seem to be the case, therefore, that Hitler and Göring would give out this account of what has happened only if they knew that this account would reach the people in any event—which, in turn, would appear to indicate that the generals must have gotten access to German radio and/or other communications.[3]

7. If it is true, as reported, that Brauchitsch[4] and Halder have been involved in the plot, then chances are, that the whole group represented by "Herman" [Helmuth James Graf von Moltke][5] must have been mixed up in it, since they were two of the leading members of the group he represented.[6] If this is the case, it would follow that our refusal to dicker with these people—or at least their inability to make a deal with us—must have convinced them that they had to do their part first, without any help or promises from us.

8. One of the most interesting, and possibly one of the most important, political warfare angles of the past several days' developments obviously is that the Fourth Reich now has its alibi for the present war. We may expect to hear between now and the next German war the claim that Germany was not defeated in the field in this war, but that it was cheated out of the war by the disloyalty of a small group of traitorous generals. I should like to suggest that both ourselves and OWI [Office of War Information] make the most strenuous efforts, in our propaganda to Germany, to put over the point that the generals are quitting *because* the German armies are, in effect, defeated in the field, and to counteract the argument that the armies are being defeated because the generals are deserting.

---

3. In the early phase of the putsch, troops loyal to the conspirators had occupied the main Berlin radio station. They failed, however, to close it down or use it for transmitting their own prepared statements.

4. Field Marshal Walther von Brauchitsch had been Supreme Commander of the Army until his retirement in December 1941.

5. See in particular document [31].

6. Neither Halder nor Brauchitsch were at the core of the resistance, however, Moltke had been in touch with both of them.

9. For the rest, I should imagine that the most effective MO (and OWI) tactics now will be those of sowing confusion.

Document 56 · 24 July 1944

Telegram from David K. E. Bruce (OSS London) to OSS Washington: Anglo-American Intelligence Cooperation[1]

TOP SECRET

TOR: 7/24/44 2:54 pm

#62869. *Breakers.* 154 from Tiflis.

Breakers material has now been pieced together, including missing cables repeated from Washington. I went over entire story yesterday with both General Betts and Winant.[2] Betts believed that this matter, especially any military action, such as bombing Berchtesgaden,[3] was for decision at level higher than SHAEF [Supreme Headquarters of the Allied Expeditionary Forces]. Leaflet campaign had already been initiated. Ambassador suggested we defer making Breakers available to Broadway[4] until after his conference with P.M. [Prime Minister Winston Churchill] last night. He and we were concerned about possible Russian repercussions based on lack of true and complete story of our relations which are, of course, above reproach. To avoid any danger repetition last winter's Cairo story,[5] we agreed that in some way true facts should be conveyed to Russians, and he is cabling State Department in this connection.

---

1. NA, RG 226, Entry 99, Box 14, Folder 58a.

2. John G. Winant was Ambassador to Great Britain and American representative in the European Advisory Commission.

3. See documents [51] and [54].

4. I.e., Special Operations Executive (SOE) in Baker Street, London.

5. Probably a reference to Helmuth James von Moltke's attempt to approach Ambassador Kirk in Cairo. See documents [31] and [32]. In the winter of 1943/1944 reports about German overtures toward the Western Allies had appeared in Russia's official newspaper *Pravda*. The affair had caused considerable tensions between the Allies.

At conference this morning, Winant fully in agreement with us here to make Breaker material available to Broadway. We are accordingly transmitting data with letter conveying our understanding we would receive reciprocal treatment. Now that intelligence available to Broadway and ourselves on combined basis, SO [OSS Special Operations Division] can work with SOE [British Special Operations Executive] should opportunities operational activities present themselves.

Advise whether Breakers material is being considered in Washington at Joint Chiefs of Staff, Combined Chiefs of Staff or Inter-Governmental level. Betts indicated yesterday he did not believe Eisenhower had received earlier Breakers material through War Department or Combined Chief of Staff.[6]

Document 57 · 24 July 1944

Memorandum from OSS Director William J. Donovan to General George C. Marshall, Chairman of the Joint Chiefs of Staff: The Attempt on Hitler's Life, Conclusions and Propositions[1]

RESTRICTED

Memorandum for General Marshall

The following report was received from our Berne representative over radiotelephone:

Germany

"Until some trustworthy persons arrive from Germany, we will not know the full story of what took place, but it seems clear now that any prospects of an armed military revolt growing out of the Putsch against Hitler have been crushed. I am inclined to believe that the Gestapo probably had a good deal of prior informa-

---

6. General Eisenhower didn't receive any Breakers material prior to the 20th of July incident.
1. NA, RG 226, Entry 99, Box 14, Folder 58a.

tion about some of the persons involved, and were ready to strike and to strike hard. Himmler was probably glad to have an opportunity to do this before the retreating German armies were themselves on German soil, as it is far easier to deal with the *Heimatheer* than it would be to deal with the troops fresh from the defeats in the East, West, and South. But, in any event, a good deal of benefit to the Allied cause can result, as this attempt at revolt should help to undermine the will of the German Army to keep up the struggle. Obviously, an attempt is being made in Germany to play down the importance of those who were alleged to be in the plot, and therefore our tactics should be just the opposite. The personality of Beck gives us a good opportunity. He was a man of the highest military attainment, who enjoyed great respect from his colleagues, and who at the same time from prewar days refused to play along with Hitler's wild program of military conquest. Zeitzler, too, is a figure who can be used, as no one believes the story of his illness. Keitel's position is still obscure, but I am inclined to doubt the story that he was implicated in the plot. Apparently [von] Manstein, too, had nothing to do with it, as according to excellent reports, he is undergoing a serious eye operation at Breslau.[2] This attempt to overthrow Hitler was largely engineered by men who desired a western orientation of German policy, even though apparently they received no encouragement from the West, and acted on their own initiative entirely. The next attempt to overthrow the Hitler regime from the inside is likely to come from an eastern oriented group, possibly after a part of East Prussia is occupied and a German government a la Seydlitz is installed there.[3] It is probable that the failure of Beck and his friends will still further increase the influence [of] Russia in Germany and somewhat decrease the influence of the West. Russia has throughout played a more realistic policy in dealing with the internal German situation than has either the United States or England, and it is possible that, from now on, the Seydlitz Committee will increase in importance and have a larger scope of action. This is a development we should not underestimate, particularly now that the western-oriented dissident group in Germany, in and outside of the army, has received a serious, if not a fatal setback."

William J. Donovan
Director

---

2. Field Marshall Erich von Manstein was never interested in anything but military matters. In 1943, he had refused to take part in the plot against Hitler. Keitel was never approached by the conspirators.

3. General Walther von Seydlitz-Kurzbach had been captured by the Soviets at Stalingrad in February 1943, and in September he became head of the Soviet-sponsored German Officer's League (Bund deutscher Offiziere). This committee was calling for the overthrow of the Nazi regime, the ending of the war, and the retreat of the German armies to the original Reich borders of 1937. Thus, the aims of the Seydlitz committee were largely identical with the Free Germany Committee. See documents [13] and [31].

Document 58 · 26 July 1944

Memorandum from OSS Adviser Walter C. Langer[1]: A Fake Assassination Attempt?

Subject: Attempted Assassination of Hitler

Although the newspaper reports on the attempted assassination of Hitler are meagre, confused and contradictory and it is difficult to formulate any clear conception of what is happening in Germany, it is my belief that the attempt on his life was staged by himself.[2] The reasons for this conclusion are:

a. The time, place and manner of execution of the plot seem clumsy and unworthy of high-ranking German generals who planned to seize the government.

b. It seems unlikely to me that high-ranking Germans, who plotted to seize the government, would want to eliminate Hitler. They are well aware of the peculiar bond existing between him and the German people and would be more inclined to hold him as hostage to guarantee order on the home front as well as on the military fronts.

c. Any comprehensive plot by the army to seize power would almost certainly include the elimination of Goebbels and Himmler as well as Hitler.

d. In view of Hitler's fear of death it is unlikely, even with his peculiar psychological make-up, that he would proceed with state business in the calm manner described.

e. The text of his address after the incident (although it is difficult to judge from a newspaper version alone) is not what I would expect Hitler to say if the attempt had been genuine.

---

1. NA, RG 226, Entry 190, Microfilm Roll 52, Frame Numbers 23–27. This report was forwarded by Walter Langer's brother William to OSS Director Donovan and Colonel K. D. Mann, Head of the OSS Morale Operations Branch. Walter C. Langer wrote several psychological analyses of Hitler for the OSS. One of them became famous after the war when it was declassified in 1972 and published in the same year under the title *The Mind of Adolf Hitler.* The study was based on hundreds of (hitherto unpublished) oral interviews with people who had known Hitler in person.

2. This opinion was shared by several observers including German Communist exiles in Sweden. See document [63].

f. The technique of staging events of this kind in order to justify a radical course of action is not uncommon in Hitler's career, the Reichstag fire being the notable example.[3]

We may suppose that the situation in Germany is, briefly, somewhat as follows: As a result of the constant air-raids, the successful invasion and the defeats on the Eastern front particularly, the German people are losing all hope of winning the war and are wondering what good purpose it serves to continue enduring hardships and making sacrifices. Their morale and their productivity are consequently diminishing. This alarms Hitler and the top-ranking Nazis. The old-line generals are undoubtedly disgruntled about the way the war is being waged, particularly in view of the fact that one member of their group after another is being relieved of his command and is being replaced by a Nazi-trained officer. Many are probably of the opinion that the wisest course would be to make peace and salvage what they can of the German military machine and traditions.

Hitler knows that the Nazis have a sufficient hold on the home front to prevent a revolt of any consequence at this time. However, he would like to raise the morale of the people. The army is the only real threat to his power and position, and especially the old-line generals who command the respect and confidence of their men and the people at home. Many of the most famous among them consistently resisted his attempts to imbue them with the Nazi ideology. These are his greatest threat [sic]. The most obvious way of combatting this danger is to replace all those whose loyalty is doubtful with ardent Nazi supporters. Hitler has been doing this for some time, but it is a slow process because he must always wait until an occasion arises on which a given commander appears to be incompetent before he can justify the replacement in the eyes of the soldiers or of the people.

The recent succession of events has been such that Hitler fears the situation is getting out of his control. Something drastic must be done which will serve to speed up the elimination of old-line generals who might organize a revolt, frighten the more timid into blind submission, and at the same time win back or strengthen the allegiance of the rank and file at home as well as on the front.

When we look at the situation in this light there is only one possible event which could serve these purposes and that is an unsuccessful attempt on Hitler's life. The immediate reaction of all Nazi sympathizers would be: "We must no longer complain of our hardships or lose courage. We must try to be worthy of our Führer who sets us such a wonderful example. He is not only exposed to the dangers of air-raids and enemy fire, but also to the bullets and bombs of a hidden assassin. Yet he carries on with undaunted courage and fortitude, confident of ultimate victory. He lives only for Germany and although the future seems dark, we must not fail him." This type of emotional appeal for his personal safety and

---

3. The Reichstag fire, which destroyed most of the Reich Parliament in Berlin on 27 February 1933, was used as a pretext by the Nazis to suspend basic rights and to persecute the political left.

comfort is an old trick in Hitler's repertoire and has been unusually successful with the women and younger people. From it he would expect a definite rise in the level of morale. On the other side, only such an attempt on his life would in any way justify the purging of large numbers of old-line generals without any waiting for a show of apparent incompetence. Since no trial is allowed, all suspects and undesirables can be permanently eliminated from the picture and their places taken by ardent supporters who can be trusted. The process is quick, thorough and impressive.

These are the more obvious aspects of the plot, but there are subtle elements which are also extremely important. As failure looms ahead the aggression which has been directed against the enemy is gradually repressed by a fear of him. A new outlet for this aggression must be found. Since it can no longer be directed to the outside it begins to attach itself to persons within. Under these circumstances it most frequently becomes directed against the leaders who are responsible for their immediate predicament. In the present German situation this would be Hitler and the Nazis and if left to itself it would, in time, as these aggressive forces became stronger, lead to a general revolt against them.

Hitler undoubtedly senses this and in order to avoid such a catastrophe he must find a scapegoat to whom he can divert the mounting aggression in the people. The Jews served this purpose for Hitler after the last war and ever since but they cannot now be used in this way because they have had no part in the war effort. The only possible group which could serve in this capacity are the old-line generals whom Hitler has always hated and feared. The problem is how to shift the aggression of the people from himself to this particular group! In order to accomplish this successfully they must be placed in a position where they can, as a group, be accused of betrayal and disloyalty to the cause, while he appears to be working in behalf of the people. The attempted assassination serves this purpose beautifully for when it is translated, it says: "Do not blame me for our present predicament. I am doing my best to save you from disaster and willingly risk my life to do so. But how can we expect to succeed when these villains whom we trusted and who should be loyal in the performance of their duty betray us. You must hate them and not me." In order to satisfy their aggressive impulses he acts as the agent of the people in slaughtering the criminals. In this way he hopes to escape their vengeance as well as to absolve himself from any responsibility for his own failure.

In addition to diverting the mounting aggression, this technique also serves as a foundation for a future Nazi underground movement. In a short time the facts could be distorted, as they were after the last war, so that it would appear that the Nazi ideology and methods were sound and would have proved victorious if they had not been sabotaged by the Junkers and the old-line generals. The Nazi underground would presumably follow the same techniques in arousing the people that they used after the last war and unless some radical measures are taken to offset them they would probably be just as successful, especially with the younger generation.

Mention should also be made of one other aspect of the assassination attempt. The miraculous escape from death is designed to strengthen the myth that Hitler is under the protection of Divine Providence which shields him from death in order that he may fulfill his mission of leading Germany to a new greatness. This is an important element in holding the German people together and helps to maintain the delusion that although things look black at the present time Adolph [sic] will yet, by some miracle, turn defeat into victory as he has done so many times in the past.

In view of all this, the conclusion that the assassination attempt was staged seems almost inescapable. Equally inescapable is the conclusion that unless German morale was actually beginning to crumble, such a drastic measure would not have been necessary. Our problem is to capitalize on this knowledge. I would suggest that one of the best ways in which this can be done is to expose the plot as an attempt on the part of Hitler to trick the German people in the ways I have described. Every attempt must be made to prevent the transfer of aggressive impulses from Hitler and the Nazis, where they rightfully belong, to the old-line generals who are more likely to use common sense in facing the reality of the situation. In order to do this we must point out in detail what Hitler hoped to accomplish and why. In this way we would be calling his cards before he can play them and at least partially explode his strategy. This part of the project can be carried out by means of leaflets as well as the black and white radio with varying emphasis. On the black radio[4] we should use every means at our disposal to persuade the Army, if there is a plot to seize the government, not to assassinate Hitler but to take him prisoner. Any assassination will tend to strengthen the Hitler Myth and make the reformation of Germany in the future much more difficult. Our task would be much easier if he could be kept alive, but powerless, in order that he can be shown to the German people in his true light and be made to shoulder the responsibility for their disaster.

A word may also be said about Hitler personally. If the purge of the Army is as extensive as the newspapers would have us believe, it is almost certain that Hitler will go into a deep depression as he did after the Blood Purge in 1934.[5] He will be unfit for human companionship and will avoid it as much as possible. He will seek it only when the ghosts of his victims threaten him and he needs others about him as protectors. The minute these "protectors" appear, he will shift his secret fears onto them and dismiss them before they have a chance to assassinate him. In his sleep as well as in his waking state, he will feel himself surrounded by avengers. His capacity for work will approach zero and he will not dare to make

---

4. I.e., broadcasts disguising their origins.

5. Between 30 June and 2 July 1934, one hundred or more actual and potential oppositionals had been shot in the so-called Röhm-Putsch. This action was designed to eliminate the Sturmabteilung (SA, Storm Division) as a possible competitor of the Reichswehr. On the Röhm-Putsch, see also document [60].

any decisions. By his own actions in the immediate future he should aggravate the dissension among the remaining officers in the army. This would be an ideal time to hasten his psychological deterioration by playing on his fears if we had the means of reaching him. Rumors and black radio programs of all kinds of plots to murder him might be helpful.

From a psychological point of view it seems certain that German morale will decline. The attempted assassination may cause a temporary upswing but the increased pressure and terror will soon make itself felt. Terror feeds on itself for a time, but when it is directed against a part of oneself it soon becomes intolerable and breaks under its own weight. From the progression of events it seems almost inevitable that Germany will sooner or later break out into a bloody revolution.

Walter C. Langer
Consultant

Document 59 · 26 July 1944

Directive by the OSS Morale Operations Branch:[1] Denunciation of German Officers and Nazis

[...]

Attempt to give SS the names of all German officers and Nazis, known to you, and state that they were involved in Putsch. This will have the effect, if it works, of creating confusion in the SS, and of liquidating the people denounced.

---

1. NA, RG 226, Entry 134, Box 303. Whereas this message was sent to OSS Stockholm, similar cables went to other OSS outposts in Europe.

Document 60 · 27 July 1944

Report by the OSS Research and Analysis Branch: The Attempt on Hitler's Life and Its Consequences[1]

SECRET

[...]

The Attempt on Hitler's Life and Its Consequences

I. The Background

A. Principles for the Evaluation of German Morale. An understanding of the political significance of the latest attempt on Hitler's life may be aided greatly by a recapitulation of principles for the evaluation of German morale. These principles have been evolved in a series of papers[2] and may be summarized as follows:

1. The ruling group in Germany is made up of four segments: Party hierarchy, Army leadership, industrial and financial leaders, and high civil servants.
2. In the course of the war, the political power of the industrial leadership and of the civil servants has diminished to such a degree that they can assert themselves only by attempting to influence either Party or Army.
3. Therefore, the Party and Army leaderships are the politically important factors of the ruling group.
4. Though the Army leadership is permeated by reliable Nazis, it still preserves an identity of its own.

---

1. NA, RG 226, Entry 99, Box 14, Folder 58a. Author of this memorandum was Franz L. Neumann.
2. *The Ruling Class in Nazi Germany,* PW [Psychological Warfare] Weekly, *23 July 1943.*

5. Since the ruling group itself must make the political decisions its morale is determined by its own evaluation of the total political situation.

6. The morale of the subordinate strata is not conditioned by their thinking and feelings but rather by the institutional controls of Nazi society which compel the subordinate strata to work and fight no matter what may be their attitudes toward war and Nazism.

7. There is no potentially powerful revolutionary movement from below, although underground organizations of considerable strength do exist. These can become active only if a *coup d'état* paves the way for the destruction of the Nazi controls.

8. Such a coup could not be expected before the invasion. It can come only if the Army leadership fears the loss of the German Army, which it needs as the instrument for domestic control and political bargaining with foreign powers.

B. Party and Army. The retention of the generals' control over the Army is the key to the understanding of the plot. Without an army which is independent of the Nazi Party, the Army leadership and its allies—industrialists, bankers, Junkers, and high civil servants—cannot possibly play a role during the collapse and the post-war period. The Army leadership cannot count again upon a Social Democratic leadership which would entrust demobilization and reorganization of the Army to the old Officers' Corps, encourage the establishment of a Free Corps, and protect the *Reichswehr* from parliamentary control. If the generals lose Army control this time, they will be unable to exert any influence upon domestic developments or foreign policy.

It may be objected that these expectations of the generals are utterly without foundation, in view of the declared policy of the United Nations to destroy the German Army and to demobilize Germany. It is true that the United Nations have stated formally this to be their policy. But there is little doubt that the German generals hope and will continue to hope[3] until the opposite is clearly demonstrated to them, that they can create differences between the USSR and the Western powers and thereby retain at least the remnants of their instrument. With regard to the USSR, they see some hope in the Free Germany Committee and the German Officers' Union.[4] They also may remember Stalin's statement of 21 October 1942, when he said that he desired only the destruction of the "Hitlerite army."[5] The Army undoubtedly will continue to hope to bring about some understanding between Germany and the Western Powers against "the danger of Bolshevism," which it will present as the major danger to Europe.

---

3. *See also OSS Source #34017, 25 July 1944.*

4. For an estimate of the Free Germany Committee by the Research and Analysis Branch see document [29].

5. See also document [46].

Futile as these hopes may turn out to be, it is likely they influence and determine the outlook of the generals, just as they shaped the policies of Hindenburg, Groener, Seeckt, Reinhardt, and Schleicher in the fateful days of 1918 and 1919.[6]

The antagonism between Army and Party is of long standing. It first manifested itself on 30 June 1934, when Hitler purged Röhm and his group, which desired, broadly speaking, to transform the Army into an affiliate of the Party. On 30 June 1934, therefore, the Party was purged in order to maintain the organizational autonomy of the Army. In 1944 the Army was purged in order to save the Party. If Hitler had not purged the party in 1934, the Army would have become a Party formation; but if he had tried to do so, the Officers' Corps would have tried to overthrow him even then. Thus 1934 was the decisive year for the Nazi Party, a year that sealed the fate of Nazism as a revolutionary movement.

But the same purge that preserved the Army's organizational independence led to its political decline. The purge was not confined to Röhm and his followers, but also included the two generals who had done most to preserve the army under the Weimar Republic—von Schleicher and von Bredow. The Army leadership accepted this development and thereby subordinated itself to National Socialism. Step by step the influence of the conservative Officers' Corps was undermined, and subservient Army leaders took charge.

While this change tended to subordinate the Army politically, a new antagonism arose over the question of strategy. This difference was clearly brought out in a speech by Colonel General Ludwig Beck delivered in 1935 on the 125th anniversary celebration of the Military Academy.[7]

"It is the imperative demand that military questions should be traced back in their inner coherence to their origins in systematic intellectual labor, penetrating the problem step by step. That demand must be fulfilled, today more than ever before, by every one who desires to lead. Only its fulfillment can give the necessary basis for the responsibility, independence and initiative of the leader.

Such systematic thought must be carefully learned and exercised. To that end above all these years at the Academy are meant to contribute. Nothing could be more dangerous than to follow sudden inspirations, however intelligent or brilliant they may appear, without pursuing them to the logical conclusions, or to indulge in wishful thinking, however sincere our purposes. We need officers capable of systematically following the path of logical argument with disciplined intellect to its conclusion, strong enough in character and nerve, to execute what the intellect dictates.

---

6. See document [19a].

7. *Quoted from H. Rosinsky,* The German Army, *Washington, 1944.*

The *coup d'oeil*, the so-called lightning-like grasp of a momentary situation, formerly so highly praised, can certainly continue to be of importance in many situations in land warfare. In general, however, it must be considered of less importance, at least in the higher regions of leadership, than an understanding of the situation matured out of an intellectual penetration endeavoring to exhaust all possibilities …"

This speech reveals, perhaps better than the history of the various campaigns, the profound differences in the strategic approach of the conservative generals and of Hitler. It is undoubtedly Hitler's strategy on the Eastern Front that has led to the annihilation of the German field army. This must have created an ever-growing antagonism between the Party and the generals, exemplified by the retirement of many leading generals (see appendix I)[8] and supported by a huge number of intelligence reports (see also below […]).

The attempt on Hitler's life can be understood best if it is assumed that the Army leadership is primarily concerned with the preservation of the Army as its instrument. Such a situation now prevails. The field army is exposed to annihilation on the battlefield. Every general officer likely has realized since 6 June 1944[9] that nothing can prevent military defeat.

All that will remain to the army leadership is the Home (Reserve) Army. But the *New York Times* published on 20 July, one day before the attempted assassination, the statement that Himmler was to be appointed dictator of the Home Front and head of the Reserve Army, with the power to appoint and dismiss generals. Such a measure, which was decided upon long before the attempt on Hitler and thus was well known to the army officers, threatened to deprive the Army leadership of its control of the Home Army, consequently leaving the leadership without any bargaining power.

It is against this background—threatened annihilation of the field army in battle and loss of control of the Home Army by subordination to the SS—that the attempted coup may be analyzed.

II. Analysis of the Attempt

A. Friction Between the SS and the Army. The impending transfer of the Home Army to Himmler explains the timing of the attempt.[10] Indications of this are contained in Hitler's speech of 2 July 1944, delivered at the funeral of General Dietl, and Goebbels' article in *Das Reich* of 7 July, in which it was stated that the

---

8. Not printed. Appendix I listed the names and dates of retirement of 54 full generals or higher-ranking general officers.

9. I.e., D day, the Allied landing in Normandy.

10. See document [54].

only danger to the Nazi regime lay in the home front.[11] There were many more signs of the growing antagonism between the Party and its SS and the Army, apart from the basic strategic differences. The Army allegedly had tried to establish "security posts" in bombed towns throughout Germany in order to counteract SS domination;[12] General von Falkenhausen and Colonel General Friedrich Dollmann were replaced by SS officers,[13] and the SS and SA apparently were destined to play the lion's part in Hitler's "People's war" at the hour of military defeat.[14]

Mounting instances of acute friction and counteraction between army and SS commanders end, not infrequently, with the recall or the death of Army generals.[15] The reckless employment of SS troops, attributed to Army generals, particularly to Rundstedt,[16] was said to have resulted in demands by the SS for a greater, if not the dominant, share in military leadership.[17] Distrust by the SS of Army officers and demands for their dismissal were grounded in instances of defeatism among Army generals.

The *coup* also coincided with what appears to be the collapse of a German plan of defense, apparently a slow withdrawal from the East and firm resistance in the West, with the West maintaining strategic priority for the time being. Dittmar indicates that this strategy has been revised owing to the "unexpectedly rapid Soviet advance," so that to some extent the center of gravity thus once more will be shifted to the East.[18] According to secret reports,[19] a number of divisions from the strategic reserves have now been sent East, and more are promised.

It is quite possible that this newest change in strategy was unacceptable to those Army circles which have retained sufficient independence of judgment to recognize the handwriting on the wall.

Their action may be motivated by recognition that further sacrifice of troops entailed in this strategy would end in the complete destruction of German manpower, and of the German armies in particular. But it was the impending appointment of Himmler as dictator of the home front that forced the conspirators' hand.[20]

B. The Peace Feelers of the Beck Group. It is also known that a group of Army generals attempted to establish contact with the Allies in order to negotiate a separate peace. It was clear, even at the time, that this peace feeler was made either

---

11. See document [54].

12. *OSS #35739, 19 July 1944.*

13. *OSS #35770, 19 July 1944.*

14. *OSS Source S, 18 July 1944.*

15. *OSS #35770, 19 July 1944.*

16. *OSS #35919, 22 July 1944.*

17. *OSS #35739, 19 July 1944.*

18. Lieutenant General Kurt Dittmar was Speaker of the German Army. His candid radio broadcasts from Berlin were systematically analyzed by the OSS.

19. *OSS Daily, 18 July 1944.*

20. There is no evidence outside OSS records for this interpretation.

with the connivance of the SS Security Service or that the Security Service was at least acquainted with it,[21] and allowed the generals to approach the Allies in order to get full knowledge of all the ramifications of the plot. It also may have been the threatened exposure of their activities which compelled the plotters to act. This is likely in view of the fact that Suendermann's[22] statement to the foreign press seems to imply that General Beck was shot before the attempt on Hitler was made.[23]

C. The Identity of the Plotters. It is much more difficult to determine the identity of the plotters and their backers. The Nazi spokesmen endeavored to create the impression that "only a small clique of inconspicuous officers"[24] had made the attempt. Göring[25] narrows it down to "a miserable clique of former generals who had to be ousted . . . because of a leadership as cowardly as it was incompetent."

Very soon, however, emphasis was shifted from retired to active generals. The statement from Berlin to the European press admitted that active officers "holding important positions in the reserve"[26] were not only concerned in, but had actually inspired, the plot. Colonel General Heinz Guderian, the new Chief of Staff, finally laid the responsibility to a "few officers, some of them on the retired list,"[27] thereby admitting the majority were active officers. Goebbels finally laid responsibility[28] for the leadership of the plot on a colonel general, retired many years ago (apparently Beck) and another colonel general removed from the Eastern Front because of cowardice.[29]

The reasons for this change in emphasis are not hard to discover. The death or execution of active officers could not be hidden and had to be justified. As a consequence, their participation in the plot had to be established. According to German statements, therefore, the plot was confined exclusively to officers, namely, retired generals and members of the Home Command.

If Zeitzler really was among the plotters, he may have been planted there by the Nazis.[30] This would explain his temporary dismissal. To the list of those who were

---

21. *OSS Source #33696, 21 July 1944.*

22. Helmut Sündermann was Deputy Head of the Reich's press and information office.

23. *The Germans asserted, however, on 27 July 1944, that Beck committed suicide. (See below.)* For a special black radio operation drawing on Beck's suicide see document [72].

24. *According to Hitler, 21 July 1944.*

25. *FCC Daily Report, 21 July 1944, p. CCA 3.*

26. *FCC Daily Report, 22 July 1944, p. CCC 6.*

27. New York Times, *24 July 1944.*

28. New York Times, *27 July 1944.*

29. *The German radio identified today (27 July 1944) the following conspirators: Col. Gen. Ludwig Beck is said to have committed suicide. Col. Gen. Erich Höpner is awaiting trial. Höpner, who was Chief of Staff to Field Marshal v. Rundstedt, was retired in 1942. General Friedrich Olbricht, Chief of the General Army office was court-martialled and shot.*

30. *OSS Source #33934, 24 July 1944, differs from this interpretation.*

probably purged may be added the name of General Georg Thomas, Chief of the War Economy and Armament Office of the Supreme Command of the Armed Forces. Up to the time of Speer's ascendancy, Thomas was the key controller of the Nazi economy. Since 1942 he has continually lost power to Speer and his Armament Office was incorporated into the Speer Ministry,[31] while Thomas himself has been made subject to Speer's orders. Thomas is the outstanding liaison officer between the army and the leading industrialists.

Appendix I gives a list of the leading German generals who have been retired since 1938.[32] Appendix II contains the names of the major officers in the Home Command.[33] There is little doubt that General Beck participated in the preparation of the *Putsch*, although it it doubtful that he plotted the assassination of Hitler. Deputy Press Chief Suendermann's speech to the Foreign Press[34] seems to imply that he was shot before the attempt was made.[35]

There is no hint in German statements that civilians were in any way involved in the *Putsch* and the attempted assassination. And yet this appears likely. The aim of the *Putsch* was not only the assassination of Hitler, but also the assumption of governmental powers by the plotters in order to surrender to the Western Powers. If this is assumed to be true—and available intelligence supports this conclusion[36]—civilians must have participated in the preparation of the *Putsch*. Without the active cooperation of leading civil servants, and possibly of industrialists, the generals could not have assumed control of the huge governmental machinery that is necessary to install a new national government. The fact that the Germans have not admitted the participation of civilians may mean either they are not cognizant of this (which is doubtful), or they are reluctant to admit the extent of the opposition to the regime. In addition, by mentioning only generals in connection with the plot, the Nazis made it possible to shift the burden of the defeat on the Eastern Front from Hitler's strategy to treason by Army officers. This point will be elaborated later.

D. The Political Character of the Conspiratorial Group. The members of the conspiratorial group did not represent a positive political program for Germany save on one point: surrender to the Western powers in order to save the Army. They clearly counted upon what they consider "natural affinities" between Germany and Western culture and society, fear of Russia, in spite of all declarations to the contrary, and aversion to a German revolution which may spread and infect Europe. The group thus "gambled on what they conceived to be latent intentions of the Western Powers and the 'hidden' antagonism between the

---

31. See document [50].
32. See footnote 8, this document.
33. Not printed.
34. *FCC Daily Report, 21 July 1944, p. CCC 5.*
35. For the actual circumstances of Beck's death see document [54].
36. *OSS Source #33934, 24 July 1944.*

Western Powers. ..." [sic] The group was "favorably disposed to the military occupation of Germany by the Western Powers."[37]

The group was probably drawn from those favoring the so-called Western Orientation of German foreign policy,[38] which was formulated most clearly by the late General Max Hoffmann[39] as against those favoring an Eastern Orientation (the late von Seeckt, von Brockdorff-Rantzau, von Kühlmann,[40] and a large number of active generals).

But apart from its hope to sell itself to the West for what it believes to be the ultimately necessary war against the USSR, the group represented nothing except bankrupt generals, nationalist intellectuals, and (possibly) nationalistic Social Democrats and civil servants. This by no means implies that the group would not have found backing if it had succeeded in its *Putsch*. The desire for peace is believed to be so intense in Germany that any group, no matter how compromised, would have found almost universal acclaim if it succeeded in ending the war, though its power would have vanished rapidly once peace was declared. The extermination of the group thus does not impede the political regeneration of Germany.

III. The Consequences of the Attempt

A. The Purge of Opposition Leaders. No matter how narrow the basis of the plot may have been, there is little doubt that it will be the occasion for a large-scale purge of generals, former political leaders, and possibly of industrialists, bankers and high civil servants. One statement in the Goebbels speech of 26 July 1944[41] indicates that there is to be a wholesale purge. Goebbels, when reporting his instructions to the Commander of the Berlin Guard battalion, Major Remer, added: "Immediately after the end of my speech officers and soldiers take up their machine pistols and rifles to *get them ready to settle accounts*."[42] Intensified attempts to exterminate the active or potential opposition were reported for some weeks prior to the attempt. These purges, of course, never were publicized. The generals' plot provides the opportunity of carrying out large-scale purges which

---

37. *All quotations from The Morale of the German Ruling Class*, PW Weekly, *21 April 1944 pp. 11–12.*

38. *OSS Source 33696, 21 July 1944.*

39. *For details, see* The Free Germany Committee and the German People, *OSS, 6 August 1943, pp. 12–14.* Not printed. Compare, however, document [14] of the same day.

40. This is a reference to World War I and to the Weimar Republic. General von Seeckt had played a prominent role in establishing secret contacts between the Reichswehr and the Red Army in the 1920s. Ulrich von Brockdorff-Rantzau had served as German Ambassador in Moscow from 1922 to 1928. Richard von Kühlmann had been German Foreign Minister in 1917/1918. In connection with the attempt on Hitler's life, he was arrested but released after a short time in custody.

41. New York Times, *27 July 1944.*

42. *Italicized by the author.*

could not possibly be hidden from the German people, but which can now not only be brought into the open but even given a convincing and rational justification.

Though it is likely that the purge will affect equally the members of the Western and Eastern orientation within the Officers' Corps, the influence of the Easterners undoubtedly will increase. This is due to two factors. The Eastern orientation has many more adherents, especially in view of the influence of the late General von Seeckt.[43] Besides, in the Free Germany Committee and the German Officers' Union, the Easterners already possess a rather strong organization abroad, staffed with well-known officers (see appendix III).[44] This fact, together with the possible rise of Communist movements in the post-hostilities period (see below), is likely to cause an Eastern orientation of important strata in the German people unless the post-hostilities policy of the USSR is held primarily responsible for the deprivations of Germany.

To some extent, the pattern of 30 June 1934 likely will be repeated. The 1934 pattern means that the Nazi leadership will publicly admit only a very limited purge while it actually will attempt to exterminate all those who could possibly organize resistance. The purge by no means will necessarily be confined to army officers and the potential revolutionary opposition.[45] There are, of course, very good reasons why the Nazi leadership cannot possibly admit that the plot has broad ramifications. To do so would be to admit the instability of the regime, and thus, while Germany is enduring one military defeat after another, to invite mutinies and desertion. The tightness of domestic controls will prevent the people from learning the extent of the purge (years passed before the seriousness of the 1934 purge was known in Germany—if it is known even now). Each local incident of the purge thus can remain isolated and justifiable, and the picture presented by the Nazis (a plot confined to a few) may thus be believed.

B. The Success of the Purge. Has opposition, actual and potential, now been purged effectively? This question cannot be answered with certainty, since two major factors are unknown: The strength of the opposition and the extent of the purge. But it is safe to assume that the rise of a new opposition within the Army leadership has been made much more difficult, while the joining of industrialists and high bureaucrats is now unlikely in view of the fear that the purge is likely to create among this group. Even those who have considered joining a *Putsch* are

---

43. A major reason for the orientation were contacts that had been established secretly between the Reichswehr and the Red Army after World War I. Von Seeckt was a prominent figure in these operations designed to circumvent demilitarization measures.

44. Not printed. This appendix lists 30 higher officers in the German Officers' Union and the Free Germany Committee.

45. *There are already reports of the execution of Schacht, von Neurath, and members of the Stauffenberg family.* (These reports were inaccurate: although Schacht and several members of the Stauffenberg family were, indeed, arrested and put into concentration camps after the 20th of July plot, none of them was executed. Von Neurath was not at all involved in the plot.)

now likely to submit declarations of loyalty. They will probably avoid even the slightest indication of a conspiratorial spirit.

On the other hand, it is impossible to annihilate the potential opposition without crippling the army, state, and industrial machines in so doing. There can be no doubt that the high Officer Corps and many high civil servants and industrialists are overwhelmingly conservative, though their great majority is non-political in the sense that it merely obeys the orders of a duly constituted central authority. Had the coup been successful, the bulk of the high Officer Corps, civil servants, and industrialists would have been likely to follow the new leadership. As the situation now stands, this potential reservoir of opposition has been deprived of a leadership which alone would have been capable of transforming oppositional feelings into concerted action.

At the same time, it must be kept in mind that without a previously successful army coup, no successful revolution from below could have been expected.

C. The Effects on Army Morale.   The outcome of the coup and purge is the tightening of Nazi controls over the armed forces, which probably will now lose their identity and become, so to speak, an affiliate of the Nazi Party. Symbolic of this is the imposition of the Nazi salute on the armed forces.[46] The Reserve Army seems destined to be thoroughly Nazified. It was, in the *Wehrkreise* (corps areas), commanded by older and often re-activated generals who were strongly imbued with the traditional spirit of conservatism[47] and constituted the most powerfully entrenched army bureaucracy. They likely are to be removed and probably will be replaced by the Higher SS and Police Leaders whose jurisdiction tallies with that of the *Wehrkreise*.

What will the reaction of the remaining officers be? It is most likely that they will continue to fight—with the one reservation mentioned below.

There are a number of reasons for this:

The first is inherent in the pattern of army organization and in the army tradition. Rebellion of the army against civil authority is, of course, the exception. Very few officers have the courage to risk their lives in this way; the great majority fights as long as a central authority exists and orders it to fight. The central authority not only exists but is now outwardly stronger than before. Considerations of pure self-interest must not be forgotten. German officers have increasingly become civil servants eager for promotion and anxious for pensions.

The second question is whether field commanders will surrender with their army units before the military situation compels them to do so. This appears

---

46. This had been one of the first reactions of the Nazi government to the failed putsch. Other measures taken were the arrests of the plotters' families (*Sippenhaft*). Altogether several hundred were taken into custody.

47. *Names and rank in* Order of Battle of the German Army, *February 1944 (MID), pp. 25–49.*

unlikely. This view is based on the case of General Hoffmeister, recently captured by the Russian army.[48] It seems clear that Hoffmeister had either some kind of contact with the Free Germany Committee and the German Officers' Union at Moscow or was acquainted previously with the aims of the Moscow organization. It is evident from his broadcast to the German army in the East that he was genuinely critical of Hitler's strategy and was in complete opposition to his leadership. And yet his broadcast reveals clearly[49] that in spite of his probable contact with the Seydlitz group, and in spite of his opposition to the personal strategy of Hitler, he fought until the military situation compelled his surrender. Military honor and tradition thus will make it unlikely that generals will surrender except under military necessity.

But the coup and the purge are most likely to influence their estimate as to what "military necessity" is. Prior to the coup, the generals fought bitterly because the whole army leadership appeared united in the determination to fight to the finish. Now it is being demonstrated to them that Germany's outstanding military leaders—whose patriotism, experience, and skill are beyond doubt—have abandoned hope and have admitted that nothing, save a miracle, can avert complete military disaster for Germany. They may now come to believe that their own contribution to the fight matters little, and they may now interpret the term "military necessity" rather liberally and surrender without putting up a last-ditch fight.

It is difficult to judge whether the morale of the Army has been adversely affected, or will be impaired within the near future. The common soldier may actually experience a certain upswing. He may even believe that the defeat in the East was due to treason rather than faulty German strategy and Russian superiority. If this is his reaction, then he will be compelled to revise his views if he is ordered to withdraw further.

In the Officers' Corps, the number of Nazis among the junior officers is very high, but is fairly small in the upper ranks. The coup and purge unquestionably will impair morale. The uncertainty about the ramifications of the plot is likely to create distrust among the Officers' Corps; fear of denunciation will grow, and initiative will be further crippled because responsible commanders will shrink from any strategic and tactical decision not approved by the Party, lest it be attributed to a treasonable spirit.

There are, however, no indications as yet that the fighting spirit has been impaired, though the Nazis tend to create this impression. Lt. Gen. Dittmar's talk[50] attributes the defeat in the East at least partly to treason. "We are," he said,

---

48. It has been suggested by some historians that the Soviet government was not only aware of the 20th of July plot against Hitler, but used captured Lieutenant-General Edmund Hoffmeister as a spokesman to support the revolt morally. Hoffmeister was indeed a member of the Free Germany Committee. His radio speech on an imminent collapse of the Reich was broadcast in German language via BBC just an hour before the plot took place.

49. New York Times, *20 July 1944.*

50. *FCC Daily Report 26 July 1944, p. H 4.*

"far from wanting to deduce the development of the situation in the East *only*[51] from detrimental influences exerted by the traitors ... For that their circle was too small and its import on the whole organization of the army not great enough." The dilemma of Nazi propaganda is clearly revealed here. Part of the blame for the defeats is shifted from Hitler's strategy to the plotters, but the whole responsibility cannot be attributed to them without admitting wide and deep ramifications of the plot.

D. Consequences for the Home Front. The direct consequence of the abortive coup is the full concentration of all powers in the hands of the triumvirate of Himmler, Göring, and Goebbels as manifested by Hitler's edict of 26 July 1944.[52] Further labor mobilization will deprive the civilian population of even the barest conveniences, will make it impossible to replace even the most primitive objects destroyed by air warfare. Many administrative offices are likely to be closed, the Economic Groups may be dissolved, and sole responsibility for war production may be given to Speer's Committee and Rings [sic]. This is probable in view of the praise which Goebbels heaped on Speer.[53] The ascendance of the *Gauleiter* over the traditional administrative agencies may culminate in the complete abolition of many administrative bodies. It is likely that *Kreisleiter* will become mayors and *Landräte*, and such offices as that of the provincial presidents may be replaced simply by the *Gau* administration.

Though Göring and Goebbels appear to share power with Himmler, they are, in reality, his subordinates and it will be their duty merely to implement his decisions on policy.

Will Himmler aim at nationalization of the means of production? Will he try to institute a system of National Communism in order to stimulate production? This appears unlikely. Himmler and the SS long since have ceased to attack industrialists. The Speer organization and the Göring combine are permeated with SS leaders who have close links with business.[54] Robert Ley referred to the plotters as "German counts," "criminal members of the nobility" and to the "reaction"[55] but made no mention of industrialists and bankers. Besides, it would be disastrous to undertake a large-scale program of economic reorganization at a time when every ounce of manufactured war material counts. All that can be expected, therefore, is a radical elimination of many administrative control agencies. Large-scale expropriations can only be expected as a last desperate attempt to organize a *levée en masse* for which the enthusiastic approval of the worker would be needed.

---

51. *Emphasis supplied.*
52. *Text* New York Times, *26 July 1944.*
53. New York Times, *27 July 1944.*
54. The Ruling Class in Germany, *op. cit.*
55. *FCC Daily Report, 25 July 1944, pp. CCB 3/4.*

E. The Pattern of German Collapse. The coup and purge are likely to change the pattern of collapse. This aspect exceeds the scope of this paper and therefore will be treated very briefly:

It has heretofore been assumed[56] that fighting is not likely to take place on German soil because generals leading a successful *Putsch* would depose the Nazi leadership and sue for peace. This now appears less likely. It can now be assumed that the Nazi leadership is committed to a fight to the finish and will not hesitate to make Germany a battlefield. But it is doubtful whether this will be possible.

It is questionable that the Nazi leadership will be successful in achieving its three major tasks:

To prepare and execute an orderly retreat;

To keep the masses of workers from striking;

To prevent the surrender of army corps commanders with their armies once this state of the war is reached.

Tentatively, the following development may be envisaged when German territory is invaded in the West and East, or if in the East, large-scale inroads are made on German territory, strikes are likely to break out.

It is doubtful that they can be suppressed. These strikes may not be revolutionary, but merely defeatist. The armies will try either to hurry home or, if obstacles exist, surrender without centralized command. There will then be no central authority unless the Nazi government itself surrenders and Germany will be in a state of chaos.

The consequences of the abortive coup may well be the rise of National Bolshevist movements in the post-hostilities period.[57] The problem which the Nationalist movement faced in 1918 and 1919 will arise again. To the genuine Nationalist youth in Germany, the solution of the problem after the defeat of National Socialism will be very different from what it was after 1918. The Nationalist groups may point to the enormous internal and external strength of the USSR. They may attribute this strength to the fact that the bourgeoisie has been eliminated in Russia and that, while the Nazis talk about the People's community, the Russians have established it by the extermination of their own industrialists, bankers, Junkers, and middle classes. These groups, therefore, may attempt to ally themselves with the German working classes, hoping to swing them in a Nationalistic direction. They may strive to bring about a reconciliation of Nationalism and Communism and orient their policy towards an understanding with Russia, hoping that with Russia's backing Germany can be restored to the position of a great power.

---

56. The Process of German Collapse *R & A No. 7477, 4 December 1943.*

57. *For details see* The Free Germany Manifesto and the German People. *R & A, 6 August 1943, pp. 6–12.*

Document 61 · 28 July 1944

Telegram from OSS Director William J. Donovan to David K. E. Bruce (OSS London): OSS Directives Concerning the "Breakers" Correspondence[1]

SECRET

TOD 28/7/44 11:48 pm

#58807. To [David] Bruce only from 109 [William J. Donovan], with reference to Bern-London

Breakers #866–7. *Action*: London; *Information*: Bern (#1881–4).

We will by no means let the Russians see the *Breakers* correspondence. It can be easily seen, especially from cable #2714–6 from Bern of April 6, 1944, that Bern did not feel that there was any possibility of our helping *Breakers*, but instead said most emphatically that we would inform the Russians of any action we might take.

This is precisely the answer I gave through Turkish channels when, about a year ago, a group much like the *Breakers*, or possibly the *Breakers* themselves, said they were ready to help us in the West as a means of keeping Russia out.[2] Simultaneously, it was reported that a similar group was inclined towards the Soviet.[3] I took up this proposition with the British, and we concluded that it would be wiser not to inform the Soviet, (1) because it might arouse their suspicions of us rather than impress them with our desire to be helpful, and (2) because there was some evidence that the eastern-oriented group had already approached them with their proposals.

I think events have already demonstrated the advisability of avoiding involvement in this matter, and I consider that, if the Germans battle it out inside Germany without help from us, it will be of more benefit to humanity.

---

1. NA, RG 226, Entry 146, Box 235, Folder 3296.

2. This is a reference to Helmuth von Moltke's approach to the Allies via Turkey. See documents [31], [32], [37a], [37b] and [37c].

3. See in particular document [57].

With reference to the type of information you mention in your #825–7, I think it unsafe to use Winant to bring it to State's attention. This is only doing what Washington does anyway, and increases the probability of leakage, as Winant will present his report to State through their channels, which may not handle this specific type of information as carefully as the channels that we have specially set up. The practice of taking this material to Winant has also brought unfavorable comment from 110 [Allen W. Dulles].

I wish strongly to emphasize that this is Washington's job, which we are doing by keeping those government agencies informed which have a legitimate interest.

WJD

Document 62 · 1 August 1944

OSS Propaganda Directive:
Faked Resistance Movements[1]

SECRET

#1911–12. Weekly directive for MO.[2]

Disseminate the information that "Das Neue Deutschland" [The New Germany] is 1 element connected with the attempt on Hitler's life.[3] Like the others, its membership is composed of assorted civilians and army officers. This entire group intend to supplant the Nazis with a new government dedicated to the following principles: Insure a speedy demobilization; provide for a better peace; prevent impending civil conflict and put an end to any additional slaughter. It makes an appeal to patriotic Germans to refuse to join SS, to strike and to hoard and to engage in other activities that will bring about a speedy Nazi downfall.

---

1. NA, RG 226, Entry 146, Box 231, Folder 1390. This weekly directive was distributed by the Morale Operations Branch in Washington to several European Outposts. Donovan took a special interest in these directives and had all of them sent to his office. Others were forwarded to the Secretariat, the Communications Division and to Counterintelligence (X–2).

2. The following slogans are examples of black propaganda. In contrast to "white" or "open" propaganda, in black propaganda, the origin of the source is intentionally concealed.

3. This movement had been concocted by the OSS. See also document [68].

Spread the report that the 4,000 kilos of gold sent to Argentina for the purpose of supporting the Nazi underground in the future will now be used by the SS officials for their personal needs.

Keep on with the practice of submitting lists of alleged conspirators to SS.

Make a statement to the effect that a good part of the *Waffen SS* volunteers joined up because they wished to secure weapons with which to protect their homes from Nazi purgers. [...]

Document 63 · 3 August 1944

Memorandum by OSS Stockholm: Position of German Communists[1]

SECRET

Position of the German Communists on Questions of the Day

(Meeting of August 1)

In an exchange of views between German Social Democrats, members of the SAP (Socialist Workers Party), and Communists on the events of July 20th in Germany, there was general agreement that the attempt on Hitler's life had been organized by the Nazis themselves in order to put suspected and possibly outright conspirational officers and industrialists out of the way, and from this starting point to introduce internal terrorism on an increasing scale. The Communists pointed out among other things that the Nazis are attempting to hold their own by capturing the imagination of the dissatisfied masses, and in particular of the workers, under the illusion that the "revolution" begun in 1933/34 was going to be carried through, particularly in taking measures against the nobility. But all of us

---

1. NA, RG 59, CDF 103.918/9–544. The information given in this dispatch, which had been translated from Swedish into English, was considered by the OSS to be "reliable." Like most other cables from Sweden it reached the OSS through diplomatic channels.

agreed that nobody believes this sort of thing any longer and that it makes no impression. The Communists said that this recent internal action of the Nazis could be traced to the fact that internal opposition appears to be more and more organized (whereby, even though they did not say so openly, they quite obviously alluded to the influence of the "National Committee of Free Germany").

When a Social Democrat speaker broached the question of the "National Committee" and evidenced a very skeptical attitude towards the further intentions of the officers represented in that group, he was refuted by a Communist speaker who pointed out that amongst the more prominent officers there were a number of men who had assumed officer positions only during the war. Moreover, it was today apparent from the public statements of the "National Committee" that soldiers were taking oppositional stands towards many of the utterances of von *Einsiedel, Seydlitz,* etc. It was consequently certain that in the future the National Committee would not play up these figures to the same extent as at the start. However, up to now this had been the right policy to follow for breaking down the morale of the officers corps and thereby the whole *Wehrmacht.* He went on to say that, should a military regime arise in Germany, such a government would very quickly be swept aside by a mass movement.

Some Social Democrats expressed their belief that, if a regime of generals or some form of interregnum should fail to come into being (presupposing the overthrow of the Nazis prior to a general collapse), the responsibility for "unconditional surrender" could not be assumed by democrat or socialist elements. Some other Social Democrats took sharp exception to this point of view on the grounds that the only consequence of such an attitude would be to abandon everything to fate, and thus to assume responsibility for continued bloodshed and ever increasing terrorism inside Germany. The principal point was to get the war over with; the myth of the "dagger thrust" could only possibly gain ground in the event that afterward a policy was followed which gave the masses no democracy and no social improvement.[2] It was only on this basis that the Nazis had succeeded in exploiting the Versailles treaty.

In opposition to the Social Democrats, who limited themselves to general discussion, the SAP members proposed the formation of a common committee of action in Stockholm, in an attempt to make a public proclamation of common aims and a common platform; in particular, to attempt to make use of the radio broadcasts from England and the Soviet Union in order to speak directly to the anti-Nazi population in Germany as a homogeneous Socialist movement, fused from the various former parties. They also introduced a resolution, which they had worked out, concerning the events of July 20.

The communists were basically in agreement with this proposal, but would not join with the SAP members obviously because they are annoyed at the intermediate

---

2. This is a reference to the so-called "stab-in-the-back" legend after World War I. See document [31].

position these people occupy between the Socialist and Communist parties. They are especially hostile towards those people who until 1928/29 were in the Communist party and consequently know it inside out. They finally concluded that all this must once again be thoroughly discussed within the individual parties. It was decided that the Communists and the Socialists should each define their own individual positions once again, and then the 5 persons (2 Communists, 2 Socialists, 1 SAP), who function as a purely technical contact committee between the various groups, are to meet.

Document 64 · 18 August 1944

Telegram from Allen W. Dulles (OSS Bern) to OSS Washington: Eastern and Western Oriented Resistance[1]

SECRET

TOR: 8/19/44 4:16 am

#4532–4. *Breakers*. To Jackpot, wishing him a pleasant journey. In reference to your #1955.

I interpret the situation in the following way: some little time prior to the putsch, some type of union existed between the eastern and western oriented factions. Both groups had identical immediate goals, the destruction of the Hitler gang. I believe that 512 [Hans Bernd Gisevius] was not aware of this move until he arrived at headquarters. The foregoing is only a guess but I call to your attention the opening paragraph of Breakers #3423–31,[2] describing the reaction 512 received when he returned the messenger with the information that there was no possibility at all of making a deal with the west on the basis of allowing the Nazis to maintain the Eastern Front. In addition, refer to the answer which 512 received. It is entirely probable that Breakers decided at that point to collaborate with the east oriented faction. Even though the identities of several generals involved were

---

1. NA, RG 226, Entry 99, Box 14, File 58a.
2. Not printed.

furnished to me in advance, the fact that participants who were just as prominent (possibly those who were eastern oriented) were not mentioned makes me think that 512 had no knowledge of this development before he returned.

This appears to be the most probable answer to your query rather than any change in the policy or mentality of Becky-Leper [Beck-Goerdeler] and their group.

Document 65 · 18 August 1944

Report by OSS Rome: An Interview with Father Georg Leiber in the Vatican[1]

CONFIDENTIAL

Subject: Interview with Father Georg Leiber, Professor at the Papal Universities Gregoriana, Piazza della Pilotta, Rome, 18 August 1944

1. Biographical Details

A Jesuit of Bavarian origin, Father Leiber was teaching in the Theological Faculty of the University of Munich when Cardinal Pacelli, as Papal Nuncio to Germany, visited Bavaria. Pacelli was so impressed with Father Leiber's ability that he took him on his staff as private secretary. Father Leiber has remained with him ever since, working apparently in intimate contact with him both during his years as Cardinal Secretary of State and since his elevation to the Papacy. At the present time, Father Leiber's official position is simply that of professor at the Gregoriana.[2] His friends know, however, that he is also serving as confidential secretary to the Pope, whom he sees almost daily. These friends (who include Baron Froelichsthal of the Austrian Office) consider him a thorough anti-Nazi.

---

1. NA, RG 226, Entry 136, Box 14. This interview, which had been conducted by members of the 2677th Regiment OSS, was forwarded on 20 August by H. Stuart Hughes to R&A Director William L. Langer. Hughes was at the time working with the Italian outpost of R&A.
2. I.e., Vatican University.

2. The Background of the Attempt on Hitler's Life

Although he has not been in Germany since 1932, Father Leiber has unusual sources of information on the history of conspiracies against the Nazi regime. According to his own account, the conspirators almost invariably kept him informed of their activities, in an effort to find out the Pope's reaction to their designs.[3] Father Leiber identifies three distinct plots during the years preceding the assassination attempt of last month. On this fourth effort, he has practically no information, since in this case the conspirators evidently did not care to take him into their confidence.

a. Winter, 1939–1940. The first major plot against the Nazi regime was organized under the leadership of General von Hadler [Halder] during the period just preceding the Norwegian campaign.[4] The conspirators, who were primarily members of the German nobility, hoped that the expedition against Norway would fail and thus give them an opportunity to carry out their designs. With the success of the campaign, the conspiracy evidently evaporated. Furthermore, Von Hadler [Halder] had compromised his own position by some indiscretion which had leaked out through Switzerland. The chief weakness of the whole conspiracy seems to have been its lack of support from the generals, who still remained loyal to Hitler.

b. February, 1943. The next effort, which resulted directly from the Stalingrad disaster, was far more serious and extensive in the support it obtained. Its leader was General Ludwig Beck, and its civilian adherents included Löbe, former Social-Democratic President of the Reichstag,[5] Goerdeler, former mayor of Leipzig, and Von Hassel [von Hassell], former German ambassador to Italy[6]—a range of support including all political elements under the Weimar Republic except the extreme Right and the extreme Left. Adenauer, former Centrist mayor of Cologne, refused to join the movement, since he believed that the Nazi regime

---

3. Between 1939 and 1943 the Catholic lawyer Josef Müller had been Leiber's chief contact to the German opposition. Through Müller he was in touch with oppositional circles in the Abwehr, including Hans Oster and Hans von Dohnanyi but also with the theologian Dietrich Bonhoeffer. After the arrest of Müller, Bonhoeffer and Dohnanyi, Father Leiber got his information on the German resistance through Hans Bernd Gisevius.

4. An invasion of Norway had been contemplated by Admiral Raeder and Hitler as early as October 1939. The actual invasion started in April 1940.

5.Through Social Democrats Wilhelm Leuschner and Julius Leber, Paul Löbe came in touch with the resistance circle around Carl Goerdeler in 1935. After 20 July 1944, he was arrested and taken to a concentration camp in Silesia.

6. Ulrich von Hassell who had been ambassador in Rome from 1932 to 1938 was a conservative member of the opposition. He was mainly in contact with General Ludwig Beck, Carl Goerdeler and Johannes Popitz.

should bear the onus of losing the war before the opposition should attempt its overthrow.[7]

The key figures in the conspiracy were to have been the generals on the Eastern Front, under the leadership of Marshal von Mannstein [Manstein]. Immediately after the Stalingrad defeat, these generals had despaired of holding the front together. When, however, Mannstein discovered that he could in fact hold some sort of a winter line, he refused to take part in the conspiracy. This refusal spelled the end of the whole attempt.

c. September-October, 1943. Of this third plot, Father Leiber received a somewhat fragmentary outline from a colonel responsible for cultural affairs in Rome. The attempt was to have taken place by October 15 at the latest, but was to be dependent on a previous stabilization of the Russian front. The absence of such a stabilization evidently resulted in the abandonment of the conspiracy.[8]

The failure of all these attempts Father Leiber ascribes to two causes: first, the lack of a sincere anti-Nazi outlook on the part of the conspirators, who were acting from opportunist motives; second, the constant insistance on the part of the generals that an attempt to overthrow the regime must not come at a time when the Eastern Front was in motion—that is, the conspiracy should not endanger the safety of the Reich. When the Germans were retreating, the generals refused to take political action: when the Front was stable, they claimed that an overthrow of the regime was no longer necessary. Under such conditions, action became impossible.

The aims of the conspirators in almost all cases were: first, a withdrawal to the frontiers of the "Old Reich" (whether or not it included Austria was somewhat unclear); second, a compromise peace with the Allies; third, a reconstructed government leaning on the "moderate" parties.

3. The Future of the Catholic Church in German Political Life

Father Lieber's [Leiber] own apparent sympathy with the aims of these conspiracies springs from his Centrist associations. While admitting that the Center has no national organization as a resistance movement, Father Leiber believes that it can recover its position very rapidly after the armistice. The majority of German Catholics, he claims, will again turn to the Center as their natural political affiliation. For the future, the key question will be that of education. The co-existence of a system of state and confessional schools will, in Father Leiber's opinion, best advance the position of the Church in Germany. Until such a program gets under way, however, the youth of Germany (those 10 to 30) must be considered as lost to

---

7. Nevertheless, Konrad Adenauer who was later to become the first Chancellor of the Federal Republic of Germany, was arrested by the Gestapo on 22 August 1944 together with some 700 actual or potential opponents.

8. There were plans for more than one assassination attempt in the fall of 1943. Among the conspirators were Generals Beck, Kluge, Olbricht and Tresckow as well as Carl Goerdeler.

Catholicism. For the immediate post-war period, the Church must place its reliance on the older generations and on the very young.

In Austria, Father Leiber recognizes that special conditions exist. Not the least of these is the position toward Nazism that the Austrian prelates have taken. While frankly admitting that their attitude in 1938 was "very weak", and that the position of Cardinal Innitzer still leaves much to be desired, Father Leiber points to certain of the Austrian bishops as worthy to rank beside von Gallen [Galen], von Preysing, and Faulhaber in Germany—notably the Bishops of Graz, St. Polten, and Klagenfurt.

Document 66 · 23 August 1944

Telegram from Allen W. Dulles
(OSS Bern) to OSS Director William J. Donovan:
Are the Nazis Planning to Liquidate
All Foreign Workers?[1]

SECRET

TOR: 8/23/44 10:12 pm

#4638–4643. From 110 [Allen W. Dulles].

Our number 481[2] has been given the material in our cable #4523–26 to Washington. In his cable #281135, dated the 28th of last month, of which we received an information copy, and in his flash to the Office of War Information, dated the 2nd of August, 678[3] quoted from the *National Zeitung* of Basle[4] and mentioned reports that the National Socialists were planning to liquidate all foreign workers in the Reich. In cable #2704, dated the 5th of this month, Mr.

---

1. NA, RG 226, Entry 134, Box 277, Folder 1579.

2. This agent or informant maintained regular contact between German exiles in Switzerland, German oppositional army circles and the OSS.

3. This person was exchanging information between Allen W. Dulles on one side and German labor groups and the branch office of the Free Germany Committee in Switzerland on the other.

4. The *Nationalzeitung* was the major newspaper in the Swiss city of Basle.

Cordell Hull requested more information regarding this. The Legation [in Bern] answered in their cable #5113, dated the 8th of this month.[5]

Our 481 was the originating source of both the story in the *National Zeitung* and 678's flash. He has now let me have the information given below, which I forward with reserve pending a check on 481 by you and London and additional checks on him by us. Nevertheless, I believe the source sufficiently authenticated to justify forwarding his story: 481 had not received more than brief, occasional communications from his friends in OKW [Oberkommando der Wehrmacht; Supreme Command of the Armed Forces] ever since his internment here in 1941. However, on the 11th of last month, these friends sent him a secret courier bearing a lengthy report and an appeal from Major-General Hellmuth Stieff, who was subsequently executed.[6] According to this report, toward the end of May and the beginning of June, there was a conference in Hitler's Headquarters at Berchtesgaden. Present were Hitler, Kaltenbrunner, Himmler, Guderian, Fromm, Zeitzler, and Keitel, among others. The decision was reached at this meeting to make arrangements for the extermination of alien workers in the event that the Russian, British, and American troops made any further gains.[7] The workers were placed in 5 groups at the suggestion of Kaltenbrunner and Himmler. The first of these groups, called "Very Dangerous" was to have the honor of being exterminated before the others. It seems that they were to be disposed of, starting at once, the whole 2,000,000 of them. In order to provide a legitimate excuse for this massacre, it was agreed that the 2,000,000 who were to be liquidated first would be taken from one work camp to another and on the way would be shot down by *Schutzstaffel* [SS] troops on the pretext that they had attempted to revolt or escape. In this same report received by 481, there was also the statement that a number of the Wehrmacht generals, such as Von Rundstedt, Zeitzler, Von Bock, Fromm, Von Witzleben, as well as General Otto, 481's closest friend, had declined to associate themselves with this mass murder. It was because of this that some of them later took part in the attack on the Fuehrer, which was foreshadowed in the report.

In their report to 481, General Hellmuth Stieff and his friends requested that he contact the Allies and warn them of what was to come, urging them to drop leaflets telling the German people about it and suggesting that prominent refugees, political leaders and men of letters such as Professor Dessauer, Bruening, Thomas Mann, Wirth, and others, make an appeal.[8] General Von

---

5. Not printed.

6. Stieff had stored explosives for an assassination attempt against Hitler in 1943. He was again involved in the preparations for the anti-Hitler plot in July 1944. Having been among the first officers to be arrested and tried, Stieff was hanged on 8 August in Plötzensee prison.

7. As a result of this information the War Department had General Eisenhower issue a statement in the early fall that severe penalties would be inflicted upon anyone mistreating forced labor units in Germany.

8. All the persons mentioned were German exiles who were at the time living either in the United States (Brüning, Mann) or in Switzerland (Dessauer, Wirth).

Modtlas, an army chief, was also mentioned by the report, which said that it might be possible to persuade him to turn his army on the Nazi Government. The writers of the report, however, had no love for the Russians and wanted nothing to do with General Seydlitz's Committee.

The contents of this report were given by 481 to his friends Professor Dessauer and Alfred Kober of the National Zeitung. I saw the former a short time ago; he confirms this and vouches for 481. There is nothing impossible about the plan, as put forth by the report. However, although I have no cause to question 481's good faith, before I accept his evidence I would like to have more proof that he is acting in all sincerity.

Document 67 · 15 September 1944

Memorandum from William A. Kimbel (OSS Washington)[1] to OSS Director William J. Donovan: Additional Information About the July Plot

SECRET

General Donovan,

The attached came to us from Spain, as having been presented to them[2] by a German official having some connection with Breakers.[3] We also present the background of those personalities mentioned, concerning whom we have a previous record.

This report may serve to emphasize the far-sighted intelligence developed by OSS. No dissemination is being given to this material, pending your decision as to how it may be best utilized.

W.A. Kimbel

---

1. NA, RG 226, Entry 99, Box 14, Folder 58a. Kimbel was Donovan's liaison to Adolf A. Berle in the State Department.

2. I.e., the OSS outpost in Madrid.

3. This official was Otto John, an attorney for Lufthansa and Abwehr agent. See documents [34] and [35].

The Events of July 20, 1944[4]

The following information must not be used as propaganda. It must be placed only at the disposal of such persons who will promise that the names followed by an X will remain secret, as the fate of these persons is still uncertain, and they would run the risk of being exposed to reprisal action by the Nazi terror if their names were to be linked in a general way with the attempt against Hitler.

On July 14, I was notified through Stauffenberg's closest military collaborator, Colonel Hausen (?) X, [Georg Hansen][5] that I was to leave for Berlin immediately. I was given to understand that the action against the Nazis was to be effected within the next few days, perhaps even before my arrival in Berlin. I was told that if I did not arrive in Berlin on time, I was to act on my own initiative, following up any action indicated by Stauffenberg und Hansen.

I arrived in Berlin the afternoon of July 19. I telephoned the OKH [*Oberkommando des Heeres;* Supreme Command of the Army] in the Bend-lerstrasse[6] and was told to hold myself in readiness for the following day and to call again early in the morning. I returned home, and that same evening I was interrogated by some friends on the political and military situation. The following morning, I called Stauffenberg's aide, as pre-arranged, and was informed by the secretary that a message had been left for me and that I was to come to the Bendlerstrasse toward 6 p.m. that evening.

When I arrived at the appointed time, the iron gates of the main entrance were closed and the guard had been reinforced. The command of the guard had been entrusted to a young captain who had been notified of my arrival and who wrote down my name in the log without asking any questions. On my way to see Stauffenberg, I met Colonel Jaeger X at the main entrance to the second floor. Colonel Jaeger [Fritz Jäger] was awarded the Knight's Cross after Stalingrad and belonged to our group. At this time, however, I found him in a situation which, to me, was almost incomprehensible. He was standing in front of the entrance without his hat and unarmed. Behind him, to the right and the left, were two armed soldiers. In front of him, to one side, there was an *Obersturmbannführer*[7] holding his hat in his hand and pointing a pistol. At first glance I did not realize at whom he was pointing it. After the radio broadcast announcing the failure of the attempt against Hitler, I was already convinced that everything had gone wrong. But from the manner of Jaeger's greetings to me, I noticed very quickly that he, as well as the Wehrmacht, was master of the situation.

---

4. This report was translated by OSS officials from German into English.

5. Colonel Hansen was the successor of Admiral Canaris, the Chief of the Abwehr who had been removed from office in February 1944 and arrested after the 20th of July.

6. The street in Berlin where the Ministry of War was located. Used as a synonym for Ministry of War or Supreme Command of the Army Forces.

7. I.e., a Lieutenant-Colonel of the SS.

After I had talked to him (Jaeger) for a moment, Stauffenberg's aide, First Lieutenant von Haeften,[8] arrived. He talked for a while about the situation and told me that Colonel Hansen had not yet arrived at the rendezvous and that I was to wait for him. I went into Stauffenberg's outer office where Major Count von Schwerin X [Ulrich Wilhelm Graf Schwerin von Schwanenfeld][9] received me with these words: "How lucky that you arrived in time. Hansen is not here yet. We must wait. The situation will not be completely cleared up for twenty-four hours." He left and Stauffenberg entered the room at the same moment. He greeted me rapidly and rather gravely. At the same instant, his secretary called him to the telephone. "Minister Speer wishes urgently to speak to Count von Stauffenberg." Stauffenberg excused himself and walked into General Fromm's outer office.

In the interval, Count Schwerin had returned and given me a general outline of the situation. According to him, the attempt had not succeeded completely, but it seemed that Hitler was seriously hurt and at least in danger of losing his life. Unfortunately, it had not been possible to seize radio facilities and, in this way, the Nazis were still in possession of the most powerful instrument.[10] However, it was necessary to proceed, as retreat was no longer possible. Orders to establish a state of siege had been issued. Beck was determined to go ahead and had already assigned the Supreme Command of the Wehrmacht to v. Witzleben. Fromm was not raising any objections, but agreed completely (however, Fromm had never been a member of the opposition).

On the whole, I had the impression that the matter was taking its course and would develop for better or for worse. At this moment, moreover, it seemed a favorable circumstance that incoming information appeared to indicate that the Wehrmacht in the Reich and the occupied territories were ranging themselves against the Nazis.

To accomplish my task, I had to wait for Colonel Hansen, with whom it was impossible to get in touch. Stauffenberg and his officers were very busy (I was the only civilian on the spot). I had every opportunity to observe the course of events. Stauffenberg was constantly on the telephone speaking to the commanding officers in the Reich and the occupied territories. He had the necessary contacts and was confirming that the instructions he had sent by wire for the establishment of a state of siege (*Ausnahmezustand*-state of emergency) had actually been received.

Meanwhile, Beck and Witzleben had exchanged views in Fromm's office. Soon after, Witzleben, accompanied by his aide, left the building to take over the

---

8. Werner von Haeften had assisted Stauffenberg in bringing the explosives to Hitler's headquarters. He was court-martialed and shot on the evening of July 20.

9. Schwerin von Schwanenfeld had been in close contact with oppositional trade unionists and Social Democrats, including Mierendorff, Leber and Leuschner. He was arrested on 21 July and executed on 8 September 1944.

10. See document [55].

Command of the Wehrmacht at Headquarters.[11] Little by little the chiefs of services and the OKH generals arrived to confer with Fromm. Suddenly, the news came from a military source that contrary orders had been issued by the Führer's Headquarters. Stauffenberg answered by telephone that these contrary orders had not been "autorisiert" (authorized), that the Wehrmacht was in complete control under the command of Fieldmarshal Witzleben, and that the nation was in the greatest danger. In this hour of grave peril it was the duty of soldiers to act and to crush any opposition which might manifest itself. All radio stations and all information centers were to be seized immediately. The only center of command in the Reich must be the Chief of the Reserve Army, to whom all other military chiefs must be subordinated. General Olbricht spoke similarly to the outlying posts.

The orders issued were followed to the letter by the chiefs of the Reserve Army, but little by little, and with increasing frequency, news arrived concerning contrary orders issued by the Führer's Headquarters and a mounting uncertainty made itself felt among the chiefs of local commands in the Reich. Nevertheless, Stauffenberg, Olbricht and his officers carried on. It was under the impression that our undertaking was not going too badly as, at any rate, the administrative machinery had been put into action, and even if civil war should break out, we had the cooperation of the majority of commands.

After a certain length of time, von Haeften came to tell me that there was still no way of establishing contact with Hansen. I was obliged to return home and was to try to reach Hansen early the following morning at his office, as contact with him had to be established at all costs. With this hope and with the conviction that matters would develop favorably for us in the end, I left the OKH toward eleven o'clock, leaving instructions that I was to be summoned by telephone the following morning. I had considered paying a visit to Minister Popitz,[12] but on the way I gave up this idea, as it was already very late and returned home. This was fortunate, as Popitz' daughter [Cornelia Popitz] informed me the next day that he had been arrested the same night.

When I arrived home, I heard the radio announce a message by Hitler. I could not believe my ears and was convinced that the Nazis were using a double. I was unable to contact the OKH by telephone and remained sitting at my radio until the following morning.

In the meantime, I heard the speeches of Hitler, Goering, and Doenitz,[13] and I got a clear idea of how our affairs were progressing. In spite of that, I tried early the next morning to telephone Hansen and Stauffenberg. There was no

---

11. General Erwin von Witzleben was taken into custody on 21 July 1944 and executed on 8 August.

12. Johannes Popitz was the only minister in office among the conspirators. He was designated to become Minister of Education and Cultural Affairs. In spite of his connections with Himmler, whom he tried to win over for a plot against Hitler, Popitz was sentenced to death in October 1944 and executed on 2 February 1945.

13. For the contents of these speeches see document [60].

longer any way of reaching Hansen even for official business. On the twenty-second, I received a telephone message that Hansen had gone on a trip. I concluded from that that he had either been arrested or was being followed.[14] Stauffenberg and Haeften had also taken a trip. As yet I had no idea that they were already dead. The message that was given to me by telephone by his secretary disturbed me to such a point that I did not even mention my name, and I tried to get information about the situation from other friends. As cautiously as possible, I telephoned several people from a post office and was only able to determine that most of our friends did not answer or "had gone on a trip". Saturday afternoon I managed to meet a friend of the Foreign Office who was in a position to give me information on the development of events after my departure from the Bendlerstrasse.

Olbricht and Stauffenberg, being undeterred by the contrary orders issued by Hitler's (the *Führer's*) Supreme Headquarters, continued preparation of measures, intended to set up a state of siege. In the meanwhile, it had been learned at home by radio announcements that Hitler was only slightly wounded and still alive. This circumstance made many people waver and provoked a reaction even among officers of the *Oberkommando des Heeres*, Army High Command. Several officers, Colonel von der Heyde at the head, burst into Stauffenberg's anteroom and recalled the oath of fidelity that they had made to their *Führer*. "The *Führer* is still alive; he will be Supreme Commander as long as he lives." Stauffenberg had deceived them by announcing to them the death of Hitler. They would never have taken part in the "putsch" against the Führer, instigated by Stauffenberg and the Nobles' Club.[15] They demanded the immediate arrest of all of the leaders of the conspiracy. At the same time, machine guns were brought out. At this point, Fromm also must have returned and used the same arguments against Stauffenberg. A shot rang out; Stauffenberg was hit in the back. That was the signal to attack the others. Olbricht, Stauffenberg, and von Haeften were immediately put to death,[16] all the others arrested and led away. I have learned nothing of their final fate. It is virtually a certainty that they were shot at once. In any case, Beck certainly took his own life.[17]

After the plot had been thus nipped in the bud at the OKH by officers faithful to Hitler, it was easy for the Nazis—that is to say, Himmler—to take matters into their own hands. All that was needed was a housecleaning. That night and the following day, arrests were carried out on a vast scale. In my opinion, almost all those who were under suspicion of belonging to the opposition in any form were caught in the net.

---

14. Georg Hansen was court-martialed on 10 August and executed on the same day.

15. This is a reference to the so-called Deutscher Klub (German Club), otherwise known as Herrenklub, a circle of national-conservative intellectuals opposed to the Nazi-regime.

16. Together with the three officers mentioned, also Albrecht Ritter Mertz von Quirnheim was put to death.

17. See document [54].

That morning I read Goebbels' message in the press. It was entirely possible that Stauffenberg had in his pocket the draft of a ministerial list. This would explain the arrest of Popitz, who, personally, had not taken any part in the action. But that can also mean that all the leaders of the opposition were arrested and actually shot without delay. I intend to make a special note of the connection between the opposition and the personalities who handled the affair.

Goebbels' account of the events of the twentieth are partly correct. In fact, during the afternoon of July 20, the Military Commander of Berlin, General von Haase [Paul von Hase] was informed by General Olbricht that the attempt on Hitler's life would occur that very day and that he should make the necessary preparations at Berlin to take possession of the official government headquarters. General von Hase called together the officers of the Guards of the regiment under his command and issued instructions. Among these military leaders was Major Remer, a Nazi who promptly notified Goebbels by telephone that he had been given the unusual order to occupy Official Headquarters on the pretext that Hitler was dead. Goebbels advised Remer to conduct himself as if he were a participant in the putsch. Goebbels then contacted the Führer's General Headquarters and informed them of the measures taken at Berlin. From that time on he was in a position to take counter-measures based on Hitler's personal order. A detachment of the regiment quartered at Doebritz School received the order to occupy the headquarters of the Commanding Officer of the city,[18] but this had already been done by a certain battalion of the Guards. From his balcony, von Hase saw the arrival of new troops and at first believed that they were reinforcements being sent to him. However, these troops promptly surrounded the others, and Hase was invited by a lieutenant to leave the balcony and enter into the house.

A short time later, Hase received a call from Goebbels to come to see him. Hase, not having an overall picture of the situation, went to Goebbels's home. The latter was not himself certain that the counter-measures by Hitler's General Headquarters would succeed. He offered Hase some wine, and while they drank and chattered together, neither knew which would be the prisoner of the other. An aide of Goebbels entered, whispered something to him, and Goebbels then declared that General von Hase was his prisoner. The General, a sturdy person known as an athlete, made no attempt to resist and let himself be arrested. Close watch was kept on his family in the C. O. [Commanding Officer's] Headquarters. I have not discovered what became of them.[19]

In my opinion, the Wehrmacht could continue its activities against the Nazis despite Stauffenberg's failure.

For a long time Fieldmarshal von Kluge has belonged to the opposition party of generals. He was not involved in the actual preparations of Stauffenberg's plot, although he would have thrown in his lot with them had Hitler been killed. In

---

18. I.e., Berlin.
19. Paul von Hase was arrested on the evening of 20 July and executed on 8 August 1944.

fact, von Kluge, after the attempt on Hitler's life, also took the necessary measures in order to assure the control of state affairs as far as his powers and duties were concerned. Accordingly, he permitted the SD [*Sicherheitsdienst*; Chief Reich Security Office] to occupy the head office of the Gestapo at Paris. Unfortunately, a teletype machine in the cellar of the Gestapo building was overlooked which enabled the Nazis locked in there to contact their central office at Berlin. Apparently, Kluge, after having seen that the affair would not succeed and that events were not going well, once again placed himself on Hitler's side. In spite of this, there is no doubt that he sympathizes with the opposition and that he might reform and continue the aims of the Wehrmacht, provided that he is handled skillfully and influenced in a clever and diplomatic manner. On the Allies's side, he should be encouraged to withdraw from the West. At present, there is as yet no way of knowing what persons in our circle at Berlin are still alive or free to contact Kluge. Of necessity, influence should be brought to bear upon Kluge by reminding him of March 1943, and that it was with his consent and under his authority that an attempt was prepared against Hitler and even executed but failed as the bomb did not explode.[20] At present there is no way of evaluating the opportunities and possibilities of effecting this contact with Kluge.[21]

Through an appropriate use of BBC propaganda in Germany, a very considerable influence can be exerted. This would be to broadcast an eulogy of Stauffenberg which would result in reestablishing the influence of those of the opposition still remaining in Berlin.

As far as the military plans of Hitler are concerned, it may be said that he has none. His only demand is that each soldier fight until death, wherever he may be. The Guderian plans can only be those which General Headquarters had at the time when he accepted his position; i.e., shortening of the front and the establishment of a new line of defense on the Weichsel (Vistula).

But the rapid Russian advances make it too late for the execution of such a plan. Beck himself judged as very dubious the ability to hold a new front line on the Weichsel (Vistula) since the Russians had already advanced too far.[22]

In the opposition there exist today persons belonging to all the former parties of the Right, including Social Democrats such as Ministers Schacht and Popitz,[23] the former Oberbürgermeister Goerdeler, the Secretary of State Plank [Erwin

---

20. This attempt was primarily conducted by Henning von Tresckow and Fabian von Schlabrendorff. It occured on 7 March 1943.

21. On 15 August, Field Marshal Kluge drove into the Falaise pocket on the Western front possibly to get in touch with the Allies. On the way he was held up by bomber attacks and lost his radio truck. By the evening, Hitler was convinced that Kluge had deserted to the enemy. He appointed Field Marshal Walter Model to succeed Kluge as Commander in Chief West. On 19 August, Kluge committed suicide.

22. In August 1944, the uprising of the Polish resistance had started in Warsaw. The Soviet troops remained on the eastern side of the Vistula until the Germans had crushed the uprising in October.

23. Neither Schacht nor Popitz were Social Democrats. They were both national conservative members of the opposition.

Planck], and Harnatk [Ernst von Harnack]. I would like to emphasize this point and can speak for these people. For many years, I have personally known the circles comprising the leaders of the opposition. The below mentioned persons are only a few examples.

OFFICE OF STRATEGIC SERVICES

Washington, D. C.[24]

Beck. General Ludwig von Beck, one of the leaders of the opposition group. Committed suicide after the 20 July plot.

Fromm. General Fritz Fromm, Chief of Army Equipment and Commander of the replacement training Army. Member of the opposition group. A report received on 2 September 1944 stated that he was being held in custody, but was not yet executed.

Goerdeler. Dr. Karl [Carl] Goerdeler, former Mayor of Leipzig and one of the leaders of the opposition group. A report from Berlin on 11 September 1944 states that he was sentenced by the People's Tribunal and hanged.[25]

Guderian. General Heinz Guderian was reported on 21 July 1944 to have replaced General Zeitzler as Chief of the General Staff, after Zeitzler had been retired "for reasons of health".

von Haase. [von Hase]. Presumably Lieutenant General Paul von Hase. An official German report monitored by the F.C.C. [Federal Communications Commission] on 5 August 1944 states that he was held under arrest by the Court of Honor. A later report stated that he had been hanged.[26]

von Haeften. Ober Lieutenant of the Reserve Werner von Haeften was officially reported shot on 20 July 1944. His brother, Hans Gustav [Hans-Bernd] von Haeften of the Foreign Office, was reported on 3 September 1944 to have been tried in secret and hanged.[27]

Hansen. This may be the Colonel Hansen who became Acting Director of the Abwehr under Kaltenbrunner, after Canaris was ousted. He was one of the principal contact men for Gisevius and Waetjen. He was placed under arrest by the Court of Honor, according to a DNB broadcast monitored by the F.C.C. on 5 August 1944. See also: Haensen.

---

24. The following is a list compiled by OSS research analysts giving biographical background information on the persons mentioned in the report.

25. Goerdeler had been sentenced to death on 8 September 1944; he was, however, not executed for another five months.

26. Von Hase was hanged on 8 August 1944.

27. Lieutenant (Res.) Werner von Haeften's brother Hans-Bernd, a Legation Counselor at the Foreign Office, was arrested on 22 July and executed on 15 August 1944.

Haensen. This may be the Colonel of the General Staff Hansen reported to have been placed under arrest by the Court of Honor, according to the broadcast mentioned above.

von der Heyde [Lieutenant Colonel Bolkow von der Heyde]. This may be Major von der Heydte, Commander in Chief of the sixth Parachute Regiment.

Leber. Dr. Leber, former Socialist member of the Reichstag (1924, 1928, 1930–1933); imprisoned 1933 to February 1937.[28]

Leuschner. Dr. Wilhelm Leuschner, Minister of the Interior for Hesse 1929–1933, member of the underground, allegedly scheduled by the opposition group to become Vice-Chancellor. Sentenced to death by the People's Tribunal on 11 September 1944.[29]

"Niklaus". Believed to be Herr Otto [Otto John] who is, or has been, Director of the Deutsche *Lufthansa.*

Olbricht. Brigadier General Friedrich Olbricht, German Air Force, a member of the opposition group. Court martialled on 20 July 1944, according to an official German broadcast monitored by F.C.C. on 4 August 1944.

Popitz. Hermann [Johannes] E. J. Popitz, former Minister of Finance for Prussia. Reported on 11 August 1944 to have been imprisoned after the failure of the 20 July plot.

Schacht. Dr. Hjalmar Schacht, former head of the *Reichsbank,* reported under arrest on 24 July 1944.[30]

Speer. Dr. Albert Speer, Reichs Minister [sic] for Armaments and War Production and Chief of the Four-Year Plan.

Stauffenberg. Colonel Graf Claus von Stauffenberg served as liaison between the older officers on active duty at General Headquarters and the younger group formerly headed by Helmuth von Moltke (former advisor to OKW on International Law). He was killed during the plot of 20 July, and his whole family is reported to have been put to death.[31]

von Witzleben. Field Marshal Erwin von Witzleben, retired. An official German report states that he was found guilty of treason in the plot of 20 July, was sentenced to death and hanged, according to the *New York Times* of 8 September 1944.

---

28. Julius Leber had been arrested by the Gestapo on 5 July 1944. He was executed on 5 January 1945.

29. Leuschner was sentenced to death on 8 September 1944, and hanged on 29 September.

30. The arrest took place on July 29, 1944.

31. The information concerning Stauffenberg's family is incorrect.

Document 68 · October 1944

Memorandum by the OSS Morale Operations Branch: *Das Neue Deutschland*— An Example of a Propaganda Newspaper[1]

Example of an MO [Morale Operations] Newspaper
Das Neue Deutschland (*The New Germany*)

Story

This newspaper purports to represent a fake Peace Party inside Germany, whose overall aims are:

1. To put an end to the war.
2. To liquidate the Nazi Party.
3. To set up a new German State on democratic principles.

Produced/Printed

First in MO/Algiers, then in Rome, in collaboration with the Plans and Production Section of the Washington Base.[2]

---

1. NA, RG 226, Entry 99, Box 69, Folder 306.

2. The material that went into *Das Neue Deutschland* was constantly reviewed by the Editorial Board in Psychological Warfare Against Germany. This Board was composed of James Riddleberger of the State Department, Hans Speyer of the Office of War Information, and Wallace Deuel of the OSS.

Dissemination

By secret air lift to pin-points, where the material is received by OSS agents or Partisans. Also by infiltration of German POWs of the "Sauerkraut" Missions,[3] and by special mail air drops by the 15th Air Force to Resistance Group in Southern France, and one mass drop over Vienna of a million copies overprinted to read "This fell into Allied hands when Paris was taken".

Date

August 1944

Comebacks

German deserters have come over the lines carrying copies of the *Das Neue Deutschland*, quoting from it.

A POW Unteroffizier [Sergeant] of the 8th Battery, 165th Artillery Regiment, 65th Division, located south of Bologna, stated that he and some comrades thought the material came from German underground.

Enemy recognition of *Das Neue Deutschland* appeared in a special warning to the German troops by the National Socialist Leadership "Information for the Troops", No. 371, October 1944. [...]

The program of the movement is stated as follows:

"Our Program: A Call to Germany"

(1) It is proposed that an immediate request be made of the Allied Governments for an armistice and honorable peace terms, negotiations on Germany's behalf to be carried on by a commission representing every class of German;

(2) That all political prisoners be immediately released from confinement and that governmental assistance be provided for them in locating their families and reestablishing their homes;

(3) That freedom of the press, speech and religion be immediately restored to the German people and that the formation of new truly representative political parties be encouraged;

(4) That an immediate general election be held to choose representatives to the Reichstag and other national offices. This is to be followed by local elections throughout the Reich;

---

3. This OSS initiative had been sparked by the failure of the 20th of July plot. During a OSS meeting held in Italy on the very night of the plot, it was decided to use the novel and rather daring method of employing trustworthy German prisoners of war for distributing propaganda behind enemy lines. Until that time, aerial distribution, although often discounted for ineffectiveness, had been the only means of infiltrating OSS material. The "Sauerkraut" project proved to be quite successful. "Sauerkraut" missions provided the 5th Army (G–2) with tactical intelligence. They also planted MO leaflets, stickers, false orders, and proclamations. The reactions of German soldiers to the OSS printed material were also gauged. See documents [78] and [79].

(5) That a commission be immediately appointed to organize post-war recon-struction and to provide employment for those being released from the army and war industries;

(6) That a charter of rights for labor be published immediately, establishing the right of collective bargaining through its own representatives;

(7) That a free educational system be immediately restored inside the Reich and that the nation's text books be purged of all Nazi doctrine;

(8) That a commission be immediately appointed to study the development of Germany's post-war trade and to meet with the representatives of other nations for the purpose of signing trade agreements;

(9) In order to revive agriculture, that a system of farm subsidies be set up to pro-vide farmers with necessary funds to purchase seed and farm equipment. [...]

Document 69 · 16 October 1944

Telegram from Myron Taylor (OSS Stockholm) to OSS Washington: German Peace Overtures in the East[1]

SECRET

TOR: 10/17/44 10:38 am

#140. 155 [Taylor] to 109 [Donovan]. In connection with your #94.

We have obtained no evidence that Kleist, who is well known to us, has defi-nitely attempted to repeat his contacts with local Russians which we reported in cable #303, dated July 6, and later cables.[2]

---

1. NA, RG 226, Entry 134, Box 304, Folder 1690.

2. Bruno Peter Kleist, one of Ribbentrop's chief advisers in the Foreign Office on East European Affairs, was striving to launch peace overtures in the East ever since the fall of 1942. In his efforts he was backed by Admiral Canaris. Likewise, Adam von Trott zu Solz had tried to contact both the Western and Eastern Allies through Stockholm. The OSS was aware of these peace feelers. After 20 July 1944, Myron Taylor, the head of the OSS outpost in Stockholm, claimed he had never possessed any reliable intelligence on the intentions of von Trott.

We constantly keep tabs on his travels in and out of Sweden and have uncon-firmed report he is here at present. We have arranged to have him put under sur-veillance whenever he is here.

For your personal information: At time we reported Kleist's contact with Russians here Herschel Johnson[3] was skeptical and personally questioned Madame Kollontay,[4] who blandly denied actual meeting but admitted Kleist had made attempt meet Russians. Herschel also pursued matter further by querying Boheman[5] on point who also stated personal doubts as to alleged fact but said Russians had exhibited to him note transmitted by Kleist suggesting possibility of meeting. However, we were satisfied by our sources that at least one meeting did take place.

---

3. Herschel V. Johnson had been Minister to Stockholm since 1941.

4. Aleksandra Kollontai, the daughter of a Czarist general, had fallen from grace under Stalin. She was therefore sent off to Stockholm as a minister for Russia. In German opposition circles Kollontai was thought to be able to influence Soviet politics from her post in neutral Sweden. Her power was, however, more fictional than real.

5. Erik C. Boheman was Secretary General of the Swedish Ministry for Foreign Affairs.

Document 70a · 17 October 1944

Letter from Stewart W. Herman (OSS Washington)[1] to Allen W. Dulles (OSS Bern): A Recent Report on the German Protestant Church

SECRET

Subject: Recent Report on German Protestant Church

For your own information it may be interesting to have certain comments from me regarding Dr. S.'s [Hans Schönfeld's] report on the present status of the resistance movement within the German Protestant Church.[2]

First of all, I should like to confirm from my own knowledge virtually everything that was stated in the report. Up until the time I left Germany after Pearl Harbor Day, I was in close touch with the German Church and its leaders. It is quite true that the protest made on behalf of Russian prisoners of war, action taken on behalf of non-Aryan Christians and Jews, steps taken against euthanasia, etc., were energetically pursued by church leaders. I was not aware that Bishop Wurm was leading a movement to take over certain civilian controls at the time of the collapse but this step, which is perfectly logical, does not surprise me. Furthermore from my own experience I would say that the church has been relatively successful in preserving in the Christian tradition large numbers of so-called Nazi Youth who should certainly be taken into consideration in the post-hostilities period. And, I think we will find that the churches of the occupied countries will pay a certain debt of gratitude to the German Church and its representatives for the help which was provided during the "Quisling Period".

---

1. NA, RG 226, Entry 125, Box 8, Folder 133; Stewart W. Herman Papers, Shelter Island, N.Y.; Besier, Ökumenische Mission, pp. 160–161. Stewart W. Herman had been pastor of the American community in Berlin from 1936 to 1941. After the German declaration of war in December 1941 he was interned for several months before he could return to the United States. After publishing a book about his experiences in Nazi Germany in 1942, he was drafted for the OSS. When the OSS was dissolved in October 1945, Stewart W. Herman became Deputy Head of the Reconstruction branch of the World Council of Churches.

2. Document [70c].

These considerations lead me to observe that a German Church provides the strongest organized basis for stabilizing post-war Germany. In a certain sense it seems to me that OSS should think of the German Church along the same lines as it thinks of the trade union movements for which it has even gone so far as to set up special apparatus.[3] By this I do not mean that an ecclesiastical mission be established in OSS but rather that an effort be made to establish church contacts whereby information may be obtained regarding any Nazi "Flare-ups" and whereby support may be brought to the church for re-knitting broad international connections during the period of occupation.

It may interest you further to have some comments of mine regarding the persons mentioned in Dr. S.'s statement. The contact between Bishop Wurm, Bishop Meiser, Dr. Koch and their opposite numbers in the Catholic Church is a matter of common knowledge. Bishop Wurm has emerged as the strongest of the Episcopal leaders in the Lutheran Church. Unfortunately Bishop Maharhens [Marahrens], titular head of the Lutheran Church in Germany, has proved to be a relatively weak character.

On the other hand Dr. Hanns Lilje, who is the general secretary of Lutheran World Action, which is a combination of Lutherans around the world, is a very strong member of the Confessional Church. I know him very well and was in close touch with him until December 1941. In my mind he is the most capable leader among the younger men in Germany. He was general secretary of the Christian Student Movement.

I also know Dr. Eugen Gerstenmeier who has consistently undermined the compromising position of his superior, Bishop Haeckel [Heckel] of the Church's Foreign Office.[4] Gerstenmeier is from Wuerttemberg and in very close touch with Bishop Wurm. He was largely responsible for the good relationship which the church enjoyed with certain influential members of the foreign office in Berlin. He has an exceptional amount of physical and moral courage.

Pastor Grueber I knew in Berlin before his arrest.[5] He knew no hesitation in combatting the Nazi regime at every turn and distinguished himself particularly for his ability to organize aid on behalf of the persecuted Jews. Another person of the same category is Pastor Kurtz of Berlin who likewise bearded the Gestapo in its den on more than one occasion.

Dr. Otto Dibelius is a church statesman of great stature and has performed a great deal of good work even after the Nazis deprived him of his office. He was head of the Evangelical Church in Prussia.

I am not sure about Dr. Bachmann who seems to me to be a fairly weak character although, later on, he may have been considerably influenced by Ger-

---

3. This is a reference to the Labor Section in the Office of Strategic Services. See in particular documents [11] and [33].

4. I.e., the Kirchliches Außenamt der Evangelischen Kirche in Berlin.

5. This arrest took place in late December 1940 when Heinrich Grüber was detained in a concentration camp for his support of German Jews.

stenmeier. I am certain that he is not a fighter like the rest of the men in this list. Before the war he was pastor of the German Church in Nice, France.

The only other man I know is Dr. Asmussen whose name ranks along with that of Pastor Niemoeller as one of the most courageous of the leaders of the Confessional Church.

In addition to these personalities, there are many others in Germany whose names should be known to anyone attempting to provide Germany with a new government. This would unquestionably be a full job. I know that the Biographical Record Section has already done a great deal toward the collection of the names of confessional pastors but I do not know whether plans have been made to put them to use.[6]

In line of our recent conversation I wrote to Dr. Leiper[7] outlining the proposal whereby a representative of the World Council may proceed to Switzerland and then into Germany as soon as [it] becomes possible to do so. When he replies I shall let you know at once. So far as I am concerned, I remain perfectly neutral until I am sure that I can be of special service in this connection.

Incidentally, a translation of the report was made and put into Comdr. Armour's hands the day after you called me about it.

> *Stewart W. Herman*
> **Chief Central European Section**
> **SO Branch**

---

6. At the time of this report, Emmy Rado, head of the OSS Biographical Record Section, had authored a study on the Confessional Church in Germany and collected background information on 174 protestant theologians in Germany. These lists were taken to Europe by Rado in late 1944. To what extent they were put into use, cannot be determined. For Rado's work on churches see also document [71].

7. Henry Smith Leiper was an American theologian involved in ecumenical work.

Document 70b · 31 October 1944

OSS Director William J. Donovan
to President Franklin D. Roosevelt:
A Report from Switzerland
on the German Churches[1]

Knowing of your concern that Nazism should not survive war by going underground, I believe you may want to see the attached memorandum[2] on the anti-Nazi activities of the Protestant and Catholic Churches in Germany. This memorandum was prepared early in September 1944 by Dr. H. Schoenfeld [Hans Schönfeld], an outstanding figure in the Evangelical Church who left Germany in June of this year and now maintains his German contacts from a residence taken up in Switzerland.[3]

Already the anti-Nazi church elements, organized in cells and "leading groups" of both the clergy and the laity, have saved thousands of Jews, hostages, prisoners of war, foreign churchmen and labor draftees from extermination, deportation and other Nazi control measures. This was accomplished not only through intercession with government officials but also by clandestine action undertaken at great personal risk. Dr. Schoenfeld's memorandum, which emphasizes the collaboration between the Catholic and Protestant clergy, provides a list of prominent personalities and an outline of their activities in this movement. Foreseeing the collapse of Nazi Germany, this movement has formed a Self-Help ("Selbsthilfe") organization, headed by a central commission responsible for maintenance of transportation, distribution of food, protection of spiritual welfare and reorganisation of the German educational system. In his memorandum Dr. Schoenfeld

---

1. NA, RG 226, Entry 162, Microfilm 1642, Roll 24, Frames 662–663.

2. Document [70c].

3. As he was working both for the Church Foreign Office (Kirchliches Außenamt der Evangelischen Kirche) in Berlin and for the World Council of Churches in Geneva, Hans Schönfeld traveled frequently to Switzerland where he met with Allen W. Dulles on many occasions. Schönfeld was also affiliated with the Kreisau resistance circle around Helmuth von Moltke.

includes a proposal for close liaison between the Self-Help organization and the Allied forces of occupation.

William J. Donovan
Director

Document 70c · Early September 1944

Memorandum by Hans Schönfeld (World Council of Churches) to Allen W. Dulles (OSS Bern): German Church Opposition Against the National Socialist Regime[1]

The Service of the Church Within the Framework of the Resistance Movement Against the National Socialist Regime in Germany

I. In the dispute with the Nazi Regime during the past seven or eight years in general, and during the recent years in particular, the main decisive contribution of the German Evangelical Church, and the Roman Catholic Church, has been the bitter, constantly renewed, successful battle of resistance of these churches against the repeated attempts of the Party and Reich Government to disrupt the unified structure of the church body as a whole, and to destroy the administrative structure of the church in order to divide the corporate Church into individual church communities. Such a division would have placed the individual church communities in a situation of penury. Three attempts have been made during the war to destroy the corporate character of the churches. This destruction was only avoided through the energetic intervention of the most courageous among leading Churchman, and through the efforts of prominent Christian laymen in Government, Army, industry, and agriculture. At the same time, it was possible to

---

1. NA, RG 226, Entry 190, Box 27, Folder 99; original German version: Heideking/Mauch, USA und deutscher Widerstand, pp. 205–215.

save the church centers of the Home Missions and other organizations, from seizure and expropriation; thus preserving the basis for further development of the battle waged by leading groups and community "cells".

II. This also made it possible to preserve the material basis for a collective spiritual orientation of the broad strata of the population in all communities and churches. Through sermons and pastoral counsel, through lectures and evangelization, foundations were laid among all classes of the people for a determined struggle against those principles of national socialist ideology which represent lust for power, the theory of the master race, lawlessness, and the lust for revenge. Thus, the work in this domain, repeated week after week, succeeded in sustaining broad strata of the population in their resistance against hate. This was especially true at the time when hundreds of thousands of evacuees found themselves in desperate circumstances and were, therefore, often in danger of succumbing to National Socialist propaganda or nihilism. Noteworthy is the success of the leading church forces in bringing about the reestablishment of Christian instruction for tens of thousands of young people and children from the evacuated communities, thereby establishing the basis for reorganization of education, and providing a foundation upon which it will be possible to build, once National Socialism has been abolished.

III. In the collective action of the resistance movement in Germany in behalf of the non-Aryan population, and especially of non-Aryan Christians, the leading churchmen of the Evangelical and Catholic Churches have often constituted the deciding, crystallizing nucleus, by their ability to mobilize Christian lay forces in all districts of Germany. Around this nucleus were prominent members of the armed forces, industry and agriculture. In this way, the steps taken with the Reich Government carried sufficient weight to become a deciding factor. Furthermore, through open, as well as secret collaboration of the leading groups and the "cells", it was possible in many thousand individual cases, to save non-Aryan members of the German population from deportation and extermination. It was possible to hide many thousand persons in the large cities, although by this act clergymen and Christian laymen risked their lives. Through collaboration of the leading groups with the "cells", it was possible to remove threatened persons to other districts, thereby saving lives. There were thousands of cases where efforts to save the threatened persons were not successful. However, the struggle was continued without interruption until the last few months. The churches also contributed in a decisive manner toward preventing the deportation of 400,000 non-Aryans of mixed parentage.

IV. In the collective activity of the resistance forces to obtain humane treatment for the millions of prisoners of war, the churches mobilized their own forces within the Christian laity as extensively as possible. Furthermore, through their defense of collective Christian care for prisoners of war, as carried out by the organizations of the entire oecumenical movement of the Vatican, the churches have lent direct support to resistance forces in key positions in the Army and Government. This proved especially useful in the effort to rescue one million Russian prisoners.

V. On the basis of their experience in the struggle against the National Socialist Regime, the representatives and liaison agents of the Evangelical and Catholic Churches among the leading Christian elite in the occupied countries have offered their constant and useful support. It was necessary to acquaint the leading men of the Christian elite with particular resistance methods over a wide area. Through close collaboration between the churches' liaison agents and the political resistance forces in Germany and the occupied countries, it was possible to lend particular weight to the collective action of the church in the occupied countries. This was particularly useful in the struggle to bring about the preservation of the corporate organization of the churches in Holland, France and Denmark. The struggle for the preservation of Christian schools in Holland was likewise supported in this manner. Furthermore, it was often necessary to protect the safety of leading churchmen in occupied countries through the efforts of the churches' liaison agents in the resistance movement in Germany. Through this action it was possible to liberate the two leading Dutch churchmen, Prof. Kramer and Dr. Gravemeyer, from the hostage camp where they were being held. This method alone made it possible to protect the well-known leading French churchman, Dr. Marc Boegner, and to obtain the liberation of many members of the French clergy from detention by the Gestapo. Through the efforts of these liaison agents, it has also been possible, so far, to protect Bishop Berggrav from further seizure and to maintain personal liaison with him.[2]

VI. The central liaison agents of the Churches in Germany—in this case particularly the German Evangelical Church—have interceded in favor of an all-embracing support of the spiritual welfare and rallying of the 450,000 Dutch workers and clerks in Germany. At the risk of the agents' own lives, this work was often carried out for the benefit of French, Norwegian and Danish labor draftees. In all districts of Germany, community houses, churches, church homes, and rooms in the houses of the clergy, were placed at the disposal of foreign workers, to collect them and provide for their spiritual welfare. Collections taken up in German communities often made it possible to procure the services and provide for the support of Dutch and French vicars. The functioning of Christian laymen was also made possible through efforts of the church and its agents. This was accomplished only by bitter struggles against both the Gestapo and Dr. Ley's Labor Front organization. A relationship of mutual trust was created between the leading church groups and the prominent church representatives of the German Evangelical Church, as well as the Catholic Church, a relationship which proved valuable in the work of collaboration in matters pertaining to the "Self-Help" organization (Selbsthilfe).

---

2. In the course of the war years, Eivind Berggrav had become a prime symbol of defiance to the German occupiers. On several occasions he met with Theodor Steltzer, an official of the German occupation administration and member of the Kreisau resistance circle, with whom he shared thoughts on the ecumenical movement and concerns over Nazi persecution of both churches and Jews. Steltzer saved Berggrav's life on at least one occasion.

Oecumenical Contacts of Dr. H. Schönfeld which he has been able to maintain in a large measure throughout the war.

I. Contact maintained since 1929–30 with Dr. Leiper and Dr. Cavert, U.S.A.

Contact maintained since 1937–39 with Rev. Roswell P. Barness and Mr. John Foster Dulles.

The first three, named above, are secretaries-general of the American Federation of Churches; collaboration embraces social-ethical, economic and international problems.[3]

II. a. In contact since 1930 with Lord Bishop of Chichester [George Bell] for collaboration in spiritual matters, as well as for the support of the church's work in assistance to non-Aryan Christians.[4]

b. Since 1932–33 in contact with Dr. J. Oldham [Joseph Houldsworth Oldham], the spiritual director of the oecumenical preparatory work, presiding the World Church Conference at Oxford on "Church, State and People". Through him many contacts have been maintained with the representatives of the British trade unions and industrialists, with leading men in the British educational field, as well as politicians. At present, contact has also been established with Dr. Oldham's work as the author of "Christian Youth Letter".

c. Since 1935–37, in contact with W. Tempel [William Temple], then Archbishop of York, now Archbishop of Canterbury; collaboration in the preparation of the Oxford Conference, especially in the treatment of social and economic problems.

III. a. Since 1936–37 in contact with Prof. Dr. H. Kramer, the spiritual leader of the eight Dutch Reformed Churches.

b. Since 1940–41 in contact with Dr. Gravemeyer, The Hague, in central organizational management of the convention of the eight Dutch Reformed Churches; collaboration during the war, especially in matters pertaining to the mobilization of the church's resistance forces in Holland; participation in the action which led to the liberation of Dr. Kramer and Dr. Gravemeyer, who had been arrested as hostages.

c. Since 1931–32 contact has been maintained with the French church leader, President Dr. Marc Boegner; participation in the action insuring Dr. Boegner's protection from the Gestapo.

d. Since 1931 in contact with Dr. Conrod, secretary-general of the French Reformed Church; collaborative action during the war, particularly in intervention on behalf of French prisoners of war, as well as of French workers in

---

3. All of them were involved in the ecumenical movement. At the time, John Foster Dulles was Chairman of the American Commission to Study the Bases of a Just and Durable Peace, which took particular interest not only in war and peace aims but also in the Christian opposition against Hitler.

4. In May 1942, Schönfeld met Bishop Bell secretly in Stockholm giving him detailed information about the opposition against Hitler. Bell's subsequent efforts to bring the British government to support the German resistance were, however, to fail.

Germany; participation in the protective action on behalf of arrested French clergymen and non-Aryan Christians.

e. Since 1936–37 in contact with Bishop Dr. Berggrav, Norway. Collaboration during the war in matters pertaining to international questions and the organization of oecumenical collaboration between the leading Scandinavian, British, French and other church leaders; in the oecumenical movement in behalf of a just and lasting peace, support of the Norwegian resistance forces within the church; participation in the protective action in behalf of Bishop Berggrav; support of the action for the care of Norwegian workers and clerks in Germany.

f. Since 1936–37 in contact with Bishop Fugelsang-Damgaard, Copenhagen, the leading Bishop of the Danish Church; collaboration during the war for the support and protection of the church resistance forces in Denmark; support of the spiritual care of Danish workers in Germany.

Nomenclature.

The following lists the names, and gives a brief summary of the activity, of vitally important personalities in the German "Self-Help" organization of the Church. (Selbsthilfewerk der Kirchen).

I. A close relationship was established between leading representatives of the German Evangelical Church and the Roman Catholic Church in Germany for the purpose of building up the "Self-Help" organization.

a. Bishop Dr. Wurm of Stuttgart, the speaker of the entire German Evangelical Church (compare further on with II, a), kept in continuous contact with the Catholic *Archbishop Gröber* of Freiburg (responsible for all of Baden) on vital questions pertaining to the development of the organization. Archbishop Gröber is known, through his statements and speeches, as one of the most courageous leaders in the Catholic Church, a man who has played an outstanding part in rallying together the Catholic forces of resistance.

b. Contact was maintained in Bavaria between the well-known Lutheran *Bishop Meiser* and *Cardinal Faulhaber* in Munich; these two men and their colleagues are responsible for the Bavarian leading group.[5]

c. A corresponding collaboration came into existence for the Rhineland and Westphalia between the leader of the Protestant Church in Westphalia, *Dr. Koch,* and the well-known Catholic Bishop of Münster, *Count Galen.*[6]

d. The central collaboration directives emanating from Berlin were shaped jointly by *Dr. Eugen Gerstenmaier,* leader of the oecumenical central office of the German Evangelical Church [Kirchliches Außenamt], and the Catholic Bishop of Berlin, *Count Preysing,* who is also well-known for his courageous participation in joint church action against the Party and the Government of the Reich.

---

5. These two bishops did not play prominent roles in the German church opposition. Interestingly, Faulhaber was involved in peace overtures initiated by Nazi governor Ritter von Epp of Bavaria in April 1945. See documents [95a] and [95b].

6. The OSS kept several copies of von Galen's courageous anti-Nazi sermons in their archives.

e. Collaboration between Protestant and Catholic representatives of the leading groups in the various districts, who are responsible for the development of the German "Self-Help" organization, is accomplished in a similar fashion.

II. The participation of the German Evangelical Church in the entire "Self-Help" organization is led by:

a. *Bishop Wurm* of Stuttgart who, together with the heads of the secret Reich Advisory Council of the German Evangelical Church, has succeeded in rallying to the cause an overwhelming majority (85–90 percent) of the established Protestant churches and parishes in Germany, and has recruited and guided the application of Christian principles in the resistance movement. In the battle against euthanasia he became well-known, carrying out a joint action for the protection of thousands of medical cases from destruction, as well as for protection of thousands of Non-Aryan Christians. He is also noted for the protection of oppressed populations in occupied territories and for the protection of foreign workers. Evidence of his activity can be found in statements made by him, which are known to the British and American public.

b. *Dr. Eugen Gerstenmaier,* Berlin, who is the head of the oecumenical central office of the German Evangelical Church, which is also the central office for the direction of Group A II. Dr. Gerstenmaier is known for his unusually capable and energetic leadership in the mobilization of the church's resistance forces, and for the development of the entire network of leading groups in the struggle against the Gestapo on behalf of foreign workers, as well as for his participation in liberating and protecting clergymen and leading laymen in the resistance forces of the occupied territories. He maintains extensive contacts with representatives of Christian and socialist labor in the development of the "cell" system. He also maintains close contact with Christian groups in the armed forces and, outside of Germany, with Barness, Leiper, Temple, Chichester and Oldham.

c. *Rector Grüber,* Berlin, known in Germany, the United States, Great Britain, France, Holland and Norway for his extraordinarily courageous intervention in behalf of Non-Aryan Christians. He has outstanding organizational capacities for large scale relief action. For almost two years he maintained contact in the concentration camps at Oranienburg and Dachau with captive French, Polish, Czechoslovakian and Dutch clergymen. Above all, he has contacts among the workers, as well as representatives of the "Red Aid" (Rote Hilfe).[7] At present he has emerged as one of the leading spirits representing the church's attitude in the struggle waged by the church resistance forces. On the basis of this he is especially well qualified to handle the central organization of the work to be done by the Central Commission for the provision of material care.[8]

d. *Rector (licenciate) W. Menn,* Andernach (Rhineland) is particularly qualified as liaison agent of the Central Commission A, by reason of his extensive contacts with industrial and labor representatives throughout the entire Rhineland and

---

7. Communist underground organization.
8. For Grüber see also document [70a].

Westphalia. He was formerly the head of the Church Office for Social Work of the Rhenish Protestant Church and was responsible, at the same time, for the oecumenical work and organization within the association of clergymen (Pfarrer-Bruderschaft) of the Rhineland and Westphalia. Since 1929–30 he has been in close contact with all oecumenical activity and especially with Barness, John Foster Dulles, Leiper and Cavert in the U.S.A., as well as with the Archbishop of Canterbury, the Lord Bishop of Chichester, Dr. Oldham in Great Britain and Prof. Dr. Kramer in Holland.

II. The following are some of the leading personalities in the Central Commission B, for spiritual care within the framework of the German "Self-Help" organization.

a. *Dr. Otto Dibelius,* Berlin, is well-known in Germany, as well as on the European Continent and in the Anglo-Saxon Churches, for the extensive services he has rendered in the struggle against the National Socialist regime and its intrusion into the domain of the church, as well as for his close collaboration with leading forces in the resistance movement. On the basis of the distinguished organizational capacities he has shown in rallying the best evangelizing forces to the cause, he was entrusted with the management of Central Commission B. He maintains liaison with other churches, notably with the Lord Bishop of Chichester.

b. *Dr. W. Bachmann,* Berlin. As head of the services for the spiritual welfare of prisoners of war and internees, he has shown outstanding abilities in mobilizing the forces of the church in spiritual matters and under difficult circumstances. He is known for his courageous intervention in behalf of American, Anglo-Saxon, French, Dutch, Serbian and Russian prisoners of war. He holds a key position in the defense of an all-embracing Christian service by other organizations and churches in Germany for the spiritual welfare of prisoners of war and internees. He has also intervened for the spiritual welfare of foreign workers.

c. *Dr. Thielicke,* Stuttgart, is entrusted with the spiritual education of the leading groups in Württemberg and beyond. He has developed a distinguished literary activity in the analyzation of National Socialist ideology and has opposed it uncompromisingly. He has done outstanding work for spiritual welfare in the younger generation, especially among the laboring classes. Because of this and because of his many years of evangelizing activity in all parts of Germany, and the contacts he has thereby established with leading groups in many districts, he has also been chosen as a liaison agent in the Central Commission B.

d. *Dr. Hutten,* Stuttgart, has been a liaison for many years between the central leading groups and the resistance movement of the church. He has been extremely valuable in the shaping of a Christian point of view in the public, a point of view which has penetrated to all districts and communities. For this reason he has been entrusted with work of this nature in the Central Commission B.

e. *Dr. H. Lilje,* Berlin, is one of the most distinguished Evangelists and speakers of the German Evangelical Church. He has done extensive work in the uncompromising opposition to the attacks of National Socialists on Christian thought and life in all districts of Germany. He maintains excellent relations with all oecumenical activities, especially with Dr. Oldham and the Lord Bishop of Chichester, and with the leading younger generation of Christians in Great Britain. He is also in contact with leading men in the Lutheran Churches of Europe and the U.S.A.

III. The following are included in leading Württemberg and Baden groups.

a. *Dr. W. Collmer* [Paul Collmer], Stuttgart, holds a leading position in the struggle for the settlement of great questions of social import in Württemberg and Baden. Therefore, he is in close collaboration with the representatives of labor and their liaison men in the development of the "cell" system. At present, he also has special contacts with the resistance forces in concentration camps, and the labor liaison agents who are active in this connection. He formerly participated in the collaboration with leading resistance forces of the church and the political works [sic] in Holland. He has outstanding organizational and administrative abilities.

b. *Dr. Plappart*, industrial representative in Württemberg and Baden. He has done distinguished work in organization and the instruction of leading groups and "cells" in these districts. He enjoys the special confidence of labor.

c. *Oberbahnrat X* (high official in the transport system), Stuttgart. Holds a central position in the entire transport system of Württemberg, Baden and Bavaria.

d. *Dr. W. Hoffmann*, Stuttgart. He has performed leading functions in the schooling of correlated leading groups and in the struggle against National Socialist ideology. He is the central representative for the re-formation of the educational system.

e. *Prof. Erik Wolf*, Freiburg (Baden). Holds a central position in judicial affairs and government administration. He is noted for his courageous stand as legal counsel of the militant churches, as well as educator of a younger generation of jurists and administrative officials who have adopted an uncompromising attitude toward the National Socialist regime, and who have joined the leading groups and "cells" under the direction of the churches. He is in very close contact with President Max Huber of Geneva and Prof. E. Brunner of Zurich.

IV. The following are included in leading groups in north Germany, especially Hamburg, Bremen, Sleswick-Holstein and Lower Saxony.

a. *Dr. Asmussen*, outstanding Hamburg churchman, has a leading position in the management of the collective church initiative undertaken by the German Evangelical Church. He is known for his courageous stand in the opposition to the National Socialist State. He maintains extremely close relations with leading Catholic circles.

b. (Licentiate) *Herntrich*, Hamburg, has shown outstanding ability and leadership in organizing matters pertaining to spiritual welfare, particularly in the case of hundreds of thousands of evacuees who have been indoctrinated with an uncompromising collective policy of resistance against a spirit of hatred or a lust for revenge.

c. *Dr. Steltzer*, Sleswick-Holstein, is a distinguished expert on the entire transport system. He holds a central position in the schooling of experts in the administration of leading groups and "cells". He participated in the protective action undertaken in behalf of Bishop Berggrav.

d. *Rudolf Petersen*, Hamburg, is a representative of the leading commercial circles. He has confidential contacts in Anglo-Saxon countries.

e. *Police-president Schrors*, Bremen, holds a key position in the entire administrative and transport system. He has confidential contacts with all circles in the population, including labor.

Among others, the two following central circles have been formed in Germany since 1938 for the purpose of combating the National Socialist regime. These circles have undertaken the task of organizing the totality of resistance forces in Germany.

I. The Circle around Count Helmut Moltke and Count Peter Yorck von Wartenburg* (Circle A I)

a. Political attitude toward the outside: Germany can only be capable of existing as part of a unified federative Europe, developed along Christian-social lines. Political attitude toward the interior: after the fall of centralization, a political structure corresponding to the above must be built.

b. Composition: officials and workers from Christian and socialist unions, industrialists, agriculturalists, and officers, all of whom are in key positions in the social and economic life of the army, and the governmental and communal administrative machine.

c. Aim: Preparation of a democratic self-governing administrative body in Germany, which, after the collapse of the National Socialist regime, will be capable of taking over the administration of the country even to the village committees.

II. The circle around Dr. Eugen Gerstenmaier (Circle A II)

a. Political attitude: the same as in Circle A I.

b. Composition: Church leaders, members of the clergy, and laymen of the German Evangelical Church including every class of the population, especially the laboring classes who, until recently, had not evidenced any interest in the church. This central group is in close contact with representatives and laity of the Catholic Church (and the Catholic population) correspondingly engaged in activities in the same field.

c. Aim: orientation, within the framework of the church revival, of the entire public and civil life according to Christian principles.

III. Since 1940 there has been a *growing fusion of the two central groups of Circle A I and Circle A II*. This was brought about especially by the fact that leaders of A II were in a position to bring to the cause results of their extensive mobilization of broad strata of the population against National Socialism in all districts of Germany and particularly the benefits of their extensive relations with labor.

As a result of the events on July 20, Count Peter Yorck von Wartenburg was executed.

This resulted in a close collaboration for the following purpose: penetration of Germany and Austria by reliable liaison men; formation of leading groups and subordinated "cell" systems in all districts.

Of value in this collaboration was the fact that in the struggle against party and Reich Government, the Evangelical Church, as well as the Catholic Church in Germany had preserved the corporate organization of the church communities in every part of Germany and Austria. On the basis of the preservation of this organization, it has been possible to develop the system of small groups in all districts, even down to individual communities. This system of leading groups and "cells" was organized to provide the services of experts in every domain, such as, the church, government, self-government, educational system, industry and agriculture. These leading groups and "cells" educated broad masses of the people for a realistic opposition to Nazi propaganda. The collaboration of both Circles (A I and A II) and the support of the resistance movement embracing the entire German territory, proved valuable for the execution of large unified actions. For example, the constantly renewed success in obtaining humane treatment for prisoners of war and especially in the action undertaken to save about one million Russian prisoners from extermination during the winter of 1941/42.

Such action saved about 400,000 Non-Aryans of mixed parentage from deportation and saved thousands of hostages and Jews in the occupied territories. It also provided care and support for hundreds of thousands of Dutch, French, Norwegian, Danish and Ukrainian workers.

The particular role played by the churches in this joint action by both circles is presented in a special report.

IV. With a constant view toward the possible collapse of the Nazi system and the subsequent occupation of the Reich territory, a "Self-Help" organization of the German Evangelical Church and the Catholic Church in Germany was prepared in conformity with the aims of Circle A I. It is to be expected that the collapse of the National Socialist system will result in the complete discontinuation of the functions of the central and local Nazi food and transport authorities, for all leading offices of the administrative machine are held by Nazi officials. After the collapse, these officials will, in all probability, no longer be tolerated by the workers, and it must be expected that they will be immediately eliminated. In such a situation the churches will have the only organization embracing the entire German territory and reaching into the most isolated communities of the country. At that moment they alone will be in a position to handle the entire food and food distribution system.

Therefore, a Central Labor Commission (Central Commission A) was formed in the German Evangelical Church under the direction of Bishop Wurm of Stuttgart. Central Commission A is managed by Friedrich v. Bodelschwingh, Bethel, and Rector Grüber, Berlin, for the assumption of the supply system. Central Commission A is supported by the leading groups (mentioned in paragraph 2), who are responsible for the individual districts and who, in turn, will call upon the services of the subordinate "cells" in the communities. As mentioned, these leading groups are composed of especially energetic members of the clergy and of experts among industrialists, workers, officials and professional men. The assumption of the transport system has been prepared with special care. The elements constituting Central Commission A also insure close contact with the secret organization "Red Aid" (Rote Hilfe).

V. Beside Central Commission A for food supply, a further Central Commission to safeguard spiritual welfare and the reorganization of the educational system was organized in close collaboration with the Catholic Church. This is Central Commission B and is managed by Dr. O. Dibelius and Dr. W. Bachmann. Parallel with Central Commission A, Central Commission B has worked in close collaboration with leading groups and "cells" and has obtained full support from the established churches and parishes in combating the spiritual disintegration and great mental void which will befall the population after the collapse of Germany. Together with pastoral activities, this will include an all embracing spiritual orientation of broad masses of the German population through sermons, publications, radio broadcasts and all possible personal efforts by Christian forces for the accomplishment of this enormous task. Furthermore, based on the expert knowledge of the leading groups, the reorganization of the educational system will be initiated with a radical purging action which will eliminate all Nazi elements from the teaching body.

The work of both Central Commissions and their organs is undertaken in behalf of all strata of the population, regardless of the church they belong to, and especially in behalf of the millions of foreign workers. Thanks to the churches' efforts, they have their own confidential liaison men among these workers (see Memorandum on the churches).[9]

VI. In consideration of the expected collapse of the National Socialist regime, and the fact that the Allied military command must be strongly interested in a rapid return to calm and order, and as smooth as possible a resumption of work in German industry and agriculture, the following is hereby proposed:

The establishment of an advisory group attached to the general staff of the Allied occupying forces in Germany. This advisory organ would represent the liaison with the German "Self-Help" organization described in paragraphs 3 and 4. Upon the withdrawal of combat troops, this advisory group would be taken over by the highest echelon of the occupying authorities (Inter-Allied Commission).

The first concern of this mediator board would be to regulate collaboration between the highest Allied occupation authorities and the "Self-Help" organization (as described in I) and its subsequent development, German self-government.

---

9. Not printed.

Under no circumstances should the leading organs of the German "Self-Help" organization be regarded by the German population as "Quislings" as a result of their close contact with the victorious powers. Therefore, the above-mentioned advisory organ should immediately be represented as a liaison agency between the oecumenical aid society of the World Council of Churches, the "Self-Help" organization of the Roman Catholic Church and, above all, the corresponding American and British aid societies and the German "Self-Help" organization. In this manner, immediate collaborative work will be freed from a considerable danger which it would be impossible to overlook. Thus, the work of collaboration will be raised from a purely political form of contact to that of a solitary aid organization composed of the Christian elements recruited by the large churches, elements who have stood together throughout the entire war despite any political differences of opinion.

It may be advisable to include men from the oecumenical aid society of the World Council of Churches and the collective aid society of the Roman Catholic Church in the above-mentioned advisory group. These men could act as advisory liaison men, as their long-standing collaboration with the personalities in the German "Self-Help" organization (I) have made them thoroughly acquainted with the personalities in question.

The "Self-Help" organization, embracing the entire Reich territory and described under I, is the only remaining organization capable of functioning immediately in post-Nazi Germany. Only [by] establishing a collaboration devoid of friction between the provisional occupation authorities and the "Self-Help" organization can chaos be avoided in Germany.

Document 71 · November 1944

Memorandum by Emmy Rado
(OSS New York): History and Significance
of the Confessional Church in Germany[1]

SECRET

Mrs. Rado's Biographical Records Section in New York has just prepared a memorandum on the history and significance of the Confessional Church in Germany which I think you will find of considerable interest.[2] I am sending you herewith two copies of the same with the suggestion that you may wish to keep one for your files or to show to a few people in SI-Washington who are interested in the subject, and to forward the other to the German desk in London, if you believe it would be of value to them in their work. A copy has already been delivered to General Donovan as he expressed interest in receiving information on this matter.

Outside of copies to him and to you, I am making no further dissemination of this memo except to forward one copy to Hugh Wilson and one copy to [Allen W.] Dulles. I am sure you will find it of considerable interest and after you have had an opportunity to look it over, I would appreciate your opinion of the same.

JCH [John C. Hughes]

---

1. NA, RG 226, Entry 92, Box 588, Folder 6. This memorandum was forwarded on 5 December 1944 by John C. Hughes of OSS New York to Whitney H. Shepardson, Chief of OSS Secret Intelligence in Washington, D.C.

2. In mid-1943 Emmy Rado had started the so-called "Biographical Records" project of the OSS. Its aim was to accumulate as much biographical information as possible on different professional groups in Germany and the individual's pro- or anti-Nazi attitudes. See also document [70a].

Memorandum on the History and Significance
of the Confessional Church *(Bekenntniskirche)* in Germany
and Brief History of the Relations Between State and Church
in Germany during the Weimar Republic and Before 1918

Chapter I: State and Protestant Church Under Hitler

1) Some time before Hitler came to power the Nazis organized a campaign designed to conquer the German Protestant Church from within. The "German Christian Movement", created for that very purpose, used in its early stages fifth column tactics within the Protestant Church: ostensibly prompted solely by religious motives, it advocated disassociating the religion of Christ from its Jewish background. It disowned the Old Testament and refused to accept it as the word of God. Next, it attempted to interpret and express the religion of Christ in terms of the Nazi doctrine of "blood and soil" and the superiority of the "Aryan" race. After Hitler's advent it gradually dropped the pretense of being concerned solely with the interpretation of the Gospel of Christ. Its object became more and more openly the glorification and sanctification of Nazidom, and it used to that end spiritual propaganda as well as threats. In other words, the German Christian Movement became in due course a Nazi organization in the guise of a Church but claimed to be the legitimate Protestant Church of Germany. Its supreme aim was more complete Nazification of Germany by making Nazidom palatable to Germans desiring to retain, at least superficially, a Christian tradition.

2) Immediately after Hitler's accession to power the Nazis, in line with their policy of unifying and centralizing the administration throughout the Reich— ostensibly to promote its efficiency, in reality to infiltrate it with Party members— tried to centralize the Government of the Protestant Church. To that end a Ministry for Church Affairs and the position of Reichsbischof[3] were created. Moreover, the exercise of all functions of supervision and the administration of the Church affairs the State had retained were put in the hands of the Nazis. Wherever vacancies occured in the theological faculties of universities or State-owned theological seminaries, they were filled with Nazis (German Christians.) As a result, the Board of Examiners for the theological examinations soon consisted only of Nazis, and only Nazi candidates had a chance of passing and thereby of qualifying for the Ministry; but all these steps and measures were of merely secondary importance. To nazify the Protestant Church and its following, the men who had to be won over or, if they resisted, curbed or removed, were the Protestant pastors.

---

3. With the Reichsbishop, for the first time in German history, the Protestant Church had a single head.

At first Hitler proceeded with considerable caution. Friedrich von Bodelschwingh Jr. of Bethel near Bielefeld was nominated to the office of Reichsbischof upon the unanimous vote of representatives of the various Protestant Churches. Representing the best conservative tradition in the Protestant Church, he was known throughout Germany for his exemplary social and charitable work. (He had continued with marked success the religious and charitable institutions his father had founded.) In short, a man who enjoyed universal respect and had nothing whatever to do with the German Christian Movement. But this conciliatory gesture failed completely. After less than six months von Bodelschwingh resigned and returned to Bethel. His successor as Reichsbischof was an Army chaplain from Königsberg, Ludwig Müller, a German Christian and Nazi. Known to only a few German pastors, he had neither a good theological background nor a forceful personality. In fact, he was an insignificant person— vain, conceited, ruthless, mean, and fairly stupid.

From the moment he was appointed Reichsbischof the fight in the Protestant Church was on. Individual pastors had been aware of the danger Nazidom represented for their faith and their Church already when Hitler took over; but the majority indulged in wishful and confused thinking, some swayed by the appeal of Nazi slogans to their patriotic traditions and instincts, other succumbing to their desire for peace and for social reform. Müller's appointment as Reichsbischof aroused not only a flood of protests (thousands of pastors read from their pulpits a declaration expressing their determination to disobey and resist Müller and the Nazi-controlled Administration of Church Affairs) but was the beginning of a concerted movement which called itself "Bekennende Kirche" (Confessional Church).[4]

The origin of the Confessional Movement cannot be localized at any one point. It arose simultaneously throughout Germany, as the expression of a spirit of resistance to the Nazi encroachment on the independence of the Protestant Church. Martin Niemöller, pastor of a small church in Dahlem, a wealthy suburb of Berlin, and famous as a hero of World War I,[5] enjoys perhaps the highest prestige and appears as its leading figure today, because of the fanaticism with which he advocated the movement in the beginning and because his martyr role received the widest publicity. However, he was not alone in initiating the movement, nor can he be called its true spiritual leader, or even its most fundamental thinker.

The growth of the Confessional Church is the more remarkable when one considers that it occured against the will of the Nazis and despite their active opposition—yet under their very eyes. Synodical meetings were held, attended by representatives from all over Germany, most of them pastors but many of them laymen. A "Provisional Government of the Church" was established, a "Pastors'

---

4. See also documents [21] and [70c].

5. On Pastor Martin Niemöller compare also documents [20] and [21]. Niemöller had been commander of a U-Boat in World War I.

Emergency League" was organized to help pastors when financial support was withheld by the Nazi-controlled Church Government. Substantial funds were collected, theological schools to train ministers were organized and staffed, and boards of examiners set up to qualify students of theology for the Ministry. Above all, the Confessional Church Movement intensified religious life and theological thinking, preached and practiced tolerance and helped not only the sick and the poor but also the persecuted.

The Nazis did everything in their power to crush the movement. Pastors who had joined the "Confessional Church" were deposed by decree of the Nazi-controlled Government—their salaries stopped; but the pastors often simply disregarded the order and stayed on, continuing to preach and to perform all their duties, supported by their congregation or by the "Pastors' Emergency League". Thereupon a German Christian pastor was usually sent out to take over the church building and the parsonage by force (often with the help of Stormtroopers). If that was impossible, because the new pastor could not expect any support from the congregation in question, the church building was locked. If all this proved ineffective because the pastor would not yield to threats and had too much support from his congregation to be removed by physical force, he was denounced to the Gestapo, whereupon he was either arrested and sent to a camp or, at least, ordered to leave the district and forbidden to speak in public. After the outbreak of the war these measures were supplemented by drafting recalcitrant pastors for military service whenever their age and physical fitness permitted.

Occasionally the Nazis tried to appease the Confessional pastors. So-called "Kirchenausschüsse" (church committees), composed mainly of pastors who were known as "irenic", i.e. opposed to every kind of radicalism, were organized to act as a consulting body to the Government of the Church. Whenever a pastor fell for their ruse, he was given a larger congregation or a promotion or some other reward. But the "Kirchenausschüsse" did not function long. When the Confessional members saw that they could not carry their views, they resigned. The whole measure, like many other measures and institutions the Nazis tried, finally had to be abandoned. Nor was the Confessional Movement always in the defensive. In many instances it sent its ministers out to reconquer congregations from a German Christian pastor. When its publications were suppressed, mimeographed sheets were circulated, and if they were confiscated, the Church news was spread by word of mouth. Prayer services for pastors who had been arrested and imprisoned were held—if a church building was found locked against them, congregations met in the streets. In short, it was the kind of struggle that could not but kindle a spirit of resistance, conspiracy, and eventually open revolt.

[...]

3) As a result of the fight in the Protestant Church, three groups can be distinguished among the Protestant pastors in Germany:

a. The German Christians who put Nazism first, Christianity second.
b. The active and militant members of the Confessional Church who are willing

to make every sacrifice, and who suffered persecution and hardship to preserve a truly Christian Church and the freedom to preach the true Gospel.

c. A middle group, whose members may or may not have joined the
Confessional Movement but who, while definitely opposed to the German
Christians, are so much inclined to peaceful cooperation with the State that
they abstain from any participation in active resistance.

Chapter II: Political Significance of the Confessional Movement

As we saw, the Nazis set out to apply their method of unification
(*Gleichschaltung*—coordination) to the Protestant Church. They used every
weapon—compromise, intimidation, threats, persecution, bribes, as well as
promises, rewards, and appeasement. They succeeded in every field except this
one. The Confessional Movement grew and spread despite all their efforts to
crush it. This fact alone gives the Confessional Movement great political significance. By its nature that significance is symbolic or potential rather than actual.
The Confessional Church never aspired, much less achieved, political influence,
but it instilled a spirit of resistance in its adherents, it made them critical of the
Regime and its basic philosophy, and it afforded Germans at least one forum
before which they could register a protest, however silent and meek. And, under
the circumstances, this protest could not help but have a political flavor: Pastors
as well as laymen who joined the Confessional Church thereby professed that they
were not Nazis, at least in one important respect.

Nevertheless, in evaluating its potential value for political reconstruction in
Germany, great caution is indicated. Most of its leaders are interested in the tenets
of their religion, in social work, or in Church policy, but not in political ideologies
and institutions. Their fundamental attitude to "the government" is the traditional Lutheran obedience in all "temporal" matters owed to the "ruler", whoever
he may be. Democracy means nothing to them. In fact, many of them are by tradition against it. Yet, for the purpose of finding the men and women who might
be the nucleus and the leaders of a German democratic regeneration, the existence of the Confessional Movement is of inestimable value, because the minds of
its members have not been poisoned, because they will have the prestige of having
resisted the Nazis, because they have learned to operate as a coherent group, and,
last but not least, because they must feel an urge to find a new political system
preventing the recurrence of Nazism and similar philosophies.

From this viewpoint the Confessional Movement is undoubtedly a great assest
for German political reconstruction. However, a word of caution is perhaps not
out of place also here. The Nazis are, of course, well aware of the potential significance of the Confessional Movement in Germany's political life. It would be in
keeping with their fifth column tactics if they were themselves to choose a religious movement as a cloak for their nefarious ends. Cooperation with Protestant
pastors of undoubted sincerity and independence may be the sole means of
unmasking attempts they may make along such lines. In this field these pastors

can be counted upon to cooperate, whereas it is by no means certain that they will cooperate with the Allies in all other respects.

...⁶

Document 72 · 31 October 1944

OSS Black Radio Speech:
General Beck Speaks Again[1]

Beck I (Final)[2]

I'm calling Germany. I'm calling not only my comrades of the *Wehrmacht*. I'm calling the whole of Germany. I do not *beg* for your attention. I *demand* your attention. In the name of Germany, in the name of our Fatherland so gravely endangered, I demand that each of you listen and that each of you do whatever your patriotic duty commands you to do. I do not act, as the saying goes, by order; not on command of some leader. There is only *one* leader; and that is our patriotic conscience. My conscience commands me to speak to Germany.

I don't need to introduce myself. My voice betrays me. My voice speaks for me. My comrades of the OKW [Oberkommando der Wehrmacht] and of the General Staff, and all officers and men who at any time have had anything to do with me have, of course, recognized me by now and they know: This is Beck, Ludwig Beck. Yes, no other than Col.-Gen. [Colonel General] Beck, former Chief of the General Staff. The big crowd, of course, does not know my voice. I'm not accustomed to

---

6. The third chapter of Rado's study covers the relations between state and Protestant Church under the Weimar Republic. In the fourth she traces the history of this relationship back to the Reformation.

1. NA, RG 226, Entry 139, Box 115, Folder 1539; German original on tape: NA, Audiovisual Records 226.01.

2. This is the first of a number of Beck speeches scheduled for broadcasting. For this radio operation, (Operation Joker), the OSS Morale Operations Branch had compiled a detailed biography of Beck using documents at the Wiener Library and secret intelligence material. Several prisoners of war who were interned in Brondsbury, England, had helped the OSS writing team to "nazify" the speeches. One prisoner of war, a major, was persuaded to read the text, another one was selected as the lead-in announcer for the broadcast.

appear more or less regularly before the microphone like Hitler and Ley and Goebbels to make demagogic speeches *in a professional way.* We, of the General Staff, are accustomed *to act* ... and to keep silent. But the desperate position of our Fatherland forces us to break this professional silence. Therefore, the *entire* people is now going to get to know my voice. This is *not* the voice of the dead which speaks to you. On the contrary! My voice is very much alive; and the Nazi leaders who declared me dead though they knew better will soon find out with the *deepest* regret *how* alive I am!

Goebbels declared on the radio that I had committed suicide.[3] This was really very nice of him, for whoever has been declared dead erroneously is—so the saying goes—supposed to live particularly long. According to that I'll get to be very old. For it is now the second time that the Nazis declared I had taken my own life.[4] The first time was in 1938 when I resigned.[5] Any other Chief of the General Staff would have done the same if such a ... layman[6] would have continually stuck his nose into his business. Of course, I know that the fact that I resigned could have endangered my life. That time, which was six years ago, Himmler had given the orders to get me out of the way, just as he has done recently. At that time I upset the calculation of these "gentlemen". I owe it to my friend Freiherr von Fritsch that I got away alive. His news service was a hundred times better than the entire spy system of the Gestapo. This was one of the reasons Fritsch was subsequently assassinated.[7] Half an hour after Himmler had given the order to shoot me, Fritsch knew of it. So I simply disappeared ... and they spread the rumor I had committed suicide.

[...]

I know the significance of the oath to the flag. I don't mean the involuntary oath that we were forced to take when Hitler, using a counterfeited testament of Hindenburg, put himself at the head of the Wehrmacht in 1934.[8] No, I mean the oath to the flag, which I swore in 1898, when, at the age of eighteen, I entered the Army.

After the revolution we spoke once in a smaller circle about the question of how the present situation was compatible with our former oath to the flag. I then

---

3. See document [54].

4. Before broadcasting the Beck speech, prisoners of war had been interviewed about the believability of rumors concerning General Beck being alive. The OSS found out that most prisoners believed them.

5. As he did not agree with Hitler's plan to conquer Czechoslovakia, Beck resigned as Chief of the General Staff in August 1938.

6. This is an allusion to Hitler.

7. As Commander in Chief of the Army, Fritsch was formally in charge of military intelligence. In 1938 he had been removed from his position, and in September 1939 he sought and found death on a Polish battlefield.

8. After Hindenburg's death in August 1934, Hitler arbitrarily took over all of the *Reichspräsident*'s official functions, including the Supreme Command of the Armed Forces. From then on, every soldier had to swear a personal oath to Hitler.

pointed out: The Emperor has freed us from the loyalty we owed to his *person*: but no human being can free me from my oath of loyalty to Germany. I am proud to admit, to this very day, here before all Germany: I myself belonged to the group of staff officers who, in 1918, forced the Emperor to abdicate.[9]

The Emperor had led Germany to the brink of catastrophe. We prevailed upon him to take the consequences. By this means Germany was spared gigantic losses, her towns were saved from destruction, and the bulk of the country from foreign occupation. That happened then. And now: The catastrophe into which Hitler has plunged Germany is far worse than any disaster that ever threatened us. *Therefore* we have come to the conclusion to get Hitler out of the way. Together with all of my comrades I deplore that our attempt of July 20th failed ... and that it cost the lives of some of the best of us. But I am proud that, just as in 1918, I belonged to this group of men who valued loyalty to their Fatherland higher than anything else.

We cannot accomplish it alone. *Everyone* must do his duty. Everyone is needed if we are to accomplish our task: to save that part of the Army that can still be saved, and to free our homeland from the criminals who have plunged it and our people into ruin.

[...]

A few important points: First, the invasion of England: For it, too, Freiherr v. Fritsch and I had prepared everything in detail. The maps that *we* had prepared were even much better than the maps of the British General Staff. Everything was ready. The troops were poised in the ports of the Channel. The necessary tonnage was available. But then ... Hitler left us in the lurch. Till today, we members of the General Staff[10] could not understand why the order had not been forthcoming from the headquarters of the Fuehrer. We asked for it again and again. Again and again we received an evasive answer. Today we know the reason: Goering's *Luftwaffe* [air force] did not come up to our expectations. The battle of the air over England—planned by Goering and Hitler—had been lost; and with it the possibility of an invasion of England.

Number two: The attack on Russia: The plan for this campaign, also, had been worked out by Col.-Gen. [Colonel General] v. Fritsch, and I had served as his adviser. Never before in our glorious history had our troops experienced such unprecedented victories as in the Summer and Fall of 1941. Everything went along with the precision of clock work, in exact accordance with the plan until ... here again, Mr. Hitler with his intuition interfered. Col.-Gen. Hoeppner [Hoepner] asked urgently for reinforcements for the final attack on Moscow. Hitler refused them ... [11]

---

9. Since 1912, Beck had been a member of the Prussian General Staff.

10. Actually, Beck had been living in retirement since 1938.

11. In the winter of 1941, General Erich Hoepner had called his troops back from the Moscow front against Hitler's express orders. Thereafter, he was released from his post, and in August 1944 he was executed for his participation in the plot against Hitler.

Number three: The catastrophe of Stalingrad. Up to now, the dreadful truth about Stalingrad probably has been known only to the General Staff. Part of the city was already in our hands. We had figured out exactly the number of days required to occupy the whole of it ... which would have meant complete control of the Volga. But here, again, the amateur commander of the Wehrmacht, Mr. Hitler, interfered with his intuition. On his own initiative, he gave the order to change the battle line. On his own initiative he ordered the troops to take up new positions. Moreover, he did it without having the sectional commanders notified of the change he had ordered: This was the definite turning point of the war. There the stone, or better the avalanche, of our retreat got into motion.

Number four: The catastrophe in the West: From the Maginot Line, I had learned that there is no defensive wall that cannot be breached.[12] Fieldmarshal v. Rundstedt too, had warned emphatically against offering senseless resistance along the Atlantic Wall.[13] He called it "propaganda warfare". But, again, Hitler knew better: and again, his decision was against us generals. [...]

It is easy to command "Hold out to the last drop of blood! Resistance to the last cartridge!" But our great Clausewitz, the preceptor of our entire General Staff, held a different opinion from Mr. Hitler's. In his standard work, "On War", Clausewitz teaches ... I quote literally ... "We *protect* ourselves against defeat, if we give up the soil for which we have fought in *just time*". Yes, "in just time" ... exactly what we wanted to do in France! Aachen, the resplendent Imperial city with its irreplacable historic monuments, is now but a heap of ruins. Aachen is dead, irrevocably swept from the face of the earth.[14] Thousands of brave soldiers, thousands of innocent civilians, were senselessly butchered, only because—here, too—Mr. Hitler did not act "in just time". But Hitler loses his sense of proportion when it comes to sacrificing the lives of *others*. Here again I must mention what Clausewitz says: "The losses suffered by a retreating defender will be much greater if he retreats after having lost the battle, than if he does it voluntarily". On all fronts, Hitler has waited *until* the battle was lost. Therefore, our losses on all fronts are so unproportionally greater than anybody in the General Staff could have dreamed.

A whole world has taken up arms against us, a world whose human resources are just as unlimited as its production facilities. But nevertheless a reckless and amateurish government tells you: "Hold out! We shall catch up with the material superiority of the enemy. In summer, it is true, we have been forced to retreat by the crushing superiority of the enemy; but soon we shall have caught up with the enemy. Just as in 1939, we are on the eve of a great and victorious offensive". This they dare to tell you, German men and women, at the threshold of the sixth war

---

12. French line of defense against Germany in the western and northwestern parts of France, constructed between 1929 and 1932.

13. A fortification built by the Germans along the Atlantic Coast.

14. Aachen was the first major German city that had been taken by the Allied troops in October 1944.

winter! This they dare to tell you … after Stalingrad … after the loss of France … after Aachen!!!

[…]

Never has such a crime as the calling up of the *Volkssturm* [people's armed resistance] been committed against our people.[15] Perhaps, if you have no feelings, you may say: "What good are the old men!" I am of a different opinion: Everyone will be needed whose life can be saved! Everyone will be needed for the reconstruction of the Fatherland. But more than any other age group, we shall need our children! The future of Germany, any future that our people can still expect, is being buried if we permit that even the youngest of our youth are being sacrificed for Hitler.

Therefore, there is only *one* remedy, only *one* slogan: away with Hitler! Away with the Nazi rule! This sounds like a call to mutiny, particularly in the mouth of a former Chief of the General Staff, it *is* a call to mutiny. In this particular case, I can refer you to an authority whom the Nazis, yes even the Nazis, must recognize: Mr. Hitler, Mr. Adolf Hitler, writes in his book "Mein Kampf" … I've written down the quotation. Here it is. The author, Adolf Hitler, writes on Page 590: "In the hour when the organization of a people is breaking down, and it becomes apparent that, thanks to the action of a few scoundrels, the people will be subjected to the worst oppression, obedience towards them and fulfillment of duty seem nothing but doctrinary madness. At such a time, duty and responsibility to the entire nation become paramount".[16] This is not good German. But it is a good rule. Thanks to "the action of a few scoundrels" Germany is about to collapse. And Hitler himself teaches that responsibility towards the nation must be held higher than any other consideration. Therefore, my listeners, I stand before you today. Therefore, I speak to you.

And therefore I have to quote again, as main witness, this very same Mr. Hitler. At another place in his book … you can find it in Chapter 31 … "State Authority Not Purpose in Itself" … there Hitler writes *literally* … "When the government uses its power to lead a people towards destruction, then rebellion is not only right but the duty of each citizen of such a nation". I should like to underline each word: The rebellion of our people is, as Hitler himself declares, not only our right but our duty […]

Hitler knows that only Himmler can still keep him in power. But we know that Himmler's power has been very much overestimated. I do not deny that Himmler's power is still great. But I stand here before you, so in my case Himmler has failed! My younger friend and collaborator, Werner Graf v.d. Schulenburg, has been sought in vain by Himmler since July 20th. SS-Obergruppenführer [Lieutenant General] Nebe, who joined us, has not yet been arrested, despite the

---

15. On 25 September 1944, the Nazi government had called up all German men from age 16 to 60, who could bear arms, for the *Deutscher Volkssturm*.

16. Parts of the original quote are here omitted.

fact that Himmler offered a reward of 50,000 Marks for his capture. You have been told that Head-Mayor Goerdeler was caught by the Gestapo, sentenced to death by the Peoples' Tribunal [Volksgerichtshof], and hanged. This is not true. Head-Mayor Goerdeler is still at liberty.[17] You see: whoever wants to be free … whoever has the unbreakable will to freedom … does not fall into the hands of the Gestapo. Therefore, I call upon you, my listeners: Do not make the mistake of being despondent! Think of Germany! Of nothing but Germany!

[…]

Listen attentively and follow my instructions:

Thousands of like-minded people have already joined our movement. It is everyone's duty to enlarge the circle of our movement more and more. Ask your friends to […][18] listen with you to my messages.

Elect from among you energetic and determined men and women as your representatives! Select from among your friends technically experienced people. When I give you the signal for action, these experts must assume control over all important establishments such as means of transportation, broadcasting stations, newspaper plants, etc. […] Organize yourselves into committees to prepare for united and effective action: Officers and non-coms on leave should be called in for organizational work.

Arm yourselves! Be prepared particularly to take over depots of arms of the Wehrmacht, and especially of the Party, at the decisive moment, and to put these to use for our purposes.

These are my instructions for today. For reasons which, quite naturally, I cannot explain over the radio, I can give you no further instructions at this time. We must not endanger our organization by premature actions. For the same reasons, you will not hear from me in the next few days, the next week, or even *longer*. In the meanwhile, you must still be careful. However, you should try our wavelength every day for five minutes at this hour.[19] Everyone should listen in case we should bring you some important messages.

You, German Wehrmacht, who have served in happy and unhappy days, your courage and bravery are acknowledged throughout the world. A courageous army, when defeated, yields to superior force however painful and bitter that may be.

And now to work! Remember the old adage: The individual may perish, but Germany must live! And Germany will live! If we all do our duty and put an end to the despised Nazi regime!

---

17. Friedrich-Werner Graf von der Schulenburg had been arrested after the 20th of July; he was executed on 23 October 1944. Goerdeler had been arrested on August 12 and was executed in February 1945. Only Nebe was able to keep in hiding until early 1945; he was, however, executed in March 1945.

18. Illegible word.

19. The Nazis successfully jammed the second broadcast. However, reports about the speech appeared in Swedish, French, British and U.S. newspapers.

Document 73 · 15 November 1944

Report by the OSS Research and Analysis Branch: Some Criteria for the Identification of Non-Nazis and Anti-Nazis in Germany[1]

CONFIDENTIAL

Some Criteria for the Identification of Anti-Nazis in Germany

Description. A Political and Social Analysis

[...]

I. Introduction. At the time of the Allied occupation of Germany, almost everyone who is not unmistakably identified with the Hitler regime by his position and activity will represent himself as a non-Nazi or anti-Nazi. Those who did actively cooperate with the regime will declare that they did so only under threat to themselves or their families or in order to protect their business or their employees; the vast majority of people will say that they collaborated with the regime only insofar as they were obliged to in order to earn their living. The decision as to the truth of such claims will not be easy, since numerous Nazi organizations and agencies were indeed compulsory, as for example, the German Labor Front, the Hitler Youth, the NS [National Socialist] Teachers League, the *Reichsgruppen* of industry, banking, trade, etc. Cooperation was unquestionably in many cases the prerequisite to maintaining one's bare existence. The development of some criteria for the identification of anti-Nazis is therefore of the utmost importance for Military Government officials. It should be emphasized from the beginning that the criteria suggested in this paper should serve only as a guide for spot investiga-

1. NA, RG 59, R&A No. 2189. This paper, like document [52], was part of the so-called Civil Affairs Guide project commissioned by the War Department in preparation for American Military Government in Germany. An earlier version of the report had been prepared in June 1944 by Herbert Marcuse.

tions and that they are subject to corroboration or correction by any evidence produced by such investigations.

Willingness to cooperate with the occupation authorities is no criterion for anti-Nazi attitudes. It may be assumed that many persons will seek the favor of the occupation authorities in order to retain the position they held under the Nazi system. For example, industrialists or bankers who increased their power during the Hitler period and who participated in the spoliation of the occupied territories, in the "Aryanization" of property, etc., may offer their services to the occupation authorities in order to avoid identification with Nazi policies. This will be especially true if they held no political position under the Hitler regime, but served it merely as businessmen. On the other hand, many active and convinced anti-Nazis may be extremely reluctant and even unwilling to cooperate with the Allies because they may fear the accusation of working against their own country in the interest of foreign powers.

The problem is further complicated by the fact that even the active and passive opposition to the Hitler regime includes certain groups which, from the point of view of MG [Military Government] and of the democratic forces in German society, cannot be classified as anti-Nazis. To these groups would belong, for example, the followers of Otto Strasser and other "National Bolshevist" circles which accuse the Hitler regime of not being National Socialist enough;[2] also there are some nationalistic-reactionary cliques which resent the *parvenu* character of the Nazi regime.

II. General Considerations. There is no clear-cut group of anti-Nazis which can be defined by a single set of criteria. There is instead a sliding scale of dissension with and opposition to Nazism, ranging all the way from dissatisfied cliques within the Nazi leadership itself, through various gradations of collaboration and "neutrality," to the active opposition of the underground movement.
… [3]

IV. Anti-Nazis and Non-Nazis. For the present purposes a general distinction is made between *anti*-Nazis and *non*-Nazis. The latter category includes all those who cooperated with the regime only under compulsion and to earn their living, while the former category applies to those who opposed the regime. An essential requirement for either category is that the anti- or non-Nazi attitude must have been evinced while the Nazi controls were still intact, i.e., while the Hitler government (or succeeding Nazi government) was still in power, the Nazi administration still functioning, and the Nazi police and SS still working. One important

---

2. Otto Strasser was an advocate of an independent, decidedly anti-capitalist line of National Socialism.

3. In the omitted passages, the study deals in particular with the non-Nazi's and anti-Nazi's relation to established social and political groups. It is argued that the line dividing Nazis from non-Nazis and anti-Nazis cuts across the traditional social and political groups.

exception to this must be made: in view of the fact that any revolutionary movement in Germany is likely to arise only when the Nazi controls are disintegrating, persons who participate actively in such movements must be considered anti-Nazis, provided that they do not belong to the dissident Nazi groups mentioned above. [...] Distinction must, however, be made between genuine revolutionary movements which aim at the overthrow of the Nazi system in all its social and political ramifications, and *coups d'état* or palace revolutions which seek only to replace one form of authoritarian and anti-democratic government by another. Participation in such movements cannot be taken as a criterion for anti-Nazi attitudes.

A. *Anti-Nazis.* This category includes only persons who have given evidence of their active opposition to the Nazi regime and who are opposed not only to some incidental aspects of the Nazi regime but to its basic social, political, and ideological structure.

In all cases, the evidence collected about the attitudes of individuals should be supplemented and confirmed by consultation with anti-Nazis among the local population who have proved to be reliable. Subject to this stipulation the following categories may be considered as anti-Nazis:

1. Political Prisoners. Persons who have been arrested because of their hostility or opposition to the Nazi regime and who have not subsequently made their peace with the regime. An exception to this category is the Nazi opposition within the Party (for example, the Strasser group).[4]

2. Persons who have promoted or participated in acts of oppositional activity such as strikes, sabotage, slow-downs, production of anti-Nazi leaflets, and any other kind of "underground" activity, aiming at the overthrow of the Nazi system.

3. Persons who have been dismissed or removed from their positions because of their hostility or opposition to the Nazi regime (especially civil servants, teachers, writers, etc.).

During the last years of the regime, owing to the manpower shortage, the Nazis may have reinstated such persons in office. These cases should be examined with particular care.

4. Persons who have publicly criticized the Nazi regime or who have published books, papers, or articles which are clearly recognizable as criticism of the Nazi regime and which, in the public mind, have become identified with such criticism.

On the other hand, persons who have made remarks critical of the Nazi regime while on official trips to foreign countries, but have continued to work in leading cultural positions should not be considered anti-Nazis. Moreover, if they have travelled in foreign countries in the exercise of their functions and with the support of the German authorities, they should be considered "cultural agents" of the

---

4. *This exception holds true also for categories 2, 3, 4, and 6.*

Nazi regime (for example, Wilhelm Furtwängler, Ferdinand Sauerbruch, Eduard Spranger, Nicolai Hartman, Edward Wechsler [Eduard Wechssler]).[5]

5. Members and clerics of the Confessional Church (_Bekenntniskirche_) and other clergymen who have voiced their opposition to the Nazi regime in sermons, pastoral letters, etc.[6]

Quite a few members of the clergy (especially high Catholic dignitaries) have protested against certain Nazi ideologies and practices which were repugnant to religious morality or organization, but have at the same time endorsed the Nazi government's national and social policies. The record of these persons does not in itself warrant their classification as anti-Nazis.

6. Persons who have given support and shelter to victims of Nazi persecution, if they have given no evidence of pro-Nazi activities in other connections.

B. Non-Nazis. This group would include the large number of persons who have not given any evidence of anti-Nazi activity, but who have never been identified with the Nazi regime.[7]

The concept of non-identification is difficult to define since its content and political implications vary considerably according to social status and position. The criteria for non-identification in the case of an industrial leader, for example, who can live without continuing in his job, must be different from that of a worker who must work to live. Moreover, non-identification coming after a long period of identification and arising only from Nazi interference with one's private business interests (as in the case of Fritz Thyssen)[8] should not in itself be taken as a sign of non-Nazi attitude; such a person may again become an ardent supporter of a new aggressive militaristic policy if he deems it profitable for his business interests.

The following (negative) criteria may be indicative of non-identification:

1. Non-membership in the Nazi Party and its affiliated organizations, and non-participation in Party activities. Where membership and participation were compulsory (for example, Hitler Youth, NS Teachers Association), a careful examination of each individual's record must be made.

---

5. The famous surgeon Dr. Ferdinand Sauerbruch was a friend of Beck and Stauffenberg and had been aware of the preparations for the coup. After the war he was acquitted of collaboration with the Nazis. The brilliant conductor Wilhelm Furtwängler who was likewise acquitted, served as a cultural figurehead and willing instrument of the Nazis.

6. For the situation of the German churches see in particular documents [22], [31], [70c] and [71].

7. _It should be borne in mind that since the distinction between anti-Nazis and non-Nazis is based primarily on overt acts, there may be many persons generally non-active politically who have been consistently and wholeheartedly anti-Nazi in attitude but who, for lack of evidence, can only be classified as non-Nazi._

8. The Ruhr industrialist Fritz Thyssen had financially supported the Nazi movement from early on; in the 1930s, however, he objected against the persecution of the Jews. Having been forced to emigrate in 1939, he was arrested in France in 1941 and put into a concentration camp.

2. Refusal to accept Party honors and awards.

3. Refusal to accept government or party positions (see below).

More specifically, the following additional criteria for defining a non-Nazi attitude are suggested:

1. *Businessmen.* Refusal to accept government or Party positions is particularly important in the case of businessmen. Since all enterprises which could be used for war production were incorporated into the Nazi machine, the mere fact that a man continued his business under the Nazi regime is no criterion for determining his political attitudes. However, businessmen who went beyond this and accepted positions in the governmental organizations of the economy or in the self-administration of business, should be considered Nazis until evidence to the contrary is forthcoming.

2. *Intellectuals.* German intellectuals have had the freedom to refrain from publishing books or pamphlets which were not indispensable to the exercise of their specific functions. If persons whose intellectual province was essentially affected by Nazi ideology and practices (for example, constitutional lawyers, sociologists, modern historians, philosophers) still refrained from publishing under the Nazi regime or dealt only with strictly technical and scientific problems, this may be taken as a sign of non-cooperation (for example the constitutional lawyer, Rudolf Smend).

3. *Workers.* In the case of workers and of all those who had to continue in their jobs because they had no other means of making a living, non-identification can only be determined through the testimony of people who had an opportunity to watch their behavior on the spot. As a rule, no person should be considered as non-Nazi who was entrusted with the function of a subleader, who was a member of the *Werkscharen* or Political Shock Troops in the plants, who was *Vertrauensmann*[9] of the German Labor Front, or who was distinguished for efficiency at his work (the "efficiency books" given out by the works leader in conjunction with the Labor Front are excellent evidence in such cases since efficiency ratings had to take into consideration the employee's political reliability).

If persons claim that they became subleaders or representatives of the Labor Front only in order to protect their anti-Nazi fellow workers or in order to cover up their own anti-Nazi activities, their claims should be investigated in consultation with the colleagues whom they claim to have protected. In addition to the negative criteria mentioned above, instances of poor workmanship, frequent absenteeism, complaints, solidarity with foreign workers may be indications of non-Nazi attitudes.[10]

9. I.e., confidential person.

10. On further considerations about the relationship between German and foreign workers see document [23].

None of these criteria is a test demonstrating non-Nazism. At most they form a basis for disqualification. Further examination of the person will be required, plus testimony from those in a position to verify his repute as a non-Nazi.

Document 74 · 16 November 1944

Telegram from Myron Taylor
(OSS Stockholm) to OSS Washington:
Simulating a German Underground[1]

SECRET

[...]

Would instead appreciate receiving copy for leaflets in German for distribution in Germany. Contents should clearly indicate existence of powerful underground movements within country. We now have excellent distribution facilities and possibilities of frequent delivery such material to Germany. Air pouching all *Harvard* issues.[2]

---

1. NA, RG 226, Entry 134, Box 304, Folder 1691.

2. This is a reference to a periodical produced by the OSS over a short period of time in 1944 giving misleading data and information on German economic developments. Officials of the OSS Morale Operations Branch claimed this paper got limited yet effective dissemination among industrialists in Germany.

Document 75 · 20 November 1944

Memorandum from Paul Mellon
(OSS Morale Operations Branch)
to Colonel David K. E. Bruce (OSS London):
C. G. Jung and OSS Propaganda[1]

SECRET

Subject: Project for Obtaining General and Specific Information Useful for Implementing Black Propaganda Plans, from Sources in Switzerland

Outline of Project

1. It is requested that the undersigned be sent to Switzerland, under suitable diplomatic or other civilian cover, to contact Dr. C. G. Jung, eminent Zürich psychologist. Contact would be made upon a purely personal basis, interviews being easily arranged due to the former relationship of the undersigned to Dr. Jung as student and friend.

2. The purpose of the interview or interviews would be to obtain, by indirection and deduction, information regarding the psychological state of the German civilian and soldier with a view to incorporating such information in all MO Black Propaganda plans. It is believed that Jung, due to his unique position in the psychological and medical world, and as a result of his widespread practice as consultant and analyst to Germans of all classes, would be an ideal source of information of the above type. It is known beyond the shadow of a doubt that though neutral in action, as a Swiss citizen by birth and residence, his political sympathies are definitely pro-Allied and pro-democratic.

[...]²

---

1. NA, RG 226, Entry 190, Box 31, Folder 128. There had been previous contacts between the OSS and C. G. Jung ever since Allen Dulles had established his Bern office in late 1942. See document [9].

2. The omitted passage contains biographical information on Jung.

6. In the light of past experience (and it must be remembered that the war was at that time well developed, and that Jung believed the entrance of the United States inevitable) it is believed that little difficulty would be encountered in persuading him to talk, even if in the most general terms, regarding the present state of Germany. It must be remembered that Jung was the original exponent of the theory of the Collective Unconscious, the stream of which appears faintly from time to time in the dreams and fantasies of children and grown-ups as individuals, as well as in the mass mind of whole nations. It is Jung's hypothesis that Germany, because as a geographical territory it was never penetrated by Ceasar's legions (beyond the Rhine) never became a Christianized nation. Christianity came to the small countries of Germany in diminished waves and in diluted forms, long after the main wave of spiritual power had engulfed the rest of the Continent. It came to Germany already tainted with intellectual doubt, and hence it was Germany that contained the seeds of Protestantism. In a sense, therefore, Germany has always been a pagan nation, and it has always been subject to the powerful sway of its own barbarian soul.[3] Hitler, with his appeal to the forces of war and destruction, has crystallized the innate, uncivilized, unconscious forces in each individual German, until Germany has exhibited, as a nation, the greatest example of mass psychosis ever witnessed in the history of the world.

7. In view of Jung's historical, philosophical, and psychological grasp of the underlying factors in the nation's life, and in view of his intimate knowledge of the individual German mind, it would seem worth the effort and time to glean whatever truths he may have deduced from his study of Germany at war, and his practice in treating the German individual. The nation is the aggregate of the individuals it contains, and the psychosis of the individual reflects the psychosis of the nation, and vice versa.

General and Specific Information to Be Sought

8. a. General information re morale & economic conditions.
    b. Historical parallels that could be used effectively in preparing propaganda, and their implications.
    c. Types of rumours that have found current widespread belief in Germany.

---

3. For a different interpretation of Germany as a barbaric state see document [6].

d. Fears & psychoses uppermost in German patients in the war years.
e. Evidences of the psychological effect of air warfare on the average German soldier, and child and adult civilian.
f. Symbolical representations (symbols, words, pictures, books, songs etc.) most effective in influencing the German unconscious.
g. What the average German thinks about, wants, fears, dreams.

[...]

Paul Mellon
Capt. Cav.

Document 76 · 27 November 1944

Memorandum from OSS Director William J. Donovan to the Joint Chiefs of Staff: Black Propaganda Treatment of Unconditional Surrender[1]

SECRET

Subject: Black Propaganda Treatment of Unconditional Surrender

I. Discussion

1. Analysis of German propaganda for home-front consumption discloses that while a literal translation of the phrase "unconditional surrender" has rarely been employed to convince the German people that there is no alternative but to con-

---

1. NA, RG 226, Entry 139, Box 176, Folder 2327.

tinue the war, the concept of surrender has become associated in the German mind with the worst catastrophies which could befall the population. The horrible prospects of exile to Siberia, eternal slavery, de-industrialization, break-up of Germany, and even sterilization, have been carefully portrayed to the Germans by their Nazi leaders.[2] It is considered that the German spirit of resistance has been bolstered greatly by fear of the consequence of unconditional surrender.

2. Black propaganda disseminated by wholly secret means and purporting to originate from within enemy countries could:

a. Diminish the propaganda value of this theme by attempting to *dissociate* "unconditional surrender" from the afflictions Nazi leaders have been predicting to their people.

Typical Black Theme: "Unconditional surrender" is demanded of "our" Government by the Allies, but it applies only to the Nazi Government and the *Wehrmacht,* and *not* to us as individuals. Behaviour of Allied Forces in Italy, Rumania, Bulgaria and occupied areas of Germany disprove the Nazi predictions of horrible conditions resulting from unconditional surrender".

b. Convert the theme to a black propaganda weapon of our own by *associating* "unconditional surrender" with desirable rather than fearsome prospects.

Typical Black Theme: Unconditional surrender means "our" delivery from the Nazi yoke and would represent a new beginning for the German people wherein "our" biological strength, shrewdness, and scientific prowess would soon lead "us" to a healthy economic and social position. Homes, industries, national wealth, and the framework of the German Army would be conserved for the future. The destruction of Germany is too high a price to pay for saving the Nazis for another four or five months, by which time military defeat is inevitable.

c. Suggest that continuation of the war would expose the German people to a fate worse than that threatened by Nazi propagandists.

Typical Black Theme: The traditional humanitarian tendencies of the democracies may change to vindictiveness if the war is allowed to continue. The chaos, disease, and privation predicted for us in the event of unconditional surrender will develop by prolonging the war. "Our" continued resistance protects only the Nazi leaders.

d. Give the German people a vague and wholly spurious idea of the "terms" of unconditional surrender which the Allies will impose.

Black Treatment: "Terms" would *not* be specifically set forth, but "interpreted" in general terms based upon the principles enumerated at TAB 'A'.[3]

3. *Methods:* At the present time a spurious and purportedly clandestine newspaper, *Das Neue Deutschland,*[4] is being printed in Europe by this organization and

---

2. This is an allusion to the Nazi propaganda campaign against the so-called Morgenthau Plan, which had been discussed in the United States in the fall of 1944.

3. Not printed.

4. See document [68].

distributed by means of agents to the German troops on the Western Front and the Italian Front, in Hungary and in Austria. Future editions of this publication, whose cover is still considered to be secure, can develop the themes enumerated in Paragraph 2 above. Rumors currently being carried through neutral countries to Germany and initiated among German troops by means of agents can portray the inevitability of defeat and the reasons for unconditional surrender now. A false document setting forth actual terms of unconditional surrender may be "planted" in such a manner that its content would be appropriately published, or the secret Allied intentions after surrender could be "disclosed" by rumor alone.

4. It is recognized that in conducting black propaganda operations, the real source of the propaganda may be suspected, but its dissemination is handled in such a manner that neither the Allied Military Commanders nor their Governments can be implicated, and all such propaganda may, if necessary, be officially disavowed.

II. Recommendations

1. That the Morale Operations branch of this organization be authorized to undertake a black propaganda campaign, directed at the German people's fear of the consequences of "unconditional surrender."

Suggested Black Statement of Allied Intentions After Unconditional Surrender of Germany

I. Territorial

1. Germany will be entirely occupied by Allied troops.
2. Although Russian, British and American troops will occupy three separate sections of Germany, it is not intended to partition the German Reich.

II. Military

1. Internal order will be maintained by Allied forces until a German Government is formed.

III. Judicial

1. War criminals will be tried by special international tribunals. Impartial justice will be meted out.

2. War criminals are defined as leaders of the National Socialist Party, certain general officers in the Wehrmacht, police officers of high rank, and any other persons who have committed criminal acts.

3. Persons accused of being war criminals will be committed to trial only after the establishment of their probable participation in criminal acts by an impartial international body.

IV. Political

1. Germany will eventually be allowed to choose its own form of government and the Allies will establish the machinery for registering the expression of popular will.

2. The National Socialist Party will be stamped out. No member of that party will be allowed to hold any office or position of trust.

3. Germany will be admitted to participation in whatever association of nations is formed after proving its good intentions.

V. Economic

1. The establishment of a prosperous Germany as a self-sustaining member of the family of nations is desired by the Allies. To this end the Allies will restore the basis of sound German currency, assistance in the restoration of German industry will be provided with a view to absorbing the unemployed, and Germany will be allowed access to raw materials and markets in order to support its industry.

2. Germany will be forbidden to manufacture airplanes, guns over 20 mm. calibre and warships. Allied control will be exercised to insure that German industry will be directed only toward the production of non-military goods.

VI. Reparations

1. Property acquired by Germans in any other country will be returned to its owner or compensation made.

2. Property destroyed or damaged by Germans in any other country will be rebuild and restored by Germany.

VII. Cultural

1. Freedom of religion is guaranteed.

2. Education, speech and the press will be controlled only to the extent necessary to insure that National Socialism and similar doctrines are not advocated.

3. Organizations of a non-military and non-political character will be permitted.

[...]

William J. Donovan
Director

Unconditional Surrender

I. Situation

Nazi propagandists have been using U.S. [Unconditional Surrender] phrase to convince Germans that there is no alternative but to fight.

[...]

II. Objective

Undo work of Nazi propagandists, and diminish desire to resist by:

- a. Destroying the propaganda value U.S. phrase has had for German leaders. This can be achieved by *dissociating* it from all the afflictions the Nazis have been threatening the Germans with in case of U.S.
- b. Turning U.S. phrase into a propaganda weapon of our own. This can be accomplished by *associating* U.S. with desirable rather than feared prospects.
- c. Persuading Germans that further continuation of the war would bring about practically all the evils they have been told would follow if they accepted U.S. now.

III. Implementation

Three separate campaigns, which may be run simultaneously, can be organized around the three phases of our objective.

Using all available channels, but especially the "New Germany Party" and its publication "The New Germany", such ideas as the following should be hammered at the Germans continuously:

- a. With respect to objective-phase (a):

    1. Play up theme that U.S. is nothing but a term. Situation in Italy, Finland, Rumania shows that Nazi interpretation of U.S. is not true.
    2. U.S. is asked of us Germans by the Allies because Nazis have violated every treaty they have made, and therefore no one is willing to deal with them otherwise. Allies have no other choice.
    3. U.S. applies only to Nazi leaders, not to us Germans as people.
    4. We have nothing to fear from U.S. America and England would save us from Bolshevization.
    5. Only Nazi criminals fear U.S.; German people would not be affected.
    6. We are of more value to the Allies here in an industrial Germany than in the barren Siberia.
    7. Democratic countries are humanitarian, and therefore soft. We can play upon their softness, if the Nazis didn't represent us—we are realistic, and therefore, smarter than they.

- b. With respect to objective-phase (b):

    1. U.S. now would mean delivery of the German people from the Nazi yoke.
    2. U.S. would mean a new beginning for the German people, and the possibility to start bargaining for a "negotiated peace" where our economic power, biological strength, and German shrewdness would play the main role.

3. U.S. would save German homes, industry, soil, future prospects for jobs, etc.

4. U.S. would help us preserve at least the framework of a German army, with the possibility for a *next* time (this especially for the German military classes).

5. U.S. would mean demobilization and the return of sons, sweethearts, husbands, to their beloved.

6. The war is lost for us, anyway. Our choice is between U.S. now, or in four or five months.

c. With respect to objective-phase (c):

1. If we wait another four or five months, our bargaining power would be lost.

2. We now have strong and influential friends in the democratic countries. We may lose them if we continue the war.

3. Millions of men, women and children would die if the war is prolonged, with no prospect of improving our condition.

4. Our factories and cities, our soil and livestock would probably be totally destroyed.

5. Disease and suffering would increase as we enter the winter months without food, shelter, clothing, medicine, or other protective measures.

6. Spirit of humanitarianism among Allies may turn into one of revenge.

7. The German army may be completely obliterated during or after the inevitable surrender, if we decide to go on.

8. Germany may not be able to rise again, and may become another Carthage.

General Themes

Rather the end of the Nazis, than that of Germany.

U.S. now means the end of the Nazis; a new beginning for Germany.

U.S. now is a good investment in the future of Germany.

Destruction of Germany is too high a price to pay to save the Nazis for another four or five months.

We have the choice of U.S. now; or an unconditional peace later on.

Document 77 · 1 December 1944

Memorandum from OSS Director William J. Donovan to President Franklin D. Roosevelt: OSS Preparations for the Post-War Period[1]

SECRET

Memorandum for the President

[...]

1. We have set up an intelligence service, both tactical and strategic.

In the tactical sense we are making available to the armed forces through the service of OSS Detachments with our forward divisions agents whom we have passed through the lines. We are also employing Alsatians, French workmen and other foreigners now in Germany.

In the strategic phase we have already penetrated certain German government offices (which intelligence you have received over a period)[2] and have been particulary fortunate in establishing contact with certain elements of German labor groups who have been helping us with great gallantry and efficiency.[3]

In addition we have been working with the French organization charged with aiding French Prisoners of War and deported laborers, and have made arrangements with the Danes and Norwegians for cooperation in the underground phase.

---

1. Roosevelt Library, Hyde Park, F. D. Roosevelt Papers. President's Secretary's Files, Box 171, Folder OSS/1–15 December 1944.

2. This refers particularly to German Foreign Office official Fritz Kolbe (code-named George Wood) who supplied OSS Bern with hundreds of microfilm copies of secret German Foreign Office documents between the summer of 1943 and mid–1944. This material (code-named Kappa or Boston series) contained high-level information on military and political developments and on Germany's cooperation with its allies and satellites. The information was invariably passed on to the White House.

3. See for instance document [11].

We have been undertaking this work from Sweden and Switzerland, as well as from the front lines.

2. We have in operation with the forward elements of the Allied Armies in Germany units engaged in counterespionage against the Germans. […] In addition to work against Nazi agents, valuable data has been obtained on potential [Nazi] underground leaders. We have information on more than 250,000 agents and suspects. SHAEF [Supreme Headquarters of the Allied Expeditionary Forces] has been supplied with data on more than 50,000 suspects and underground personalities. Many German agents have been identified; several hundred have been arrested.

[…]

In order to carry on this work in Germany after the cessation of organized military resistance, OSS has been asked by the Allied Control Council to participate as a unit in their work. Our services would be employed for intelligence, counterespionage and countermeasures against enemy sabotage. The Joint Chiefs of Staff have already approved this proposal in principle.[4]

Some time ago I sent you a memorandum setting forth in detail the activities of a group of German nationals identified with the labor movement and an active group in the Lutheran and Catholic Churches,[5] with both of which we have established contact. They will provide invaluable aid in meeting the underground.

> *Donovan*
> **William J. Donovan**
> **Director**

---

4. Proposals for continuing the OSS into the post-war era leaked to the U.S. press, however, and caused a storm of protest. The OSS was dissolved by President Truman in September 1945.

5. See documents [70a] and [70c].

Document 78 · 5 December 1944

Report by Eugene Warner (OSS Rome): German POWs as OSS Agents in Italy[1]

SECRET

Example of Agent Distribution: German POW's as Agents on "Sauerkraut" Missions

Situation

The attempted assassination of Hitler on July 20, 1944 provided an unrivalled psychological opportunity for attacking the morale of the German Army, if appropriate propaganda could be circulated without delay.

Objective of Mission

To undermine the will-to-fight of enemy troops by using subversive materials based on new discouragement, and discord among some of the top Nazis, MO hoped to demoralize the German front-line soldiers and cause them to desert or surrender.

Implementation

By passing agents directly through the front lines to distribute freshly conceived rumors, leaflets, fake orders and proclamations as well as long ranged arousers of homesickness, such as the rumor that a German women's "Lonely Hearts Club" existed.

---

1. NA, RG 226, Entry 139, Box 160, Folder 2144.

Operations

Need for swift action suggested the novel use of a small group of captured, carefully screened German POW/s as agents to infiltrate the lines. Subversive materials were distributed and the German POW/s watched the propaganda being read by enemy soldiers, including members of the SS.

Comebacks

1. General Kesselring[2] was forced to deny authorship of an "official" proclamation posted in his name.

2. Intelligence brought back by the POW agents aided in an eight mile advance of the Fifth Army whose G-2[3] suggested citation for the conception of the Mission and requested

3. that greatly expanded PW agent infiltrations be planned and put into operation as soon as possible.

Herewith some charcoal sketches of the first Sauerkraut operations run by MO Medto,[4] unique, it is believed, in this war. Sketches were made by one of the German agents who has considerable artistic talent, Willi H.

1. July 24, 1944, the men were behind barbed wire. This was four days after the attempt on Hitler's life. To capitalize on this historic moment, MO decided a special operation was called for, and on the suggestion of Lieut. Burkhardt of R&A, who knew of the existence of several anti-nazi Germans at the cage, the first Sauerkraut was planned and initiated, all in the space of a few hours.

2. Major Dewart and Pvt. Barbara Lauwers (who speaks German)[5] drove about 150 miles at night, interviewed PWs during the next day, obtained a truck, loaded the men, and started for Rome the following night, arriving July 25.

3. In Rome, Lt. Jack Daniels joined the party and so did Eddie Zinder [Lindner]; Pvt. Lauwers, her work excellently completed, dropping out dead tired. The truck loaded with men and Dewart, Zinder and Daniels in a jeep, shoved off for the front. Daniels portrait is No. 3, Zinder No. 4, and Dewart and Daniels in their jeep is No. 5.

6. At a forward base near Florence, Zinder is seen improvising with whatever tools and documents he could find, the necessary credentials and papers for the men to carry with them in case they were halted or arrested.

7. Uniforms and equipment were a serious problem, as well as proper papers. Dewart and Daniels roamed the front all day and most of the next night searching for odds and ends such as belts, helmets, boots, etc. Meanwhile the men them-

---

2. General Albert Kesselring, Commander in Chief of the German Armed Forces in Italy.

3. Counterintelligence division

4. Mediterranean Theater of Operations.

5. Lawyer Dr. Barbara Lauwers, a young Czech emigré, had volunteered to be dispatched to Italy in 1944.

selves helped prepare and No. 7 shows (left) an agent fixing an improvised lining into a steel helmet, and (right) another agent with anvil and hammer making his own German dogtags from scraps of metal.

8. Zinder, by candlelight, briefs the men on the exact routes they shall take, what their cover stories are to be, and what they are expected to do once they are across the lines into enemy territory.

9. Daniels hands one of the agents the MO material, including a specially printed "proclamation" signed by General Kesselring which stated that Kesselring was a member of the group which attempted to assassinate Hitler.[6]

10. Entire group gathers for final briefing. Daniels listens as Zinder gives the men a pep talk. At extreme left is Cpl. Alfio D'Urso, MO printer, who had been pressed into service as a guard.

11. Mission required the agents to be led into No-Man's land by Capt. Abrigagni's detachment, to the shores of the Arno River and from there the men were to swim or ford the river as best they could, climb the opposite bank, and make their way back into German territory, distributing MO material among enemy troops and gathering whatever tactical intelligence they came across.

12. Whole area was under shellfire, heavily mined, and defended with barbed wire, etc. German patrols were numerous both on North and South shores of the river. Great caution had to be used to keep from being captured.

13. Distribution begins. The agents fanned out in various directions. Proclamations were posted, leaflets tossed in vehicles, left along roads, placed in CPs, etc. This operation was experimental, since it was the first of its kind ever tried anywhere, and while it did not extend over more than a quick and shallow penetration, it did prove that similar ops on a larger scale were practicable. Some mistakes were made, due to its haste, but they were corrected in later infiltrations.

14. MO German agents creep under cover of darkness through a battered town in No-Man's land. Note German gas-mask container in man's hand. These made ideal containers for leaflets, etc. Each man carries about 15 pounds or about 15,000 items.

15. A German patrol halts to pick up and read MO leaflets. Some spectacular results were observed by our agents hiding nearby on several similar occasions— one patrol threw down its guns, shouted "The war is over!" and began racing at top speed for the rear.

16. A different kind of incident occurred on a later Sauerkraut when an SS captain spotted our men posting bulletins and called his guard. Our men were cornered. They dropped into a ditch and began shooting their way out, killing the captain and killing or wounding two or three others, before they could make a getaway.

17. Artist allows himself to become cartoonist in final sketch which shows his conception of a German field-grade [sic] officer reading the Kesselring proclama-

---

6. For MO efforts to denounce SS officers and German generals as members of the conspiracy against Hitler, see documents [62] and [85].

tion. This drawing has no basis in fact. However, it is known that Kesselring was forced to go on the radio to deny the authenticity of one of our proclamations bearing his name.

Since the first Sauerkraut, five more have been completed as this is written 5 Dec., 1944, and many more are in the making. The original group of 16 recruits was cut down to 8, and this 8 are still with us. They have just finished a long rest and are scheduled to begin operations again very shortly, their next mission being an extremely complicated and hazardous one which will be part maritime and will take them far behind the lines. Meanwhile, 20 more agents have been recruited and are being put through the lines at regular intervals from a new holding area North of Florence, their last mission, dated 1 Dec., being requested by the Fifth Army to gain some much-needed tactical intelligence. As this is typed, a phone call has come down from Florence to Rome, advising that it was successful and all the men returned.

(sgd) *Eugene Warner*
Chief, MO Medto
[Mediterranean Theater
of Operations]

Document 79 · 19 December 1944

Lieutenant Colonel K. D. Mann
(OSS Morale Operations Branch)
to OSS Director William J. Donovan:
The "Sauerkraut" Missions[1]

A Brief of Three Missions "Sauerkrauts"
I-II-III Covering July to October 1944

[...]

Situation

On July 21, 1944 after word was received of the attempt on Hitler's life, a special meeting was held to devise ways to exploit the situation to the fullest. Ordinary methods of infiltration via plane drops were not judged speedy enough. After careful deliberation by OSS representatives in Rome, the MO Branch decided to use the novel and daring method of employing friendly, trustworthy German Prisoners of War who had been security-checked and drawn from the POW cage at Aversa—200 miles from Rome. Private Lauers [Barbara Lauwers] with the assistance of P.W. officers in charge of the POW cage made the final selections of men who were then indoctrinated, trained, equipped and briefed in MO tactics to be sent back into the enemy lines.

Objectives

1. To plant MO leaflets, stickers, false orders and proclamations in bivouac areas, on trees, buildings, trucks and other places accessible to the German front-line troops.

---

1. NA, RG 226, Entry 99, Box 69, Folder 306.

2. To assess and observe at first hand the reactions of these German soldiers to the MO printed material particularly designed for them.
3. To expose the troops to a MO barrage properly timed and coordinated with the political implications and confusion ensuing from the attempt on Hitler's life.
4. To obtain and return with Order of Battle and Morale intelligence for G–2 and the MO Branch, on the disposition, strength and character of the German Front Line troops facing the Fifth Army.

Purpose

1. To exploit a new technique for infiltration of MO propaganda behind the enemy lines in Italy.
2. To observe at first hand the over-all morale of the German front line troops.

[...]

Accomplishments of Mission I

The optimum results may not have been attained, partly due to the exploratory character of Mission I, also because all of the men who did go in, did not penetrate as deeply into the lines as was hoped.[2] However, both the fact that the enemy lines were penetrated and that this was accomplished by POW/s who proved both reliable and effective, adds a new chapter to the technique of front line infiltration.

Mission II

On September 7, 1944 seven German POWs trained, security checked and prepared at a holding area were put through the enemy lines in the Fifth Army Sector near the village of Prato, 10 kilometers north-west of Florence.
[...]

Difficulties

One of the teams of POWs were challenged as to the authenticity of their papers. Apprehensive that their papers, stamped with rubber instead of the official steel stamp, might betray them, the men had dumped their MO material in a ditch just before the encounter. One of the team explained that his unit had lost their regu-

---

2. Altogether out of a stockade of 200, 14 German prisoners of war had been selected for the mission.

lar stamp and the German MP [Military Police] seemed to accept the story though he took their names and number.

Accomplishments of Mission II

1. MO literature was disseminated and MO rumors spread by word of mouth all along the front from Prato west of Pistoia and as far north as Bologna. MO/POW teams watched German soldiers reading the material and heard them discussing its messages with credulity.
2. On September 11, the POW cage at Livorno reported the arrival of about 30 new German POWs who had carried or seen MO material and generally believed it. They all credited Das Neue Deutschland [The New Germany] with being an authentic German paper put out by a Communist group.[3]
3. On September 13, Fifth Army G-2 received a report that General Kesselring had found it necessary to deny authorship of a "proclamation", "denouncing Hitler's policy of destroying the German Wehrmacht for the sake of the Party", signed by the General, which was the most important MO item carried in by the POW agents.
4. The teams brought back:
   a) tactical intelligence for the Fifth Army G-2
   b) a report on German front line troops morale for the MO Branch.
5. Major Blom, Fifth Army CIC [Counterintelligence Corps], expressed great satisfaction with the Sauerkraut Missions and a desire to have them repeated.

Mission III[4]

[...]

Operations

On October 3, an alert was dispatched to intelligence officers of front line echelons to be ready for an attempt by our German POW agents to infiltrate the enemy lines to carry out a mission similar to Missions I and II of this report. Team "Maria" returned via the 6th South African Armored Division Sector. On October 7, the two remaining teams "Ada" and "Rosie" returned, their mission accomplished.

[...]

---

3. On *Das Neue Deutschland* see document [68].
4. This mission consisted of three teams made up of two or three agents.

Incident

On October 4, two of the agents placed MO leaflets in trees on the outskirts of Sibano not noticing that they were being observed by a German officer, presumably a Captain of SS who went out to read the leaflets. Discovering the material was anti-Nazi propaganda, he alerted his men, causing 16 soldiers to start firing at the two agents. Both agents fired back, hitting and wounding three Germans. The team ran up the road meeting another group of Germans and fired at them, wounding two. After hiding in the mountains for three hours, the POW agents joined the Allied lines, fearing a general alarm. It is believed that this incident possibly might have started the rumor among German troops that actual street fighting had occurred between SS and regular troops and that MO could use this point for propaganda.

[...]

Final Conclusions

The new technique of infiltrating POW agents back into enemy lines as demonstrated by "Sauerkraut" Missions I-II-III and IV,[5] has proved successful in spite of skepticism on the part of some OSS and Army officials and British opposition to employing the same agent more than once on a fixed front.

Over a period of three months in which some 14 POW agents were infiltrated three different times into the lines:

1. No instance of their acting as double agents occurred.
2. Their security was never blown.
3. Instead of "dumping" their MO propaganda material, it was definitely proved that the POW agents took it deep into the lines in some sections and planted it in proper places as evidenced by its appearance on regular POW/s and deserters.

At present, the POW agents are being held in a villa, where MO Rome is using them to check the exactness and accuracy of details to be employed in writing MO material. The familiarity of the POWs with the current homely expressions used by the German troops and the home front, is being exploited.

---

5. Mission IV is mentioned briefly in the document. It was credited with providing OSS with invaluable morale intelligence.

Document 80 · 30 December 1944

Telegram from OSS Washington to Allen W. Dulles (OSS Bern): OSS Agents for Germany[1]

[…]

1. As you must know, intelligence from Germany during the next few months will undoubtedly be of extreme importance. Therefore, besides interviews with third parties who have traveled through or just returned from Germany, it is highly important to get our own agents' first hand observation.

2. We understand completely the vast practical difficulty of planting and supporting agents in Germany, therefore, we think you should focus your greatest effort on the other choice, specifically, efforts to find agents in Germany itself who are capable of building intelligence networks there, passing out information either through channels now growing elsewhere or through you.

3. We know that lack of any concrete policy on part of the Allies which might attract certain German types is a serious difficulty with respect to the above. However, inducements and incitements of another nature, with which you are familiar, can be used.[2]

4. We surmise from your past cables that there are groups and individuals with whom you are in contact, who might be developed to the point of being actual agents, either in cellular networks or individually.

5. Very interested in learning your ideas on all this when we can confer with you further in order that most possible benefit can be obtained of all connections, both present and past.

---

1. NA, RG 226, Entry 146, Box 235, Folder 3296.

2. In general, the OSS did not hesitate to employ Communists as agents even though they were released almost automatically after the war. Moreover, the OSS was prepared to turn into an agent almost any "type" who was anti-Nazi. Dulles and others promised these agents material support and assistance in a postwar world.

1945

Document 81a · 5 January 1945

Memorandum by the Supreme Headquarters Allied Expeditionary Forces (France): OSS Black Radio Project "Matchbox"[1]

TOP SECRET

The following proposed psychological warfare operation (code name *Matchbox*) is designed to undermine German resistance knit together through Wehrmacht discipline, party control and "strength through fear" propaganda, by providing evidence of existence of powerful faction inside Germany defying this control and anxious to end war at once from patriotic motives.

The medium is a "Black" radio station ostensibly situated inside Germany and operated by a group representing Wehrmacht, industrial, and other important elements who have reached conclusion that the war is irretrievably lost, that continuation will ruin German human and material resources and only increase harshness of Allied terms and that Germany's future is entirely bound up with the attitude and decisions of the Allies.

The group will show that a great internal struggle is proceeding between two opposing factions. The one for which it speaks demands peace now from realistic and patriotic motives. The other represented by the Himmler group is guided by self motive [sic]. Realizing that its members' past actions make dealings with the Allies impossible it is determined to fight to the last even though this means the utter destruction of Germany.

Broadcasts will be made in German and English. The object of the latter is cover to support and substantiate the real aim which is to convince *Wehrmacht* and civilians that internal forces already exist sufficiently powerful to make peace now, and that attempts are being made to reach Allied world to this end.

This operation can only succeed if audience is convinced of its genuineness. To achieve this, broadcasts will go out on shortwave giving impression of emanating

---

1. This copy was signed by General Eisenhower and forwarded from SHAEF in Versailles, France, to the War Department and to the Combined Chiefs of Staff (CCS). For the British response see document [81b], which follows.

from mobile military transmitter; knowledge of operation will be confined to smallest possible circle. No request will be made for dog (censorship) stop, thus allowing free reporting of broadcasts which will increase station's verisimilitude. (It is however pointed out that those broadcasts would be picked up in Britain and probably also in the United States.)

A dog stop would prevent comment by press and radio in Britain, but no such censorship is possible in the United States. Nor could publicity in Britain be avoided of reports if broadcasts came from the United States or neutral countries. Open discusison of these broadcasts might cause following reactions:

To engender the belief among Allied civilians and troops that a breach now exists between the Wehrmacht and the party, and that an enemy collapse is imminent. This belief might slow down production and lessen the will to fight of our troops.

To stimulate "soft peace" discussions in Allied political quarters in the belief that there was a sufficiently powerful group in Germany capable of suing for peace now.

Operation *Matchbox* is concurred in by Chief of Staff SHAEF subject to your approval particularly in regard to possible political reactions in the United States and Britain. Chief of Staff SHAEF is satisfied that dangers of ill-effects on Allied troop morale in this theatre can be dealt with here.

This whole problem, because of its possible far reaching effects, is forwarded to the Combined Chiefs of Staff because it crosses fields of interest to the highest governmental authorities. The Russians also might be affected. So far as our own operations are concerned it appears to be promising and if other considerations do not outweigh this fact, its approval is recommended.

Document 81b · 18 January 1945

Memorandum by the Representative of the British Chiefs of Staff: Veto Against Project "Matchbox"[1]

TOP SECRET

[...]

Plan "Matchbox"

1. The proposals put forward by General Eisenhower in SCAF [Supreme Commander of the Allied Forces] 166 (Enclosure)[2] have received most careful examination by all the interested authorities in London.

2. The report by these authorities, with whose conclusions the British Chiefs of Staff are in agreement, points out that General Eisenhower's plan is unacceptable for the following main reasons:

a. Psychological warfare plans involving the deception of the British and Allied publics by broadcasting could not commend themselves to His Majesty's Government. This attitude could only change if the military importance attached to any given plan were of such a decisive nature as to justify what would undoubtedly be a serious risk. We do not think that this can be said of the plan in SCAF 166.

b. There is a serious risk of exposure by the enemy. While it is true that hitherto the Germans have not made any serious attempt to denounce our black broadcasting other than by secret instructions to their own troops, we feel that if the plans received publicity in Britain and the United States, the enemy would not hesitate to expose the fraudulent nature of the operation.

c. The broadcasts in support of the plan would have to be made in English as well as in German if they were to carry full weight and it would therefore be easy for the enemy to point out, also in English broadcasts, to the British and American publics that they were being wilfully deceived by their own governments about peace prospects.

---

1. NA, RG 165, ABC 384 Europe (5 Aug 43) Sec 1-B, C.C.S. 771.
2. See document [81a].

3. The British Chiefs of Staff ask that the Combined Chiefs of Staff should inform General Eisenhower that his plan is unacceptable for the reasons given above.

Document 82 · 10 January 1945

Minutes of OSS Inter-Branch Meeting[1]
OSS Relations with the CALPO Resistance Group[2]

Subject: CALPO[3]—Minutes of inter-branch meeting held in Director's office, 1500 hours, 10 January 1945.

A. Background

Major Black reviewed the course of OSS relations with CALPO, which began with the preliminary report on CALPO prepared by R&A (23 October 1944)[4] and included preliminary negotiations by Mr. Cassady for SI [Secret Intelligence]. He read portions of Mr. Cassady's memorandum to, and endorsed by, General Donovan which stressed the probable predominance of SO [Special Operations] interest in the employment of persons supplied by CALPO and the importance of segregating SI agents from SO agents. The present meeting was the outcome of an inter-branch discussion in London and the resulting OPSAF Mission to Paris.

---

1. NA, RG 226, Entry 190, Box 424, Folder 882. This meeting was held in the Director's Office. It was attended by Major Black, Executive Office (presiding), Mr. Cassady (SI), Lt. Col. Colby (Field Detachments), Major Runkle (X–2), Major Pusey (SO), Comdr. Breckinridge (Security), Mr. Bagier (MO), Lt. Gould (SI, for OPSAF Mission), Cpt. Kull (R&A).

2. I.e., Comité Allemagne Libre Pour l' Ouest.

3. The members of CALPO considered themselves to be the Western wing of the Moscow Free Germany Committee. Moscow, however, ignored CALPO almost entirely. Beginning in late summer 1944, the OSS had increased their contacts with CALPO resistance groups. CALPO was delivering secret intelligence to the OSS; in turn OSS lent support to this organization of German anti-Nazis. CALPO-OSS relations culminated in early 1945 in a top secret plan to assassinate high-ranking members of the Nazi Party and of the Gestapo, using approximately 100 German nationals, recruited from the CALPO organization. See documents [84] and [96]. As long as OSS contacts remained secret or did not involve the U.S. government such cooperation could be carried out rather undisturbed in the shadow of Allied warfare.

4. Not printed. R&A officials had been aware that the CALPO group was predominently Communist; nevertheless, the evaluation of the group was clearly favorable.

B. OPSAF Mission: Lt. Gould's Report

Lt. Gould reported on the inter-branch negotiations in London and the several branch requests relayed by him in his conferences during the last few days with Maurel (Hauser) and Horteck (Niebergall), Secretary-General and President of CALPO, respectively.[5]

Summaries of Lt. Gould's discussions with Maurel and Horteck are as follows, on behalf of:

1. SI

Safe Addresses. CALPO is willing to make its lists of various types of safe addresses in Germany available, to assist in securing addresses from the *French Comité des Prisonniers et Déportées,* and to organize its safe addresses in the border regions of Belgium, Luxembourg, and Mulhouse. CALPO's safe addresses will be available only to its own agents employed by OSS, agents of the Free Germany Movement in Great Britain, and such other operations as its representatives, either in France or Britain, approve.

Communications. Communications are effected by two courier chains from within Germany, one reaching Paris via Switzerland and involving a Swiss representative of CALPO, the other controlled by the Swiss Free Germany Movement and originating in its own zone of operations in Germany. (Operational zones have been agreed upon by CALPO and the Swiss and Swedish Free Germany Movements). The chain to Paris from the Swiss border takes eight days normally and could be facilitated with technical assistance.[6]

[...]

Agent Personnel. CALPO will supply SI with agents, understanding that they are to be used for all types of information, priority reserved at all times for military information, and CALPO will have opportunity to exchange political information with returning agents.

---

5. Joseph Gould, a young lieutenant, was a prominent member of the OSS Labor Section in London. Harald Hauser, alias Jean Louis Morel, was CALPO's Secretary General, Otto Niebergall-Florian, alias Horteck, was the President of the CALPO group. Niebergall-Florian had fled from Germany to France in 1935 where he referred to himself as "chef du T.A. [Travail Allemand] et de la Résistance des Allemands anti-hitlériens en France depuis 1940".

6. One of the major figures involved in this communication was Noel H. Field, CALPO's representative in Marseilles, who kept wires to Swiss Communists and members of the Free Germany Committee and also to OSS representative Allen W. Dulles in Bern.

2. SO

General. Maquis groups, organized by CALPO and known as *Freischaren* [Free corps] under three leaders—political, charged with ultimate decisions; military, charged with operational plans; and technical, responsible for care of weapons and other materials—are operating currently, primarily in the Saarbrücken area, around Trier and Koblenz. Eight groups are definitely placed. The Swiss representatives (see above) will bring further reports on their activities.

CALPO was informed that OSS is prepared to create SO missions for reinforcement of existing groups and to institute original operations. They would have both military and political objectives and regard contact with existing Maquis groups as basic to their operations.

Agent Personnel. CALPO will supply the names of PWs who are bona fide antifascists for short penetrations and of personnel from its own membership for operations inside Germany, both as reinforcements and as new groups. CALPO is best equipped to operate in the Saargebiet.[7] It has formed a group which is familiar with the area, the people, and the Nazi apparatus and whose mission is to destroy Nazi, particularly Gestapo, organizations, SS remnants, etc., working on the principle of seeking to enlist the assistance of the local population.

3. MO

General. All CALPO groups and representatives in Germany have high priority propaganda directives. All material is prepared in Germany on the basis of local information within the framework of basic directives from CALPO via the courier chain.

[...]

4. X–2 [OSS Counterintelligence]

War Criminals. CALPO is prepared to make its dossiers on war criminals available to X–2.

Vetting. CALPO is agreeable to the X–2 proposal for assistance in vetting and will supply all of its personality information to X–2 when it is desired to check

---

7. Until 1935 the Saargebiet had been under French control. After Hitler's rise to power in 1933 numerous Communists had fled to this region. Many of them decided to leave the Saar district, however, after it fell back to Germany. As CALPO's President, Otto Niebergall-Florian had been a Communist City Councillor of the Saargebiet Capital Saarbrücken, he disposed of a network of actual and potential anti-Nazis in this region.

such files. In return, CALPO would appreciate an opportunity to submit names for X–2 checks.

5. R&A

In response to specific requests, and without prejudice to future requests, CALPO will permit OSS representatives to microfilm its files, excluding its membership list. CALPO will submit a chart of organization, data on the number and political character of its members, and information concerning its relations with other organizations, both German and French.

C. OPSAF Mission: Comments on Lt. Gould's Report

Representatives of the several branches commented on Lt. Gould's report with the view of informing him of additional recommendations to OPSAF in respect of benefits which may be expected from CALPO and the machinery for securing them.

1. *SI*. Mr. Cassady remarked that SI interests had been handled by Lt. Gould.

2. *SO*. Major Pusey expressed optimism about the potential value of CALPO. Without additional German-speaking SO personnel, SO would have to depend on SI screening. It was agreed that SO's operational interest in CALPO is the greatest.

3. *MO*. Mr. Bagier said he would withhold special recommendation until he has met Mr. Kuhnert (CALPO propaganda chief).

4. *X–2*. Major Runkle stated that, given the current X–2 concentration on security in Paris, X–2/Paris has no use for CALPO agents until the armies advance well into Germany. Mr. Cassady pointed out, however, that General Donovan instructs that CALPO be dropped once we are in Germany in order to guard against the penetration of OSS. Major Runkle remarked that CALPO's war criminal information would be useful in Washington and London and that assistance to CALPO on its own security checks could be granted in return for access to CALPO files of personality information.

5. *R&A*. Kull recommended that R&A representatives have an opportunity to brief agents on political questions. It appears that cooperation and facilities now offered by CALPO, as described by Lt. Gould, are adequate to satisfy R&A interest in CALPO itself, its activities, and relations with other organizations.

D. General Discussion

CALPO's Financial Position

Mr. Cassady observed that CALPO is financially sound, having been informed by Maurel (Hauser) that it has about thirty-four million francs at its disposal.

CALPO's Relations with British Agencies

No one has any knowledge of such relations.

Agent Personnel

Lt. Gould calculated that the probable total number available, after screening, will be approximately one hundred and fifty, seventy-five to one hundred of whom will be SO material. This conforms to Mr. Cassady's previous estimate. [...]

E. Decisions and Recommendations to OPSAF

[...][8]

What CALPO will receive from OSS:

   a. Agents will receive money, cover, communications and equipment.
   b. Transportation assistance will be made available to move proposed CALPO agent personnel, for screening and recruiting purposes, to and from the Paris and Lyon bases.
   c. The matter of expediting dispatch of CALPO intelligence from the Swiss border to Paris (now requiring eight days) will be discussed with the interested parties.
   d. Maurel will be assisted in the matter of transportation for his trip to Lyon and southern France.

[...]

I. Safe Addresses SI

1. CALPO has the following categories of safe addresses:

   a. Through penetration into the Wehrmacht by its members, CALPO has created Stützpunkte (Points des Appui) [Bases]. *Wehrmacht* men and the correspondents for furloughs established, and positions to the central organization; correspondents indicated the development of the Stützpunkte and of the work involved. [...]

   b. Political safe addresses operating during the period 1935–40 developed by CALPO activities during the war. [...]

   c. "Exchange" or "Relief" Stützpunkte. CALPO had a member in the German Bureau of Placement for the region of Toulon, Marseilles, and Lyon during the occupation. The German arrangement was an exchange of three

----

8. The omitted paragraphs deal with mere technical details, for instance on security checks and briefing and training. It is also stated that 110 [i.e., Allen W. Dulles] as the only OSS member based outside London would receive these minutes and all subsequent minutes and reports concering the mission.

Foreign workers for one French prisoner (although the French prisoners never did return) and through this arrangement and their contact, CALPO placed their German members under the cover of other nationalities, in particular places within Germany. Their agent[s] in the Bureau of Placement know exactly what needs the Germans had and called for particular persons by pre-arrangement. [...]

d. Personal political safe addresses where the political feature is not the dominant character. CALPO regards this classification as the least reliable of its resources.

e. Foreign workers' operations by other nationalities. The French, Italian, Spanish, and Czech have organizations doing the same work by their nationals within Germany.[9] CALPO has official liaison with the Comité des Prisonniers et Déportées. CALPO believes that this committee would grant to it their safe addresses.

[...]

II. SO

1. General. CALPO was informed that OSS is prepared to create SO missions carrying arms and Allied SO material[10] into Germany as reinforcing groups and on original missions. Basic to the work would be the establishment of contacts with existing Maquis groups. The missions would have military and political objectives. The combinations would be indicated clearly in training and briefing.

Present Maquis groups organized by CALPO known as *Freischaren* groups [...][11] Also these groups are organized into those with only German personnel and into those including other nationals. Further, there are city groups, usually no more than five in number, and field groups, which are larger. All groups have been formed inside Germany. The foundation of the German group was laid in 1944. Eight such groups are now known, including their physical position, main district for operations in Saarbruchen [Saarbrücken], including Traire [Trier] and Goblensk [Koblenz]. The Swiss man (see Communications above) will bring a late report on the activities of these groups. [...]

III. MO

1. General. [...] CALPO agents have as their most important instructions the pro-duction of propaganda. All material is prepared in Germany, contents receive some direction through the courier chains from CALPO, with basic amendments, of

---

9. Later on in the discussions, Lt. Col. Colby expressed concern about the effect of the SHAEF directive regarding organization and OSS operations among foreign worker groups inside Germany. See document [84].

10. In particular booby traps and explosives.

11. On the organization of the *Freischaren* groups see above.

course, on the ground. CALPO declares that its information is limited to regional operations and that there are atomic developments beyond these organized regions. There is no central organization of this work within Germany. CALPO characterizes its approach as sober and realistic. As to the tone of the propaganda, CALPO declares that there is now a general tendency to the positive in terms of unity of all groups in opposition to Hitler. This is regarded as a sharp advance of the negative approach which characterizes the preceding period. There is no central organization but all groups—even without central guidance—are going within the direction of unity. CALPO concludes that if there were the technical possibility of a central organization, this positive political unity would develop quickly and in considerable degree.

[...]

Document 83a · 20 January 1945

Memorandum from OSS Assistant Director Charles S. Cheston to Secretary of State Edward R. Stettinius: Last Effort to Save Helmuth James Graf von Moltke[1]

SECRET

Memorandum for the Secretary of State[2]

The OSS representative in Bern has transmitted the following information obtained from a reliable source:

Helmuth von Moltke, 37, a member of the conspiratorial group behind the 20 July coup has been condemned to death.[3] In view of the important role which he

---

1. NA, RG 226, Entry 99, Box 14, Folder 58a. This memorandum was attached to a letter from Charles S. Cheston, Acting Director of the OSS, to James C. Dunn, Assistant Secretary of State.

2. *Bern Cable #3689—19 January 1945.*

3. On 9 and 10 January 1945, Moltke had been tried together with other members of his resistance circle. He was to be executed no less than three days after this document was written.

played in the conspiratorial group [he was head of the younger group of officers], his death would represent a serious loss. Source has suggested to the British that they might consider whether there is any possibility of taking action to delay the execution in view of the fact that von Moltke's mother was British or South African. [His mother was the former Dorothy Innes of Capetown who married his father, Helmuth von Moltke, in 1905 and died several years ago.][4]

The OSS representative comments that while the hope of saving von Moltke is obviously slim, experience has shown that if some stir is created, the Germans at this stage may consider a person more valuable alive than dead.

The OSS representative cites the case of Erwin Planck, former confidential secretary to Bruening [Brüning] and former Secretary of State in the Schleicher and von Papen cabinets, and son of the noted physicist Max Planck.[5] Planck was accused by the Germans of complicity in the 20 July putsch and condemned to death. Oshima, the Japanese Ambassador in Berlin, intervened, on the ground that Erwin Planck had taken part in the conclusion of certain agreements with the Japanese. Oshima declared that Planck's execution would offend Japanese dignity. As a result Planck's sentence was commuted and he was sent to a concentration camp.[6]

The OSS representative also cites the case of Dr. Eugen Gerstenmeier, one of the leading men in the Confessional Church who was sentenced to six years' imprisonment. [Gerstenmeier, a member of the Christian opposition to the Nazis, was reported on May 4, 1943, in contact with a member of the British Embassy staff in Stockholm. It appears probable that he was in some way connected with the conspiratorial group behind the 20 July *coup,* but received only a comparatively light sentence.]

Source also has learned through well informed circles in Berlin that the Germans had very high hopes of taking Antwerp in the Ardennes offensive[7] and are very deeply disappointed by this failure.

Charles S. Cheston
Acting Director

---

4. Dorothy von Moltke had died in 1935. On her father's side—Sir James Rose Innes was South Africa's Chief Justice—the family held friendly relations with Field Marshal Jan Christiaan Smuts, former Prime Minister of South Africa, and Winston Churchill.

5. Erwin Planck became Undersecretary of State in 1932. He was released from duty, however, with Hitler's appointment to chancellorship.

6. Nevertheless, Erwin Planck was executed together with von Moltke on 23 January 1945, in Berlin Plötzensee.

7. Otherwise known as the Battle of the Bulge which lasted from mid-December 1944 until the end of January 1945. In spite of surprising success in the beginning, the Germans never got anywhere near Antwerp, Belgium.

Document 83b · 2 November 1943

OSS Biographical Files: Personal Data of Helmuth James Graf von Moltke[1]

Germany

I

1) von *Moltke,* Count
   Berlin, Pariserplatz. 7
   and Kreisau, near Schweidnitz,
   Silesia

2) Attorney at Law and Co-manager of a family estate in Silesia

3) [born] about 1903[2]
   German

[...]

9) Married

10) a. Nee Deichmann[3]
    c. Several children
    d. She comes from a family of bankers in Cologne

11) The wife of the late Baron Bruno Schroeder of London, England, senior part-
    ner of the banking firm of J. Henry Schroeder & Co. is her [Freya von Moltke's]
    aunt; a brother of his, an architect, is in the United States Army.[4]

---

1. NA, RG 226, Entry 99, Box 14, File 58a.
2. Helmuth James von Moltke was born on 11 March 1907.
3. This is a reference to Moltke's wife, Freya von Moltke.
4. Wilhelm Viggo (Willo) von Moltke. "Willo" served in the U.S. Army from 1943 to 1947, first in the Far East and later in Germany.

13) Studied law in England (see 15 below) as well as in Germany. b. Has complete command of English; also speaks French.

14) Widely travelled.

15) While admitted to the Bar in Berlin, he never tried very hard to establish himself seriously as a practicing attorney; he divided his time between Berlin and his farm in Silesia,[5] spending about four days a week in Berlin and three on the farm. Moreover, to have another iron in the fire, he registered as an undergraduate at the "Inner Temple"[6] between 1935 and 1937, attending "terms" whenever he could (attendance is a mere formality). In 1937, after passing the examinations required, he was called to the English Bar as a member of the "Inner Temple"; in this war he is reported to be working in the Admiralty Court in Berlin.

16) Thoroughly Democratic and Liberal; interested in history and politics; outspokenly anti-Nazi; went out of his way to avoid contact with the Nazis and their organizations and made only such concessions as were unavoidable as long as he lived in Germany. He frequently considered leaving Germany but could not make up his mind. Despite his title, he is by nature and inclination anything but a "Prussian", "Junker" [Prussian nobleman] or reactionary. Thoroughly European-minded.

21) *Physiological:* Unusually tall (about 6' 5"), inclined to stoop, dark hair, dark eyes, tanned complexion.

   Intellectual: Has many interests; is well-read and well-educated.

   Emotional: Very quiet and reserved/strong sense of decency, justice, and fairness/likes to help others and takes a genuine interest in their problems/not without ambition but on the whole more interested in family life than in his career.

   Operational: It is difficult to evaluate von Moltke's skill as a lawyer; everyone who knows him agrees about his integrity, his intelligence, and his seriousness. He might be useful as a source of information through his knowledge of people in his local district (Silesia); moreover, his close international connections and his genuinely cooperative spirit might be useful in the reconstruction period.

   Memory: good Judgement: fair Objectivity: good

   [Source]: 1028 and interviewer's own knowledge

---

5. The anti-Nazi Kreisau Circle which was founded in 1933 was named after the Moltke family estate in Silesia.

6. A prestigious law school in London.

Document 84 · 22 January 1945

Memorandum from the OSS to General Dwight D. Eisenhower: Arming of Foreign Workers in Germany[1]

TOP SECRET

Subject: Clandestine Supply to Foreign Workers

[...]

Object:

1. To present a study of the foreign worker situation in *Germany* and to give consideration to the possibility of clandestine delivery of arms to foreign workers formed into *Maquis* Groups.

Discussion:

2. SHAEF Policy. [...]

Informal discussion has arisen at SHAEF [Supreme Headquarters of the Allied Expeditionary Forces] over the question of whether support should be given to foreign worker *Maquis* groups in *Germany* in the event that they should form. The political policy at the present time does not countenance the support of any indigenous group of *Germans;* but it is conceived that circumstances might arise in which a *Maquis,* consisting of foreign workers only, would form and serve a useful purpose.[2]

---

1. NA, RG 226, Entry 190, Box 284, Folder 1252. This memorandum had been drawn up by members of the Special Operations Branch in the European Theater of War.

2. While material support of resistance groups in Yugoslavia, Poland and France was generally practiced, it had been ruled out by the Joint Chiefs of Staff from the very beginning that Austrians and Germans should receive any such support.

3. Nazi *Policy Toward Foreign Workers.* a. The *Nazi* policy toward foreign workers has in recent months followed a dual tendency: measures of conciliation in matters of physical welfare, but measures of control in relation to the movement and contact of the foreign workers with the *German* population. For example, under *Himmler's* order, dated 17 October 1944, foreign workers may no longer be billeted in cities, and must spend the night in their barracks. This policy is based on the fact that the *Germans* consider the foreign workers not so much a positive revolutionary force as an element of social disorder in a totalitarian society. However, it is evident that the *German* authorities reckon with the possibilities in the near future of an *Allied* inspired uprising among foreign workers.

Frequent reports indicate that *Himmler* is planning to eliminate all men capable of leading an organized opposition when the time comes, or of collaborating later with an army of occupation when it finally arrives.[3] In addition, the authorities have shown a tendency to transport as many foreign workers as possible from *Berlin*, and to replace them by *Germans* or workers of the "*German* race" from various *Reich* territories.

b. A serious obstacle to cooperation among foreign worker groups of different nationalities is presented as the result of an inherent distrust on the part of each national group for the others. The *Nazi* authorities have recognized this fact, and, in order to realize the fullest dividends from foreign labor, they have, therefore, segregated the various national groups. In addition, they have transferred workers from Western *Europe* to the Eastern borders of the *Reich,* and *Russian, Polish* and *Slavic* workers have been transported to Western *Germany.*

c. Because of the stringent *Nazi* controls and the mixed character of foreign labor, individual rather than group action appears to be the rule. There are indications, however, that as the *Allies* move farther into *Germany,* mass dislocation, if not mass uprisings, will be the result. With the controls loosened, foreign workers are apt to disorganize the *German* system by leaving factories and camps and by endeavoring to infiltrate behind the *Allied* lines or break for home. Yet, there is a strong hope, based on various sources, that foreign workers will cluster around any effective resistance groups that might emerge.

4. *Prevailing Organization Among Foreign Workers.* a. While a unified resistance movement against the *Germans* does not yet exist, *Nazi* authorities are becoming more apprehensive as an "inner determination" among the foreign workers becomes increasingly manifest through a sudden reserve, clandestine sabotage, sullenness, simulation of illness, and deliberate silence.

b. There is little evidence in any group of foreign workers of a spontaneous resistance organization; in fact, the *French* and *Polish* workers appear to be the only groups with any significant organization at all. The small nuclei of resistance that do exist appear to be underground trade union organizations rather than political activist groups. However, foreign workers have recently displayed a more

---

3. For rumors of Nazi plans to liquidate foreign workers see document [66].

decided tendency to unite and to follow the suggestions which are being broad-cast over the *Allied* radio.

c. The following are evidences of attempts at organization among the deportees:

(1) Reports have been received discribing small underground organizations of foreign workers in the *Rhineland, Prussian Saxony,* and *NE [Northeast] Germany.* Occasionally, sabotage is carried out, but in general it may be said that the foreign worker is far more interested in seeking flight to his homeland than in causing an uprising in *Germany.*

(2) The *Enemy* has admitted the existence of opposition elements among for-eign workers, but he cannot be certain of what organizations do exist which may be aroused to anti-*Nazi* action. The warning addressed by the *German* press to *German* workers against collaboration with the foreigner and the admission that such cases of collaboration have already taken place reveal the general political fears of the *Germans* toward foreign worker elements.

(3) […] The existence of the *Amicale des Travailleurs Francais,* an organization existing among *French* foreign workers in *Germany,* used as a front for anti-*German* activities, is known.

(4) SOE [Special Operations Executive] has recognized the existence of an organized *Polish* underground in *Germany,* particularly in the following regions: (a) *Hannover-Westphalia-* [and?] the *Rhineland;* (b) *Baden-Württemberg;* (c) *Hamburg-Kiel.* Accordingly, a project has been created for the purpose of organiz-ing and preparing *Polish* workmen in these areas for effective action upon collapse or upon the withdrawal of *German* troops.

5. Evidences of Maquis Formations and Uprisings Among Foreign Workers. a. It is pointed out by OSS, R&A Branch, 23 October 1944, in a report on the *Comite "Allemagne Libre" Pour L'Ouest* that *CALPO* was advised c. 10 October 1944, by clandestine radio, of *Maquis* groups, numbering up to 20,000,[4] composed partly of foreign workers, who are operating in the Southern *Schwarzwald* [Black For-est]. The members of the *Maquis* are reported to have come from *Stuttgart, Mannheim, Baden, Ludwigshafen,* and some from the *Ruhr.* In the same manner, *CALPO* received news, c. 15 October 1944, that SS troops had been sent to clean up these guerrillas. A report in the *Daily Telegraph,* 4 December 1944, seems to tie in with *CALPO*'s claims, and reads as follows:

"*Berlin* officially estimates that about 50,000 escaped prisoners of war and for-eign workers are now pursuing a roving existence in *South Germany.* This figure is certainly an underestimate.

"Many thousands who are living the life of outlaws in the *Black Forest* had been sent by the *Nazi* authorities to Western *Germany.* They seized the opportunity

---

4. This number seems grossly exaggerated.

during air raids of breaking out from prison camps or taking French leave from factories.

"There are believed to be secret organizations in the *Reich* which are helping such escapes. Most of the men are striving to reach the *Allied* lines or the *Swiss* frontier."[5]

b. During September 1944, 300 *French* workers deserted to *Slovakia* from *Hungary* and were of great assistance during resistance uprisings. Judged by the *Czechs* to be good fighters, these foreign worker forces were obliged to disperse at the end of operations.[6] It is believed that these troops still exist in the mountains of *Central Slovakia,* awaiting the *Russian* advance before showing their hand again.

c. A report from *Basle.* 27 September 1944, after General *Eisenhower* had made his appeal to foreign workers,[7] stated that many attacks had been made on *German* policemen. It is assumed that such activity was the direct result of an attempt on the part of the foreign workers to obtain arms.

[...]

6. Present Location and Strength of Foreign Workers. a. According to recent and most available estimates there are between 7,000,000 and 8,500,000 foreign workers in *Germany,* including roughly 2,000,000 working P/Ws. Among these workers those nationals whose countries are at war with *Germany* have by far the most numerous representation:

(1) *Russians*	2,500,000	
(2) *French*	1,750,000	
(3) *Poles*	1,500,000	
(4) *Belgians*	500,000	
(5) *Dutch*	350,000	
(6) *Yugoslavs*	325,000	
(7) *Czechs*	350,000	
(8) *Italians*	400,000	
Total:	7,675,000	

[...]

---

5. Although isolated incidents along these lines were reported by the SS and Gestapo, the information as given here is inaccurate.

6. On 29 August 1944, Slovak partisans had started an uprising against the Wehrmacht. This liberation attempt was, however, suppressed by the retreating German armies.

7. On 5 September 1944, General Eisenhower had addressed foreign workers through BBC, calling for sabotage.

7. Estimate of Foreign Workers Who Will Form Maquis Groups. a. The Direction Generale des Etudes et Recherches (DGER)[8] has estimated that a minimum of 100,000 political deportees and 400,000 workers of *French* nationality would be able to form some kind of *Maquis* Groups at the time of the German collapse.

b. Based on this estimate, it could probably be said that, in general, 25% of all foreign workers in *Germany* might be expected to form *Maquis* Groups.
[...]

8. Supply Considerations.

a. Basis of Estimates. (1) In order to facilitate the consideration of the supply problem to foreign workers in *Germany,* and in order to have a simple mathematical basis upon which to calculate estimates, a unit of 50 men is suggested, equipped with the type of arms employed by the *Maquis* in *France.*
[...]

b. Requirements. (1) Should the potential estimate of 1,981,250 foreign workers, who it is believed could be expected to form *Maquis* groups, prove sound, the supply situation would be a critical one. Procurement might well be impossible in view of the existing shortage of *American* weapons required for combat troops.

(2) Since it is considered that supplies for such a large number of foreign workers could not be met by OSS (SO), requirements are put forward for 500,000 individuals. It is assumed that no more than 500,000 foreign workers would require arming in the indeterminate future and that it would not be practical to consider the establishment of a stockpile at this time for a larger number of *Maquis* forces in *Germany*.

(3) 500,000 foreign workers would thus require the following equipment, based on the proposed organization of foreign worker *Maquis* units:

American Weapons	Quantity	Initial Ammunition Supply
Pistol, automatic, cal. .45 or Revolver, cal. .38	80,000	400,000
Rifle, cal. .30, M1903	340,000	68,000,000
Launcher, Rocket AT 2.36" M1A1	40,000	560,000
SMG cal. .45 M3	100,000	10,000,000

...

---

8. French Security Service.

Document 85 · 24 January 1945

Letter from David Williamson
(OSS Morale Operations Branch)
to Lieutenant Colonel John S. Roller:
A Successful Denunciation[1]

SECRET

Subject: List of Names

With reference to our letter of 7 December 1944, attached is a list of prominent German officials with pertinent data concerning each. It may be possible for you to denounce some of them to an appropriate German security organization. This list has been cleared with X-2.

It will interest you to know that the Germans have recently announced (13 January 1945) the dismissal of Gen. Walter Schieber, one of Speer's right-hand men. You will recall that on September 26, 1944, the MO Weekly Directive[2] suggested denouncing this man. The apparent connection between the two events is cause for congratulation.[3]

DW

---

1. NA, RG 226, Entry 139, Box 113, Folder 1569/70.
2. Not printed. See, however, 62.
3. For this strategy used by the MO Branch see document [62].

Document 86 · 24 January 1945

Telegram from Allen W. Dulles
(OSS Bern) to OSS Washington:
The Escape of a "Breakers" Emissary[1]

SECRET

TOR: 1/24/45, 10:45 p.m.

#4039. Bern-Washington. From 110.

#4839. Bern-London.

#4289. Bern-Paris.

512 [Hans Bernd Gisevius] has just escaped from Germany on last express train running from Berlin on papers prepared by C and D London[2] (congratulations to London, particularly on Geheimstaatz* [sic] Polizei [Gestapo] identification disk, which was particularly useful). He has been in hiding in Berlin since he left the Bendlerstrasse[3] at 1830 hours1 July 20, $\frac{1}{2}$ hour before the plotters were arrested. His friends' fate and 6 months hiding have shattered his nerves and it may take a few days to piece together his story, which [we] will send soonest possible.

For 154. See #179.** It might have good psychological effect if you could give any encouraging reaction regarding manuscript.

---

1. NA, RG 226, Entry 99, Box 14, Folder 58a.

2. I.e., the OSS Censorship and Documents Branch. This branch was in charge of preparing counterfeit identification documents such as passports and visas.

* *Received as Geheimstaatr.*

3. The Berlin headquarters of the conspiracy during the 20th of July incident.

** *Number cannot be identified.*

Document 87 · 25 January 1945

Telegram from OSS Assistant Director Charles S. Cheston to Allen W. Dulles (OSS Bern): Congratulations on OSS Bern's Work[1]

SECRET

TOD: 1/25/45, 16:02

#2747. 110 [Allen W. Dulles] from Cheston and 154 [Whitney H. Shepardson].

Please replace our #2717 (*Out* 1991) with following: delighted to hear 512 [Hans Bernd Gisevius] safe. Please tell him that manuscript already proved of greatest value and being further studied.[2] You are authorized to pay him one thousand dollars for valuable intelligence obtained from it. As you can appreciate believe it inappropriate to make arrangements with publisher to have it published now. When security and official reasons permit he will of course be at liberty to arrange for publication. Looking forward to receipt of full story. Congratulations.

CSC

---

1. NA, RG 226, Entry 146, Box 235, Folder 3296.

2. The Gisevius manuscript gave details about the rise of National Socialism and the events leading up to the 20th of July. It was first published in Zurich in 1946, then in Boston (1947) and finally in London (1948) under the title *To the Bitter End (Bis zum bitteren Ende)*.

Document 88 · 25 January 1945

Telegram from Allen W. Dulles (OSS Bern) to OSS Washington: Secret OSS Channels to German Commanders in the West[1]

SECRET

TOR:26/1/45, 0:20 a.m.

[...]

Endeavoring to explore possibilities of secret line to Rundstedt[2] and already have a line to Kesselring via contact who is seeing 476 [Gero von Schulze-Gaevernitz] today before proceeding to Italy to see Kesselring.[3] Could anything along following lines be given discreetly to cut outs[4] who have contacts in high Wehrmacht circles? (1) Unconditional surrender remains unaltered policy but problem for German military leaders to face is future of own country in face of inevitable and rapidly approaching military defeat. (2) In both west and east Germany faces the choice of making each German city an Aachen, Warsaw or Budapest,[5] or of facilitating entry of the Allied forces and orderly transfer of authority to forces of occupation under conditions which would (a) spare unnecessary destruction, (b) facilitate distribution of food and raw materials so as to render possible an earlier resumption of economic life and, (c) render possible orderly evacuation of prisoners and foreign workers, (3) Officers of *Wehrmacht* who contribute to such constructive policy, assuming war criminals not involved, would be treated with consideration due their rank and in relation to the services they thus render in

---

1. NA, RG 226, Entry 138, Box 2.

2. For Rundstedt, see documents [43], [53], [54] and [60].

3. Since December 1941 General Wilhelm Kesselring had been Supreme Commander of the German Armed Forces in Italy and the Mediterranean. Gaevernitz had been in contact with Kesselring through the German consul in Lugano, Konstantin von Neurath, since late December. This was the first episode of an action backed by Allen W. Dulles, which later became known as Operation Sunrise. See documents [91], [93] and [94].

4. I.e., liaison agents who are not aware of the contents of their messages.

5. These cities were among the first in Central Europe to be occupied by the Allies. In all these places German resistance had been strong, resulting in massive destruction.

facilitating liquidation of the Nazi regime and those forces which have supported it.

This is merely rough outline of ideas, but some affirmative program along some such lines may help to drive a wedge into German Army and to facilitate American and British occupation of at least Western Germany before effects of Russian successes in east create situation of complete chaos thruout [sic] Germany. Even though Russia may not, and probably does not, desire to see a Bolshevized Germany, many Germans believe this would facilitate an understanding with Russia and are working in this direction aided by events, by the distress incident to the slowly creeping paralysis in German transportation and the suffering resulting from air bombardments and the presence in Germany of millions undernourished and desperate prisoners of war, foreign workers and bombed out population.

Document 89 · 27 January 1945

Memorandum from OSS Assistant Director Charles S. Cheston to the Joint Chiefs of Staff: The Danger of a Bolshevized Germany[1]

SECRET

Memorandum of Information for the Joint Chiefs of Staff:

The following communication has been received from the OSS representative in Bern:

One of the two emissaries of the conspiratorial group behind the 20 July putsch who was previously reported arrested by the Nazis has escaped to Switzerland,[2] and has supplied further information on the divergence of opinion which devel-

---

1. NA, RG 226, Entry 99, Box 14, Folder 58a. This memorandum, based on a telegram of 25 January by Allen Dulles, was forwarded to the President, the Secretary of State and the Joint Chiefs of Staff.
2. I.e., Hans Bernd Gisevius.

oped among the conspirators as previously reported in a memorandum dated 17 August 1944.[3]

Source declares that Colonel von Stauffenberg, who made the attempt on Hitler's life, had planned to conclude a peace with the Soviets, if the putsch were successful and proposed to announce the establishment of a "workers and peasants" regime in Germany.[4] The old-line Generals did not agree with this plan and continued to favor a peace arrangement with the Western Allies to the exclusion of the Soviets. They did not oppose von Stauffenberg, however, since he was the only one willing to risk his life and was the only person in a position to place the bomb. They hoped that they would be able later to direct developments along more conservative lines.

The OSS representative comments that:

The present situation on the Eastern Front and the general trend of the situation in Germany indicate that an eastern solution of the war may now be more attractive to Germany. It is not impossible that Germany will maintain stubborn resistance in the West even though the Soviets have pressed deep into the Reich, unless some means is found to break the resistance of Wehrmacht forces opposing the British and Americans.

A subtle, psychological approach may help the Anglo-American military forces. The following points might be suggested to high Wehrmacht circles:

1. Unconditional surrender unalterably remains the Allied policy, but German military leaders must, in the face of the inevitable and rapidly approaching military defeat, consider the future of their country.
2. In both the East and the West Germany faces the choice of making each German city an Aachen, Warsaw, or Budapest, or of facilitating the entry of Allied armies and the orderly transfer of authority to occupation forces under conditions which would spare unnecessary destruction, facilitate the distribution of food and raw materials and a resumption of economic life, and make possible the orderly evacuation of prisoners and foreign workers.
3. Wehrmacht officers who contribute to such a constructive policy, assuming they are not marked as war criminals, would be treated with consideration due their rank and according to the services which they render in the liquidation of the Nazi regime and the forces which have supported it.

An affirmative program along these lines, the OSS representative believes, may help to drive a wedge in the German army before the effects of the Soviet successes in the East create chaos in Germany. Even though the USSR probably does not

---

3. Not printed.

4. Stauffenberg's alleged sympathy with the Soviets was later exploited in the German Democratic Republic's historiography on the German resistance. There is some evidence that Gisevius exaggerated the eastern leanings of the German population in general. He may have hoped that Dulles could convince Washington to soften the policy of unconditional surrender.

wish to see a Bolshevized Germany, many Germans appear to believe that a Bolshevized Germany would facilitate an understanding with the USSR. They seem to be working in this direction, aided by current military developments, by the distress incident to the slowly creeping paralysis of German transport, by the suffering resulting from air bombardment, and by the presence in Germany of large numbers of undernourished and desparate prisoners of war, foreign workers, and bombed-out peoples.

Charles S. Cheston
Acting Director

Document 90 · 5 February 1945

Telegram from Allen W. Dulles (OSS Bern) to OSS Washington: How Should the United States React to the Russian Free German Committee[1]

TOP SECRET

TOR: 5/2/45 23:50

#4909. Bern to Washington. #5979. Bern to London. #4869. Bern to Paris. *Breakers.* Carib from 110. Information: Forgan and 140.

Answering your #3057 (OUT 2782)[2] inquiring re 512's [Hans Bernd Gisevius] estimate of Russian Free German Committee and its probable use. 512 is convinced that Russians will come to Germany with carefully assembled and thoroughly indoctrinated group of Germans probably including Paulus, Seydlitz et al.[3] If they can succeed in putting this over as the government of Germany they will do so but more likely, in view of probable American and British opposition, they will at first merely use this in Russian zone. However, as this will be the only German organization and as it will profit from its long advertisement and prestige of Russian backing, it will more and more be looked to as the government of

---

1. NA, RG 226, Entry 138, Box 2.
2. Not printed.
3. See in particular documents [14] and [15].

Germany since USA and Britain will have nothing comparable. It may, of course, be initially set up as a committee and procedure followed similar to that in case of Lublin Committee.[4]

512 believes we have only 3 alternatives: 1). Accept Russian German committee; 2). Set up rival committee or probably 2 rival committees in respective Anglo-Saxon zones,[5] or 3). Organize jointly with Russians some type of German committee which is subject to Allied occupation authorities and will assist in transacting current affairs as successor to German government on the understanding, of course, that final authority rests solely with military occupation. Such committee might be largely of technical men, experts in their respective fields such as finance, transportation, food rationing and distribution, public works, labor relations, police and the like but we would probably have to accept some of the Paulus, Seydlitz crowd.

512 feels, and I agree, that if we go into Germany without any plans along this 3rd line, something like the Seydlitz committee will eventually be imposed on us.

512 stresses importance, particularly from our viewpoint as regards South America, of controlling German Foreign representation. He believes that if this is properly handled we might be able to infiltrate and break up entire Nazi espionage ring in South America.

Certain German diplomats here who are not too compromised as Nazis are expecting early summons to adhere to Seydlitz committee or alternatively that Seydlitz committee will send its own people here and endeavor to infiltrate German diplomatic, consular establishment.

Some weeks ago 476 [Gero von Schulze-Gaevernitz], at invitation of General Sibert, G-2, 12th AG [Army Group], visited 12th AG and later London and SHAEF and with my backing presented plan for getting together small group of high anti-Nazi German Officers, whom he interviewed in France and England to advise on certain phases of German matters and methods of penetrating OKW. This group was not to have any political functions and was to work secretly. This plan which I consider constructive has apparently died in SHAEF, or, at least, I have heard nothing further about it, possibly owing to Gen. Betts' illness as he had matter in hand.

While agreeing that we should not set up German committee of political refugees such as Bruning [Brüning], Wirth, Braun, Treviranus et al, I feel we should prepare quietly and without formality in Switzerland, France and elsewhere certain individual Germans who have maintained close contact with Germany and who would be suitable to advise on certain phases German matters and possibly serve on technical administrative committees which any occupying authorities in Germany will find absolutely essential. I have several candidates here including 512 who was slated for high post if the July 20th affair had succeeded.[6]

---

4. Since January, the Soviet-sponsored Lublin Committee (Polish Committee for National Liberation) functioned as the Government of Poland, although a Polish government-in-exile resided in London.

5. For plans to set up a western-oriented German committee, see documents [26] and [42].

6. Gisevius was to become head of the Reich Chancellery.

If we do nothing of this nature, the ready made Russian German committee may monopolize the field.

Document 91 · 26 February 1945

Memorandum from OSS Director William J. Donovan to President Franklin D. Roosevelt: Possibilities of Ending the War in the West[1]

TOP SECRET

Memorandum for the President:

The following information, transmitted by the OSS representative in Bern, is a sequel to a memorandum dated 9 February:[2]

Alexander Constantin von Neurath, the German Consul at Lugano, while visiting his father (the former Foreign Minister and Protector of Bohemia and Moravia) near Stuttgart on 10 February, received a telephone call from Marshal Kesselring, advising him to go to a secret rendezvous where he found Lieutenant-General Siegfried Westphal, chief of staff to Rundstedt, and Marshal Johannes Blaskowitz, former (?) commander of Army Group "G" on the Western Front.[3]

---

1. Roosevelt Library, Hyde Park, F. D. Roosevelt Papers. President's Secretary's Files, Box 171, Folder OSS/February 1945.

2. Not printed. In this memorandum Donovan had reported to the President about a prospective meeting between Allen W. Dulles and German military and SS leaders. On 8 February, the German Consul at Lugano, Alexander Constantin von Neurath, asserted to the OSS representative in Bern that he had just returned from a meeting with Field Marshal Albert Kesselring, Rudolf Rahn (German Ambassador to the Mussolini regime in North Italy) and Karl Wolff, the higher SS and police leader in Italy and Chief of Himmler's personal staff. At that time, however, neither Kesselring nor Field Marshall Gerd von Rundstedt were ready to surrender to the Western Allies.

3. In January 1945, Blaskowitz had changed from Army Group G to Army Group H where he took over the command in Holland.

Von Neurath knew Westphal well, having served with him for two years as liaison officer in North Africa; he knew Blaskowitz less well.

The three frankly discussed the possibility of opening the Western Front to the Allies. Westphal and Blaskowitz questioned the value of taking such a step, if they were merely to be considered as war criminals. They added that it was increasingly difficult to organize any large-scale move to open the front because of the technical difficulties presented by the SS and the state of mind of the troops. They said that their armies included large elements of Germans from East Prussia and eastern Germany whose fighting qualities had been stiffened by the Soviet occupation of their home areas.[4]   These troops, they explained, motivated by the feeling that they have lost everything and having no homes or families to which to return, consider it better to stay on and fight. Westphal even declared that the troops sometimes refuse to obey orders from headquarters to retire, stating that since they are holding good positions and may not find as good ones in the rear, they prefer to fight it out where they are.

Neither Westphal nor Blaskowitz made definite suggestions. They appear, however, (a) to be working with Kesselring, (b) to have uppermost in their minds the idea of opening up the Western and Italian Fronts to the Allies, and (c) to be approaching the point where they might discuss such an arrangement on purely military lines with an American Army officer. Prerequisites to such a discussion would be adequate security arrangements and personal assurances that they would not be included in the war criminals list but would be granted some basis to justify their action, such as an opportunity to help in the orderly liquidation and to prevent unnecessary destruction in Germany.

Von Neurath, now back in Switzerland, plans to report to Kesselring his conversation with Westphal and Blaskowitz and to determine whether a routine reason can be found for Westphal to visit Kesselring.

[The OSS representative comments that while von Neurath may obtain further direct access to Kesselring without arousing SS and SD [*Sicherheitsdienst;* security service of the SS] suspicions, he must exercise the greatest care. The representative doubts that von Neurath will be guilty of indiscretion, since his own life is apparently at stake and since his background is non-Nazi. The representative describes von Neurath as not brilliant but a reasonably solid type who has excellent relations with the Reichswehr as a result of his long liaison work in North Africa. If Westphal makes the trip to Italy he could probably stay only a very short time without arousing suspicion, since Kesselring himself is already the subject of press rumors which may result in his elimination by Himmler.]

[(The London *Daily Dispatch* on 24 February carried a story from its Bern correspondent stating that Kesselring has offered secretly to the Allies to withdraw under pressure, leaving North Italian cities intact and preventing neo-Fascist destruction, in return for which he has asked for assurances that he would not be considered a war criminal and would be allowed to retire his troops to Germany to maintain order.)]

---

4. Beginning on 12 January 1945, a major Soviet offensive destroyed the German forces between the Vistula and the Oder River.

[The OSS representative declares that while he cannot predict the chances of successfully persuading Westphal and Kesselring to open up the Italian and Western Fronts simultaneously, he judges them to be sufficient to justify careful consideration of the idea. He believes that no political *quid pro quo's* or impairment of the unconditional surrender principle would be involved if conversations were held between an American officer and these German officers. Such conversations, which could be held in the Lugano area on the Swiss side of the Italo-Swiss border, would have to await the outcome of von Neurath's forthcoming meeting with Kesselring.]

(The OSS representative in Caserta reports that AFHQ [Allied Force Headquarters, Mediterranean] is interested in obtaining positive and authentic confirmation of Kesselring's disposition to negotiate with the Allies. AFHQ feels that if Kesselring wishes to dispatch an emissary with an official message, he could find means to do so.)

Charles S. Cheston
Acting Director

Document 92 · 27 February 1945

Telegram from OSS Washington
to Allen W. Dulles (OSS Bern):
Guideline for Recruiting German Agents[1]

SECRET

[...]

As to the question of any measure of protection which might be held out to those who retain their official positions and render service to us, we wish to point out that a similar question was raised with the President in December last respecting Germans in general who assist us and that he has gone on record with us to the following effect:

He does not believe that we should offer any guarantees of protection in the post hostilities period to Germans working for our organization. He considers that the carrying out of such guarantees would be difficult and probably widely misunderstood both in this country and abroad. He anticipates that an increasing

---

1. NA, RG 226, Entry 138, Box 2. The same message was sent to the OSS outpost in London.

number of Germans will try to save themselves by coming over to our side at the last moment and he points out that among this group there will probably be some who should properly be tried for war crimes or at least arrested for active participation in Nazi activities. Even with necessary controls he is not prepared to authorize the giving of guarantees.

This question has been discussed with General Holmes[2] who agrees with us that it would, however, be in order for you to make a general statement to the Germans in question to the effect that due note will be taken of any activities on their part tending to assist the allies and bring the war to a prompt conclusion. That such activities would tend to improve their standing with the Allies, and that in the event they should become involved in future trials reports of such activities would be introduced in evidence.

This general statement is believed by both us and the State Department to be entirely within the framework of the President's views as stated above but it should of course not be expressed in writing nor should there be any possibility of its being construed as in the nature of a guarantee or basis of exemption from trial.

Both the State Department and we here believe that it would be unwise to foster any public movement of secession or to permit the German activities to assume a political character. Certainly none of the group should be encouraged to believe that we are fostering any German committee for political purposes.[3] It should be made clear beyond doubt that their contribution must be entirely on the basis of furnishing intelligence.

---

2. General Julius Holmes was Assistant Secretary for Administration in the State Department.
3. See document [90].

Document 93 · 8 March 1945

Memorandum from OSS Director William J. Donovan to President Franklin D. Roosevelt: Hopes for Secret Surrender[1]

TOP SECRET

Memorandum for the President:

The following information, transmitted by the OSS representative in Bern, is a sequel to memoranda dated 9 and 26 February[2]:

Obergruppenfuehrer [Lieutenant-General] and General der Waffen SS Karl Wolff, the Higher SS and Police Leader in Italy, and a German High Command representative presumably from General Kesselring's staff, arrived in Lugano, Switzerland on the morning of 8 March. They are allegedly prepared to make definite commitments in regard to terminating German resistance in North Italy.

The OSS representative in Bern believes that, if Wolf is really working with Kesselring, the two Generals might effect an unconditional surrender. Absolute secrecy is essential to a successful surrender, and the OSS representative is ready to arrange with complete secrecy for the entry into Switzerland in civilian clothes of fully authorized representatives of the Supreme Allied Mediterranean Command.

It is not clear whether this move is separate from the Neurath negotiations [described in the memoranda of 9 and 26 February], but the OSS representative in Bern believes they will merge in so far as the North Italian situation is concerned.

Wolff is accompanied by Standartenführer [Colonel] Dollmann, who has in the past claimed that he represented Kesselring, Rahn, Wolff, and Harster. Dollmann and his aide, Zimmern [Guido Zimmer], had made indirect contact

---

1. Roosevelt Library, Hyde Park, F. D. Roosevelt Papers. President's Secretary's Files, Box 171, Folder OSS/February 1945.
2. Document [91].

with the OSS representative on 2 March, and promised to return on 8 March with credentials and definite proposals. On the earlier date the suggestion was made to Dollmann that he bring with him an important Italian partisan leader as evidence of his good faith and ability to act. Dollmann has reportedly brought along Ferruccio Parri, Chief of the North Italian Patriots Unified Command.

The above information has been given to AFHQ [Allied Force Headquarters, Mediterranean] by our Caserta representative.

Document 94 · 10 March 1945

Memorandum from OSS Director
William J. Donovan to President Franklin D. Roosevelt:
Secret Talks Between Allen W. Dulles
and Nazi Leaders[1]

TOP SECRET

Memorandum for the President

The OSS representative in Bern has forwarded the following information, supplementary to my memoranda of 8[2] and 9 March[3]:

Obergruppenfuehrer [Lieutenant-General] and *General der Waffen SS* Karl Wolff, who has arrived in Zurich to discuss a definite program for taking German forces in North Italy out of the war, is accompanied by the two men who made the preliminary contact with the OSS representative (Standartenfuehrer [Colonel] Dollmann and his aide, Zimmer) as well as by Wolff's military expert, Sturmbannfuehrer [Major] Wenner, and an Italian intermediary, Baron Pirelli.

---

1. Roosevelt Library, Hyde Park, F. D. Roosevelt Papers. President's Secretary's Files, Box 171, Folder OSS/March 1–15, 1945.
2. Document [93].
3. Not printed.

The OSS representative consented to see only Wolff, who came to the former's apartment with a Swiss intermediary on the evening of 8 March. The OSS representative and an associate, a former German Consul in Zurich,[4] then talked with Wolff alone. The former Consul later saw Wolff and Dollmann together.

Wolff is a distinctive personality, and evidence indicates that he represents the more moderate element in Waffen SS combined with a measure of romanticism. He is probably the most dynamic personality in North Italy and, next to Kesselring, the most powerful.

Wolff stated that the time had come when some German with power to act should lead Germany out of the war in order to end useless human and material destruction. He says he is willing to act and feels he can persuade Kesselring to cooperate, and that the two control the situation in North Italy. As far as the SS is concerned, Wolff states that he also controls Western Austria, since his authority includes the Vorarlberg, Tyrol, and the Brenner Pass with both its northern and southern approaches. Wolff declares that joint action by Kesselring and himself would leave Hitler and Himmler powerless to take effective countermeasure like the ones they employed in the 20 July crisis. Also Wolff feels that joint action by Kesselring and himself would have a vital repercussion on the German Army, particularly on the Western Front, since many Generals are only waiting for someone to take the lead. Wolff made no request concerning his personal safety or privileged treatment from the war criminal viewpoint.[5]

Wolff envisages the following procedures to bring about action: (1) He will meet Kesselring during the week-end of 10 March in order to obtain a definite commitment to joint action. Wolff says he has had the closest possible personal relations with Kesselring for several years, and indicated that Kesselring's problem was to reconcile such action with his oath of allegiance. Kesselring has insisted that, after a long military career throughout which he had always kept his oath, he was too old to change. Nevertheless Wolff believes he can be won over to see the senselessness of the struggle and admit that his duty to the German people is higher than that to the Fuehrer.

(2) With Kesselring, Wolff will draft an appeal to be signed by themselves, Rahn (the German Ambassador to the Mussolini regime in North Italy), and others. The appeal will set forth the uselessness of the struggle and the signers' responsibility to the German people to end it, will call on military commanders in particular and Germans in general to dissociate themselves from Himmler-Hitler control, and will state that the Germans in North Italy are terminating hostilities.

---

4. I.e., Hans Bernd Gisevius.

5. Nevertheless, Karl Wolff was spared from being sentenced in the Nuremberg Trials. Instead, he served as witness for the prosecution, appearing in court in full SS uniform. It was not before much later that a Bavarian court found him guilty of participating in the deportation of Jews. His 15 year sentence was suspended after less than half of his imprisonment.

(3) Wolff will make preparations to get this message to the German people and military commanders via radio and wireless.

(4) Provided Kesselring is won over, Wolff believes that he and Kesselring would come clandestinely to Switzerland within the week in order to meet Allied military men and coordinate purely military surrender moves with the appeal. Apparently no one on Kesselring's immediate staff is suited to represent him for this purpose, his chief of staff not yet having been acquainted with the plan.

As evidence of his ability to act, Wolff has already unconditionally delivered Ferrucio Parri, Italian patriot from North Italy, and [Antonio Usmiani][6] (a former OSS agent in Milan), to the OSS representative in Bern. Parri had been imprisoned in Verona [Usmiani] in Milan. Their release was requested of Dollmann during the preliminary negotiations of 2 March, and both men assumed at the time they were taken away by the SS that they were being led to execution. Neither yet knows the reason for the release. Wolff fully realizes Parri's importance, and remarked to an intermediary that he was giving up his most important hostage.[7]

Wolff is prepared to demonstrate further his ability to act by: (1) discontinuing active warfare against Italian partisans, merely keeping up whatever pretense is necessary pending execution of the plan; (2) releasing to Switzerland several hundred Jews interned at Bozen (Bolzano); Wolff claims he has refused any ransom money offered in this connection although some has possibly already been swallowed up by intermediaries; (3) assuming full responsibility for the safety and good treatment of 350 British and American prisoners at Mantua, of whom 150 are in the hospital and 200 on the southern outskirts; Wolff claims that these are all the British-American prisoners held in North Italy, since they had been currently transferred to Germany; (4) releasing to Switzerland, if he can be found, [...],[8] an Italian patriot working with CLNAI[9] and the British; his release is particularly desired by Parri; (5) facilitating as much as possible the return to North Italy of Italian officers presently held in Germany, who might be useful in the post-hostilities period.

In reference to Alexander Constantin von Neurath, the German Consul at Lugano [whose part in earlier peace feelers is described in my memoranda of 9 and 26 February[10]], Wolff will welcome von Neurath's help since he feels that von

---

6. Name deleted in the original.

7. Parri, who had been a leading figure in the anti-fascist movement since the early 1920s founded the resistance group Giustizia e Libertà in French exile. Since 1943 he had been one of the leading members of the military resistance against Hitler and Mussolini in Northern Italy; he became Italy's first postwar Prime Minister.

8. Name deleted in the original.

9. The Committee of National Liberation in Upper Italy was the coordinating body of the resistance in northern Italy.

10. Document [91].

Neurath has considerable influence on Kesselring. Wolff will invite von Neurath to join him in Italy on 10 March.

Wolff claims that Himmler knowns nothing of his present activites. He saw Himmler and Hitler early in February and advised them of the general hopelessness of the North Italy situation, but received no definite instructions from them.

The OSS representative has made no commitments, merely listening to Wolff's presentation and stating, with no refutation from Wolff, that unconditional surrender was the only possible course. The OSS representative comments that, if the results of the Wolff-Kesselring talks are favorable, this plan may present a unique opportunity to shorten the war, permit occupation of North Italy, possibly penetrate Austria under most favorable conditions, and possibly wreck German plans for establishment of a maquis.[11]

The OSS representative in Caserta has advised AFHQ [Allied Force Headquarters, Mediterranean] of the information transmitted by the OSS representative in Bern. General Alexander has outlined to Marshal [Sir Alan] Brooke the procedure which AFHQ proposes to follow, including a plan for two senior staff officers to go to Switzerland to meet with German representatives. Apparently Alexander has furnished this information to Brooke as a matter of courtesy and will go ahead on his initiative, although he will cooperate with Brooke if London wishes to send other people to join in the meeting. OSS has been directed to submit a plan to carry out all necessary steps, including arrangements for a Swiss meeting place, transportation to and from that place to the French-Swiss border, as well as transportation from the Annemasse airport or vicinity to French-Swiss border. In addition, OSS will be called upon to provide communications, clerical assistance (including interpreters), and all necessary safeguards for the security of operations. The OSS representative in Bern will select a safe meeting place, arrange transportation from Annemasse to and from that place, and issue appropriate instructions to secure and provide arrangements for meeting the party at the Annemasse airport and supervising arrangements to and from the French-Swiss border. The total number of the party is unknown at this time, but all plans are being made to include arrangements for 15 to 20 people. OSS is

---

11. This is a reference to Allied fears of a Nazi attempt to make a last stand in the Alpenfestung (Alpine Fortress).

withholding all these plans from the German representatives until directed by AFHQ to suggest a date for the meeting.[12]

> *Donovan*
> **William J. Donvoan**
> **Director**

Document 95a · 27 March 1945

Memorandum from OSS Director William J. Donovan to the Joint Chiefs of Staff: Approaches from Austrian and Bavarian Nazis[1]

TOP SECRET

Subject: Approaches from Austrian and Bavarian Nazis

The following information, transmitted by the OSS representative in Bern [Allen W. Dulles], summarizes approaches by Ernst Kaltenbrunner (Tab A), Chief of the Nazi Security and Police Service, and by Franz Xaver Ritter von Epp (Tab B),[2] *Reichsstatthalter* (Governor) of Bavaria.

---

12. In a handwritten message Donovan added that he was planning to go to Italy "to set up communications etc." if this "looks feasible." Donovan did not get personally involved, but Dulles and Schulze-Gaevernitz continued this operation, code named Sunrise in Switzerland and northern Italy. After Stalin became aware of these dealings, he lodged strong protest with Roosevelt and Churchill and demanded the participation of Soviet representatives in the negotiations. The affair led to a first major dispute between Washington and Moscow. After long delays caused by political as well as technical difficulties, Operation Sunrise ended with the separate surrender of the German forces in northern Italy on 29 April 1945, eight days before the general capitulation.

1. NA, RG 226, Entry 190, MF 1641, Roll 21, Frames 197–207.

2. Tables not printed.

Through two Emissaries, Kaltenbrunner reports the existence of an opposition group within the Austrian SS which is anxious to liquidate the Nazi Party in Austria and to arrange for the orderly transfer of administrative functions to the Western Powers. This group is apparently anxious to gain some immunity from the Allies by serving as a "transitional regime" instead of joining the Nazi die-hards in a last-ditch struggle in the German "redoubt."[3] The Kaltenbrunner group claims to have established contact with worker and Catholic opposition groups in Austria.

Von Epp, through his emissary, claims that he wishes to spare Bavaria from becoming a battlefield and, when Nazi controls break down, intends to assume executive power in Bavaria with the help of *Wehrkreis* [army district] commanders.

Certain striking similarities are apparent between these two approaches and those of Obergruppenfuehrer and *General der Waffen SS* Karl Wolff with respect to North Italy, reported in previous memoranda.[4] Whether these are indepen-dent, spontaneous efforts of dissident Nazis to save themselves, or whether Himmler is behind these moves and is, himself, preparing to desert the Nazi die-hards, remains an open question.

William J. Donovan
Director

Approaches from the Kaltenbrunner Group[5]

On 28 February the OSS representative in Bern [Allen W. Dulles] reported that he had been approached by an Austrian industrialist[6] with whom he had had previ-ous contacts. The Austrian declared that he for several years had been acquainted with Hoettel [Wilhelm Hoettl], a Viennese SS chief, who knew vaguely that he had indirect contacts with Americans in Switzerland. Prior to the industrialist's departure for Switzerland on 18 January, Hoettel informed him that Ernst Kaltenbrunner, Chief of the Security and Police Service, wished to see him.

The Austrian industrialist saw Kaltenbrunner, who told him that he, Kaltenbrunner, and Himmler were very anxious to end the war and as a first step were contemplating the liquidation of "war mongers" within the Nazi Party, espe-cially Martin Bormann, Deputy Leader of the Nazi Party.[7] Kaltenbrunner also said that he and Himmler were very anxious to establish contact with the British and Americans and planned to send a high SS official to Switzerland to speak for

---

3. See document [94].

4. This is a reference to Operation Sunrise. See documents [91], [93] and [94].

5. The information that follows summarizes five cables from OSS Bern that were forwarded to Donovan between 28 February and 24 March 1945.

6. This person could not be identified by name.

7. During the last months of the war, Himmler was being gradually displaced at the center of power around Hitler by Bormann and his clique.

them, if a contact could be established. Kaltenbrunner asked the Austrian industrialist to do what he could to establish such a contact.

The industrialist claimed that he had suggested to Kaltenbrunner that Alfred Potocki, brother of the former Polish Ambassador to Washington, should be allowed to go with him to Switzerland, since he felt that Potocki had good contacts with the British. According to the industrialist, Hoettel immediately arranged for an exit visa for Potocki, who expected to proceed first to Liechtenstein.[8] (Potocki apparently never arrived there.)

After further conversations with the industrialist, the OSS representative on 2 March reported that other good sources tended to support the industrialist's claim that Himmler, Kaltenbrunner, and certain other high SS officials might abandon the die-hard Nazi fanatics like Hitler and Bormann, and (instead of joining them in the German "redoubt") might try to gain some immunity by serving as a "transitional regime".

(The OSS representative commented that so long as such Nazi leaders as Himmler and Kaltenbrunner believe that it might be possible to obtain some immunity from the Allies, an opportunity may be offered to drive a wedge into Nazi leadership and thereby reduce the effectiveness of German "redoubt" plans. The representative said that through indirect channels he was arranging for Hoettel to come to the Swiss frontier where a trustworthy intermediary would see him.)

On 15 March the OSS representative reported that Hoettel had told the intermediary that the SS contained a so-called Austrian opposition represented by Kaltenbrunner, Hermann Neubacher (the former Plenipotentiary to the Balkans), and himself.

This opposition group, Hoettel declared, had been responsible for saving many people from SS persecution. Hoettel also said that he was responsible for the transfer of Karl Seitz (the former Lord Mayor of Vienna) from a concentration camp in Silesia to Bavaria and now hoped shortly to free Seitz. Hoettel said that previous to his present assignment (apparently as Kaltenbrunner's right-hand man in Vienna) he had acted for Kaltenbrunner in supervising the activities of Edmund Weesenmeyer, the German Plenipotentiary in Hungary. He added that he had recently been assigned by Kaltenbrunner to establish contact with opposition groups in Austria.

On 24 March the OSS representative reported that Hoettel had made a second trip to Switzerland and declared that the majority of the Austrian SS, most of whom are Austrian nationals, wish to liquidate the Nazi Party and to arrange for an orderly transfer of administrative functions to the Western Powers. This plan, Hoettel declared, would involve the elimination of those SS elements favoring a continuation of the war, especially the supporters of Bormann and a number of the Gauleiters.

---

8. I.e., the neutral Alpine republic situated between Austria and Switzerland.

(The OSS representative, on 24 March, also reported that the Austrian industrialist, who had seen Kaltenbrunner between Hoettel's first and second trips, had declared that Hoettel's second trip was made at Kaltenbrunner's special request. The industrialist supported Hoettel's statements.)

Hoettel declared that Kaltenbrunner had assigned him to contact Austrian opposition groups in order to support anti-Communist elements. Hoettel said he was selected for this task because he is a Catholic and because his father is a Social Democratic school reformer.[9]

[...]

Hoettel said his task had been facilitated by the anti-Communist leanings of Austrian workers. Hoettel claimed that he had established contact with anti-Nazi worker leaders in Steiermark, Wiener Neustadt and Vienna, and with Catholic opposition groups. He cited the name of a Catholic leader, which already had been supplied the OSS by representatives of the Provisional Austrian National Committee (POEN),[10] but claimed that he knew other opposition leaders only by their cover names.

[OSS Washington Comment. POEN representatives reported to the OSS representative in Paris recently that they had established contact with some of the higher SS officers in Vienna.]

Hoettel promised to return to Switzerland with certain of these opposition leaders, and hinted that he might even bring out the former Lord Mayor, Seitz, as well as representatives of the workers and Catholic opposition.[11]

(In September 1944, the OSS representative reported that Glaise-Horstenau had, following his removal from his liaison post, sent a message to the representative indicating his desire to work with the Allies for the liberation of Austria.[12] The OSS representative then commented that Glaise-Horstenau apparently wished, through his friends in Army circles, to open to the Western Allies the route to Vienna via Zagreb in the hope of avoiding a Soviet occupation of the Austrian capital.) [...]

---

9. Karl Hoettl, a teacher for many years until 1934, was an outspoken anti-Nazi serving on the Vienna board of education.

10. This is a reference to the resistance circle around Fritz Molden that was established in Vienna in late 1944. Molden, who was in contact with OSS Bern, wished Austria to be treated as an independent state and spared occupation as a conquered enemy after the war

11. Hoettl reappeared in Switzerland on 9 April and reported that his relations with Kaltenbrunner had become rather strained. By that time, Kaltenbrunner had been drawn into the Hitler camp and was spending considerable time with the Führer who had offered him von Ribbentrop's post as Foreign Minister. At the Nuremberg Trials, Kaltenbrunner was condemned to death and later executed.

12. Lieutenant-General Edmund Glaise von Horstenau had been the former Liaison Officer for the German Army with the Croatian Government.

With regard to the general situation, Hoettel declared that the Nazis expect and wish to exploit a wave of anti-Communism in the Balkan area. For this reason, he said, despite the pressure on other fronts, SS divisions had been kept on the Lake Balaton front in Hungary, and von Weich's army held relatively inactive in Croatia. Hoettel said that the Alpine "redoubt" would be finished and stocked in about three months. The *Steyrwerke,* he said, is already underground, producing such defensive weapons as *Panzer Faeuste* [anti-tank grenade launchers]. The Nazis intend to take Wehrmacht as well as SS units into the "redoubt", he added, and even the families of the troops.

With respect to the situation within the Nazi Party, Hoettel said that the split between the western and eastern oriented groups was becoming increasingly apparent. Robert Ley and his followers in the Labor Front, plus Bormann and many of the Gauleiters, he declared, belong to the Eastern orientation, while Kaltenbrunner and his followers belong to the western-oriented group. Hoettel predicted a kind of Tauroggen movement[13] in which the Western Front would be opened, the troops would be marched towards the East to fight as free corps bands, while the government of Germany would be left to the Western Allies.

(The OSS representative comments that there are other indications that certain SS elements are trying to save themselves by turning to the West, by ignoring or even favoring local anti-Nazi movements, and by preparing to avoid a last ditch "redoubt" struggle with the die-hards. The representative points to the similarity of these activities inspired by Kaltenbrunner, efforts by Obergruppenfuehrer and General der Waffen SS Karl Wolff to arrange a surrender in North Italy, and a recent approach by von Epp with respect to Bavaria, summarized in Tab B.)[14]

Approaches from von Epp[15]

On 23 March, the OSS representative in Bern reported that Heinz Adolf Heintze of the German Foreign Office arrived in Switzerland with a message from Franz Xaver Ritter von Epp, Lieutenant-General, retired, the *Reichsstatthalter* (Governor) of Bavaria. Von Epp declares that, although he has served the Nazis, as an old-school Bavarian officer he wishes to spare Bavaria from becoming a battleground. When central Nazi government controls break down, he intends to assume executive power in Bavaria, aided by several *Wehrkreis* [army unit] commanders in charge of Bavarian reserve units. The most energetic of these, he says, is General Kriebel, commanding *Wehrkreis* VII. Von Epp and these *Wehrkreis* commanders believe that the troops under their command would follow orders to take action against Himmler and the SS.

---

13. On the Tauroggen Convention see document [31].
14. For the Epp approaches see documents [95b] and [98].
15. The following is a summary of Bern cables dated 23 and 26 March 1945.

Von Epp declares that he has acquainted Cardinal Faulhaber and other Bavarian Catholic leaders with his plans and had tried to contact the Vatican through Faulhaber. This contact could not be safely established, he claims, because the Gestapo is represented in the Cardinal's entourage. Von Epp apparently asked his emissary, Heintze, to find out whether his appearance at the head of a Bavarian anti-Hitler movement would tend to prejudice the movement in Allied eyes, in view of his own Nazi background and the fact that he had remained in office under Hitler.

(The OSS representative comments that this group may not have sufficient energy and determination to carry through its plans.)

[OSS Washington Comment: Von Epp, now 76, has been a confirmed Nazi ever since he joined the Party in 1923. He was instrumental in Hitler's rise to power and delivered Bavaria to Hitler on 9 March 1933. Following World War I, he founded the Epp Free Corps and put down the revolt in the Ruhr in 1919–20, then returned to the German Army until his retirement in 1923. He became *Reichskommissar* for Bavaria in March 1933 and was made *Reichsstatthalter* the following month. In recent years he actually has been subordinate in power to the *Gauleiter*. He is anti-Communist and probably pro-monarchist at the present time.]

Document 95b · 9 April 1945

Memorandum from OSS Assistant Director G. Edward Buxton to President Franklin D. Roosevelt: Bavarian Surrender Proposals[1]

TOP SECRET

Memorandum for the President

The following information, transmitted by the OSS representative in Bern, is a sequel to a memorandum dated 27 March concerning approaches via Heinz Heintze of the German Foreign Office, from a Bavarian Nazi group headed by Franz Xaver Ritter von Epp, the *Reichsstatthalter* (Governor) of Bavaria:

A trusted messenger who is working with Heintze returned to Switzerland on 6 April from Munich, where he made contact with the von Epp group. Source confirms that von Epp and several other high-ranking officers are prepared to do everything within their power to cut short warfare in Bavaria, and, if possible, to prevent unnecessary destruction in Bavaria, and, if possible, to prevent establishment of the "redoubt". Among those working with von Epp are General Karl Kriebel, commanding *Wehrkreis* VIII, Munich; Generalleutnant (Lw) [Lieutenant-General, Air Force] Wolfgang Vorwald, commandant of *Luftgau* VIIIl, Munich, who controls the ground personnel of the large airfields in the Munich area (including Schleissheim and Riehm) and at the Reichenhall airdrome near Salzburg; and Obergruppenfuehrer [Lieutenant-General] Benno Martin, Higher SS and Police Leader for *Wehrkreis* XIII, Nuremberg. The group also includes several younger officers and government officials.

---

1. Roosevelt Library, Hyde Park, F. D. Roosevelt Papers. President's Secretary's Files, Box 171, Folder OSS/April 1945. Included with these documents were some handwritten notes by the President's private secretary Grace G. Tully written some four weeks after Roosevelt's death. Tully explained she had found the Epp material in FDR's basket and briefcase. As far as Tully remembered, no action had been taken on any of these matters. She assumed "the President was following them to discuss with various people and take action on them at the proper time."

The messenger reports that the group is prepared immediately to receive a radio operator [operational details are here omitted].

(The OSS representative comments that while the von Epp group may not be able to take effective action against the SS in Bavaria, the dropping of a radio operator appears worth the gamble and should at least produce useful military information.)[2]

G. Edward Buxton
Acting Director

Document 96 · 31 March 1945

Memorandum from Colonel Edward W. Gamble Jr. (OSS Washington) to General Dwight D. Eisenhower: Special Sabotage Operations Against Nazi and Gestapo Personnel[1]

SECRET

Subject: Special Sabotage Operations Against Nazi and Gestapo Personnel

1. Reference is made to SHAEF Directive, 29 Jan 45, subject, "OSS (SO) and SOE Activity in Germany," (SHAEF/17240/13/Ops(C)).[2]

2. Under SHAEF Directive, in reference above, OSS (SO) is ordered to conduct activities to hasten the surrender or disintegration of the German armed forces by

---

2. On 28 April 1945, Governor Franz Xaver Ritter von Epp was arrested by the Bavarian Freedom Movement under Captain Gerngroß who brought him to the studio of Radio Munich. When placed before the microphone and told to broadcast a surrender statement to the Allies, von Epp refused. For the Bavarian Freedom Movement see document [98].

1. NA, RG 226, Entry 148, Box 122, Folder 2113.

2. Not printed.

subversive activities in Germany, directed towards bringing about the downfall of Germany from within. In order to accomplish this purpose, it is believed that the following program of special sabotage operations against Nazi and Gestapo personnel will be the most effective means at this stage of the war.

3. It will be our objective[3] to concentrate our primary efforts on the single mission of assassination of high-ranking members of the Nazi Party and of the Gestapo, using approximately 100 German nationals, recruited from the CALPO organization.[4] These will be commanded by American officers and provided with the necessary communications.

4. In order to utilize the number of operational personnel to the maximum, their efforts will be concentrated in an area of operations generally north of the reduit. (See map attached[5]). Agents will be dispatched to local points near known concentrations of Nazi or Gestapo officials. Personnel targets will be generally fixed on any person with or equalling the rank of Major and higher, in the Nazi Party, with preference to *Schutz Staffel* [SS] and *Sturm Abteilung* [SA], and in the *Polizei* [Police], with preference to *Sicherheits Dienst* [Security Service], *Geheime Staatspolizei* [Gestapo] and *Kriminal Polizei* [Criminal Investigation].

5. By a coordinated effort in eliminating Nazi and Gestapo officials, it is believed that the German effort will be weakened from within, particularly as to the following factors:

a) Continuing activities in the area contemplated would tend to undermine the fear complex of the *Wehrmacht, Volkssturm,*[6] and the populace in general, concerning the invincible strength of the Party and the Gestapo.

b) The organized killings should reduce the effectiveness of the operations of the Nazi Party and the Gestapo, because of the measures they will have to take to protect themselves.

c) As news of these activities is spread, similar acts on the part of those local Germans opposed to the Nazis will be encouraged.

6. It is requested that the above program for special sabotage operations against Nazi and Gestapo personnel by OSS (SO) be approved.

Edward W. Gamble, Jr.
Colonel—G.S.C.
Deputy

---

3. I.e., the objective of the OSS Special Operations agents attached to U.S. army units.
4. See in particular documents [82] and [84].
5. Not printed.
6. I.e., the last-minute call to arms of the whole male population by the Nazis.

Document 97a · 15–30 April 1945

Field Report by the OSS Morale Operations Branch: Comebacks on Black Newspaper *Das Neue Deutschland*[1]

SECRET

Comebacks on *Das Neue Deutschland.*
Excerpt from MO/Mediterranean Field Report
of 15–30 April 1945

Effectiveness of MO [Morale Operations]

a) Early returns from outlying precincts indicated that MO had scored a much greater success than had been dreamed of in its operations in the Mediterranean Theater.

b) As hordes of prisoners came in,[2] it was possible to gain a first good glimpse of the results of the past year's operations, although complete surveys have been quite impossible because of the enormous masses of troops to be interrogated. Fragmentary interrogations, however, showed that surprisingly large numbers of Germans knew about DND [*Das Neue Deutschland;* The New Germany], and some of them even claimed to be active "freedom fighters" for DND.

For instance, Feldwebel Milch while taking a course at Swinemuende on the Baltic in July 1944, met a soldier by the name of Richard Meyer. They became very friendly and Meyer confided to Milch that he was a member of the German underground *Das Neue Deutschland*. He claimed to be a very active member, and urged Milch to join the movement, but before Milch had made up his mind, he

---

1. NA, RG 226, Entry 99, Box 69, Folder 306. The following is an excerpt from the Mediterranean Field Report of the OSS. On the effectiveness of the *Das Neue Deutschland* newspaper see also document [97b], which follows.

2. In early April 1945 the Allied Armies had started their final offensive in northern Italy.

was transferred. They kept up a regular mail correspondence, and Meyer often mentioned the active underground he was doing for DND.

Another prisoner, Uffz. [Sgt.] Oscar Lehmann, 37, from Vienna, a shoe designer 42nd Jaeger Div. [Infantry Division], stated he had often heard about this DND movement while talking with civilian friends in Vienna. He had a copy of the paper with him in his pocket. He stated his copy of the newspaper had been read by many of his friends, that other copies were in great demand, but almost impossible to obtain.

...[3]

But the outstanding prisoner who came to light was Feldwebel Richard Neuendorfer, mentioned above,[4] who claimed he is still a good Nazi. He told the following story: While still a member of the 26th Panzer Div. [Division] in February two men in his platoon received copies of DND *through* the mail postmarked Berlin. Neuendorfer immediately notified his commanding officer, who in turn informed 1-C (Intelligence) of the 26th Panzer Div. The two men in question were arrested and copies of DND were found in their belongings including leaflets. Neuendorfer remembers distinctly one signed "Bund Deutscher Grenadier[e]". Thereupon other soldiers in the division were searched. The two men were forced to stand a court martial. Neuendorfer attempted to impress interrogators that he was convinced, after seeing so much evidence, that there actually was an underground publishing propaganda within the Reich, after first believing that it was enemy propaganda. This testimony is the first proof MO has had of the success of its Cornflakes operation which consisted of dropping mailbags filled with self-addressed stamped envelopes alongside shot-up trains in the Reich. It is reasonable to assume that if two such letters dropped in Austria found their way through the German mail system to Berlin, and then clear down to troops on the Italian front, and were discovered in a first cursory interrogation, that many more of the letters likewise reached the target and were successfully sent through the Nazi's own mail system. These two letters are an example of MO propaganda working to perfection—(1) The recipients were convinced of the genuineness of the propaganda, and (2) Disruption of the Wehrmacht, resulting in official investigations and courts-martial.

...[5]

---

3. The omitted passage lists numerous similar statements by German prisoners of war.

4. Feldwebel [Technical Sergeant] Richard Neuendorfer, 45, from Hamburg, stated he saw DND in Bologna in February 1945.

5. The following passages give further examples of the effectiveness of MO propaganda, including reports obtained not only from POWs but also from OSS field teams that had been overrun by the advancing armies.

Document 97b · 9 July 1945

Report by Robert M. Allen
(OSS Morale Operations Branch):
Evidence of the Effectiveness of
Das Neue Deutschland [1]

SECRET

Subject: MO Interrogations
of German PWs, May and June 1945

Evidence of Effectiveness of DND

1. The following statistics on the effectiveness of MO propaganda are based upon interrogations by MO personnel of German PWs during May and June 1945. [...] Total number of prisoners questioned was 5698.[2] [...] Most of the PWs received DND from their comrades or from civilians (many of them women). Nineteen claimed to have received DND by mail. The Austrian paper was delivered by mail in three cases. Others found the material in railroad stations, waiting rooms, busses, trains, etc. One stated that he had seen DND being thrown from a moving military vehicle. Of the 3050 cooperative PWs the percentage runs as follows: 44.9% knew of DND, 14% had read it. 27% knew about the Austrian newspaper, 9.3% had read it. 48.8% knew about *Frontpost*,[3] 46.9% had read it. After including

---

1. NA, RG 226, Entry 99, Box 69, Folder 306. This report was sent to Colonel K. D. Mann, Chief of the Morale Operations Branch.

2. These persons included internees at Leghorn camp and German hospital personnel and patients at Mantova, Italy.

3. Another subversive newspaper produced by the OSS Morale Operations Branch. The vast majority of *Frontpost* information was correct, and only a small portion was designed to delude the Germans.

those who refused to answer questions pertaining to this and other subjects, in considering the total of 5698 we get the following percentages: 23.9% knew of DND; 7.6% read it. 14.4% knew the Austrian paper, 5% read it. 26.6% were familiar with *Frontpost,* 25% read it. Of the 104 questionnaires that were brought back, 52 contained no information of interest to MO, X–2, or R&A. The following is perhaps of interest to MO: only one man said that the effect of the propaganda material mentioned in the questionaires was sometimes doubtful. Many answered the question "What impression did this material have on you?" in the following way:

"Good."

"Very good."

"It was believable."

"It stimulated distrust of the German newspapers and radio to the point that we didn't believe the papers and radio any more."

"The papers and leaflets gave us hope that we will be able to live as free Germans again when the Hitler system has collapsed."

...[4]

Robert M. Allen
1st Lieut., TC, MO Branch

---

4. In the omitted passages many similar samples are given.

Document 98 · June 1945

Report by the OSS Morale Operations Branch: Black Radio *Capricorn*[1]

SECRET

Black Radio "Capricorn"

Situation

To exploit collapsing state of the *Wehrmacht* on all fronts as well as tottering condition on German home-front, MO/ETO joined SHAEF in all out psychological warfare campaign to induce Germans to accept unconditional surrender.

Objective

To induce German soldiers and civilians to give up losing fight leading them surely to total annihilation.

Implementation

Daily short and medium-wave programs of 10 minute duration repeated at various times.

Operations

A speaker, "Hagedorn", broadcasting inside military information, purporting to represent a German Underground movement, exhorts his listeners to (1) overthrow immediately Hitlerism, Germany's arch enemy. (2) submit to Allied control of Germany, to enable the nation to recover from its 12 year old ordeal. (3) accept unconditional surrender as only way to avoid complete annihilation.

---

1. NA, RG 226, Entry 139, Box 11, Folder 1569.

Swedish newspaper, *Svenska Dagbladet* reported Program most effective of all "German Underground" activities.

Personnel

3 Officers, 8 Enlisted Men, 8 Civilians.

Equipment

100 KW [Kilowatt] daytime transmission; 7 1/2 KW evening transmission, over powerful British Station.

On 10 February [1945], Lieutenant John Reinhardt, USNR, submitted a black radio project, the code name for which was "Capricorn" to the chief of the MO Branch ETO, Lt. Colonel John S. Roller, AC. Earlier in that same month of February, the MO Branch had submitted another black radio project, called "Matchbox"[2] to General Robert A. McClure of Psychological Warfare Division-SHAEF and to OSS Washington for clearance. Since the latter named project called for a direct peace appeal in English and German, clearance at high levels was considered doubtful and "Capricorn", while not as inflammable as "Matchbox", was considered an alternative for immediate radio action on the part of MO. [...]

Objective

The objective of "Capricorn" was to undermine further German continuance of the war by evidence of the existence of a group of underground patriots referring to themselves as the "*Neue Deutschland Partei*" from within Germany addressing the German people, informing both of their post war plans for a healthy and useful Germany.

Three Themes of Hagedorn

1. Condemnation of Naziism As the Greatest Enemy of the German Nation. That Hitlerism was responsible for Germany's misery; that the Nazi leaders, knowing full well that they were doomed, had decided to drag all Germany down with them using every means at their disposal. All patriotic Germans must disassociate themselves from the Nazi criminals by their actions and help in bringing them to trial.

2. End the War Before Everything Is Lost. The German audience was told to refuse evacuation orders. It was explained that it was the most devilish Nazi plan to delay an East-West juncture of the enemy by compressing the German popula-

---

2. See documents [81a] and [81b].

tion into a writing wall of human flesh without regard for their sufferings. The refrain continued to the German listening audience to disobey the Nazi orders; refuse to fight and die for a criminal cause; revolt openly against the Nazi executioners.

3. Reconstruction of a New Germany. The audience was warned that after the actual cessation of hostilities Germany would have to face problems that must be solved if she were to survive.

Transmission

The transmission of the program was by short wave on the British facilities at MB [Mutual Broadcasting], which have been previously mentioned in the story of *Soldatensender*.[3]

Time of Transmission

Commencing on 26 February 1945 with two days of teaser announcements, the program continued daily until 28 April 1945 from 8:15 A.M. to 8:15 P.M. every hour a quarter after the hour, the program enduring from ten to fifteen minutes.

Personnel

The personnel engaged on the production of Hagedorn were headed by Lieutenant John Reinhardt, USNR, who then replaced Mr. F. C. Oechsner as Editorial Chief of the MO Branch. Others were:

Announcers: Mr. Egon Jamieson; Mr. Douglas Bagier; Lt. John Reinhardt, USNR

The Voice: Mr. Stephan Schnable [Schnabel]

Intelligence: PFC Carl Selby; PFC Rudi Weiss; Mr. Howard Becker; Mr. Heinz Peters

Chief Writer: Mr. Hans Rehfish

Reaction

This independently operated radio program, commencing on 26 February 1945, can claim positive reaction to one of its instructions for action to the German people to hasten the day of peace.

---

3. I.e., the British black radio station Soldatensender Calais.

On 21 March 1945, "Hagedorn", after supporting the SHAEF Directives signed by General Eisenhower to the German population of the industrial areas that they should evacuate before the Allied offensive (later changed), directed that those Germans living in towns and villages outside of the industrial areas who did *not* have to be evacuated right away:

"Hang a piece of white material, any white rag, out of your window. That would not be an actual action, but at least it would result in everybody knowing what his neighbor feels about the situation. It would overnight establish contact between millions of isolated fellow-Germans who before did not dare to face each other. As innocent, as harmless as this would look, it would be a millionfold demonstration for immediate peace. What could the police, the Party do against it! Nothing. Nothing whatsoever. ...

"Away with the Swastika banner, the symbol of Death!
"Hoist the white flag of peace!"

Eighth and Ninth Air Force fighter pilots, returning from missions over Germany, reported sections of Germany and particularly those regions skirting the densely populated *Rhineland* as resembling a "sea of white flags." This intelligence showed direct results of "Hagedorn's" initial plea for White Action.

A report, compiled by Messrs. Howard Becker and Edmund Reiss, and PFC Rudi Weiss in Munich on 15 June 1945 reveals a satisfactory reaction to the MO radio operation known as Hagedorn. Their intelligence was gained through interrogating three German officers of the Wehrmacht,[4] who formed the leader nucleus of an anti-Nazi movement in Bavaria known as the FAB (*Freiheitsaktion Bayerns*—Freedom and Reconstruction Action in Bavaria).[5] This report may be found in full in the MO Reports office in Washington, but the pertinent intelligence on listener reaction in Germany to the independent MO radio operation known as Hagedorn follows:

"Did we hear Volkssender Drei [Peoples Radio Three]? No, we didn't. But we did hear a station called Hagedorn, or a man who broadcast under the name of Hagedorn. Do you know who he could have been? He must be a remarkable person. Oh, you are looking for him yourselves in order to see of what service he can be in the new Germany? I do hope you find him. Hagedorn wasn't widely heard, for the waveband was hard to get, but he deeply influenced those who did hear him. Many times

---

4. The OSS interrogators were Calhoun Ancrum and John Weitz.

5. This anti-Nazi resistance movement was established during the last weeks of the war. Under its leader, Captain Rupprecht Gerngroß, the group was able to seize a Munich radio station on the night of 28/29 April 1945. In spite of initial success, several members of the FAB [Freiheitsaktion Bayerns] were caught and shot by the Gestapo. The *New York Times* promptly reported this incident in its Sunday edition of 29 April.

we said to each other, "What Hagedorn says is exactly what we think." Examples? Why, along in February, I think it was—Hagedorn was first heard by us towards the end of February—and we listened until Hagedorn said, "The time for revolutionary action has not yet come." He was right; if we hadn't waited our effort would have been a complete failure. (The report deals in part with a putsch that was brought about in Munich by the FAB against the Wehrmacht). Finally, he said that the time was ripe. He also expressed our ideas when he said, "Don't try to make a putsch that depends on the German generals; the revolt must come from the people." We didn't want one of these officers' affairs like July 20th; even if that had succeeded you would still have been confronted by a closeknit *Wehrmacht* bargaining to save the officers' caste. Yes, here was a parallel between our ideas and those of Hagedorn. When you finally discover who he was, please let us know; he must be a remarkable person."

[...]

Document 99 · June 1945

Memorandum from OSS Director
William J. Donovan to the Joint Chiefs of Staff:
OSS Penetration of Germany[1]

Memorandum of Information for the
Joint U.S. Chiefs of Staff

Subject: OSS Penetration of Germany

1. During the eight months preceding the unconditional surrender more than 100 OSS intelligence missions penetrated into Germany to obtain information on the enemy's situation and movements, on hidden factories and storage dumps, on the effectiveness of Allied bombings, on the treatment of Allied prisoners-of-war, and on the strength of Nazi control over the civil population.[2] Information from these missions reached Allied military headquarters promptly and in a steady stream throughout the rapid advances in March and April and into the last weeks of crumbling Nazi resistance.

2. The activities of these missions were directed and coordinated from the principal OSS headquarters in England, France, and Italy, in cooperation with OSS offices in Switzerland and Sweden and the OSS units in Brussels, Belgium, and Endhoven [Eindhoven], Holland. In addition there were OSS detachments on the staffs of the Sixth and Twelfth Army Groups, the First, Third, Seventh and Ninth Armies and the 18th Airborne Corps of the First Allied Airborne Army. All were in radio contact with each other to assure quick and immediate dissemination of intelligence.

---

1. Archives of the Army War College, Fort Carlisle, Pa., William J. Donovan Papers, Box 67A, File 261.

2. For the planning and early stages of this program see documents [1], [11] and [33]. Most of these OSS missions, the first of which was carried out on 2 September 1944, consisted of two agents. The majority of the agents entered the Reich during the last few months of the war, and several of them were dispatched via parachute. In contrast to similar operations in France that were jointly carried out with the British (SOE), all missions to Germany were launched by the OSS alone. SOE had feared that all agents would be killed quickly. This was, however, not the case.

3. Long-range penetration was begun in September 1944 when an intelligence agent was parachuted into the Ruhr area where he successfully made contact with Socialist anti-Nazi elements.[3] The first operative to reach Berlin proper crossed through the lines of the Western front in November and in February had established himself within the German *Sicherheitsdienst*. A team dispatched from Italy was parachuted into southern Germany in November. Entry of operatives across the Swiss border was initiated in December. Three missions dispatched from Sweden were by February operating successfully in Hamburg, Berlin and Leipzig. Also in February another mission from Italy was parachuted into Austria near Innsbruck to report on traffic through the Brenner Pass. Aside from reporting intelligence these missions served as pathfinders for further penetrations.

4. Additional intelligence was obtained through contacts with potential anti-Nazi groups. Austrian resistance centers supplied information on German installations in Austria as well as on defenses of the Nazi "Redoubt" area. Operatives dispatched from Sweden joined with secret German anti-Nazi nuclei among labor union men.

5. Shorter-range intelligence penetrations were carried on by the OSS detachments with the Armies. "Tourist" agents were infiltrated through the German lines on two-or-three-day missions to gather information on the enemy's tactical situation and report to OSS officers on their return. In January the intensified German counter-activity and the heavy use of land mines made it preferable to parachute the "tourists" ahead of the lines. The Seventh Army officially commended OSS for the timely and accurate intelligence received from such sources.

6. After the crossing of the Rhine[4] high-frequency ground-to-air radio-telephone was used to supplement coded wireless-telegraphy for communication with agents. Radio-telephone not only permitted greater speed in reporting intelligence but also afforded the agents less danger of radio detection. Agents parachuted deep into southern and central Germany were frequently in daily radio-telephone communications with OSS officers in specially equipped American bombers on clandestine missions. The effectiveness of this system was proven in March when an agent urged immediate bombardment of a railroad station through which heavy enemy traffic was passing. The bombardment took place the next day and by nightfall the agent's eye witness account of the damage was received at Air Force Headquarters. This action drew a commendation from the Eighth Air Force.

7. By mid-April, when organized resistance along the central southern German front began to disintegrate, the OSS penetration program was adopted to permit

---

3. The name of this agent was Jupp Kappius. With the help of his wife, Änne, who had entered Germany in the disguise of a nurse, Kappius was able to instigate acts of sabotage among former trade unionists in the *Ruhr* area.

4. In early March 1945.

last-minute changes whereby agents could be prepared on very short notice to be parachuted many miles deeper inside Germany than originally planned. In this manner OSS kept pace with the speed of the Allied advance and continued until the surrender[5] to intensify reliable first-hand intelligence coverage of areas still in enemy hands by newly dispatched "tourist" agents.

8. In addition to agents reporting by radio, "sleeper" teams were dispatched into enemy territory to "lie low," observe local military and political conditions, and upon being overrun to report directly to Allied intelligence and civil affairs officers. Other such teams were assigned to observe atrocities, prisoner of war camps, and Nazi attempts to go underground.

9. Over 30 intelligence operatives were by 1 May successfully installed in the German "Redoubt" area, in preparation for extensive reporting on that region had the Germans sought to make a last stand in the Austrian Alps. Further reports on movements of German units continued to be received even after the official unconditional surrender became effective. They provided useful information on enemy troops preparing for surrender, on war criminals seeking to escape or hide, and on caches of weapons, food, material and Nazi loot.

WJD

Document 100 · June 1945

Memorandum by OSS Wiesbaden (Germany): Views of a Group of Reliable and Democratic Germans[1]

[...]

This report is based upon a trip taken through Germany between the above dates,[2] covering as principal points Cologne [Köln], Bochum, Dortmund, Hannover, Gottingen [Göttingen], Kassel, Frankfurt [Frankfurt am Main], and Freiburg in Bresgau [Freiburg im Breisgau]. It was made in the company of the

---

5. On 8 May 1945.

1. NA, RG 226, Entry 125, Box 11.

2. The information given in this report was gathered in Germany in the period between 5 and 13 June 1945. The source, whose code number was 399, could not be identified. It was, however, considered by the OSS to be especially reliable.

leader of a German Socialist resistance group with membership in workers', trade union and intellectual circles, and there was opportunity at each of the cities named (and at some other points) to talk to a representative group. It must be borne in mind that the views here expressed are a reflection of the views of persons nearly all of whom had been for a time in prison or concentration camps, had been trailed by the Gestapo and are deeply pro-Allied and anti-Nazi, and that they cannot therefore be taken as typical of present-day German opinion.

1) Background

It need not be amplified, but should not be forgotten, that the anti-Nazi resistance in Germany operated in the latter months of the war and the first days of the occupation under entirely abnormal conditions. Lack of transport, inadequate communications, and a bad food situation were added to the always existent work of the Gestapo as real hindrances to effective action. Time and again we were told of efforts to build groups which succeeded or were about to succeed when an effective bombardment would kill some of the troop, force factories to move and take away others, and disrupt existing communications between those remaining with the necessary result that they were compelled to begin once more. The almost complete absence of transport in the first weeks of the occupation delayed (though it did not prevent) normal political and trade union developments. Preoccupation with getting food, and the difficulty of accomplishing any task in completely ruined and smashed cities, the frequent forced movings or evictions, are the background upon which any developments must be projected.

2) Political Trends

a. *Socialist:* The Socialist and Social Democratic opposition in Germany achieved only the slightest results before the occupation. Most of those with whom we spoke were apologetic that this should have been true, while recognizing the fact. They attributed this to the following factors:

Terror: Each person had, expectably, his personal account of brushes with the Gestapo, of concentration camps, of prison, of beatings and of questionings, and gave this the greatest weight in explaining their inactivity. We were told of several groups which had made substantial progress in getting together a nucleus of resistant Germans which were broken up through the Gestapo counter-espionage services; the remaining members were then faced with the problem of starting again under more dangerous circumstances. That in many cases they did is a tribute to their courage; many of them made efforts over a period of ten years or more and were forced to several new beginnings.

Lack of Direction: The absence of clear and regular contacts with the allies (or with the outside world) made most anti-Nazi efforts seem pointless and the atomization of resistance which was the result of Gestapo activity prevented the growth of any clear lines or plans.[3] While the persons with whom we talked had worked actively, directly or indirectly, for the Allies, they recognized that among many oppositional elements acts of isolated sabotage, attacks upon Nazi personalities and similar plans were thought to involve a personal hazard with no chance of equivalent contribution to the anti-Nazi cause; the Nazi system of exacting retribution from families of the guilty led many to feel that they were not alone risking their own lives (as they were in many cases willing to do) but the lives of other innocents as well, without their consent. [...]

Leadership: Many of those with whom we spoke felt that the same inertia and bureaucracy which had prevented decisive action against Hitler in 1932 or 1933 (contrary to the behavior of the Austrian Socialists)[4] had operated to dampen resistance during the period of Hitler rule; the same persons, unequipped for decisive action, remained the leaders. The passage of years further weakened their spirit of resistance; their inability to get at the younger workers because of the Gestapo and mobilization prevented the rise of a new leadership. The best and most active were almost without exception cleared out by the Gestapo or other Nazi units, by killing, imprisonment or such close observation that any action was unthinkable.

Lack of Unity: There was no apparent effort to form a united front of resistance, apparently again out of fear of the Gestapo; in only one town (Hannover) had our contacts been approached by the July 20 group and then very late while there was no longer time to organize any active assistance. Each political party continued its efforts to organize a resistance independent of all others, and there was no trace of contacts (except on a personal level) between members of the right resistance, church groups, the left resistance or the trade unions. In general, the attitude toward July 20 was that it was "putschist", condemned to failure from the beginning.

As far as could be observed, the Socialist resistance succeeded only in maintaining alive a small circle of friends, opposed to the regime, and in supplying some intelligence of use to the Allies. Upon occupation by Allied troops of their localities, they presented themselves to the authorities and were accepted for important posts in the government. Since that time they have been engaged principally in the duties assigned them by MG [Military Government] but have also done preparatory work for the reestablishment of the trade unions and of a Socialist party. In general, their views may be summarized as follows:

1. They feel that the old Social Democratic Party was too bureaucratic, and its mistakes too glaring, to warrant its revival. They look forward to the founding of a new Socialist party which will find its leadership among younger elements and

---

3. The same diagnosis had been delivered by R&A in September 1943, see document [22].

4. In 1934 in Austria, Social Democrats had shown open resistance against the Dollfuß regime and participated in street fights in Vienna and other cities.

work toward an independent regime through Allied military government which will be socialist and democratic. They feel that this end can only be attained if they show the ability to organize the German people on non-nationalist lines (for this reason they fear the influence of the German Nationalists—even those who were non-Nazi—since they fear a new German militarism through them) through friendly co-operation with the Allied services.

2. They are determined to do everything in their power to root out all vestiges of Nazism; they are timid about taking practical steps (other than supplying information to Allied services) since they have not yet assured themselves how far they may safely go in this direction without coming in conflict with MG. To date their activity has been limited to the removal of Nazi signs and some harrassment of known Nazis remaining in office.

3. They feel that the trade union movement should be rebuilt from the bottom upwards, basing itself on the younger workers now in the factories [...] and without regard to political orientation. [...]

4. They partially understand, but regret, the MG rules which limit their activity. These are principally those limiting meetings to five persons, prohibitions against the distribution of leaflets and other printed matter and limitations on movement within occupied areas. [...]

5. They fear the remaining and potential power of the Nazis; in several cities they reported that, were complete freedom of action allowed, the Nazis would still be in power, or would shortly win it back. They attribute this not to the number of the Nazis (their estimates of those whom they would describe as true Nazis were surprisingly low, averaging about 1 in 50–100 of the adult population) but to the apathy of the population and the absence of an effective opposition. It was their opinion that the Nazis would become steadily more discredited in the eyes of the population as the stories of the terror in Germany came out through concentration camp inmates, now being released and repeating their stories throughout Germany, as returning soldiers reported what they had seen in Greece, France, Norway, and the other Nazi occupied countries, and as Allied propaganda made more and more evident to the people the causes of their present misery.[5] They were also certain that there were at present contacts among the Nazis on an informal and personal basis which would, in the course of the next months, ripen into some form of organization, carefully guarded and thoroughly clandestine.

The chief problems which they discussed were, in that order:

1. The cleaning out of the Nazis from official positions and posts of importance in factory and professional life; 2. The reconstruction of political parties and trades [trade unions]; 3. the plundering of the population by foreign workers and the economic situation. Other problems which concerned them were the rebuild-

---

5. The major instrument of educative Allied propaganda was the medium of documentary film showing atrocities and horrors inside concentration camps.

ing of intellectual life (including the problem of teachers), radio, newspaper and other information, the housing problem, relations with the Allied forces, divergences between the zones of occupation, relations with the Russians and Communists, communications with similarly minded groups in other countries, and similar problems discussed further in this report.

b. *Communist:* We spoke with no representatives of the Communist Party but many of our informants had maintained contacts with the Communist Party and had a general view of their activity. It was agreed that their contribution in the way of resistance activity had been, if anything, less than that of the Socialist opposition and for largely the same reasons, with the additional one that the position of the Communist Party after the Russo-German Pact of 1939 had exposed their membership more clearly to the Gestapo and had so confused the membership of the Party that effective opposition thereafter was even more difficult than for the Socialists.

It was unanimously felt that, since 1941,[6] the Communists had had no contacts with the Communist party in Russia or in other countries and had not, therefore, had any clear directives. [...]

The members of the Communist party have been ready to take places in factory committees, trade unions, and local government with the Socialists and Centrists; it was felt by our informants that MG officials had made a wise decision in allowing the CP [Communist party] a place in local governments, since this made them responsible along with all other Nazi oppositionals for local government and prevented their organizing criticism from the outside. [...]

There was no mention by anyone throughout our trip of the Freies Deutschland Committee (the name was unknown to practically all of them) which seems to have played no role whatsoever. The Seydlitz Committee had been heard of by a few through the Russian radio or the BBC, but was dismissed even by those who had heard of it as Russian propaganda; it seemed to have played no role of any significance.[7] The *Antifa*[8] had been quite active in the Ruhr area and was mentioned at several other points; in at least two places it had been dissolved by MG because all Nazis had flocked into it upon its being set up. [...]

The picture of the remaining Communists which emerged (it was realized that their losses to the Gestapo were the heaviest of any oppositional groups) was that of a small group, deeply divided within itself and without clear direc-

---

6. I.e., after the German invasion of the Soviet Union and the German breach of the Hitler-Stalin pact.

7. For OSS evaluations of the Free Germany Committee, see in particular documents [14] and [15]. In Soviet-occupied East Germany members of the Moscow committee such as Walter Ulbricht and Wilhelm Pieck became leading functionaries of the Socialist Unity Party (SED) and later of the government of the German Democratic Republic.

8. Spontaneously organized Anti-Fascist Blocks on the local level that worked toward the removal of Nazi authorities.

tives, apologetic for the mistakes of the past, ready to work with all other anti-Nazis and with MG, but regarded with scepticism as to its long range objectives by the Centrists and Socialists. For the present there appeared no long range objectives, but only the immediate one of rooting out Nazi influence and personalities.

c. *Centrists:* The influence of the Centrists was, expectably, confined to the Catholic parts of Germany, notably in the Cologne and Baden areas. Where they were a political force they had, again, contributed little in the way of active resistance, and for the same reasons as in the case of the Socialists. Some Church officials had, on an intellectual level, courageously withstood the Nazis and had done much to keep alive a spirit of resistance. Immediately upon the arrival of the Allied armies they had put themselves at the disposition of MG, and it was the opinion of the Socialists that, as between non-Nazis, the MG officials were most ready to use the Centrists. There was a general impression that many Nazis had joined, or returned to, the Church in the last days of the war in order to get a protection after the collapse. Where the Centrists represented a political force they had shown a willingness to cooperate with Socialist and Communist resistants on committees, in self-government, and in the trade unions; in certain places (notably the Ruhr), there were not sufficient Centrists available to make this tri-partite cooperation feasible.

The over-all pattern which emerged in the political field is one of nascent political groups, as yet of very limited scope, with the general direction of the pre–1933 period, but more ready to cooperate with one another. Their immediate objectives are cleaning out of Nazis, cooperation with MG, rebuilding of their party apparatus, and concentration on the reconstruction of the trade unions. They are hampered by lack of information and communications, MG rules concerning size of meetings and kinds of permissible activity, the apathy of the German people as a whole, and the disappearance of many of their best leaders. Their activity to date has been confined principally to discussions among a few people by way of preparatory work; other overt activity is almost entirely lacking.
 ... [9]

Summary

[...] Apart from the all-too-small nucleus of reliable persons whose views are herein covered, the impression of the mass of the Germans is one of almost complete apathy. Years of Nazi rule have schooled them to await orders and not to

---

9. The omitted passages contain a comparison of the zones of occupation in the public mind. It is stated that U.S. occupation is most liked, then the British, then the Russian and French, with only the slightest distinctions between the first two and an unknown gap between the last two. Also, the report gives some details about the German population's relation with displaced persons.

exercise any initiative; they will await and execute orders of MG in much the same fashion, for some time to come, as they once did for the Nazis. The Nazis all vehemently deny their former activity, or complain that whatever action they took was under compulsion; one of the results has been that the claims of those who actually engaged in anti-Nazi work are not, without careful checking, believed by the occupying armies.

The impression remains that the Nazis represent a strong force in Germany; that they intend to reorganize, are now laying low, but will exploit a bad economic situation and any slightest tension between the Allies for their purposes. To date the policies of MG have allowed anti-Nazi groups sufficient play, and enough hope, so that they are in a position to present an alternative to the mass of Germans along democratic and progressive lines; it would seem essential that a larger measure of freedom be slowly yielded in order that they not be allowed to feel that the policies of MG are hostile to their own and in order to find a considerable support among the population for the difficult task of combatting Nazi underground work.[10]

10. In reality, a Nazi underground never materialized.

Document 101 · 10 September 1945

Army Intelligence Consolidated Interrogation Report: The Political and Social Background of the 20 July Incident[1]

CONFIDENTIAL

Consolidated Interrogation Report

The Political and Social Background of the 20 July Incident

[...]

Preamble. A thorough study of the German opposition—what little there was—to the *Hitler*regime might help to uncover the constructive elements in Germany, their background, and their thinking. Such a study involves of necessity not merely historical investigations, but straight political intelligence, for it acquaints us with personalities and trends of political thought whose effects reach into the future, and into the reconstruction of a country the responsibil-ity for which we, by conquest, have partly assumed. Already the men and ideas of the 20 July incident have become political tools within Germany. All the po-litical parties active in Berlin and in the Russian zone of occupation, with the exception perhaps of the Communists, claim a share in this unsuccessful conspiracy. Men have entered the political limelight because they have or claim they have participated.

This investigation of the background and events of 20 July, based on interviews with individuals in Berlin,[2] is only a preliminary one. In collating the information received, an attempt was made to picture the actual events and to eliminate the

---

1. NA, RG 165, Entry 179, Box 702. All purely descriptive parts of this lengthy report, drawn up by the Counterintelligence Division of the U.S. Army (G–2) are omitted although the more interpretative passages are printed here.

2. The following personalities served as sources for the report: Dr. Hellmuth Dix, Dr. Friedrich Ernst, Lieutenant-Colonel Josef Ertel, Ludwig von Hammerstein, Amalie von Harnack, Ilse von Hassell, Wolf-Ulrich von Hassell, Andreas Hermes, Sidney Jessen, Jacob Kaiser, Ernst Lemmer, Hans Joachim von Reclam, Eduard Spranger.

retrospective wishful thinking which appears to characterize many of the statements. If parts of this report seem vague, it must be borne in mind that almost all the key participants were executed by the Gestapo and that this conspiracy was undertaken and discovered within one of the most thorough police states the world has ever known. But it is believed that further investigations in other parts of Germany will fill out the picture and that the investigation of documents which are beginning to come to light will help to substantiate evidence introduced in this report.

I. Introduction. On 20 July 1944 an explosion was heard in one of the huts of Adolf *Hitler's* supreme headquarters in Angerburg. For a few hours in the early afternoon of that day many Germans believed Hitler was dead. At 1800 hours the German radio announced an attempt on the Fuehrer's life had been made but that he had miraculously escaped.

The explosion had two general effects:

(1) Probably the greatest single purge that even Hitler's Germany had ever seen took place. A large number of high-ranking officers were arrested immediately. Some were shot at once; some were tried and then hanged; and many others escaped a similar fate by committing suicide. Civilians, too, were purged. Although it was not evident at first, it gradually came to light that practically all the remnants of the German intelligentsia, all the potential leaders of a non-Nazi Germany, were put into Gestapo prisons. Very few ever came out again.

(2) *Hitler's* narrow escape from death on that day apparently renewed his conviction that a higher destiny protected him. His certainty that he was the chosen leader was stronger than ever. He therefore continued the war with increased viciousness. The Nazis felt sure the last opposition from within had shown itself and had been wiped out. The last men of reason had been eliminated and the Nazis remained supreme. To replace the executed and arrested officers, fanatics took over, and the SS gained final control over the prosecution of the war. Inside Germany *Himmler* and his henchmen ruled unchecked. At last the gigantic war which the Nazis had provoked had become entirely their own.
...[3]

---

3. The passages omitted give a detailed analysis of the composition of the German resistance, the beginnings of the conspiracy, the aims of the plotters, the execution of their plans and the aftermath of the attempted coup d'état.

VII. Political Significance. If the plot of 20 July 1944 had succeeded it would have undoubtedly saved the lives of thousands of Allied soldiers and the victors would have found Germany and Europe in a far better condition than it is in now. On the other hand the total defeat of Germany seems a far better guarantee for world security than might have been created by a peaceful entry of Allied armies into Germany in July or August 1944. As in 1919, a "stab in the back" legend, the famous "Dolchstoss-Legende," would no doubt have sprung up again.[4] Many Germans might have believed the German Army really was not defeated and that surrender was only brought about because a clique of traitors sold the country out to the Allies. And *Hitler* would have been the great martyr. It would have been said, "If the Fuehrer had not been murdered we would have won after all." Such an attitude on the part of a people not really convinced the war was lost might easily have given rise to still another nationalistic movement, perhaps still another war, in a decade or two. German arrogance and the "Herrenvolk" [master race] complex had to be defeated utterly and decisively.

One source calls the men who planned the revolt the "men of yesterday." Undoubtedly the vast majority of them were honest, honorable, and decent men. But neither the world nor Germany herself would have found them imbued with a true democratic spirit or with the vitality and zeal which is a prerequisite for the leaders of the geographical center of Europe in a democratic world. Again, as in 1919, a new Germany would have started off with men of compromise. (The following section on personalities (*VIII.*) will show how many of them supported the Nazi regime or militarism before they finally felt compelled to turn against *Hitler.*)[5] If it is Germany's inherent fault that she never had a real revolution in the sense of a complete political upheaval, the total collapse of 8 May 1945[6] should

---

4. For the "stab-in-the-back" topos see also documents [31], [55] and [58].

5. The following personalities are listed: Willhelm Adam, Ludwig Beck, Albrecht Graf von Bernstorff, Eugen Anton Bolz, Wilhelm Canaris, Ludwig Diels, Dr. Friedrich Ernst, Paul O. H. Fechter, Dr. Otto Karl Gessler, Carl Friedrich Goerdeler, Max Halermann, Hans Berndt [Hans-Bernd] von Haeften, Kurt Lebhard, Adolf Freiherr von Hammerstein-Equord, Karl Paul Immanuel von Hase [Paul von Hase], Christian Albrecht Ulrich von Hassell [Ulrich von Hassell], Dr. Theodor Haubach, Georg Albrecht Haushofer [Albrecht Haushofer], Andreas Hermes, Jans [Jens] Peter Jessen, Jacob [Jakob] Kaiser, Dr. Julius Leber, Paul Adam Franz Lejeune-Jung, Bernhard Letterhaus, Wilhelm Leuschner, Karl Mierendorf [Carlo Mierendorff], Graf Helmuth [James] von Moltke, Gustav Noske, Friedrich Olbricht, Hermann Oncken, Hans Oster, Hans Eduard Popitz [Johannes Popitz], Ernst Ferdinand Sauerbruch, Franz Rehrl, Hans Heinrich Schaeder, Graf Friedrich Werner von der Schulenburg, Karl Seitz, Eduard Spranger, Graf Berthold Schenk von Stauffenberg, Graf Klaus Schenk von Stauffenberg, Theodor Steltzer, Elisabeth von Thadden, Adam von Trott zu Solz, Hans Ludwig, David Carl Maximilian, Peter Graf York von Wartenburg [Peter Graf Yorck von Wartenburg], Freiherr Ernst, Heinrich von Weizsäcker, [Josef] Wirmer, Erwin Job and Wilhelm von Witzleben.

6. The day of Germany's capitulation to the Allies.

have shaken the country hard enough to provide for a renewal of political thought. The 20 July 1944 incident would at best have directed a slightly altered German political philosophy into more civilized and more acceptable forms. ...[7]

Steckert, Capt.
For Frederick Sternberg
Maj, CAC Commanding

7. The omitted appendices contain biographical information on the personalities of the conspiracy; they also list actual and potential sources of additional information.

Document 102 · 15 October 1945

Field Intelligence Study by Franklin Ford (Strategic Services Unit, Germany)[1]: Political Implications of the 20th of July[2]

CONFIDENTIAL

Field Intelligence Study 31
Political Implications of the 20th of July

I. Introduction. The dramatic putsch attempt of 20 July 1944 occupies a place in the history of the Third Reich which six months after the final collapse of Nazi power still has considerable significance in the politics of Germany. Participation in the conspiracy or even personal knowledge of its composition and aims has become a political asset which Germans in all parts of the former Reich have been quick to utilize in asserting their fitness for leadership in the reconstruction period. The peculiar interest which the 20th of July has aroused among American, British, French and Russian occupation authorities is evidenced by the early use in civil administration of survivors of the conspiracy. Conversations with Military Government officers and references to implicated German politicians in Allied intelligence reports furnish frequent examples of the assumption that the bomb

---

1. U.S. Army Military Archives, Lexington, Va. Francis P. Miller Papers, Box 8, Folder 10; Bundesarchiv, Militärarchiv Freiburg i. Br., Gero von Schulze-Gaevernitz Papers. Historian Franklin Ford was a member of the OSS Research and Analysis Branch. He had been recruited by Harold C. Deutsch from the University of Minnesota. Right after the war, Ford was stationed in Biebrich near Wiesbaden, Germany, where he was preparing Field Intelligence studies under Felix Gilbert. In Biebrich, the OSS had established their quarters in an abandoned champagne factory, lately owned by the Ribbentrop family. Most of the reports that bear Ford's name were prepared in collaboration with Leonard Krieger, Perry Miller, and Hans Meyerhoff.

2. This is an excerpt of a report comprising 60 pages.

attempt against Hitler's life was the one creditable act performed by Germans in Germany during the 12 years of Nazi rule.[3]

The putsch unquestionably represented a high degree of physical courage on the part of the principal activists involved. Furthermore, in the cases of many of the participants it stemmed from a genuine moral revolt against the Nazi program. To this extent, connection with the 20th of July clearly deserves to be viewed as an important element in the personal record of any emergent German political figure. So wide were the ramifications of the plot, however, and so complex the variety of interests which motivated the hundreds of individuals concerned, that participation can scarcely be accepted *a priori* as constituting an absolute assurance of democratic impulses and personal reliability. [...]

II. Current Importance of the 20th of July. The events of 20 July 1944 and the complex conspiracy which produced them have not lost their significance in the politics of Germany, even under the present circumstances of defeat and foreign occupation. Part of the explanation for the aura of prestige which now surrounds the putsch group may be found in the desire of a nation which within the space of three years fell from its highest point of military power to the worst defeat in its history, to find some event in those years to which it can still point with pride. Another contributing factor is undoubtedly the interest which representatives of the occupying powers have continued to feel toward the event and toward those who took part in it. As in the case of all such historical crises, the 20th of July has taken on a half-legendary character in the public mind and has begun to be surrounded with nuances of political significance scarcely justified by the facts themselves.

A. The Berlin Press and the Putsch in Retrospect. ...[4] A critical analysis of the press debate concerning the 20th of July makes clear that the event lends itself to interpretation by party groups in terms of present-day political interests. The conservative tendencies of most of the putsch leaders have the full support of such parties as the Christian Democratic Union,[5] while a portion of the Social Democrats, also presented with an opportunity to capitalize on the participation of at least [two of] their own party's representatives, tend to emphasize the roles of the Socialist conspirators. The Communists and also the left-wing Socialists, although the latter have at present no independent voice in the Berlin press, call attention to the fact that the putsch, had it succeeded, would have brought the

---

3. Although there had been some 40 attempts to kill Hitler during the 12 years of his rule, it was generally believed that the 20th July attempt was the only serious incident.

4. The omitted passage paraphrases numerous postwar German press reports of the July incident.

5. Newly founded by, among others, Konrad Adenauer, with the intention to broaden the social basis of the former Catholic Center (Zentrum) party.

war to a close, but under conditions which would have confused the significance of defeat in the minds of the German people and would have constituted a brake on leftist progress for the future.

B. Importance of Survivors Under MG [Military Government]. The purge which followed the 20th of July eradicated a whole class of anti-Nazi Germans, the majority of whom would unquestionably have been welcomed into administrative posts by the four powers now occupying Germany. Even out of the small remnant of survivors, several have either been given appointments under MG or have been allowed to assume leading positions in activities having direct relevance to the revival of German political life.

In Berlin Andreas Hermes was appointed food administrator for the city by the Soviet command in May 1945. Although dismissed in July, he retains his chairmanship of the Christian Social Union there, with Jakob Kaiser, another July 20th survivor, also a member of the party's Central Committee. Another Berlin political figure who has benefited from his association with the putsch is Gustav Dahrendorf, who has taken a leading place in the reorganization of the Berlin Social Democrats. In addition to his party position, Dahrendorf occupies the post of assistant to the Administrator for Coal and Fuel in the Russian Zonal Administration. Willy Ernst, former councillor in the Finance Ministry during the 1930's and the chairman of the 20th of July memorial service in the Lehrterstrasse prison, has been used by the Russians as an adviser on financial matters in Berlin. Ernst cannot be counted an active participant in the revolt attempt, but he has at least produced evidence that he was well-informed on the putsch plans and stood ready to act as an assistant to the scheduled Finance Minister,[6] had the attempt succeeded.

Two important political figures in Bavaria have records of complicity in the Beck-Goerdeler conspiracy. One is Otto Gessler, Reich War Minister from 1920 to 1928, who was appointed Deputy Prime Minister and Chief of the State Chancellery (July-September 1945) under former Prime Minister Schaeffer [Fritz Schäffer]. Since the latter's removal, Gessler has been out of public office; but his standing in Bavaria was unquestionably enhanced in the first weeks of occupation by the fact that he was arrested by the Gestapo because Goerdeler had listed him as a prospective chief of one of the provincial administrations. The other Munich figure, to whose participation in the plot reference is constantly made, is Josef Mueller [Müller], the conspirators' agent in Rome. Mueller's importance is such that for a time he was considered a possible successor to Schaeffer,[7] but his allegedly leftist sentiments have aroused the animosity of the older Catholic leadership in Bavaria.[8]

---

6. Either Ewald Loeser or Johannes Popitz.

7. Fritz Schäffer's successor was Wilhelm Hoegner who had been in close touch with Allen W. Dulles and Gero von Schulze-Gaevernitz in Switzerland.

8. On Müller see also document [65].

Two more examples of the political value of connection with the putsch are Emil Henk of Heidelberg and Peter Bielenberg of Frankfurt-am-Main. Henk, a Socialist friend of the putschists' Vice-Chancellor-designate, Wilhelm Leuschner, shared with his friend Professor Alfred Weber of Heidelberg University, detailed knowledge of the preliminary planning for the revolt and conferred on several occasions with Leuschner. Under American Military Government, Henk was chief of the Department of Education and Religious Affairs in the Mittelrhein-Saar administration until that regional government was dissolved with the turning over of the Mittelrhein-Saar area to French occupation. Bielenberg had connections with the plot through several conspirators in the Berlin civil servant group, since he was an official in Funk's Economics Ministry on July 20th. Released from imprisonment by the Russian invasion of Germany, he proceeded to Frankfurt, where he now occupies the post of deputy to the President of the Chamber of Commerce (*Industrie- und Handelskammer*). His position takes on political importance because of the substantial semi-governmental functions exercised by the Chamber of Commerce in German municipal administration.

In the sphere of intellectual reconstruction, the Freiburg professors, Ritter, Dietze and Lampe, appear likely to play large roles.[9] The three are already members of the five-man committee which has been drawing up plans for a new program for Freiburg University, and the prestige lent them by their narrow escape from execution after July 20th assures them a receptive national audience for their future political and economic writings. Another university leader associated with the Goerdeler circle through Confessional Church contacts is Rudolf Smend, former professor of public law at Berlin and now rector of Goettingen [Göttingen] University. The type of political influence represented by these professors, who occupy no public office but who may well exercise considerable leadership in the reconstitution of German government, is to be found also in certain churchmen whose connections with the 20th of July, as well as the prestige of their offices per se, lend weight to their utterances in the minds of many Germans. Bishop Dibelius of Berlin[10] and Superior Church Councillor Wilhelm Pressel of Stuttgart are examples of this type. Finally, the political influence of certain private citizens has, to judge from MG reports, been enhanced by even the most tenuous connection with the conspiracy. Werner von Trott zu Solz, although not personally involved in the putsch plans or even aware of the full extent of his brother Adam's activities, has been given a respectful hearing by American authorities in the presentation of his recommendations for the re-education of Germany.[11] The surviv-

9. All three were members of the so-called Freiburg resistance circle.

10. For Dibelius see document [70c].

11. The Americans were not aware that Adam had a second brother, Heinrich, who had deserted to the British after the failed plot against Hitler. In England, Heinrich von Trott wrote reports about the background of the conspiracy. These reports circulated in the Foreign Office. Had the coup succeeded Heinrich was to be given command of an army unit in France.

ing Trott, who lives in Imshausen bei Bebra, is invariably referred to in MG memoranda concerning his activities as "brother of the July 20th Trott zu Solz".[12]

The lines and personalities of future German politics are still too obscure to permit any definitive judgment on the eventual importance of the July 20th tradition. For the present it is possible only to call attention to the strong interest in the affair being displayed by Germany's political press, the emergence in influential positions of specific survivors of the putsch or relatives of dead conspirators, and the extent to which any connection with the conspiracy continues to be featured in Allied intelligence reports on German personnel. In view of these evidences of the continuing significance of the affair, some basis for judging the relevance of participation may be of value for the remainder of the occupation period.

III. Background: History of the Conspiracy.

A. Composition of the Putsch Group. To the anti-Nazi world the forms and extent of opposition to Nazism on the part of Germans themselves have since 1933 been shrouded in the secrecy which necessarily attended such activities in the most ruthlessly efficient police state in history. The foreign enemies of Hitler's regime, aware of the high degree of national discipline which has for so long characterized the German population and impressed by the energetic mobilization of Germany's resources in support of the Nazis' vast military projects, tended to take a skeptical view of the possibility of any active resistance on the part of groups inside Germany. Yet there was opposition, as the 20th of July attempt eventually proved. It was an opposition which in the early years of the regime could express itself only in the form of clandestine discussions concerning methods to save Germany from the results of Nazism. Only after the resistance groups were able to win the cooperation of influential Army men was it possible to plan for a forceful overthrow of Hitler, for only the Army offered a source of physical power to outweigh that of the Nazis' SS.

The composition of the conspiratorial group which engineered the putsch attempt of July 20th by no means represented the whole range of German opposition to Hitler. Conversely, many of the participants were clearly motivated by self-interest rather than by fundamental disagreement with Nazism's political aims. But at least six distinguishable groups took part: Army dissidents, civil servants, renegade Nazis, Social Democratic leaders, churchmen and intellectuals. Within each of these groups were to be found examples of most of the various forms which opposition thinking took in the closing period of Nazi power: intellectual rejection of Hitler's philosophy and program, moral indignation at the excesses of the regime, fear of the effects on Germany following the Nazi leadership to the end, the desire for a return to old institutions and standards, the diametrically opposite aim of achieving some degree of social revolution and the professional

---

12. Adam von Trott zu Solz who had been one of the first members of the German opposition to approach Allen W. Dulles in Bern, was executed on 15 August 1944. See document [8].

soldier's impulse to salvage out of defeat at least a portion of the German Army's structural continuity. To these broader political and social concepts must be added such motives as personal ambition, fear on the part of individual conspirators, desire for revenge against the regime for old slights and the bureaucratic rivalry of whole departments within the German Government. Obviously, however, each of the component groups was motivated by a central impulse, varying from one group to the next depending on the background and interests of most of its members.
...[13]

IV. Conclusion. The basic difficulty encountered in attempting to judge the reliability of the individual German who claims connection with the 20th of July as proof of his anti-Nazi convictions lies in the wide variety of motives which formed the background of the putsch. The present report has sought to emphasize these differences of motivation among the implicated soldiers, civil servants, left-wing political leaders, churchmen and intellectuals. At the same time it has sought to illustrate the danger of making such categories too rigid, pointing out that in Stauffenberg the Army produced a man less interested in the survival of military institutions than in the reform of political institutions and that the civil servant group included men as widely different in background and ethics as Adam von Trott zu Solz and Count Wolf von Helldorf. The complexity of the problem is further increased by doubt as to the real roles of certain of the now emergent "brotherhood of July 20th". The information concerning the putsch possessed by the latter does not always bear close examination or checking against other, better-authenticated reports. In any case, an important *caveat* is suggested by the plain fact that connection with the conspiracy has become a valuable political asset to whoever can claim it. Hence the temptation to exploit to its fullest whatever knowledge he has concerning the 20th of July becomes an important factor in the individual's presentation of his personal history.

One other consideration which suggests itself is that of the individual's date of association with the plotters. To illustrate the significance of this time factor, it is only necessary to point out the difference between the fundamental rejection of Hitler exemplified by Beck from 1938 onward with the last-minute desperation of

---

13. The omitted passage comprising some 40 pages, gives a detailed account of the composition of the "Putsch group." The paragraph on the "Putsch and its Aftermath" contains a propositional list for a post-putsch cabinet. The panel of ministers is almost identical with the July 1944 list of the conspirators: Ludwig Beck (Chief of State), Carl Goerdeler (Chancellor), Wilhelm Leuschner (Vice Chancellor), Ulrich von Hassell (Foreign Minister), Friedrich Olbricht (Minister for War), Erwin von Witzleben (Commander of the Armed Forces), Julius Leber (Minister for the Interior), Paul Lejeune-Jung (Minister for Economics), Ewald Loeser (Minister for Finance), Josef Wirmer (Minister for Justice), Eugen Bolz (Minister for Education and Religious Affairs), Andreas Hermes (Minister for Agriculture), and Bernhard Letterhaus (Minister for Reconstruction). The information given in the omitted passage formed the basis for Franklin Ford's articles on the German resistance, which were published in 1946 and 1947.

Rommel, faced in the last month before the putsch with the Fuehrer's determination to continue what seemed certain to be a disastrous resistance in Normandy. Beck's and Rommel's are obviously extreme cases; but the anti-Nazism of the Germans who entered the opposition in the period of Nazi success just as obviously to be distinguished from that of the other Germans who gravitated to Beck's movement only after military defeats on all fronts had made unequivocally clear the hopeless future of the Hitler regime.

If any principle for judging the individual conspirators can be evolved from the complex of motives and degrees of active anti-Nazism, it is probably the following: that participation in the 20th of July can not be said to have political relevance except as it is viewed in relation to the individual's other qualifications. Whether he joined in the attempt out of respect for justice and enlightened patriotism or whether his personal ambition and fear of going down with the Nazis led him to take part can scarcely be expected to emerge from his connection with the event viewed in isolation. Dramatic as it was and costly though it proved to potentially valuable leadership for post-war Germany, the conspiracy can not be taken as endowing all who were connected with it with a special degree of political reliability and moral worth.

Bibliography

Note on Sources

The majority of documents printed in this volume are part of the National Archives collection of OSS records (Record Group 226). Its range and completeness mark it as a unique source on many aspects of the World War II. After the dissolution of the OSS in October 1945, the OSS material was distributed among two government agencies: The reports of the Research and Analysis Branch were sent to the Department of State; operational, administrative and support materials for all branches of the OSS were forwarded to the War Department and later entrusted to the Central Intelligence Agency. Whereas the Research and Analysis reports were declassified in 1976, the other records have been in the process of being transferred to the National Archives since 1980. Most of these materials have only been available for a few years, and a small portion are still on their way from the CIA to the National Archives where they will undergo a process of transfer, declassification, sorting and indexing. Most OSS records are kept in the Modern Military Branch of the National Archives, but there is also some OSS material in Record Group 59 in the Diplomatic Branch. This material includes in particular the documents pertaining to peace-feelers by actual anti-Nazis or people posing as anti-Nazis. Record Group 59 also holds many Final Reports of the OSS Research and Analysis Branch.

Outside Washington, D.C., the most important archives for OSS research are the Roosevelt Library in Hyde Park, N.Y. (especially the President's Secretary's Files) and the Military Archives in Carlisle Barracks, Pa., which holds a set of the Papers of William J. Donovan. Some interesting documents were also found in the George C. Marshall Library in Lexington, Va.

The records in this volume are printed from the above collections. In addition, a lot of background information was found in other archives, such as the Hoover Institution in Stanford, Cal., the Seeley G. Mudd Library in Princeton, N.J., the Harvard University Archives at Cambridge, Mass., the Library of Congress, and the Eisenhower Library in Abilene, Kan. Some information contained in the footnotes of this volume also comes from the Foreign Office Files in the Public Records Office, London and from the collections of the Archives of the World Council of Churches in Geneva.

The Bibliography of this volume is far from a complete bibliography of the topic. It offers, however, a list of books and articles from which the editors have gained important insight. The Bibliography places special emphasis on primary sources, such as memoirs of OSS members and other first-hand accounts of persons identified in this volume.

Over the course of the last two decades, the study of intelligence has become a genuine scholarly discipline, at least in the United States and Great Britain, and to a certain extent in Germany. Thus, there exist not only sensationalist spy stories but also numerous first-rate books and articles; there are even some professional journals dedicated to the subject of intelligence. The majority of the titles included in the Bibliography are reliable accounts.

Tendentious exposés have only been included when it was felt that they provided important information that could not be found elsewhere.

A number of OSS documents have been published so far. Some appear in the Foreign Relations of the United States (FRUS) series, and several were published in periodicals. The most far-reaching attempt to make intelligence documents available to the public, was through the 18-volume *Covert Warfare* series, edited by John Mendelsohn. This publication of facsimile documents is, however, not footnoted and addresses mostly specialized topics such as the Jedburgh Teams.

For a more complete bibliography on all aspects of U.S. intelligence, Neal H. Petersen's excellent work, *American Intelligence, 1775–1990: A Bibliographical Guide* (1992) should be consulted. Another important bibliographical volume is George C. Constantinides's slightly outdated, but nevertheless very valuable, *Intelligence and Espionage: An Analytical Bibliography* (1983).

As to the Office of Strategic Services, one of the most important studies is the official OSS history, also known as *The War Report*. At the time of its release in 1976, two versions appeared almost simultaneously: One was edited by Anthony Cave Brown, another by Kermit Roosevelt. Although Cave Brown's edition has been used more widely, the Roosevelt edition is more complete. Both editions had a stimulating effect on OSS research and are, despite their obvious gaps and a general lack of names, a most essential mine of operational and organizational facts pertaining to the OSS.

Quite a few OSS histories were written prior to the release and declassification of the OSS documents. Most of them are, however, largely panegyrics, or simply focus on very limited aspects of OSS history. The most substantial of the early accounts is undoubtedly the work of former CIA analyst R. Harris Smith, *OSS: The Secret History of America's First Central Intelligence Agency* (1972). Another important work (much less sensational than its title, *Undercover Girl*, suggests), was authored by Elizabeth McDonald [i.e., Betty MacIntosh] in 1947. MacDonald, a former member of the OSS and CIA was a personal friend not only of William J. Donovan but also of Allen W. Dulles. Thus, her account, which (like H. Harris Smith's book) is basically an oral history, contains some personal recollections that are not to be found elsewhere.

Possibly the best study ever written on the OSS is Bradley F. Smith's *Shadow Warriors: OSS and the Origins of the CIA* (1983). Although heavily attacked for its open criticism of covert action, *Shadow Warriors* is a great piece of research leading into numerous areas of inquiry. Another significiant work is the one by former CIA historian Thomas Troy, *Donovan and the CIA* (1981). For anybody interested in organizational aspects of the U.S. intelligence community, this volume, although dry to read, is indispensable. Despite what the title suggests, however, Troy's book is not a work on William J. Donovan. Of the three biographies published so far (by Corey Ford, Richard Dunlop and Anthony Cave Brown), Cave Brown's *The Last Hero: Wild Bill Donovan* (1982) (although in parts rather unreliable) is an invaluable source. Being far more than a Donovan biography, this thrilling account touches upon almost every aspect of OSS history and operations. Similarly, Barry Rubin's *Istanbul Intrigues* (1989), although not footnoted and often flawed, is a valuable addition on OSS operations in the Middle East.

Other books worthy of note are two volumes on the OSS-initiated secret surrender of German armed forces in northern Italy in early 1945. The first one, *The Secret Surrender* (1966), was written by Hans Bernd Gisevius and Allen W. Dulles (the English version was published under Dulles's name alone); the second is the revisionist study by Bradley F. Smith and Elena Agarossi, *Operation Sunrise: The Secret Surrender* (1979). Both of them are equally important and they complement each other.

Furthermore, two high-spirited and scholarly studies by Barry M. Katz (*Foreign Intelligence;* on the OSS Research and Analysis Branch) and Robin Winks (*Cloak and Gown*) offer amazing insights into the links between academia and U.S. intelligence. Next to William Casey's account, *The Secret War Against Hitler* (1988), Joseph Persico's *Piercing the Reich* (1979) is the only work covering intelligence operations inside Germany. Based mainly on oral interviews and on the unpublished OSS London War Diary (now available on microfilm), it is both sensational and reliable. The first scholarly collection of essays on the OSS was published in 1992. Edited by George C. Chalou of the National Archives, it presents the papers of an international OSS conference held at the Archives in July 1991. For several years to come, this significant volume will mark the frontier of academic research on the OSS in numerous fields.

Among the many dictionaries on U.S. intelligence, by far the most accurate and comprehensive is George J. A. O'Toole's, *The Encyclopedia of American Intelligence and Espionage: From the Revolutionary War to the Present* (1988).

Another important reference work for many aspects of this book, is the *International Biographical Dictionary of Central European Emigrés 1933–1945*, which was edited by Werner Röder and Herbert A. Strauss (1980–1983). The three volumes of this dictionary offer a lot of information about German exiles: Many of them were, indeed, members of the OSS or of the anti-Nazi opposition movement.

Of the many dictionaries on the German resistance, only the most recent ones (edited by Wolfgang Benz/Walter H. Pehle [1994] and Peter Steinbach/Johannes Tuchel [1994]) are listed. Both volumes contain a wealth of further reading suggestions; the latter one concentrates in particular on the oppositional's biographies. In his large bibliography on the subject of the German resistance against Hitler, *Widerstand*, Ulrich Cartarius claimed in 1984 that there is hardly any other other topic in German contemporary history that has been studied as thoroughly as the anti-Nazi movement. Even though over the course of the 1990s German research interests focused more and more on postwar topics, hundreds of books and articles about the anti-Nazi movement have been published in recent years. Unfortunately, only a small fraction appeared in English. The anti-Nazi movement has never been a favored topic among U.S. or British scholars of the World War II. It is thus not surprising that some of the most groundbreaking English-language research was done by German emigrés to the United States, in particular by such scholars as Hans Rothfels, Peter Hoffmann, Beate Ruhm von Oppen, Klemens von Klemperer, Armin Mruck and Michael Geyer.

Of the books that are readily available in the United States, two volumes on the German resistance must be singled out as outstanding research. The first is Peter Hoffmann's thousand-page-volume *The History of the German Resistance 1933–1945*, published by Cambridge University Press in 1979, the second is Klemens von Klemperer's solid and comprehensive study on the foreign relations of the German anti-Nazi opposition, *German Resistance against Hitler: The Search for Allies Abroad, 1938–1945*, published by Oxford in 1992.

In addition, the resistance history by military historian and former OSS analyst Harold C. Deutsch, *The Conspiracy Against Hitler in the Twilight War* is still worth consulting. The same is true for Hans Rothfels's very early account, *The German Opposition to Hitler: An Appraisal*, which appeared in 1948. Other important comprehensive studies are the ones by Michael Balfour, *Withstanding Hitler in Germany 1933–45* (1988), and Ger van Roon's *German Resistance to Hitler: Count von Moltke and the Kreisau Circle* (1971). Some stimulating research has been provided recently by four collective volumes; the first, *Germans Against Nazism: Nonconformity, Opposition and Resistance in the Third Reich* (1990) was edited by Francis R. Nicosia and Lawrence D. Stokes in honor of Peter Hoffmann; the second, *Resistance Against the Third Reich*, was edited in 1992 by John W. Boyer and Julius

Kirschner as a supplementary volume to the *Journal of Modern History;* the third is a collection of essays, entitled *Contending with Hitler* and edited by David C. Large; the fourth, *Widerstand gegen den Nationalsozialismus,* was edited by Peter Steinbach and Johannes Tuchel.

One cannot reexamine the literature of the last fifty years on the topic of this book without arriving at a new appreciation of two books that were published shortly after the war. One is Allen Dulles's *Germany's Underground* (1947), which (although written essentially by Wolf von Eckardt) remains an important first-hand account and a mine of information about the plotters against Hitler and their relationship with the OSS. The other volume, entitled *To the Bitter End* (1947), is Hans Bernd Gisevius's rather lengthy account. The author, one of the few surviving members of the 20th of July plot against Hitler, was also one of Allen Dulles's major informants in Bern during World War II.

I. Documentations, Memoirs and Other Primary Works

Bancroft, Mary. *Autobiography of a Spy.* New York: 1983.

Beer, Siegfried. "Exil und Emigration als Information. Zur Tätigkeit der Foreign Nationalities Branch (FNB) innerhalb des amerikanischen Kriegsgeheimdienstes COI bzw. OSS, 1941–1945." *Dokumentationsarchiv des österreichischen Widerstandes, ed. Jahrbuch 1989* (Wien: 1989): 132–144.

———. Kärnten im Frühsommer 1945. Drei Berichte und Analysen des amerikanischen Geheim-und Nachrichtendienstes OSS zu Politik, Wirtschaft und Gesellschaft in einem britisch-besetzten Bundesland. *Carinthia* 177 (1987): 415–452.

Bell, George. "The Background of the Hitler Plot." *The Contemporary Review* 168 (1945): 203–208.

Bentley, James. *Martin Niemöller.* New ed. London: 1986.

———. *Martin Niemöller. Eine Biographie.* Munich: 1985.

Besier, Gerhard, ed. Ökumenische Mission in Nachkriegsdeutschland. Die Berichte von Stewart W. Herman über die Verhältnisse in der evangelischen Kirche 1945/46. *Kirchliche Zeitgeschichte* 1 (1988): 151–187; 316–352.

Boberach, Heinz, ed. *Berichte des SD und der Gestapo über Kirche und Kirchenvolk in Deutschland 1934–1944.* Mainz: 1971.

———. *Meldungen aus dem Reich 1938–1945. Die geheimen Lageberichte des Sicherheitsdienstes der SS.* Herrsching: 1984.

Boegner, Marc. *The Long Road to Unity. Memoirs and Anticipations.* London: 1970.

Bonhoeffer, Dietrich. *No Rusty Swords: Letters, Lectures and Notes from the Collected Works.* Ed. Erwin H. Robertson. London: 1974.

———. *Letters and Papers from Prison.* Ed. Eberhard Bethge. London: 1971 [New York: 1972.]

Brandt, Willy. *My Life in Politics.* London: 1992.

———. *Links und frei. Mein Weg 1930–1950.* Hamburg: 1982.

———. *In Exile: Essays, Reflections and Letters 1933–1947.* London: 1971.

Cave Brown, Anthony, ed. *The Secret War Report of the OSS.* New York: 1976.

Coffee, Edwin R., ed. *From Normandy into the Reich.* New York/London: 1989.

Cole, R. Taylor. *The Recollections of R. Taylor Cole—Educator, Emissary, Development Planner.* Durham, NC: 1983.

Corvo, Max. *The OSS in Italy 1942–1945 A Personal Memoir.* New York/Westport, CT/ London: 1990.

Deutschlandberichte der Sozialdemokratischen Partei Deutschlands (Sopade) 1934–1940. 7 vols. Frankfurt/Main: 1980.

"Documents on Allen Dulles's Secret Negotiations with the Nazis in 1943." *New Times* [Moscow] (July 1960).

Documents on German Foreign Policy 1918–1945. Series D, vols. 2, 4, 7, 11. Washington, DC: 1949, 1956, 1956, 1964.

Dokumentationsarchiv des Österreichischen Widerstandes, ed. *Widerstand und Verfolgung in Oberösterreich 1934–1945—Eine Dokumentation.* 2 vols. Vienna: 1982.

———. *Widerstand und Verfolgung in Niederösterreich 1934–1945—Eine Dokumentation.* 3 vols. Vienna: 1987.

Dokumente zur Deutschlandpolitik Sept. 1939–41 Dec. 1941. [1. Reihe.] vol. 1: 3 Ed. Rainer Blasius. Frankfurt/Main: 1984.

Dossier: Kreisauer Kreis. Dokumente aus dem Widerstand gegen den Nationalsozialismus. Aus dem Nachlass von Lothar König S. J. Ed. Roman Bleistein. Frankfurt/Main: 1987.

Eade, Charles, ed. *The War Speeches by the Rt. Hon. Winston S. Churchill.* vols. 2, 3. Boston: 1953.

Einsiedel, Graf Heinrich von. *I Joined the Russians: A Captured German Flyer's Diary of the Communist Temptation.* New Haven, CT: 1953.

Eisenhower, Dwight D. *Crusade in Europe.* New York: 1949.

Elser, Johann Georg. *Autobiographie eines Attentäters.* Stuttgart: 1970.

Generäle. "Neue Mitteilungen zur Vorgeschichte des 20 Juli." *Die Wandlung* 1 (1945–1946): 528–537. [Hermann Kaiser]

Gerstenmaier, Eugen. *Streit und Friede hat seine Zeit—Ein Lebensbericht.* Frankfurt/Main: 1981.

———. "Zur Geschichte des Umsturzversuches vom 20 Juli 1944." *Neue Zürcher Zeitung* 23 (June 24, 1945).

Gisevius, Hans Bernd. *To the Bitter End.* Transl. Richard and Clara Winston. Boston: 1947. [London: 1948].

Görlitz, Walter, ed. *Generalfeldmarschall Keitel: Verbrecher oder Offizier? Erinnerungen, Briefe, Dokumente des Chefs OKW.* Göttingen, Berlin, Frankfurt: 1961.

Groscurth, Helmuth. *Tagebücher eines Abwehroffiziers 1938–1940, mit weiteren Dokumenten zur Militäropposition gegen Hitler.* Krausnick, Helmuth, and Harold C. Deutsch, eds. Stuttgart: 1970.

Grüber, Heinrich. *Erinnerungen aus sieben Jahrzehnten.* Köln/Berlin: 1968.

Haeften, Bernd von. *Aus unserem Leben 1944–1950.* Heidelberg: 1974.

Hagen, Paul. *Will Germany Crack?* New York: 1942.

Halder, [Franz]. *Kriegstagebuch.* vols. 1–3. Stuttgart: 1962, 1963, 1964.

Hartgrove, J. Dane, ed. *The OSS-NKVD Relationship, 1943–1945.* New York/London: 1989.

Hassell, Ulrich von. *Die Hassell-Tagebücher 1938–1944. Aufzeichnungen vom anderen Deutschland.* Ed. Friedrich Freiherr Hiller von Gaertringen in collaboration with K. P. Reiß. Berlin: 1988.

———. *Diaries.* New York: 1947; *The von Hassell Diaries 1938–1944.* London: 1948.

[Hitler, Adolf]. *Hitler's Table Talk 1941–1944.* London: 1953.

Hoegner, Wilhelm. *Der schwierige Außenseiter. Erinnerungen eines Abgeordneten, Emigranten und Ministerpräsidenten.* Munich: 1959.

Hoettl, Wilhelm. *Hitler's Paper Weapon.* St. Albans: 1955.

————. *The Secret Front: The Story of Nazi Political Espionage.* New York: 1954.

Hoover, Calvin B. *Memoirs of Capitalism, Communism, and Nazism.* Durham, NC: 1965.

House of Commons, House of Lords. *Parliamentary Debates,* 5th Series, London: 1938–1944.

Jens, Inge, ed. *Hans Scholl, Sophie Scholl. Briefe und Aufzeichnungen.* Frankfurt/Main: 1984.

John, Otto. *Falsch und spät. Der 20 Juli 1944.* Munich: 1984.

————. *Twice Through the Lines. The Autobiography of Otto John.* London/New York: 1972.

Keesing's Contemporary Archives: Weekly Diary of Important World Events. vol. 5: Bristol 1943–1945.

Kennan, George F. *Memoirs 1925–1950.* Boston: 1967.

Kleist, Peter. *Zwischen Hitler und Stalin 1939–1945. Aufzeichnungen.* Bonn: 1950.

Knoop-Graf, Anneliese, and Inge Jens, eds. *Willi Graf. Briefe und Aufzeichnungen.* Frankfurt/Main: 1988.

Kordt, Erich. *Nicht aus den Akten. Die Wilhelmstraße in Frieden und Krieg.* Stuttgart: 1950.

Kriegstagebuch des Oberkommandos der Wehrmacht (Wehrmachtsführungsstab) 1940–1945, vols. 1–4. Frankfurt/Main: 1965, 1963, 1963, 1961.

Langer, William L. *In and Out of the Ivory Tower: The Autobiography of William L. Langer.* New York: 1978.

Lankford, Nelson D., ed. *OSS Against the Reich. The World War II Diaries of Colonel David K. E. Bruce.* London: 1991.

[Leber, Julius]. *Ein Mann geht seinen Weg. Schriften, Reden und Briefe von Julius Leber.* Berlin, Frankfurt/M.: 1952.

Leverkuehn, Paul. *German Military Intelligence.* London: 1954.

Link, Werner, and Erich Matthias, eds. *Mit dem Gesicht nach Deutschland. Eine Dokumentation über die sozialdemokratische Emigration. Aus dem Nachlaß von Friedrich Stampfer, ergänzt durch andere Überlieferungen.* Düsseldorf: 1968.

Lipkens, Walter, ed. *Documents on the History of European Integration.* 2 vols. *[1: Continental Plans for European Union 1939–1945; 2: Plans für European Union in Great Britain and in Exile 1939–1945].* Berlin: 1985–1986.

Löbe, Paul. ["Anmerkungen zum 20 Juli 1944."] *Der Tagesspiegel,* 30 April 1947.

McDonald, Elizabeth. *Undercover Girl.* New York: 1947.

Mendelsohn, John, ed. *Covert Warfare. Intelligence, Counterintelligence, and Military Deception During the World War II Era.* 18 vols. New York/London: 1989.

————. *German Radio Intelligence and the Soldatensender.* New York/London: 1989.

Molden, Fritz. *Exploding Star: A Young Austrian Against Hitler.* London: 1978.

————. *Fires in the Night: The Sacrifices and Significance of the Austrian Resistance 1938–1945.* Boulder, CO: 1989.

————. *Fepolinski und Waschlapski.* Vienna: 1976.

Moltke, Helmuth James von. *Briefe an Freya 1939–1945.* Ed. Beate Ruhm von Oppen. Munich: 1988.

[Müller, Josef.] "Für das anständige Deutschland." *Telegraf* 15. October 1952.

Mulligan, Timothy, ed. *ULTRA, MAGIC, and the Allies.* London/New York: 1989.

Niebergall, Otto. *Résistance. Erinnerungen deutscher Antifaschisten.* Berlin: 1973.

Nitzsche, Gerhard. *Die Saefkow-Jacob-Bästlein-Gruppe. Dokumente und Materialien des illegalen antifaschistischen Kampfes (1942–1945).* Berlin: 1957.

Papen, Franz von. *Memoirs.* London: 1953

Poelchau, Harald. *Die letzten Stunden: Erinnerungen eines Gefängnispfarrers aufgezeichnet von Graf Alexander Stenbock-Fermor.* Berlin: 1949.

Portmann, Heinrich, ed. *Bischof Graf von Galen spricht! Ein apostolischer Kampf und sein Widerhall.* Freiburg: 1946.

Rathkolb, Oliver, ed. *Gesellschaft und Politik am Beginn der Zweiten Republik. Vertrauliche Berichte der US-Militäradministration aus Österreich 1945, in englischer Originalfassung.* Wien: 1985.

Roosevelt, Kermit, ed. *War Report of the OSS (Office of Strategic Services).* vol. 1. New York: 1976.

———. *The Overseas Targets: War Report of the OSS.* vol. 2. New York: 1976.

Rothfels, Hans, ed. "Trott und die Außenpolitik des Widerstandes." *VfZ* 12 (1964): 300–323.

———. "Adam von Trott und das State Department." *VfZ* 7 (July 1959): 318–332.

———. "Zwei außenpolitische Memoranden der deutschen Opposition (Frühjahr 1942)." *VfZ* 5 (1957): 388–397.

———. "Zwei außenpolitische Memoranden der deutschen Opposition (Frühjahr 1942)." *VfZ* 5 (Oct. 1957): 388–397.

Rothstein, Andrew, ed. *Soviet Foreign Policy During the Patriotic War: Documents and Materials 22 June 1941–31 December 1943* vol. 1: London: 1944.

Sauerbruch, Ferdinand. *A Surgeon's Life.* London: 1953.

———. *Das war mein Leben.* München: 1951.

Schacht, Hjalmar. *Account Settled.* London: 1949.

———. *Abrechnung mit Hitler.* Frankfurt/M.: 1949.

[Schellenberg, Walter] *The Schellenberg Memoirs.* London: 1956.

Schlabrendorff, Fabian von. *Offiziere gegen Hitler.* Zürich: 1946; revised and ampl. ed. by Walter Bußmann. Berlin: 1984.

———. *The Secret War Against Hitler.* London: 1966.

———. *They Almost Killed Hitler.* New York: 1947; *Revolt Against Hitler: The Personal Account of Fabian von Schlabrendorff.* Prep. and ed. by Gero v.S. Gaevernitz. London: 1948.

Schlabrendorff, Fabian von, ed. *Eugen Gerstenmaier im Dritten Reich: Eine Dokumentation.* Stuttgart: 1965. [also: Aus Politik und Zeitgeschichte B41/65. *Das Parlament,* 13 Oct. 1965.]

Schmidt, Kurt Dietrich, ed. *Dokumente des Kirchenkampfes.* 2 vols. Göttingen: 1964–1965.

Smith, Bradley F., ed. *OSS Jedburgh Teams.* 2 vols. New York/London: 1989.

———. *Other OSS Teams.* New York/London: 1989.

———. *The Spy Factory and Secret Intelligence.* New York/London: 1989.

Scholder, Klaus, ed. *Die Mittwochs-Gesellschaft. Protokolle aus dem geistigen Deutschland 1932 bis 1944.* Berlin: 1982.

Schramm, Wilhelm Ritter von, ed. *Beck und Goerdeler: Gemeinschaftsdokumente für den Frieden 1941–1944.* Munich: 1965.

Skorzeny, Otto. *Skorzeny's Special Missions.* London: 1957.

Söllner, Alfons, ed. *Zur Archäologie der Demokratie in Deutschland.* vol. 1: *Analysen von politischen Emigranten im amerikanischen Geheimdienst 1943–1945;* vol. 2: *Analysen von politischen Emigranten im amerikanischen Außenministerium 1946–1949.* Frankfurt/Main: 1986.

Speer, Albert. *Inside the Third Reich.* London: 1970.

———. *Erinnerungen.* Berlin: 1969.

Spiegelbild einer Verschwörung: Die Kaltenbrunner-Berichte an Borman und Hitler über das Attentat vom 20 Juli 1944. Geheime Dokumente aus dem ehemaligen Reichssicherheitshauptamt. Stuttgart: 1961.

Trial of the Major War Criminals Before the International Military Tribunal: Nuremberg 14 November 1945–1 October 1946 (42 vols). Nuremberg 1947–1949.

Trials of War Criminals Before the Nuremberg Military Tribunals Under Control Council Law No. 10 (15 vols). Washington, DC: 1949–1953.

Troy, Thomas F., ed. *Wartime Washington: The Secret OSS Journal of James Grafton Rogers 1942–1943.* Frederick, MD: 1987.

Vassiltchikov, Marie. *The Berlin Diaries of Marie 'Missi' Vassiltchikov.* London: 1987.

Vermehren, Isa. *Reise durch den letzten Akt.* Hamburg: 1947.

Visser't Hooft, Willem. *Memoirs.* London: 1973.

———. *Die Welt war meine Gemeinde: Autobiographie.* Munich: 1972.

Waibel, Max. *Kapitulation in Italien.* Basel: 1981.

Wedemeyer, Albert C. *Wedemeyer Reports!* New York: 1958.

———. *Der verwaltete Krieg.* Gütersloh: 1958.

Wheeler-Bennett, Sir John. *Special Relationships. America in Peace and War.* London: 1975.

Wiskemann, Elizabeth. *The Europe I Saw.* London: 1968.

II. Secondary Works

Abshagen, Karl Heinz. *Canaris.* London: 1956.

———. *Canaris. Patriot und Weltbürger.* Stuttgart: 1949.

Aigner, Dietrich. *Das Ringen um England. Das deutsch-britische Verhältnis. Die öffentliche Meinung 1933–1939. Tragödie zweier Völker.* Munich: 1969.

Alsop, Stewart, and Thomas Beaden. *Sub Rosa: The OSS and American Espionage.* 2d ed. New York: 1964.

Ambrose, Stephen E., with Richard H. Immerman. *Ike's Spies: Eisenhower and the Espionage Establishment.* Garden City, NY: 1981.

Ameringer, Charles D. *U.S. Foreign Intelligence; The Secret Side of American History.* Lexington, MA: 1990.

Andrew, Christopher, and David Dilks, eds. *The Missing Dimension: Governments and Intelligence Communities in the Twentieth Century.* Urbana, IL: 1984.

Armstrong, Anne. *Unconditional Surrender. The Impact of the Casablanca Policy upon World War II.* New Brunswick, NJ: 1961.

Astor, David. "Why the Revolt Against Hitler was Ignored." *Encounter* 32 (June 1969): 3–13.

Balfour, Michael. *Withstanding Hitler in Germany; 1933–45.* London: 1988.

———. *Propaganda in War and Peace 1939–1945.* Boston: 1979.

Balfour, Michael, and Julian Frisby. *Helmuth von Moltke. A Leader Against Hitler.* London: 1972.

Bancroft, Mary. "Jung and His Circle." *Psychological Perspectives* 6:2 (1975). [Jung Centenary Issue II.]

Bartel, Walter. "Die deutsche Widerstandsbewegung und die Alliierten zur Zeit des Zweiten Weltkrieges." *Zeitschrift für Geschichtswissenschaft* 5 (1961): 993–1013.

Becker, Howard. "The Nature and Consequences of Black Propaganda." *American Sociological Review* 14 (1949): 221–235.

Beer, Siegfried. "Der Agent 'Ernest Cole.'" *Steirische Berichte* 3 (1985): 16–20.

————. "Alliierte Planung, Propaganda und Penetration 1943–1945. Die künftigen Besatzungsmächte und das wiederzuerrichtende Österreich, von der Moskauer Deklaration bis zur Befreiung." Karner, Stefan. *Das Burgenland im Jahr 1945. Beiträge zur Landesausstellung 1945* (Eisenstadt: 1945): 67–88.

Beier, Gerhard. *Die illegale Reichsleitung der Gewerkschaften, 1933–1945.* Köln: 1981.

Benz, Wolfgang, and Walter H. Pehle, eds. *Lexikon des deutschen Widerstandes.* Frankfurt/Main: 1994.

Bergmann, Karl Hans. *Die Bewegung Freies Deutschland in der Schweiz 1943–1945.* Munich: 1974.

Bethge, Eberhard. *Dietrich Bonhoeffer.* London: 1970.

————. *Dietrich Bonhoeffer: Man of Vision, Man of Courage.* New York: 1970.

————. *Dietrich Bonhoeffer. Theologe, Christ, Zeitgenosse.* Munich: 1967.

Borsdorf, Ulrich, and Lutz Niethammer. *Zwischen Befreiung und Besatzung.* Wuppertal: 1976.

Boyens, Armin. *Kirchenkampf und Ökumene 1933–1945. Darstellung und Dokumentation unter besonderer Berücksichtigung der Quellen des Ökumenischen Rates der Kirchen.* vol. 1: *1933–1939;* vol. 2: *1939–1945.* Munich: 1969–1973.

Boyer, John W., and Julius Kirshner, eds. *Resistance Against the Third Reich.* Chicago: 1992.

Braunschweig, Pierre-Th. *Geheimer Draht nach Berlin. Die Nachrichtenlinie Masson-Schellenberg und der schweizerische Nachrichtendienst im Zweiten Weltkrieg.* 3d ed. Zürich: 1990.

Brissaud, André. *Canaris. The Biography of Admiral Canaris, Chief of German Military Intelligence in the Second World War.* London: 1973.

Bungert, Heike. "Ein meisterhafter Schachzug. Das Nationalkomitee Freies Deutschland in der Beurteilung der Amerikaner, 1943–45." Heideking, Jürgen, and Christof Mauch, eds. *Geheimdienstkrieg gegen Deutschland* (Göttingen: 1993): 90–121.

Cartarius, Ulrich, and Forschungsgemeinschaft 20 Juli e.V., eds. *Bibliographie "Widerstand."* Munich: 1984.

Casey, William J. *The Secret War Against Hitler.* Washington, DC: 1988.

Cave Brown, Anthony. *The Last Hero: Wild Bill Donovan.* New York: 1982.

Chalou, George C., ed. *The Secret War. The Office of Strategic Services in World War II.* Washington, DC: 1992.

Cline, Marjorie W., Carla E. Christiansen, and Judith M. Fontaine. *Scholar's Guide to Intelligence Literature: Bibliography of the Russell J. Bowen Collection.* Frederick, MD: 1983.

Colby, Benjamin. *'Twas a Famous Victory: Deception and Propaganda in the War Against Germany.* New Rochelle, NY: 1974.

Coleman, Archibald Frederick. "Snapdragon: Story of a Spy." *Metro: The Magazine of Southeastern Virginia* 7 (May 1977): 24–31; 64–69.

Constantinides, George C. *Intelligence and Espionage: An Analytical Bibliography.* Boulder, CO: 1983.

Conway, John S. *The Nazi Persecution of the Churches 1933–45.* Toronto/London/New York: 1968.

Corson, William R. *The Armies of Ignorance: The Rise of the American Intelligence Empire.* New York: 1977.

Coser, Lewis. *Refugee Scholars in America.* New Haven, CT: 1984.

Crankshaw, Edward. *Gestapo.* Washington, DC: 1989.

Cruikshank, Charles. *The Fourth Arm.* London: 1977.

Dallek, Robert. *Franklin D. Roosevelt and American Foreign Policy, 1932–1945.* New York: 1979.

Dallin, David. *Soviet Espionage.* New Haven, CT: 1955.

Daugherty, William Edward, with Morris Janowitz, eds. *A Psychological Warfare Casebook.* Baltimore: 1958.

Deane, John Russell. *The Strange Alliance: The Story of American Wartime Cooperation with Russia.* New York: 1947.

Deutsch, Harold C. *Hitler and His Generals.* Minneapolis: 1974.

———. *The Conspiracy Against Hitler in the Twilight War.* Minneapolis: 1968.

Döscher, Hans Jürgen. *Das Auswärtige Amt im Dritten Reich. Diplomatie im Schatten der "Endlösung."* Berlin: 1987.

Duhnke, Horst. *Die KPD von 1933 bis 1945.* Köln: 1972.

Dulles, Allen W. *The Secret Surrender.* New York: 1966.

———. *Germany's Underground.* New York: 1947.

Dunlop, Richard. *Donovan, America's Master Spy.* Chicago: 1982.

[Earle, George]. "Papen Offered to Betray Hitler, Earle Asserts in Defending Intercession." *Philadelphia Inquirer* (30 Jan. 1949).

Erdmann, James M. *Leaflet Operations in the Second World War.* Denver: 1969.

Fischer, Alexander. *Sowjetische Deutschlandpolitik im Zweiten Weltkrieg 1941–1945.* Stuttgart: 1975.

Fleischhauer, Ingeborg. *Der Widerstand gegen den Rußlandfeldzug: Beiträge zum Widerstand 1933–1945.* Berlin: 1987.

———. *Die Chance des Sonderfriedens. Deutsch-sowjetische Geheimgespräche 1941–1945.* Berlin: 1986.

Foot, Michael R. D. *Resistance: An Analysis of European Resistance to Nazism 1940–1945.* London: 1976.

Ford, Corey. *Donovan of OSS.* Boston: 1970.

Ford, Corey, and Alastair MacBain. *Cloak and Dagger: The Secret Story of the OSS.* New York: 1945.

Ford, Franklin L. "Der 20. Juli." *Die Amerikanische Rundschau* 3:11 (1947): 5–17.

———. "The Twentieth of July in the History of the German Resistance." *American Historical Review* 51 (1945/46): 609–626.

Gallin O.S.U., Mother Mary Alice. *Ethical and Religious Factors in the German Resistance to Hitler.* Washington, DC: 1955.

Garlinski, Jozef. *The Swiss Corridor: Espionage Networks in Switzerland During World War II.* London: 1981.

Georgi, Friedrich. *Soldat im Widerstand. General der Infanterie Friedrich Olbricht.* Berlin/Hamburg: 1989.

Gerstenmaier, Eugen. "Das Kirchliche Außenamt im Reiche Hitlers. Zum Gedenken an Hans Schönfeld." Gerstenmaier, Eugen. *Reden und Aufsätze.* (Stuttgart: 1962): 307–318; 421–427.

Görlitz, Walter. *The German General Staff.* London: 1953.

———. *Der deutsche Generalstab. Geschichte und Gestalt 1657–1945.* Frankfurt/M.: 1950.

Graml, Hermann, ed. *Widerstand im Dritten Reich. Probleme, Ereignisse, Gestalten.* Frankfurt/Main: 1984.

———. Hans Mommsen, Hans J. Reichhardt, and Eric Wolf. *The German Resistance to Hitler.* Berkeley/London: 1970.

Grassmann, Peter. *Sozialdemokraten gegen Hitler 1933–1945.* Munich: 1976.

Grebing, Helga, and Christl Wickert, eds. Das *"Andere Deutschland" im Widerstand gegen den Nationalsozialismus.* Essen: 1994.

Harnack, Axel v[on]. "Arvid und Mildred Harnack: Erinnerungen an ihren Prozess 1942/43." *Die Gegenwart* 2:1, 2 (1947): 15–18.

Harnack, Axel von. *Ernst von Harnack (1888–1945): Ein Kämpfer für Deutschlands Zukunft.* Schwenningen: 1951.

Hartmann, Christian. *Halder, Generalstabschef Hitlers 1938–1942.* Paderborn: 1991.

Heideking, Jürgen. "Die 'Breakers-Akte,' Das Office of Strategic Services und der 20 Juli." Heideking, Jürgen, and Christof Mauch, eds. *Geheimdienstkrieg gegen Deutschland* (Göttingen: 1993): 11–50.

———. "Amerikanische Geheimdienste und Widerstandsbewegungen im Zweiten Weltkrieg." Schulz, Gerhard. *Partisanen und Volkskrieg. Zur Revolutionierung des Krieges im 20. Jahrhundert* (Göttingen: 1985): 147–177.

———. "Gero von Schulze-Gaevernitz." Bosch, Michael and Wolfgang Niess, eds. *Der Widerstand im deutschen Südwesten 1933–1945* (Stuttgart: 1984): 281–290.

———. "Die 'Schweizer Straßen' des europäischen Widerstands." Schulz, Gerhard, ed. *Geheimdienste und Widerstandsbewegungen im Zweiten Weltkrieg.* (Göttingen: 1982): 143–187.

Heideking, Jürgen, and Christof Mauch, eds. *Geheimdienstkrieg gegen Deutschland. Subversion, Propaganda und Nachkriegsplanungen des Office of Strategic Services im Zweiten Weltkrieg.* Göttingen: 1993.

———. *USA und deutscher Widerstand. Analysen und Operationen des amerikanischen Geheimdienstes OSS.* Tübingen: 1993.

———. "Das Herman-Dossier. Helmuth James Graf von Moltke, die deutsche Emigration in Istanbul und der amerikanische Geheimdienst Office of Strategic Services." *VfZG* 40 (1992): 567–623.

Henke, Josef. *England in Hitler's politischem Kalkül 1935–1939.* Boppard: 1977.

Herbert, Ulrich. *Fremdarbeiter. Politik und Praxis des "Ausländer-Einsatzes" in der Kriegswirtschaft des Dritten Reiches.* 2d ed. Berlin: 1986.

Hinsley, Francis Harry et al. *British Intelligence in the Second World War. Its Influence on Strategy and Operations.* 5 vols. London: 1979–1990.

Hoffmann, Peter. *German Resistance to Hitler.* Cambridge, MA/London: 1988.

———. "Colonel Claus von Stauffenberg in the German Resistance to Hitler: Between East and West." *Historical Journal* 31 (Sept. 1988): 629–650.

———. "Peace through Coup d'Etat: The Foreign Contacts of the German Resistance 1933–1944." *Central European History* 19 (Mar. 1986): 3–44.

———. *The History of the German Resistance, 1933–1945.* Cambridge, MA: 1979.

Höhne, Heinz. *Canaris.* Garden City/London: 1979.

———. *Codeword: Direktor. The Story of the Red Orchestra.* London: 1970. [1971]

Hymoff, Edward. *The OSS in World War II.* New York: 1986.

Jacobsen, Hans Adolf, ed. *July 20, 1944: The German Opposition to Hitler as Viewed by Foreign Historians—An Anthology.* Bonn: 1969.

Jeffreys-Jones, Rhodri. *American Espionage: From Secret Service to CIA.* New York: 1977.

Kahn, David. *Hitler's Spies: German Military Intelligence in World War II.* New York: 1978.

Katz, Barry M. *Foreign Intelligence: Research and Analysis in the Office of Strategic Services 1942–1945.* Cambridge, MA: 1989.

———. "The Criticism of Arms: The Frankfurt School Goes to War." *Journal of Modern History* 59 (1987): 439–478.

Kennan, George F. "Noble Man: Helmuth von Moltke: A Leader Against Hitler." *New York Review* (22 Mar. 1973).

Kent, George O. "Pope Pius XII and Germany: Some Aspects of German-Vatican Relations 1933–1943." *American Historical Review* 70 (Oct. 1964): 59–78.

Kershaw, Ian. *Popular Opinion and Political Dissent in the Third Reich: Bavaria 1933–1945.* Oxford: 1983.

Kettenacker, Lothar. *Krieg zur Friedenssicherung. Die Deutschlandplanung der britischen Regierung während des Zweiten Weltkrieges.* Göttingen: 1989.

Kettenacker, Lothar, ed. *Das 'andere Deutschland' im Zweiten Weltkrieg. Emigration und Widerstand in internationaler Perspektive.* Stuttgart: 1977.

Kimche, Jon. *Spying for Peace: General Guisan and Swiss Neutrality.* New York: 1961.

Klemperer, Klemens von. *Die verlassenen Verschwörer. Der deutsche Widerstand auf der Suche nach Verbündeten 1938–1945.* Berlin: 1994.

———. *German Resistance Against Hitler. The Search for Allies Abroad 1938–1945.* Oxford: 1992.

———. "Adam von Trott zu Solz and Resistance Foreign Policy." *Central European History* 14 (1981): 351–361.

Kliem, Kurt. *Der sozialistische Widerstand gegen das Dritte Reich, dargestellt an der Gruppe "Neu Beginnen."* Marburg: 1957.

Langer, Walter C. *The Mind of Adolf Hitler: The Secret Wartime Report.* New York: 1972.

Laqueur, Walter, and Richard Breitman. *Breaking the Silence.* New York: 1986.

———. *A World of Secrets: The Uses and Limits of Intelligence.* New York: 1985.

Large, David Clay, ed. *Contending with Hitler: Varieties of German Resistance in the Third Reich.* Cambridge: 1991.

Leithäuser, Joachim Gustav. *Wilhelm Leuschner: Ein Leben für die Republik.* Köln: 1962.

Lerner, Daniel. *Sykewar: Psychological Warfare Against Nazi Germany.* Cambridge, MA: 1971.

Lill, Rudolf, and Heinrich Oberreuter, eds. *20 Juli—Porträt des Widerstands.* Munich: 1989.

Link, Werner. *Die Geschichte des internationalen Jugend-Bundes (IJB) und des Internationalen Sozialistischen Kampf-Bundes (ISK). Ein Beitrag zur Geschichte der Arbeiterbewegung in der Weimarer Republik und im Dritten Reich.* Meisenheim am Glan: 1964.

Lovell, Stanley P. *Of Spies and Stratagems.* Englewood Cliffs, NJ: 1963.

Löwenthal, Richard. *Die Widerstandsgruppe "Neu Beginnen," Beiträge zum Thema Widerstand.* Berlin: 1982.

MacDonald, Lawrence H. "The Office of Strategic Services. America's First National Intelligence Agency. *Prologue* 23 (1991): 7–24.

Maier, Hedwig. "Die SS und der 20 Juli 1944." *VfZ* 14 (1966): 299–316.

Marquardt-Bigman, Petra. *Amerikanische Geheimdienstanalysen über Deutschland 1942–1949.* München 1995.

———. *Die Deutschlandanalysen des amerikanischen Geheimdienstes in der Kriegs—und Nachkriegszeit (1941–1949). Eine Untersuchung zur Tätigkeit der Research and Analysis Branch des Office of Strategic Services und ihrer Nachfolgeorganisationen im State Department.* [PhD. Diss] Tübingen: 1991.

Martin, Bernd. *Friedensinitiativen und Machtpolitik im Zweiten Weltkrieg 1939–1942.* Düsseldorf: 1974.

Mastny, Vojtech. *Russia's Road to the Cold War.* New York: 1979.

———. "Stalin and the Prospects of a Separate Peace in World War II." *American Historical Review* 77 (1972): 1365–1388.

Mauch, Christof. "The Office of Strategic Services (OSS) and Anti-Nazi Resistance. Perceptions, Propaganda and Subversive Operations." Proceedings of the 108th Annual Conference of the American Historical Association in San Francisco (Ann Arbor, MI: 1995): 134–143.

———. "Subversion und Propaganda. Der Widerstand gegen den Nationalsozialismus im Kalkül des amerikanischen Geheimdienstes OSS." Heideking, Jürgen, and Christof Mauch, eds. *Geheimdienstkrieg gegen Deutschland* (Göttingen: 1993): 51–89.

Meier, Kurt. *Der evangelische Kirchenkampf. Gesamtdarstellung in drei Bänden.* Göttingen: 1976 ss.

Merson, Allan. *Communist Resistance in Nazi Germany.* London: 1985.

Militärgeschichtliches Forschungsamt, ed. *Aufstand des Gewissens. Der militärische Widerstand gegen Hitler und das NS-Regime 1933–1945.* Herford/Bonn: 1984.

Minott, Rodney C. *The Fortress That Never Was.* New York: 1964.

Molden, Otto. *Der Ruf des Gewissens. Der österreichische Freiheitskampf 1938–1945.* Vienna/Munich: 1958.

Moltmann, Günter. "Die Genesis der Unconditional Surrender-Forderung." Hillgruber, Andreas, ed. *Probleme des Zweiten Weltkrieges.* (Berlin: 1967): 171–198.

———. *Amerikas Deutschlandpolitik im Zweiten Weltkrieg.* Heidelberg: 1958.

Morgan, Edward P. "The Spy the Nazis Missed." *True: The Man's Magazine* (July 1950). ["The Spy the Nazis Missed. (Fritz Kolbe)," in Allen Welsh Dulles, ed., *Great True Spy Stories* (New York: 1968): 21–29.]

Mosley, Leonard. *Dulles: A Biography of Eleanor, Allen and John Foster Dulles and Their Family Network.* New York: 1978.

Müller, Josef. *Bis zur letzten Konsequenz.* Munich: 1975.

Müller, Klaus-Jürgen, and David N. Dilks, eds. *Großbritannien und der deutsche Widerstand 1933–1944.* Paderborn: 1994.

Müller, Klaus-Jürgen. *General Ludwig Beck. Studien und Dokumente zur politisch-militärischen Vorstellungswelt und Tätigkeit des Generalstabschefs des deutschen Heeres 1933–1938.* Boppard: 1980.

Müller, Klaus-Jürgen, ed. *Der deutsche Widerstand 1933–1945.* Paderborn: 1986.

Mulligan, Timothy, ed. *ULTRA, MAGIC, and the Allies.* London/New York: 1989.

Müssener, Helmut. *Exil in Schweden.* Munich: 1977.

Neuhäusler, Johann B. *Kreuz und Hakenkreuz. Der Kampf des Nationalsozialismus gegen die katholische Kirche und der kirchliche Widerstand.* 2 vols. Munich: 1946.

Neumann, Franz. *Behemoth. Struktur und Praxis des Nationalsozialismus 1933–1944.* Hrsg. und mit einem Nachwort versehen von Gert Schäfer. Frankfurt: 1984.

———. *Behemoth: The Structure and Practice of National Socialism.* New York: 1942.

Neumark, Fritz. *Zuflucht am Bosporus. Deutsche Gelehrte, Politiker und Künstler in der Emigration 1933–1953.* Frankfurt/Main: 1980.

Nicosia, Francis R., and Lawrence D. Stokes, eds. *Germans Against Nazism. Nonconformity, Opposition and Resistance in the Third Reich. Essays in Honour of Peter Hoffmann.* New York: 1990.

O'Toole, George J. A. *The Encyclopedia of American Intelligence and Espionage: From Revolutionary War to the Present.* New York/Oxford: 1988.

Padover, Saul K. *Experiment in Germany: The Story of the American Intelligence Officer.* New York: 1946.

Page, Helena P. *General Friedrich Olbricht. Ein Mann des 20 Juli.* Bonn: 1992.

Persico, Joseph E. *Casey. From the OSS to the CIA.* New York/London: 1990.

————. *Piercing the Reich: The Penetration of Nazi Germany by American Secret Agents During World War II*. New York: 1979.

Petersen, Neal H. *American Intelligence, 1775–1990. A Bibliographical Guide*. Claremont, CA: 1992.

Peterson, Walter F. "Zwischen Mißtrauen und Interesse: Regierungsstellen in Washington und die deutsche politische Emigration 1939–1945." Briegel, Manfred, and Wolfgang Frühwald, eds. *Die Erfahrung der Fremde*. Weinheim: 1988.

Peukert, Detlev. *Inside Nazi Germany: Conformity, Opposition, and Racism in Everyday Life*. New Haven/London: 1987.

————. *Die KPD im Widerstand. Verfolgung und Untergrundarbeit an Rhein und Ruhr 1933 bis 1945*. Wuppertal: 1980.

Pogue, Forrest C. *George C. Marshall*. vol. 3: *Organizer of Victory, 1943–1945*. New York: 1973.

————. *George C. Marshall*. vol. 2. *Ordeal and Hope, 1939–1942*. New York: 1966.

————. *The Supreme Command (The United States in World War II: The European Theater of Operations)*. Washington, DC: 1954.

Portmann, Heinrich. *Kardinal von Galen*. Münster: 1974.

Pütter, C. (= Konrad). *Rundfunk gegen das 'Dritte Reich'. Deutschsprachige Rundfunkaktivitäten im Exil 1933–1945—Ein Handbuch*. Munich/London/New York/Paris: 1986.

Radkau, Joachim. *Die deutsche Emigration in den USA. Ihr Einfluß auf die amerikanische Europapolitik 1933–1945*. Düsseldorf: 1971.

Rhodes, Anthony. *Propaganda, the Art of Persuasion: World War II*. New York: 1976.

Ritter, Gerhard. *The German Resistance: Carl Goerdeler's Struggle Against Tyranny*. London: 1958.

————. *Carl Goerdeler und die deutsche Widerstandsbewegung*. 3d ed. Stuttgart: 1956.

————. "Die außenpolitischen Hoffnungen der Verschwörer des 20 Juli 1944." *Merkur* 3 (Nov. 1949): 1121–1138.

Röder, Werner. *Die deutschen sozialistischen Exilgruppen in Großbritannien 1940–1945. Ein Beitrag zur Geschichte des Widerstandes gegen den Nationalsozialismus*. 2d ed. Bonn-Bad Godesberg: 1973.

Röder, Werner, and Herbert A. Strauß, eds. *Biographisches Handbuch der deutschsprachigen Emigration nach 1933/ International Biographical Dictionary of Central European Emigres 1933–1945*. 4 vols. Munich/New York: 1980–1983.

Roon, Ger van. *German Resistance to Hitler: Count von Moltke and the Kreisau Circle* [abridged]. London: 1971.

————. *Neuordnung im Widerstand: Der Kreisauer Kreis innerhalb der deutschen Widerstandsbewegung*. Munich: 1967.

Rothfels, Hans. *Die deutsche Opposition gegen Hitler: Eine Würdigung*. Frankfurt/M./Hamburg: 1958; new ed. 1969.

————. "The German Resistance in Its International Aspects." *International Affairs* 34 (1958): 477–489.

————. *The German Opposition to Hitler*. Transl. Lawrence Wilson. Hinsdale, IL: 1948. [London: 1961].

Rubin, Barry. *Istanbul Intrigues. A True-Life Casablanca*. New York: 1989.

Sainsbury, Keith. *The Turning Point. Roosevelt, Stalin, Churchill, and Chiang-Kai-Shek, 1943. The Moscow, Cairo, and Teheran Conferences*. Oxford/New York: 1985.

Scheurig, Bodo. *Verräter oder Patrioten. Das Nationalkomitee Freies Deutschland und der Bund Deutscher Offiziere in der Sowjetunion 1943–1945.* Berlin: 1993.

———. *Free Germany: The National Committee and the League of German Officers.* Middletown, CT: 1969.

———. *Freies Deutschland: Das Nationalkomitee und der Bund deutscher Offiziere in der Sowjetunion 1943–1945.* 2d ed. Munich: 1961.

Schlie, Ulrich. *Kein Friede mit Deutschland. Die geheimen Gespräche im Zweiten Weltkrieg 1939–1941.* München/Berlin: 1994.

Schmädeke, Jürgen, und Peter Steinbach, eds. *Der Widerstand gegen den Nationalsozialismus: Die deutsche Gesellschaft und der Widerstand gegen Hitler.* Munich/Zürich: 1985.

Schmitthenner, Walter, and Hans Buchheim, eds. *Der deutsche Widerstand gegen Hitler: Vier historisch-kritische Studien.* Cologne/Berlin: 1966.

Schoenhals, Kai P. *The Free Germany Movement. A Case of Patriotism or Treason?* New York: 1989.

Scholder, Klaus. *The Churches and the Third Reich.* 2 vols. London/Philadelphia: 1987–1988.

Scholl, Inge. *The White Rose. Munich 1942–1943.* Middletown, CT: 1983.

Schulz, Gerhard, ed. "'Dismemberment of Germany.' Kriegsziele und Koalitionsstrategie 1939–1945." *Historische Zeitschrift* 244 (1987): 29–92.

———. *Partisanen und Volkskrieg. Zur Revolutionierung des Krieges im 20 Jahrhundert* Göttingen: 1985

———. "Nationalpatriotismus im Widerstand. Ein Problem der europäischen Krise und des Zweiten Weltkriegs—nach vier Jahrzehnten Widerstandsgeschichte." *Vierteljahrshefte für Zeitgeschichte* 32 (1984): 9–34.

———. *Geheimdienste und Widerstandsbewegungen im Zweiten Weltkrieg.* Göttingen: 1982.

Singer, Kurt. *The Men in the Trojan Horse.* Boston: 1953.

Smith, Bradley F. *The Shadow Warriors: OSS and the Origins of the CIA.* New York: 1983.

———. "A Note on the OSS, Ultra, and World War II's Intelligence Legacy for America." *Defense Analysis* 3:2 (1987): 184–189.

Smith, Bradley F., and Elena Agarossi. *Operation Sunrise: The Secret Surrender.* New York: 1979.

Smith, Gaddis. *American Diplomacy During the Second World War 1941–1945.* New York: 1965.

Smith, Myron J., Jr. *The Secret Wars. A Guide to Sources in English.* vol. 1 *Intelligence, Propaganda and Psychological Warfare, Resistance Movements, and Secret Operations;* vol. 2 *Intelligence, Propaganda and Psychological Warfare, Covert Operations, 1945–1980.* Santa Barbara, CA: 1980–1981.

Smith, R. Harris. OSS. *The Secret History of America's First Central Intelligence Agency.* Berkeley: 1972.

Snyder, Louis, ed. *The Third Reich 1933–1945. A Bibliogrpahical Guide to German National Socialism.* New York: 1987.

Soley, Lawrence C. *Radio Warfare: OSS and CIA Subversive Propaganda.* New York: 1989.

Söllner, Alfons. "Wissenschaftliche Kompetenz und politische Ohnmacht. Deutsche Emigranten im amerikanischen Staatsdienst 1942–1949." Koebner, Thomas, Gert Sautermeister, and Sigrid Schneider, eds. *Deutschland nach Hitler. Zukunftspläne im Exil und aus der Besatzungszeit, 1939–1949.* Opladen: 1987.

Stafford, David. *Britain and the European Resistance 1940–1945: A Survey of the Special Operations Executive, with Documents.* London: 1980.

Steinbach, Peter, and Johannes Tuchel. eds. *Widerstand gegen den Nationalsozialismus.* Berlin/Bonn: 1994.

Steinert, Marlis G. *Hitlers Krieg und die Deutschen. Stimmung und Haltung der deutschen Bevölkerung im Zweiten Weltkrieg.* Düsseldorf: 1970.

Sykes, Christopher. *Troubled Loyalty: A Biography of Adam von Trott zu Solz.* London: 1968.

Thun-Hohenstein, Romedio Graf von. *Der Verschwörer. General Oster und die Militäropposition.* Munich: 1984.

Troy, Thomas F. *Donovan and the CIA: A History of the Establishment of the Central Intelligence Agency.* Frederick, MD: 1981.

U.S. Army. *The Psychological Warfare Division, Supreme Headquarters Allied Expeditionary Force: An Account of Its Operations in the Western European Campaign, 1944–1945.* Bad Homburg, Germany: 1945.

U.S. Central Intelligence Agency. *The Rote Kapelle: The CIA's History of Soviet Intelligence and Espionage Networks in Western Europe, 1936–1945.* Frederick, MD: 1979.

U.S. Department of State. *Foreign Relations of the United States.* 1945, vol. 3. *European Advisory Commission, Austria, Germany.* Washington, DC: 1968.

Visser't Hooft, Willem A. "The View from Geneva." *Encounter* 33 (Sept. 1969): 92–94.

———. "Bishop Bell's Life Work in the Ecumenical Movement." *Ecumenical Review* 11 (Jan. 1959): 133–140.

Wala, Michael. *Winning the Peace. Amerikanische Außenpolitik und der Council on Foreign Relations, 1945–1950.* Stuttgart: 1990.

The War Reports of General of the Army George C. Marshall, General of the Army H. H. Arnold, Fleet Admiral Ernest J. King. Philadelphia: 1947.

Wegner-Korfes, Sigrid. "Der 20 Juli 1944 und das Nationalkomitee 'Freies Deutschland'." *Zeitschrift für Geschichtswissenschaft* 24 (1979): 535–544.

Weinberg, Gerhard L. *The Foreign Policy of Hitler's Germany: Starting World War II, 1937–1939.* Chicago: 1980.

Weisenborn, Günther. *Der lautlose Aufstand: Bericht über die Widerstandsbewegung des deutschen Volkes 1933–1945.* Hamburg: 1953.

West, Nigel. *MI6. British Secret Intelligence Service Operations 1909–1945.* London/New York: 1983.

Williams, Leon Norman, and Maurice Williams. *Forged Stamps of Two World Wars: The Postal Forgeries and Propaganda Issues of the Belligerents 1914–1918, 1939–1945.* London: 1954.

Winks, Robin W. *Cloak and Gown: Scholars in the Secret War, 1939–1961.* New York: 1987.

Wuermeling, Henric L. *Die weiße Liste: Umbruch der politischen Kultur in Deutschland 1945.* Berlin: 1981.

Ziemke, Earl F. *The U.S. Army in the Occupation of Germany.* Washington, DC: 1975.

Zink, Harold. *The United States in Germany 1944–1955.* Princeton, NJ: 1957.

About the Book and Editors

Even paranoids have enemies. Hitler's most powerful foes were the Allied powers, but he also feared internal conspiracies bent on overthrowing his malevolent regime. In fact, there was a small but significant internal resistance to the Nazi regime, and it did receive help from the outside world. Through recently declassified intelligence documents, this book reveals for the first time the complete story of America's wartime knowledge about, encouragement of, and secret collaboration with the German resistance to Hitler—including the famous July 20th plot to assassinate the Fuehrer.

The U.S. government's secret contacts with the anti-Nazi resistance were conducted by the OSS, the World War II predecessor to the CIA. Highly sensitive intelligence reports recently released by the CIA make it evident that the U.S. government had vast knowledge of what was going on inside the Third Reich. For example, a capitulation offer to the western Allies under consideration by Count von Moltke in 1943 was thoroughly discussed within the U.S. government. And Allen Dulles, who was later to become head of the CIA, was well informed about the legendary plot of July 20th. In fact, these secret reports from inside Germany provide a well-rounded picture of German society, revealing the pro- or anti-Nazi attitudes of different social groups (workers, churches, the military, etc.). The newly released documents also show that scholars in the OSS, many of them recruited from ivy-league universities, looked for anti-Nazi movements and leaders to help create a democratic Germany after the war.

Such intelligence gathering was a major task of the OSS. However, OSS director "Wild Bill" Donovan and others favored subversive operations, spreading disinformation, and issuing propaganda. Unorthodox and often dangerous schemes were developed, including bogus "resistance newspapers," anti-Nazi letters and postcards distributed through the German postal service, sabotage, and fake radio broadcasts from "German generals" calling for uprisings against the regime.

This is much more than a documentary collection. Explanatory footnotes supply a wealth of background information for the reader, and a comprehensive introduction puts the documents into their wider historical perspective. Arranged in chronological order, these intelligence reports provide a fascinating new perspective on the story of the German resistance to Hitler and reveal an intriguing and previously unexplored aspect of America's war with Hitler.

Jürgen Heideking is director of the Institute of Anglo-American History at the University of Cologne. **Christof Mauch** is senior fellow of the German Research Foundation and is presently affiliated with The American University in Washington, D.C.

Name Index

Abrigagni, captain, Italian member of the OSS, 341
Adam, Wilhelm, colonel-general in the German army, 415
Adenauer, Konrad, lord mayor of Cologne during the Weimar Republic, first chancellor of the Fedral Republic of Germany (1949–1963), 279–280, 417
Alexander, Sir Harold, commander of the Allied Forces in the Mediterranean Theater of War, 385
Allen, Robert M., first lieutenant, member of the OSS Morale Operations Branch, 397–398
Arkel, Gerhard 'Gary' Van, member of the OSS Labor Desk in Algiers, later Berne, 188, 190
Ancrum, Paul, lieutenant, OSS interrogator, 402
Armour, Lester, commander, deputy head of the OSS outpost in London, 298
Armstrong, Hamilton Fish, journalist, editor of *Foreign Affairs*, 196
Asmussen, Hans C., theologian, member of the Confessional Church in Germany, 298, 307
Attlee, Clement R., British politician, deputy prime minister since Feburary 1942, 231

Bachmann, Wilhelm, German theologian, 297, 306, 310
Badoglio, Pietro, Italian general and prime minister, 54, 99, 103, 141
Baerensprung, Horst, lawyer, 1939 emigration to U.S., lecturer at Harvard University, 51, 82
Bagier, Douglas, member of the OSS Morale Operations Branch, 354, 357, 401
Bancroft, Mary, secretary of Allen W. Dulles in Bern, 40, 206
Barness, Roswell P., American theologian, 303, 305–306
Bästlein, Bernhard, member of the German Communist resistance, 215
"Bearcat," OSS codename. *See* Willard L. Beaulac
Beaulac, Willard L., American *chargé d'affaires* in Madrid, 193
Beck, Ludwig, German general, chief of staff of the Armed Forces (1935–1938), leading member of the German resistance against Hitler, 99, 202, 219–220, 224, 242, 244–245, 254, 262, 264–266, 278–280, 285, 287, 289–290, 319, 326, 415, 419, 422–423
Becker, Howard, sociologist, member of the OSS Morale Operations Branch, 401–402
Bell, George, bishop of Chichester (England), 303, 305–307
Berggrav, Eivind, bishop, head of the Norwegian Protestant Church, 302, 304, 308
Berle, Adolf A., assistant secretary of state (1938–44), 20, 23, 24, 144, 146, 283

Bernhard, Georg, German journalist, emigration to the U.S. in 1941, work for the Institute of Jewish Affairs, 82, 114
Bernstorff, Albrecht Graf von, retired embassy councellor, 415
Bertholet, René, OSS agent stationed in France, 206
Betts, Thomas J., brigadier general, deputy assistant chief of staff at SHAEF in London, 235, 252–253, 376
Bielenberg, Peter, civil servant in the Reich ministry of economics, 420
Bismarck, Otto von, Prussian statesman, German chancellor (1871–1890), 58, 67, 68
Black, Edwin F., member of the OSS in Washington, 354
Blankenhorn, Heber, colonel, member of the Psychological Warfare Board of the OSS, 25–26
Blaskowitz, Johannes, German field marshal, 377–378
Bliss, Robert Woods, member of the OSS Planning Group, 217
Bloch, Kurt, economist, journalist and advisor for the OSS, emigration to the U.S. in 1937, 32
Blom, major in the Fifth Army Counterintelligence Corps, 345
"Bobcat," OSS codename. *See* Helldorf, Wolf Heinrich von
Bock, Fedor von, German field marshal, 282
Bodelschwingh, Friedrich von, German theologian, member of the Confessional Church, 309, 314
Boegner, Marc, French theologian, 302–303
Boheman, Erik C., Swedish diplomat, secretary general of the Ministry of Foreign Affairs, 295
Bolz, Eugen Anton, German politician, leading member of the Weimar Center Party, 415, 422
Bonhoeffer, Dietrich, German theolgian, member of the Confessional Church, 163, 279
Bormann, Martin, *Reichsleiter*, head of the party chancellery since 1941, secretary to the Führer, 80, 221, 387–388, 390
Bosch, Robert, German industrialist, 244
Brandt, Karl, German economist, emigration to the U.S. in 1933, advisor to several government agencies including the OSS, 194, 201
Brandt, Willy, journalist, German politician (Social Democrat), emigration to Sweden, chancellor of the Federal Republic of Germany (1969–1974), evaluation of German opposition, 97, 135, 190, 210
Brauchitsch, Walther von, German general, 1939–1941, supreme commander of the Wehrmacht, 251
Brauer, Max, German politician (Social Democrat), 1936 emigration to the U.S., co-founder of the Association of Free Germans, Inc., 51, 82

Subject Index